BERLIT

DISCO
THAIL

Edited and Designed by
D & N Publishing,
Lambourn, Berkshire.

Cartography by
Carte Blanche, Basingstoke,
Hampshire.

 The Berlitz tick is used to indicate places or events of particular interest.

Photographic Acknowledgements
Front cover: detail from the Grand Palace, Bangkok.

Back cover: detail from a temple at Chiang Mai.

All photographs by the author.

Acknowledgments
Any book of this undertaking involves countless people who in some way have contributed along the way. But special thanks must go to Hermione Davies, Sarah Shaw, Yung, Noan and Christopher Gow. I would also like to thank Gary Knight and Nigel Lumsden for their help with the photographs, as well as the Tourism Authority of Thailand (TAT).

Dedication
Dedicated to my family.

Transliteration
Spelling of Thai words and place names has the same delightful flexibility as the Thai people themselves. Because there is no direct equivalent of Thai sounds in English or in any other European language, transliteration is open to endless interpretation. One place name can be spelled in any number of ways. For example Phetchburi is often spelt as Phetburi, Phetchaburi, Petburi and Petchburi—all of which are right. Generally spellings in this book follow the most common practice.

If you have any new information, suggestions or corrections to contribute to this guide, we would like to hear from you. Please write to Berlitz Publishing at the above address.

Phototypeset by Wyvern Typesetting Ltd., Bristol.

Printed by C.S. Graphics Singapore.

BERLITZ®

DISCOVER
THAILAND

Ben Davies

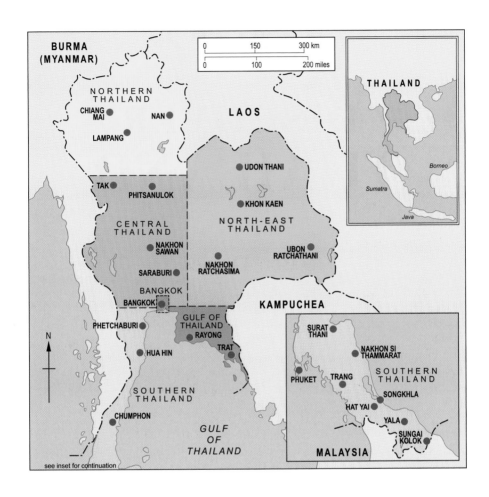

Contents

Thailand Holiday Basics

Thailand has almost everything that the visitor can dream of, and a host of other attractions too. Whether you are exploring the Kingdom by plane or train or merely on foot, there is an endless list of alternative things to do. To enjoy your trip to the full though you will need some basic nuts and bolts—practical information. Below are listed sections on how to get there and what to take as well as a few hints on how to make the best of your holiday on arrival.

When to Go

Thailand is a hot, humid, monsoon-beset country with three seasons: roughly November to February is the cooler season, March to May is the hot season and June to October is the rainy season. The ideal time to visit is between the beginning of November and the end of February when temperatures range from 18°C (64°F) to 35°C (95°F), and the rains have largely

When you have five regions, mountains, national parks and beaches to choose from there's only one satisfactory option—extend your holiday.

given way to lazy sunshine. This is the time when many of the most important festivals such as Loi Krathong are held.

Summer is from March to May. Day temperatures average from 27°C (81°F) to 35°C (95°F) and the nights are not much cooler. The humidity is extremely high. Generally the first rains begin in June and the main falls take place between July and September. This is the most unpredictable season. It can rain for up to five hours a day, flooding the streets of the capital. Often days can go by without a fall, and even when it does rain, it will normally be for only a couple of hours; then the rain stops, the skies clear, and Thailand is seen at its finest. Temperatures vary between 27°C (81°F) and

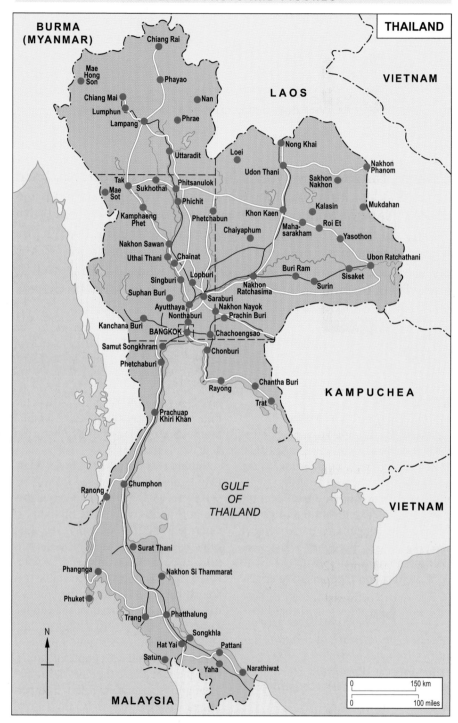

33°C (91°F). Humidity can reach 98 per cent.

In the South, the rainy season lasts longer, is more unpredictable and involves a lot more water. The region's average rainfall for the whole year is around 3,000 mm (120 inches) compared with 1,000 mm (40 inches) in the North and North-east and 1,600 mm (62 inches) in the Central Region. There is less variation in temperature with a mean temperature of around 27°C (81°F).

M *ap of Thailand.*

T *he old way of life exists side by side with tourism on the island of Phuket, the South's busiest destination.*

In the North the weather is cooler with temperatures during the winter months falling to 6°C (43°F) around Chiang Mai and Mae Hong Son. You may even need a sweater. The dry season generally lasts until June or July.

The most extreme temperatures are witnessed in the North-east, where in the hot season it can rise to 40°C (104°F). During May and June the land often suffers from drought, whilst during July and August, large areas can be covered by floods.

If you are planning to visit Thailand during the cool season, make sure you make reservations well ahead. Hotels and flights are often fully booked months in advance, and even cheaper bungalows are hard to come by.

What to Wear

Light, casual clothing is the only sensible option for Thailand's hot, humid climate. Cotton shirts, baggy trousers and dresses can be bought in abundance in almost any boutique or street market and at prices considerably lower than their Western counterparts. You should bring just a few more immediate articles.

A pair of open sandals or rubber flip-flops is a must along with a couple of pairs of shorts, a few T-shirts and several loose cotton outfits. Also take a sweater and a pair of thick socks for the cooler nights in Chiang Mai or for trekking up north. Generally it is too hot for tight trousers or jeans.

Thais usually dress impeccably. Even when temperatures are very high, they somehow maintain both their composure and their crisply ironed shirts. And whilst they are more than accustomed to the bedraggled costumes of the average *farang* (foreigner), some form of presentable attire is appreciated by Thais as a sign of respect. Beach wear should not be worn to temples or in the lobbies of some of the big hotels. For visiting government offices or for important business con-

*S*eventeen coups may have shaped the face of the Kingdom, but Thailand's soldiers still find time to dress the part.

tacts, a jacket is required. Make sure it is cotton or you'll be bathed in sweat before you make your grand entrance!

Passports and Visas

Tourists arriving in Thailand must have a valid passport and as a general rule will need a visa if they are to stay more than 15 days. Visas can be obtained from Thai embassies in most capital cities and will take around three days to be processed. Normally you need three passport-sized photos.

Multiple entry visas can also be secured on request although the cost is correspondingly higher.

At present there are three kinds of visa: transit, valid for 30 days; tourist, valid for 60 days; non-immigrant, valid for 90 days.

Extensions to both tourist and non-immigrant visas are possible but on a discretionary basis—usually for a month and costing Bt500. If you're going to do this, go to the Immigration Office at the Police Station on Soi Suanplu, Sathorn Road, Bangkok, Tel: (286) 4230/3. Alternatively go to the Immigration Office in any of the other major centres. Dress smartly and smile profusely. A daily fine is levied on tourists who overstay their welcome.

On departure a Bt200 airport tax is payable for international airlines and Bt20 for domestic airlines. Visitors who stay in Thailand more than 90 days in a calendar year or who have a non-immigrant visa will need tax clearance. This can be obtained at the Tax Office, Chahra Pong Road, near Democracy Monument and from Tax Offices at Pattaya, Chiang Mai, Hat Yai and most other major tourist centres. Failure to do this can lead to refusal to grant you an exit permit or heavy fines at the airport.

Customs Regulations

Regulations in Thailand are relatively straightforward, efficient and easy to comply with. You are allowed to bring in 200 cigarettes, 1 bottle of wine, 1 litre of spirits, 1 camera and 5 films duty free. Weapons, pornography or drugs are prohibited.

Up to US$10,000 of foreign currency may be taken into or out of the Kingdom. Foreign visitors may bring in local currency up to a maximum of Bt2,000 per person or Bt4,000 per family travelling under one passport.

Exports of Buddha images—except small ones carried on the person—antiques and genuine works of art are forbidden without export licences from the Fine Arts Department. The shop you deal with should be able to arrange the paperwork.

Finally, a word of warning. Don Muang International Airport is a centre for drug trafficking. Never look after bags for strangers, even if they are well-dressed and charming, and constantly keep an eye on your own luggage. Many a foreigner has found his stay in Thailand inadvertently extended by several years on drug charges. And once behind bars, it is very difficult to persuade anybody to let you out.

Insurance

Insurance is a necessity and you'd be unwise to leave home without it. Some tours or travel agencies will organize health and travel insurance for you at the time of purchasing your ticket. However you may prefer to look at the better known companies like American Express.

Make sure that your insurance covers transportation back home in case of an accident, as well as treatment abroad. It is also worth getting an insurance that provides indemnity for cash, as well as for valuables such as camera equipment.

Health and Medical Care

There are no immunization requirements for Thailand unless you are coming from an infected area. Health organizations do, however, strongly advise a vaccination against cholera and hepatitis and a tetanus booster to guard against accidental cuts or grazes. Some also advise typhoid immunization.

Malaria tablets are also a prerequisite, especially for those people travelling to areas outside Bangkok such as Rayong, Ko Chang and Kanchanaburi, where the disease is by no means unknown. Courses of tablets should be started at least one week prior to departure and continued for a month after returning home. Consult your doctor or a travel centre such as Thomas Cook's or British Airways' special units for further details.

If you are worried about your state of health, have a medical before you leave and try to ensure that you build up a reasonable level of fitness. Thailand is a hot country even during the so-called cooler months, and jetlag caused by the time change between Europe and Thailand can and does take its toll.

For the most part, the commonest ailments are the easiest to avoid. Beware excessive sun, and go easy on spicy food at first. Always avoid drinking tap water or eating fruit unless it is peeled, and if you don't trust ice, miss out on it.

The most insidious infections are begotten, however, not on the streets but in the Kingdom's more colourful haunts. Venereal diseases are rife and the full extent of AIDs is as yet unrecognized.

Finally, Thailand is infested with rabies. Stray dogs, of which there are literally millions, carry the disease. If you are bitten, you should be treated immediately.

Emergency Services

Thailand is as well equipped as most other countries in Asia to cope with emergency cases, but only in the big cities. Outside in the countryside services are basic, and in the really far-flung provinces the only option is immediate transportation of a sick person to the nearest big centre

Most big hotels have doctors on call and often available 21 hours a day The Tourist Police should also be able to provide immediate help. If in doubt or in an emergency, you may also contact your embassy. Emergency numbers are given on page 304.

How To Get There

By Air

Bangkok is one of the most accessible destinations in the world, albeit a long way from Britain or the USA, and is currently served by more than 40 international airlines. British Airways, Thai International and Qantas all have daily scheduled flights from London, with United Airlines, North-west and Delta serving the USA. Typical flight times are 12 hours from London, 20 hours from New York and 9 hours from Sydney.

Cheaper though less frequent alternatives range from Gulf Air to LOT

Polish Airline, Egypt Air and Aeroflot, with stopovers in the respective capitals, and sometimes other places too. There are now even direct international flights to Phuket, Hat Yai and Chiang Mai.

All flights should be booked well in advance, especially between December and March when seats are often full months ahead. For the return trip, tickets must be re-confirmed at least 72 hours prior to departure.

Don Muang International Airport lies some 32 km (20 miles) to the north of Bangkok and can be reached by taxi or bus in anything from 45 minutes to 2 hours depending on the state of traffic.

For information about flight departures and arrivals, telephone Bangkok 286 0190/9. For a list of airlines, see any of the local magazine handouts or ask at your hotel.

By Road
The only official entry point to Thailand by road is via Malaysia and the towns of Padang Besar in the west, or Sungai Kolok and Tak Bai in the east From here a variety of good tarmacked roads run all the way up the coast through beautiful scenery to Bangkok a distance of some 1,100 km (625 miles).

Drivers entering Thailand will need a vehicle registration book and a number of copies of the following: Thailand passenger's list; special import and export entry permits; Thailand Department of Customs form; Application for a Certificate of Payment; Application for Certificate of Exportation of Goods; a permit for driving your car into Malaysia. These forms can be obtained from the Tourist Authority of Thailand (TAT) or from a Thai embassy. Information about Malaysian requirements should be requested from the Tourist Development Corporation of Malaysia.

There are also buses running to Hat Yai from Bangkok, Singapore, Kuala Lumpur and Butterworth and vice-versa They depart throughout the day and night and drive at extraordinarily high speeds.

By Sea
Although there are no longer any regular passenger boats sailing to Thailand, a handful of freighters with passenger cabins still do the trip. The most frequent from Europe are Ben Line Steamers, Polish Ocean Lines and Nedloyd, and from the US, American President Lines or State Line. Cruise ships such as Cunard's Queen Elizabeth II, Royal Viking and Pearl of Scandinavia also occasionally drop anchor in Pattaya. Details should be obtained from the relevant Maritime offices.

There is also a short connection between Perlis in Malaysia and Satun in Thailand. Enquire from a local travel agent for more details.

By Train
One of the most pleasant—and if you travel first-class—comfortable and time-honoured ways of arriving in Thailand is by the rail route from Singapore and Malaysia The journey takes about 20 hours from Butterworth—Penang's mainland station—28 hours from Kuala Lumpur and 40 hours from Singapore involving two changes of train.

*W*hen a farmer has *finished in the rice fields, there is no stopping him from going home.*

Tickets can be booked in advance at the station or by some travel agents and include first-class sleepers and second-class air-conditioned or non-air-conditioned sleepers. All trains leave from and arrive at Bangkok's Hualamphong Station on Rama IV, Tel: 221 7010/20 for enquiries.

Time Difference
Time in Thailand is seven hours ahead of Greenwich Mean Time (GMT). When it is noon in Bangkok it is 3 p.m. in Sydney, 5 a.m. in London and midnight in New York.

Getting Around

One of the great delights of Thailand is the ease with which you can get around, almost at the drop of a hat.

Trains and buses are cheap. Highways are generally in good condition, and only in the far-flung provinces does the tarmac surface change to dirt. Pay tolls are limited to the area around Bangkok and petrol stations, and mechanics are to be found everywhere. However, the frantically crowded city roads, the incomprehensible Thai signs and the sheer speed and unpredictability of Thai drivers are enough to put off all but the courageous. Most people prefer to travel by train, a comfortable if somewhat slower alternative.

Thailand has buses as well, but they are fast and can test the nerves; those who opt for this method are well advised to take the more luxurious VIP buses. Local buses were made with the Thais in mind, and foreign legs and necks can suffer greatly as a consequence.

Where time is limited, the best alternative is to fly. Thai Airways, the national airline, offers efficient and comfortable domestic flights serving all the main cities. Bangkok Airways also has a small network of destinations. By European standards, both airlines are extremely cheap.

Always try to make advance bookings. This is especially true during the months of March–June (university holidays), May–July (school holidays) as well as national holidays. To avoid long queues, it is worth paying the small extra charge to buy train and plane tickets through a local travel agent. The Tourist Authority of Thailand (TAT) will normally be able to provide details of any special deals.

One last piece of advice. If you are travelling to the provinces, try to get your train/bus instructions written in Thai and always double-check that you are on the right train/bus. Many local people will often acknowledge your enquiries by nodding their head sagely when in fact they have absolutely no idea what you have said.

Air

If you are short of time and want to see as much of the country as possible, air travel is likely to prove the most sensible option. Thai Airways, the domestic airline, flies at least once daily to all the major towns in Thailand. Occasionally discounts are offered to passengers who already hold Thai International tickets. Typical fares are Bangkok–Phuket, Bt4,000 return;

Bangkok–Chiang Mai, Bt3,300 return; Bangkok–Nakhon Ratchasima (Korat), Bt2,000 return. There are several flights a day, but reservations should be made well in advance of travel at weekends or holidays, when internal flights are often full.

A new, private airline, Bangkok Airways (BA) also flies from Bangkok to Ko Samui and Hua Hin and between Phuket and Ko Samui. For the latest on services, contact any travel agent.

Trains

Thai trains are generally comfortable, inevitably cheap and, almost unique in a still developing country, normally punctual. On the *rot duan*—Bangkok's more leisurely version of the *train rapide*—there are even restaurant cars where you can tuck into a plate of fried prawns and sip on a cool beer before settling back into an air-conditioned sleeper.

The railway hub for the entire kingdom is Bangkok. From here trains run to Chiang Mai in the North, to Hat Yai in the South, and to Ubon Ratchathani and Nong Khai in the North-east. Typical first-class single fares, including sleeper are: Bt837 to Chiang Mai; Bt770 to Surat Thani; Bt730 to Nong Khai. Be warned, however—not all trains have first-class and, conversely, not all have third-class carriages. If you are thinking of taking a long rail trip, you can reserve your ticket in advance at Hualamphong station, Tel: 223 7010 or 223 7020. Failing a sleeper, don't be put off altogether as second-class seats are comfortable and recline. Even third-class seats are an acceptable standard, but only for shorter journeys.

Buses

Thailand's bus system is not for the fainthearted. It's fast, it's unpredictable and occasionally even deadly. Fortunately many of the air-conditioned buses now have video and curtains so that you can ignore the sight of the countryside passing at the speed of light and instead expend your adrenaline by watching some violent second-rate Thai movie.

Currently there are three sorts of bus. Local buses stop just about everywhere, are without air-conditioning, but have the saving grace of being extremely cheap. Air-conditioned and non-air-conditioned buses are a little more expensive and an awful lot faster and rarely stop. VIP buses are relatively luxurious, generally slower, still cheap and often provide snacks, lavatories and towels.

Addresses and telephone numbers for the bus terminals in Bangkok are:

Northern & North-east Bus Terminal
Paholyothin Road
Tel: 271 4484/1 (air-conditioned)
 271 0101/1 (non-air-conditioned)

Eastern Bus Terminal
Sukhumvit Road
Tel: 391 92274 (air-conditioned)
 391 9821 (air-conditioned)
 391 25044 (non-air-conditioned)
 391 2521 (non-air-conditioned)

Southern Bus Terminal
Charoen Sanitwong Road
Tel: 411 4978/9 (air-conditioned)

Most other cities have a number of bus terminals predictably located at opposite ends of town. Often, several bus companies serve the same route. To be safe enquire at travel agents for details and book in advance.

Some typical journey times for air-conditioned buses are Bangkok–Butterworth, 24 hours; Bangkok–Chiang Mai, 9 hours; Bangkok–Korat, 6 hours; Bangkok–Phuket, 14 hours; Bangkok–Surat Thani, 11 hours.

Boat

Thailand has thousands of km of navigable canals and waterways, with endless opportunities for the river traveller. In Bangkok alone there are no less than 22 regular boat and ferry services going as far afield as Ayutthaya and Bang PaIn. Hydrofoils also run from the Thai Intertransport Building near the Menam Hotel in Bangkok to Pattaya and Hua Hin, Tel: 291 9613/5. Enquire at local travel agents for details.

Car Hire

Driving in Bangkok sounds fun. In practice it can be a daunting experience. Thai city drivers drive like maniacs, a lot of the roads are potholed and crowded with pedestrians, and many of the road signs are indecipherable. What's more, with an excellent local transport system there is little need to splash out money or take the potential risks.

Outside Bangkok, however, those with some experience of driving in the East and preferably those who can speak a few words of Thai will find driving a less frightening experience. There are good highways from Bangkok to Chiang Rai, Nong Khai, Trat and Malaysia. Petrol at just under Bt10 a litre in 1991—Bt15 from old-fashioned suspended jars in out of the way places—is no more expensive than in Europe and there is no shortage of car-hire firms, both in Bangkok and in some of the large up-country cities like Chiang Mai and Khon Kaen, and on Phuket and Ko Samui. Most importantly, a vehicle will allow you to escape the floods of tourists and can provide a real glimpse into the unspoilt parts of Thailand—the vast areas of the North-east, the small rural villages in the North and Central Plains, and the spectacular scenery of the South.

Most agencies hire out cars on a daily basis for a fixed sum of money. This usually includes free insurance and unlimited mileage, but not petrol. An average rental for a day would be in the range of about Bt800–Bt1,400 for a Toyota Corolla and around Bt900–Bt1,600 for a Toyota Corona. Some companies like Avis will allow you to take delivery of a vehicle from one branch and return it to another so that you do not have to backtrack. They will also organize insurance and paperwork, and as an option provide you with a chauffeur.

Anyone driving must have an international driving licence and should try to get a copy of Molly Wijeysingha's book called *Thailand on Four Wheels*. The book lists the various rules, road signs, regulations and highway formalities—there aren't many of them—as well as such useful advice as not driving at night and not to expect any right of way.

International rules are generally accepted. Vehicles in Thailand are driven on the left of the road—normally.

There is a speed limit of 80 km/hour in town and 100 km/hour on open roads. One unwritten rule is that in the event of an accident, the foreigner is to blame. Another is that damages are paid immediately without calling the police.

Motorbikes

The statistics speak for themselves. In Bangkok alone there are some 25 accidents a day, with two fatalities. Outside Bangkok, the risks are considerably lower. Yet on Ko Samui more than 15 foreigners were killed or badly injured in motorbike accidents (1990), whilst in Phuket, sun-tanned *farangs* with their arms and legs in plaster casts are almost as common a sight as the proverbial water buffalo.

If you do rent a motorcycle insist that it is in relatively good condition. Most bikes are badly maintained and almost inevitably uninsured, which means that you can end up with a bill if things go wrong. Wear a helmet and protective clothing to guard against sunburn, and a pair of sunglasses to cut out the glare. Never ride alone in remote areas.

Most agents will demand a deposit and may require that you leave your passport or some other form of identification. Finally, if you're not an experienced biker, forget it. The rewards are just not worth the risk.

Local Transport

Taxis are comfortable, widely available and cheap. But you must agree a price before stepping into one. If you cannot speak Thai use fingers to denote each Bt10 you are prepared to pay. And if one taxi asks too much just wait until the next one comes along and start negotiating all over again.

Three-wheeled motorbike scooters known as *tuk tuks* are also common in Bangkok although they are less safe and more exposed to the outside fumes. And at the bottom of the scale there are pedal-power tricycles, motorbike taxis, *samlors, songthaews* (pick-up trucks)—and even horse-drawn carriages in Lampang. Make sure you bargain for all of them and enquire at your hotel or guesthouse to get an idea of the sort of price you should be paying.

Accommodation

Thailand's hotels have an unrivalled reputation for excellence and for *namchai* (an irrepressible desire to please). At least five of them are listed amongst the top 100 hotels in the world with numerous others vying for secondary honours.

Bangkok, Chiang Mai, Pattaya, Ko Samui and Phuket in particular are brimming over with luxury establishments. Even off the main tourist track top-class hotels are mushrooming.

Further down the scale there's no shortage of budget hotels, often with swimming pools and gardens, almost always clean and friendly.

At the bottom of the scale, there is a range of cheap guesthouses and hostels with spartan rooms and dormitories and a fine array of cockroaches to boot.

Prices vary as much as standards. In Bangkok, a deluxe suite at the Oriental will cost as much Bt15,000 and a standard room Bt5,000, whilst on Khaosan Road, you may be able to pick up a bed for as little as Bt60. As a general rule, however, good clean rooms are plentiful and extremely good value. Only in the really far flung provinces is choice limited, with the smaller, cheaper hotels tending to be brothels.

Most travel agencies will try to arrange accommodation for your entire stay before you leave. The advantage of this is that you get an assured room in Bangkok on arrival, which during the high season can prove quite a boon. The downside is that you tend to pay higher rates and are tied to a fixed itinerary. Probably the best idea if you are planning to travel extensively is to book a hotel for a couple of nights, and then you can either extend your stay or move on according to your mood.

Alternatively, on arrival at the airport, head straight for the hotel counter beyond customs. They will generally ring around until they get you a room. Finally, when all else fails, just jump into a taxi, ask for *rong rem* (hotel)—and wait till you find something that suits you. All the drivers have their own favourites and they often get a commission.

Camping
Several National Parks offer camping facilities, and tents can be hired out on Ko Samet and a number of the other islands. Outside in the wilds, camping is not recommended. Some years ago, two women were killed on the island of Ko Chang. It was an isolated incident, but it should serve as a reminder to anyone heading too far off the beaten track.

Money

Currency

Thailand's unit of currency is the baht. A baht is divided into 100 satang. Coins now in circulation include 25-satang and 50-satang pieces, 1-baht, 5-baht and 10-baht coins. The value of the coins is not always obvious. Older coins often exhibit Thai numerals, whilst a 1-baht coin can come in three different sizes.

Thai bank notes are easier to handle: 10-baht bills are brown; 20-baht bills are green; 50-baht bills are blue; 100-baht bills are red; 500-baht bills are purple. Notes are considerately scaled according to the amount: the larger the denomination, the larger the note. Such is the Thais' enthusiasm for this method of differentiation that it is often difficult fitting a 500 Baht note into your wallet.

Large denomination notes are often difficult to change, except in the big hotels and shopping areas. When changing money it is often worth asking the cashier for small denomination notes.

For daily foreign exchange rates, check the business section of the *Bangkok Post* or *Nation* newspaper, or any of the banks or foreign exchange services.

The current rates of exchange are: US $1 = 25.5 baht; UK £1 = 45 baht; A $1 = 19.5 baht; D M1 = 14.5 baht; S $1 = 14.2 baht.

Banks and Foreign Exchange Services

Thai and foreign banks provide standard services nationwide, and are open Monday to Friday between 8.30 a.m.

*L*uxury-seekers on Samui don't need to go far for it has many upmarket hotels.

and 3.30 p.m., but are closed on public and bank holidays. Bank currency exchange centres theoretically operate from 7 a.m. to 9 p.m. seven days a week, including holidays—though in practice when you want them they have a tendency to be closed.

Foreign currency can also be changed in most large hotels, although generally at less favourable rates. It is worth bearing in mind that outside Bangkok and the other major tourist centres, it can be extremely difficult to change money, especially if it is not US dollars.

Traveller's Cheques

Although traveller's cheques are a useful alternative to money in principle, they are not always easy to change. To save yourself problems, it is worth plumping for US dollar traveller's cheques, preferably with well-known companies such as American Express or Thomas Cook. Outside Bangkok, banks, exchange counters and large hotels will generally accept them, especially in the major tourist centres.

Credit Cards

American Express, Diners Club, Mastercard and Visa are accepted in most large hotels, restaurants, travel agents and shops, although you should always check beforehand to save yourself embarrassment. A charge of four per cent is often levied for their use.

Security

Crime and theft, although still rare in Thailand, are on the increase, especially in the big cities and around the main tourist areas. To reduce the chances of theft or mugging take a few simple precautions.

As a general rule, carry as little cash around as possible, and what you do carry, keep in a money belt tied firmly around your waist.

When staying in a hotel always make certain that the door is secure, and leave any valuables in the hotel safe, after obtaining an official receipt noting the precise contents first.

Also beware—credit card fraud is one of the Kingdom's most notorious growth industries and the arrival of large unexplained shopping bills is by no means an uncommon experience.

In some areas of the south and in all border areas you should never travel at night, nor should you go off alone on a motorcycle or in a car. Care should also be taken in the big cities where almond-eyed beauties have been known to deprive unwary tourists of more than their trousers.

The Tourist Authority of Thailand (TAT) and the police have recently issued warnings about accepting food from strangers on buses and trains. On several occasions tourists and locals have been drugged before having their belongings stolen. The offending substances are generally added to sweets and drinks, but even cigarettes can be drugged.

In an emergency, contact the Tourist Police immediately or alternatively seek advice from your embassy. Tourist Police can be recognized by the blue and yellow badges on their sleeves, their ability to speak at least a smattering of English and their generally smiling faces: they were set up in 1982.

Telephone numbers for Tourist Police Offices include: Bangkok, Tel: 225 775 or 221 6206-10 or 253 9560/1; Phuket, Tel: (076) 212 213; Pattaya, Tel: (038) 429 371; Chiang Mai, Tel: (053) 248 974; Hat Yai, Tel: (074) 246 733; Kanchanaburi, Tel: (034) 512 795; Surat Thani, Tel: (077) 421 281.

Food

Thais delight in the good things of life and nowhere is this more evident than in their enjoyment of good food and the ambience that goes with it. The Kingdom has some of the finest European restaurants but not surprisingly, it is the local food which is the real joy to savour.

*T*hailand's hottest *fiercest most delicious sauce,* nam phrik *is made from Thailand's hottest chillis, known as* prik kee noo *or mouse-shit peppers.*

Nam Phrik
Thailand's hottest, fiercest, most delicious sauce is not for the cool of heart. Nam Phrik (pepper water) is a lauded concoction made from pounded red chilli, shrimp paste, black pepper, garlic and onions. Brine and lemon juice are added, along with ginger, tamarind and gourd seeds, fish in an early stage of fermentation, and mango sprouts. Foreigners generally prefer tomato ketchup or brown source to Nam Phrik. Thais can't do without it.

Thai cuisine brings together some of the finest culinary traditions from India, China, Malaysia and even Portugal. It has the spiciness of hot

A Fearsome Hunger

"When his appetite is satisfied—and for that all that is necessary is a bowl of rice and some fish seasoned with capsicum— the Siamese is lively and happy and sleeps without care for the morrow" wrote one 19th century observer in Bangkok. Little has changed since. Recent statistics show that on average a Thai eats 22 kilos of fish a year, and more than 600 plates of rice. If that's not enough, he also consumes at least 1 kilo of chillis a year, or some 55 kilos in a lifetime. Even the thought of it is enough to reduce most westerners to tears.

chilli peppers and the sweetness of coconut milk, the pungency of fresh herbs and the saltiness of fermented fish. But more than anything it has the inspiration and the beautiful presentation which are inextricably Thai.

Altogether more than ten chilli peppers are used ranging from the famous *prik kee noo* (mouse-shit peppers) to the potent *prik chii faa*. To these are added lashings of tamarind, garlic and coriander, a sprig of lemon grass and ginger. But contrary to popular opinion, not all Thai food is fearsomely hot. Spices are used to enhance taste and not to hide it. And if you are worried, you can always ask waiters to go easy on the *mai phet* (chillis), since every dish is made to order.

Thais will generally order a selection of dishes and share them as a group. Typically, these will include a hot and sour soup (*tom yam*), a curry (*kaeng*), a steamed dish, a fried dish, a spicy salad (*yam*), some meat, some fish and steaming mounds of boiled rice or noodles. The main dishes arrive together, with the rice normally served last, as Thais believe that rice should not be allowed to detract from the quality and quantity of the other food.

If you are a newcomer to Thai food, start off with something mild (*mai phet*) and work up towards the heights of chillied serpent's heads or pigs' intestine soup. Curries (*kaeng pet*) particularly those with a coconut cream base are often less piquant than in Europe or India. Steamed sweet and sour fish with ginger and garlic (*pla priawan*) is another exquisite dish and is often served up with pineapple and and green peppers.

Other popular dishes are *mee krop* (crisp, thin noodles with bits of shrimp and egg and sweet and sour sauce); *khao phat kai* (fried rice with chicken); *kaeng som* (fish and vegetable curry without coconut milk); *pu cha* (fried stuffed crab shell); *kaeng pet phet yang* (roast duck curry); and *yam (*a spicy salad, with everything from beef to squid to papaya, served with lettuce, coriander leaves, garlic, lime juice, shallots, fish sauce and chilli pepper).

Each region of Thailand also has its own specialities. The North-east, which includes large numbers of Laotians, is famed for its sticky or glutinous rice (*khao nia*), normally served alongside barbecued meat (generally buffalo);

Table Manners

Burping, snarling and finger-licking are all considered quite acceptable in polite Thai society, but finishing your rice can be considered a serious matter. Such behaviour indicates a lack of appreciation for the good things which have been placed in front of you and may be taken by your host as evidence that he or she has not given you enough to eat.

and *som tam*, a hot salad that combines shredded green papaya, dried shrimps or curried crab claws, lemon juice, fish sauce, garlic and chillis. In the North, a local sausage called *naem* is popular. The South has numerous dishes which have been influenced by the Muslim style cooking of the Malays; and of course all kinds of seafood dishes from freshly cooked lobsters, to mussels, crabs, squid and shark.

To round off the meal, there are a variety of sweet desserts. Many are based on rice flour, coconut milk, palm sugar and sticky rice. Others are soaked in jasmine and aromatic flowers in water. A real treat is fresh mango served with coconut cream and sticky rice, or with other sweet meats such as *sangkhaya,* a kind of custard. Alternatively, ask for *pomlamay* and you will be served with whatever fruits are on offer.

If there is a difficulty in Thailand, it is more a matter of choice than of quality. Often the best restaurants are the least ostentatious, and many a gastronomic feast is prepared in nothing more than a simple shop, house or market stall. Others are grand establishments to be found in luxurious hotels or around scented lotus ponds where chefs with more than 20 years' experience create their own individual masterpieces.

If in doubt just follow your nose, latch on to the fragrant aromas wafting along the various *sois* (lanes) and take your pick. Alternatively get a list from the TAT or the *Restaurant Guide* published by Asia Books, check to see a few of the locals are there, and walk on in.

*E*ating is as much a way of life as work in Thailand.

Finally, be warned. Most Thai restaurants close early with last orders around 9.30 p.m.

Tipping

In most western restaurants tipping is expected at a standard rate of 10 per cent. Outside these veritable havens it is largely discretionary with tips rarely exceeding Bt10–20. In the really way out places, waiters will still come rushing after you with your change rather than accept it. Beware of touts who offer to show you around in exchange for a meal. Sometimes, by the time you have bought them a sumptuous dinner you won't have enough left to tip anyone.

Street Stalls

Horror stories tend to be circulated about the dangers of consuming ice or vegetables or anything from a street stall. Do not believe it. Unless you have got a weak stomach, almost anything a Thai offers you will be good. Thais do not drink the tap water which, though treated, is susceptible to rusting pipes; and when they do drink water, it is almost inevitably boiled.

As for eating in local stalls, the small noodle shop on the corner of the busy highway, or the little old lady who sells roast pigs' trotters at the market provide some of the most nutritious, tasty and typically local cuisine. A plate of fried rice or a mound of noodles and a *som tam* will probably be better for you than half a dozen hamburgers.

As a ground rule check that food is freshly cooked; and if you have just arrived in Thailand go easy to start with, as even the stomach takes time to acclimatize. Beyond that put your worries aside and feast. The Thais do and are healthy enough.

Fruits

Exotic fruits are a Thai speciality. Besides orange coloured papaya and guava, there are pineapples, tangerines, and mangoes, as well as the more illustrious-sounding longans, jackfruits and lychie. Thailand has more than 20 varieties of banana of all shapes, textures and sizes. They include seedless ones, the egg banana and even a plump cylindrical banana named *kluai khai farang* (foreign banana).

The Durian

Love it or hate it, but you can never be indifferent to it. Mouhot described the initial taste of the durian fruit to "the flesh of some animal in a state of putrefaction". King Rama II on the other hand was so enamoured with the fruit that he wrote an ode to it as he journeyed up the Chao Phya River to Ayutthaya. Encased in a thick, prickly rind that resembles a mace, and containing some ten kernels, each larger than a date, durians are found in greatest abundance during the months of April and June when the air is filled with the smell of what one British governor of Singapore called "carrion in custard". Those who take too much of a liking beware. As one eminent 19th-century gentleman put it "If you eat it often, you find yourself next day covered with blotches".

The pride of Thailand, however, is the *durian,* which is spiked like a gladiator's mace and tastes like sweet custard. To some people, the very smell is enough to send shivers down the spine. King Rama II, so loved the fruit, he composed an ode to it whilst journeying down the Chao Phya River.

Although exotic fruits are scattered throughout the Kingdom, certain regions have acquired their own reputation. Nonthaburi is famous for *durian,* Nakhon Pathom for *pomeloes,* Chantaburi for sweet tangerines and Chiang Mai for *lamyai.* Apples, strawberries and melons grow in the cooler climate of the North.

Drinks

Almost all the widely-known brands of soft drink are sold in Thailand. Even in some of the remote areas of the

Kingdom you may catch the odd hill-tribes man sipping on a bottle of Pepsi. Bottled water is sold everywhere and most doctors recommend that you drink at least one and a half litres (2.5 pints) of it a day.

In many areas, and especially the North-east, it is customary to drink *nam cha* (tea-flavoured water) or *cha jin* (chinese tea) with your meal. It is the perfect complement to Thai food, an antidote to spiciness.

Surprisingly, despite the wealth of fruits, juices are not common and when you find them they are frequently served with lashings of sugar and sometimes even salt. One pleasant drink that is widely available is *nam manao* (lime juice). If you do not like sweet drinks, emphasize that you want it *mai sai nam taan* (without sugar).

For those in search of something a little more fortifying, Thailand has two types of beer—Kloster and Singha—and its own locally manufactured whisky. Mekong is undoubtedly the most popular drink in the land. It is made from rice, is cheap, surprisingly mellow and gives staggering hangovers.

Wine is available, but generally at prices that are considerably higher than in Europe. A bottle of cheap French table wine in a restaurant will go for at least Bt300. As for anything else, it will in all likelihood cost more than the meal. Thailand also produces its own wine, but it tastes like sherry or vinegar and is not recommended.

Water

Do not drink the tap water in Thailand. Most hotels place a bottle or jug of purified water in every room for drinking purposes. When eating in a restaurant or market insist on bottled water or soft drinks and beer without ice to be safe.

Shopping and Services

Opening Hours

Opening hours are given below.

Banks

8.30 a.m.–3.30 p.m. Monday –Friday.

Department Stores

Typically 10 a.m.– 9 p.m. daily, including Sunday.

Government Offices

8.30 a.m.–noon & 1.00 p.m.–4.30 p.m. Monday to Friday.

Museums

Check before you leave, but typically 9a.m–noon & 1.00 p.m.–4.30 p.m. daily, except Monday and Friday.

Shops

From early morning to 7 or 8 p.m., often seven days a week.

Weights and Measures

Almost everything in Thailand is metric. Weights are measured in kilograms (kg), volumes in litres (l) and distances in kilometres (km).

For easy conversion: 1 kg = 2.2 lb; 1 km = 0.6 miles; 1 metre = 1.1 yards; 1 cm = 0.4 inches; 1 litre = 0.2 gallons.

Pharmacists and Opticians

Wander down any of the main streets in Bangkok or Chiang Mai and you will come across one of the hundreds of pharmacies supplying just about every form of official and unofficial drug as well as toothpastes, nappies, and all those other essentials. Pharmacists will generally be able to supply most western drugs without a prescription. However, if you think you may need one particular item, make sure you bring along the generic name as some of the brands may not be available.

Contact lens solution can also be purchased at any number of opticians. They will also fit you up with spectacles, often at less than a day's notice and for as little as Bt500.

At most pharmacists in the major shopping areas there will normally be someone who speaks English. Some pharmacists may even remain open for 24 hours. Any problems and you should ask at your hotel for advice.

Life in Bangkok's busy market starts before dawn when cartloads of fresh produce is brought in from the Central Plains.

Postal Services and Telephones

Thailand's mail service is cheap, reliable and efficient. Generally a letter sent by air mail takes 6 days to reach Europe and 9 days to reach the United

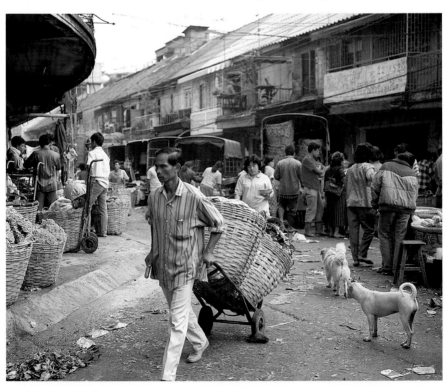

States. Parcels can also be safely dispatched and take between 7 days and 6 to 10 weeks depending on whether they go by air mail or sea mail.

In Bangkok, the Central GPO on Charoen Krung New Road is open Monday–Friday 8.00 a.m.–8.00 p.m., and 9.00 a.m.–1.00 p.m. on Saturdays, Sundays and public holidays. Outside Bangkok most post offices open from 8.30 a.m.–4.30 p.m on weekdays, and from 8.30 a.m.–12 noon on Saturdays. Almost all the big hotels offer basic mailing services and many newspaper shops sell stamps.

Telephones are located in post offices throughout the country and most of them offer a 24-hour overseas service. Hotels, railway stations, airports and department stores may also have public telephone booths. Thailand now has an IDD service with direct-dial calls available to most international destinations. The charge for a local call is generally Bt5, and for an international call to Europe approximately Bt180 for three minutes. Most big hotels and travel agents offering international dialling services normally add on a hefty surcharge.

Maps

Anyone intending to hire a car or motorbike should make sure they get hold of a detailed map of the Kingdom. A number of good country maps are available. Three of the best ones are published by APA, Bartholomew and Nelles. An extremely detailed highway map is also produced by the Department of Highways and is available from many large shopping outlets in Thailand. The map comes in four parts, marks most of the names and routes both in Thai and English and, along with a more general road map, should be a prerequisite for anyone thinking of driving in the countryside.

Newspapers and Radio

In addition to a plethora of Thai newspapers and several Chinese morning papers and an evening paper, there are also two English language dailies, the *Nation* and the *Bangkok Post*. These cover both local and foreign news and can be bought in shops in all the main tourist areas and in hotels. *Newsweek, Time,* the *Far Eastern Economic Review* and the *International Herald Tribune* are also readily available at hotel newsagents, supermarkets, department stores and leading book stores.

Thailand also has its own TV and radio stations. AM is devoted entirely to Thai language programmes. FM frequencies have several English language broadcasts on 97 MHz with news bulletins held every hour and a full round up of local and international events at 8 p.m. every weekday.

Photography

Film processing in Thailand can be done as quick as a flash. A film left in the morning will be back in the afternoon. By contrast, slides are sent to laboratories and do not always come back in good condition. Good and reliable places either for purchasing equipment or for processing film in Bangkok include AV Camera at 310/2 Silom Road, next to the Central Department Store, and Sunny Camera Trading, opposite the Oriental Hotel.

As a rule films are marginally cheaper in Thailand than in Europe, although it can sometimes be difficult

In the Central Plains farmers can harvest three crops of rice a year.

to get hold of high sensitive ASA 400 film. Some photographers claim that it is safer to bring along your own stock so that you can be assured that they have not been exposed to excessive heat.

Remember when packing your camera gear to bring along silica gel bags or any other form of drying agent. Filters, polarizing lens and a sun hood are also vital to cut out the searing glare.

Dry Cleaning and Laundry
Most hotels return laundry within 24 hours some the same day. Dry cleaning generally takes one day Besides hotels there are numerous laundrettes in Bangkok and the major towns.

Guides and Tours
Countless reliable guides and tour agencies exist in Bangkok and all the major cities Beware touts and guides who approach you on the street and offer to take you on tours or to see gem factories or shopping arcades. If in doubt enquire at the Tourist Authority of Thailand (TAT) or take an official tour with your hotel.

Touts

Be aware of self-appointed guides, touts or those who seek to sell you "special price gems". They are in all major tourist centres and are generally well-dressed and helpful, but often cost a lot more than they are worth.

Lost Property

Check first with your hotel receptionist if you lose anything, then report the loss to the nearest police station or, in Bangkok, to the Tourist Police.

Toilets

Typically a Thai toilet is of the squatting type, but most tourist facilities now have sit down loos If taken short, ask for *"hong nam"* or bathroom. To be safe bring a toilet roll with you.

Electricity

The standard supply in Thailand is 220-volt, 50-hertz A.C. Most hotels have a point for shavers and some have 110-volt sockets as well.

Religious Services

In Thailand more than 90 per cent of the population are Buddhists, but Muslim, Christian, Hindu and other faiths are also well represented The following Christian churches can be found in Bangkok.

Assumption Cathedral
21 Oriental Avenue
Tel: 234 8666

Christ Church,
11 Convent Road
Tel: 234 3634

Evangelical Church
end of Soi 10
Sukhumvit Road
Tel: 251 9539

Holy Redeemer Catholic Church
123/19 Soi Raum Rudee
Wireless (Withaya) Road
Tel: 253 0305

Tourist Information Offices

The Tourism Authority of Thailand (TAT) operates offices in Bangkok and all major cities. They distribute leaflets, maps and other useful information. For details contact:

Head Office
Ratchadamnoen Nok Avenue
Bangkok
Tel: 282 4175-9

Chiang Mai
105/1 Chiang Mai-Lamphun Road
Tel: 248 604 or 248 607

Hat Yai
1/1 Soi 2 Niphat Uthit 3 Road
Tel: 241 741 or 245 986

Kanchanaburi
Saeng Chuto Road
Tel: 511 200

Nakhon Ratchasima (Korat)
2102–2104 Mittraphap Road
Tel: 243 751

Pattaya
382/1 Chaihat Road
Tel: 428 750

Phitsanulok
209/7–8 Surasi Trade Centre
Boromtrailokanat Road
Tel: 252 742-3

Phuket
73–75 Phuket Road
Tel: 212 213 or 211 036

Surat Thani
5 Talat Mai Road
Tel: 282 828 or 281 828

Ubon Ratchathani
264/1 Khuan Thani Road
Tel: 241 770-1

Courtesy or Calculation
The Americans may have Dan Quayle, the French their Exocet missiles, but for the Thais, their biggest weapon is undoubtedly the one they carry around on their face. The Thai smile has brought them admirers, and made Thailand one of the most popular tourist destinations in the world. Teachers use it when they are embarrassed. Politicians use it to evade questions. And criminals use it when they are caught red-handed. And any foreigner worth his salt should use it if only to appease the Thais—but trust it? That's another story.

Drugs

Thailand is one of the world's major conduits for drugs smuggled over the border from the Golden Triangle. Under no circumstances carry drugs or take any luggage that is not yours. Possessing, trading or smoking drugs is punishable by prison sentences, whilst possession of heroin can carry the death penalty.

Puud Pasar Angrit? (Can You Speak English?)

The answer in most cases is likely to be no, although these days, the number of English speakers in Bangkok, Chiang Mai and Phuket is now quite high.

Given the brief nature of most people's stay and the complexity of the Thai language—it is tonal, has 48 vowels and 44 consonants—few visitors get much further than *"puud pasar Thai mae dai"* ("I cannot speak Thai"). But any one who is prepared to make the effort will find themselves bountifully rewarded. Thai is a delightful language providing a wonderful insight into both the culture and the people. What is more, even the most basic attempt is appreciated by the locals.

At the back of the book is a list of useful words and phrases. Men should always remember to say *kap* after every phrase—and women *ka.* Meanwhile start out with *sawatdee kap/ka* (hello), *khop khoon kap* (thank you) and *hong nam* (toilet). Finally, as they say in Thailand *"sanuk mak"* ("have a good time").

Sunset over the ancient temples of Sukhothai—perhaps one of many you will see during your stay in this beautiful country.

Traveller's Tips

To keep your hosts content and to enjoy your stay to the full, there are a some important things worth remembering. Respect the King and Buddhism, both of which are universally revered, dress smartly when visiting temples, and do not go nude bathing on the beaches.

Beware of touts or locals who offer to take you on tours or to show you around shops or gem stores.

Finally, you should avoid showing any anger or frustration. The Thais have unlimited amounts of patience, a smile that on the surface at least never runs out and an expectation that

The Ultimate Extremity
Feet are not a popular extremity with the Thais. If the head is the most respected part of the anatomy, the feet come bottom and are considered the lowest. As such they should never be pointed at anyone. Considering that the average western man's foot measures almost double the average Thai foot, the chances of insult are obviously much higher. The Tourist Authorities sum it up easily—"Avoid crossing your legs".

everyone else will behave likewise. Try to follow their example. Doing so will make your life easier and help preserve Thailand for everyone as "The Land of Smiles".

THE COUNTRY, ITS HISTORY AND ITS PEOPLE

Pearl of the Orient Combining the Best of East and West

With its dazzling white beaches, lush rice fields and glittering temples, Thailand sums up the unchanging image of Asia. Yet with its vibrant economy, luxurious hotels and teaming capital, it has become an increasingly progressive society. The two combine to create one of the cultural and historical experiences in the East.

No wonder the Thais are smiling. A nation of 55 million people with 22,000 glittering temples and 5 million Buddha images, who wouldn't be happy? But then Thailand also has some of the finest food in the region, a King adored by his minions and one of the fastest growing, dirtiest and most vibrant cities in the world.

Indeed whilst centuries of progress have brought unprecedented changes to this ancient Kingdom, the sheer

Sanuk or "good time" is as inbred amongst the Thais as Buddhism itself. Where better to show it than at a temple fair giving thanks for the country they live in.

wealth of culture, the sense of pride brought about by lack of colonization and the deep reverence for Buddhism and for the King remain.

Here you can see saffron-robed monks bless aeroplanes, spirit houses nestling under condominiums and thousand year old festivals. Here too, 60 per cent of the people still work the rice fields as they have for centuries.

The remarkable paradoxes are more than anything summed up in Bangkok, a city hurtling into the modern world, a world in which little thought has gone into the future and where more than 1 million vehicles pump out a ton of lead a day.

But to see another side of Thailand, you must leave Bangkok and head for the ancient ruined cities of Ayutthaya,

with colours and with contradictions, enough to turn the ordinary into the extraordinary, the unexpected into the norm.

In some ways too the people have reached a crossroads: delighted by new things and keen to show their country to westerners, but wiser to the ways of the world, surer of themselves and their place in the overall plan of things.

Yet the very essence of Thailand, which entranced early explorers, remains in the colour, the vibrancy and above all all the joie de vivre of its inhabitants. It is this which visitors will remember long after the photographs have faded.

Geography

A land of rivers, of lush rice fields and dazzling white beaches, Thailand can often seem like several different countries rolled into one. At one minute you can be on an island surrounded by limestone cliffs, the next in a deep forested plateau or on the arid plains of Isaan.

Geographically there are however five distinctive regions. Sweeping down from the foothills of the Himalayas, bisected by the rivers Ping, Yom and Nan is the Northern region, part of the geographical mass that stretches from Indochina, from Burma and Laos. The area is mountainous rising to 2,565 m above sea-level at Doi Inthanon, criss-crossed by valleys and caves.

Further south, the countryside opens into the wide open plains of the Chao Phya Valley, a vast rice bowl that is one of the most fertile areas on earth, home to 30 per cent of the national

*Y*ears ago they were everywhere. Now floating markets are a rarity. But, like many things in Thailand, they are still a dream come true.

Sukhothai and Si Satchanalai, the hill-tribes of the north or the wilderness of the border lands with dirt tracks running to endless horizons.

In Chiang Mai, Thailand's second city you will find fine handicrafts, countless temples, elephants and hill-treks. Or try one of the 53 National Parks or the islands speckled like gems around the Gulf of Thailand and the Andaman Sea. Even Bangkok is more like countless towns than one city.

Indeed wherever you are, the pervasive feel is of a country still seething population and to the sprawling capital of Bangkok.

To the north-east a vast plateau extends over one-third of the country across a landscape that is more arid, dryer and poorer, jutting out to Laos and Cambodia. Whilst to the south, along the incongruous peninsula that leads down to Malaysia, lies the region of beaches and islands and the turquoise waters of the Gulf of Thailand and the Andaman Sea.

Facts and Figures

Geography Thailand occupies a land mass approximately the size of France covering 514,000 sq km. To the north it borders Burma and Laos; to the east Cambodia; to the south, Malaysia. Major rivers are the Mekong, the Chao Phya, which is formed by the Yom, the Ping, the Wang and the Nan. The highest mountain is Doi Inthanon in the northern region which is 2,565 metres.

Population 56 million of whom 78 per cent are ethnic Thai, 15 per cent Chinese, 5 per cent Malays and less than 0.1 per cent are western residents. Bangkok, the capital has 7 million; Chiang Mai, the second largest city has just 150,000; Korat 130,000; Hat Yai 100,000.

Government Thailand has been a constitutional monarchy since 1932; the King is head of state, head of the armed forces and guardian of all religions. Legislation is exercised through the National Assembly. Administration is carried through 73 provinces (chanwat), which are in turn divided into 561 districts (tambons) and some 44,000 villages (moubans).

Religion Buddhism is the national religion and is embraced by at least 90 per cent of the population. Some 4 per cent is Muslim, 0.6 per cent, Christian and 0.4 per cent, other faiths.

Not all of the countryside has been left untouched. Rapid economic development has left deep scars on the land, depriving it of many beautiful teak trees and of the wild elephants and rich birdlife that once inhabited its vast forest canopy. But Thailand is big enough to have mountains rising to 2,565 m, national parks covering over 25,000 sq km and still some of the finest natural sights that Asia has to offer.

Diversity and Character of the People

One word more than any other sums up the character of the people. *Sanuk* is the hallmark of the Thais. Literally it means "good time", and in practice it governs much of the way people work, rest and play.

From the hospitable northerners to the cosmopolitan Bangkokeans, Thais have a relish for life, for good food and for Mekong whisky: a gaiety manifest in their Snoopy T-shirts and love for Christmas lights, in their delight with scandal, their reverence for tradition.

Beneath the light-hearted exterior, the Thais are nothing if not hard workers. They are some of the biggest producers of computer chips in the world, as well as some of the most meticulous and highly thought-of civil servants. It's just that whenever possible, non-*sanuk* activities should not interfere with the good things in life, which in practice means just about everything.

But there is little else that is uniform amongst the 55 million population. Although many of the original Thais descended from Western China thousands of years ago, many others are recent arrivals who have come from the surrounding region, intermarried and adopted Thai names. Thus there are more Lhao in Thailand than there are in Laos—some 3 million of them—as well as Khmers, Mons and ethnic hilltribes. Indeed the country has long been a melting pot for migrants from China, from Cambodia and from neighbouring Malaysia.

Thus Thais can be tall or small, squint eyed or squat. Still, as one early explorer gratefully noted even as far back as the 17th century "the women are beautiful" and "the inhabitants much given to *ryot*".

But more than anything, the people are held together by their belief in the King and in Buddhism, and by a fierce pride in being Thai—a pride that is infectious, a smile that is pervasive if enigmatic and a sense of momentum and enthusiasm found in few other places to such abundance.

Rising Star of Asia

Once it was rice and nothing but rice that was the nation's backbone. Now to the golden grain have been added tourism, finance, manufacturing, and foodstuffs, ingredients enough for some people to hail Thailand the Rising Star of Asia.

Sixty per cent of the people still work the land, and produce more than 22 million tons of rice each year. Thailand is the biggest rice producer in the world, exporting as far afield as Russia and Senegal. It's just that to rice have been added tapioca, maize, rubber, sugar cane, coconuts and cassava, as well as beans, cotton, tobacco, strawberries and even frozen chickens.

Thailand is also the biggest exporter of tinned pineapple in the world. It processes more than two million metric tonnes of marine fish a year, and is one of the largest exporters of canned tuna and prawns.

But the chief source of revenue is manufacturing. Thailand is now doing for textiles, shoes and computer disk drives what Hong Kong, Taiwan and Singapore did to cabbage-patch dolls, radios and videos. Thailand produces toys, electronics, jewellery and car components, and it does so more cheaply and more efficiently that many of its neighbours.

The biggest evidence of the boom is in Bangkok itself, where new factories and office blocks fight for space and where day and night trucks carry cement for yet more buildings to produce even more money.

Yet below the surface, Thailand remains a largely rural and relatively poor country. Daily wages in the rice fields are little more than Bt40 a day, with a minimum wage in the cities of Bt103. Even the official statistics show the average annual income per person to be little more than US$1,400 compared with more than US$13,000 in Singapore and US$24,000 in Japan. And whilst areas of metropolitan Bangkok are little different from the prosperous suburbs of almost any western capital, large tracts of the north-east remain firmly below the poverty line.

Buddhism—The Middle Way

Underlying the economy, underlying the people, underlying everything in Thailand is Buddhism, the national religion. Buddhism was first brought to Thailand in 303 BC by missionaries sent out by the emperor Asoke of India. Today more than 90 per cent of the population claim to be Buddhist— of the Hinayana, a sect that came from Sri Lanka and is less fervent, and some say better suited to the Thai character.

The cornerstone of the religion is that life is an endless cycle of birth, suffering, death and rebirth; and that only by attaining merit can eternal release (*nirvana*) be attained, or a better next life be achieved.

The Thais make merit by taking up monastic life—for anything from three weeks to a lifetime—by giving alms or robes to the monks, releasing birds or turtles from captivity, or making donations for a new temple or Buddha.. Such is their earnestness that Thailand now has more than 22,000 temples and 5 million Buddhas. Almost 50 per cent men over the age of 18 will become monks at some stage of life, even including the King. And whilst women cannot join a monastic order they will make amends by donating greater alms, or doing more charitable deeds.

Compared with Christianity, though, Buddhism has few set rules or demands. Rather it provides a medium, a way of thinking. The Thais call it the Middle Way, a philosophy that eschews extremes, encourages tolerance both of other religions and individuals and blends with animism, spiritualism—and most importantly *sanuk*.

*M*ore than 22,000 *temples and five million Buddha images are spread throughout Thailand and almost 50 per cent of men will at some stage become monks. The Thais call it a way of life.*

For those in the *Sangha* (the Holy Order) it's an arduous path. Whilst in a temple they must follow 227 rules. They must abstain from sex or alcohol, from food after midday or from mindful thoughts. They must refrain from killing even so much as an insect, or

37

having more possessions than a wooden bowl for collecting offerings, a pair of sandals, a water filter or a razor blade for shaving. But their rewards are a universal respect and a step along the path to mindfulness and to eternal release.

For the layman, Buddhism plays a no less important role. On a basic level it provides some form of moral order; but more importantly, it gives meaning to the present and hope for the future.

Buddhism may weaken as poverty gives way to prosperity, but it will remain the support and moral code of the Thais and the underlying force that will help the people through the vicissitudes of daily life and on up the ladder of success in Asia.

History

Probably in no other country in the world is the history of a nation such an inextricable source of pride as it is to the Thais. Not only was Thailand the only country in South-east Asia never to be colonized, but it also avoided civil wars and the ideological struggles that affected neighbouring kingdoms. What's more, recent discoveries suggest that it may even have been home to one of the world's earliest bronze age civilizations.

It takes more than a few skulls to prove you are one of the oldest bronze age civilizations in the world, but Ban Chiang's relics are a strong starting point.

Prehistory

It all started with a chance discovery at the small village of Ban Kao on the Kwai Noi River. During the 2nd World War, a Dutch prisoner of war came across a collection of tombs containing human remains dating back to the Neolithic Period. The finds were followed by the discovery of 4,000 year old paintings at Pha Taem in the north-east of Thailand. Then in Ban Chiang, ancient pots and weapons

were unearthed, along with fine sandstone moulds and the world's oldest known socketed tool. The pots were dated as early as 6,800 BC. Even more astounding, these same pots carried the thumb impressed patterns which been discovered as far afield as Mesopotamia, Iraq and Turkey. Some anthropologists now suggest that the people of Ban Chiang may have emigrated taking these techniques to other continents. Others claim that trade may have existed between settlements that developed simultaneously in Thailand, Asia Minor and the Americas. Yet like much of early Thai history, the exact origins of the people of Ban Chiang remain shrouded in uncertainty.

The first inhabitants of Thailand whose origins are known were the Khoms, who spread from a powerful Indian-influenced kingdom in Cambodia. From the 6th–7th century, another Indianized people called the Mons set up a collection of city states around Lopburi, which thrived until the 11th century. To the south, there sprang up the Kingdom of Srivijaya, thought to have been centred in Sumatra, which dominated the Malay Peninsula and the Indonesian Archipelago from the 8th–13th century.

Between the 8th and 11th centuries, the Khmers also arrived from Angkor—in present day Cambodia—attracted to the land by its green and fertile plains. Gradually they absorbed vast areas once ruled by the Mons, spreading as far west as Kanchanaburi, as far south as Petchburi and across the whole of the north-east region, where they left behind the great temples of Phimai, Phanom Rung and Muang Tham.

The Thais themselves are thought to have come later, originating in China somewhere on the western border of Outer Mongolia, whence they steadily migrated south and west.

From about the 10th century, the Thais started to move down river and into modern Thailand, where they split into two main groups. One concentrated in the north and formed the kingdom of Lan Na. The other gathered further south, where they defeated the Khmers and set up the kingdom of Sukhothai.

Lan Na

Early chronicles trace the origin of Lan Na (Land of a Million Rice Fields) to the principality of Chiang Saen on the south bank of the Mekong River opposite Lan Xiang (Land of a Million Elephants). Its first and best known leader was a Lawa chieftain named King Mengrai, who ascended the throne in 1259. Within his reign he extended his kingdom from the borders of Laos to present day Lamphun, and successfully captured the ancient Mon stronghold of Harupinjaya, which had ruled since the 6th century.

Mengrai also founded a new capital in Chiang Mai. It was situated on the River Ping on the spot where two white sambars, two white barking deer and a family of five white mice were seen together. Lan Na flourished for over 200 years. Its art and literature reached a peak in the middle of the 15th century under King Tilokoraj. Chiang Mai was even chosen as the spot to host the eighth world synod of Theravada Buddhism.

However, following the death of King Tilokoraj the kingdom suffered

recurrent internal conflicts. Lan Na was further weakened by wars with Sukhothai's successor, Ayutthaya, and with the Burmese. Finally the Burmese under the King of Pegu invaded in 1558, occupying much of the country until the end of the 18th century when Lan Na came under the sway of a unified Siam. Yet until 1939 and the reign of King Rama VIII, the

The Khmers from Cambodia did more than occupy parts of Thailand. They also left behind them some of the most powerful stone carvings in history.

40

region continued to have a certain amount of independence with its own *chao* (prince-governor).

Sukhothai

"This kingdom of Sukhothai is good, there is rice in the fields, there is fish in the water. The ruler does not levy taxes on his subjects.Those who want to laugh can laugh. Those who want to cry can cry." Thus reads a stone inscription from the the reign of King Ramkhamhaeng The Great.

Sukhothai, Dawn of Happiness, was the first great Thai kingdom, centre of a golden age of Thai culture. It was founded in 1238 by two Thai governors who rebelled against the Khmers; and it went on to become the dominant military power in the region.

At its peak, the kingdom's borders stretched from Lampang in the north to Vientiane in present day Laos and south towards the Malay Peninsula. Its biggest contribution though was in the arts where Sukhothai contributed some of the finest examples of Thai sculpture in history, many of which can still be found in the old city today.

Under Ramkhamhaeng (Rama the Brave), the most famous of its monarchs, Sukhothai developed strong links with neighbouring China. Potters were invited to teach the Thais the art of glazing pottery, and extensive trade was established with Cambodia and India.

Ramkamhaeng dispensed justice in public assembly, abolished slavery, established Buddhism as the national religion and is even credited with inventing the Thai alphabet.

But though a golden age of religion and culture, the rule was short-lived;

and in 1365 Sukhothai became a vassal state, relinquishing its power to the kingdom of Ayutthaya, a city lying to the south on the confluence of the three rivers Chao Phya, Pa Sak and Lopburi.

Ayutthaya

The beginnings of the great kingdom of Ayutthaya are as magnificent and as legendary as the 400-year-old history of the city itself.

Thai folklore tells of the unmarried daughter of the king of Traitrung, who became pregnant after eating an eggplant fertilized by the urine of a gardener. The gardener, Nae Saen Pom, Man of a Hundred Thousand Warts, was banished along with the princess and her son U-Thong. But the god Indra took pity, gave them a kingdom and made U-Thong, Prince of the Golden Crib, the first ruler.

U-Thong founded Ayutthaya in 1350 on an island formed by the confluence of three rivers and surrounded by rice terraces. He named it after Rama's legendary kingdom in India. The early years were spent in conflict with Sukhothai and the Khmers, but by 1431, after a series of victories against the Khmers, forces from Ayutthaya sacked the Cambodian capital at Angkor.

Over the following centuries, under King Trailokanat and a succession of legendary monarchs, Ayutthaya was to become the most beautiful and the most awe-inspiring kingdom in the East, with a population of over 1 million, hundreds of exquisite temples copied from the Khmer structures of Angkor, and more than 30 miles of waterways and roads.

The directors of the East India company compared it with London. The Abbé de Choisy, a Jesuit priest, a celebrated transvestite and a man of considerable literary powers wrote in the 17th century "The streets stretching out of sight are alleys of clear running water. The horizon is tall trees, above which are visible the sparkling towers and pyramids of the pagodas. I myself have never seen lovelier."

The kings of Ayutthaya were absolute monarchs worshipped as gods. No house outside the palace could be built more than one storey high, to ensure than no one could look down on the King. Any mortal who so much as addressed his Royal Highness was obliged to begin as follows: "High and mighty lord of me thy slave, I desire to take thy royal word and put it in my brain and on the top of my head".

The King rarely showed himself to his subjects, who were required to withdraw behind closed doors when they heard the royal musicians announce his appearance. Any loiterers who were unfortunate enough to be caught were summarily chastised with bamboos.

Being a king was still, however, a risky business. More than 10 of the 34 kings of Ayutthaya were murdered, although mainly by members of their family—cousins or nephews.

European Influence

One of the greatest periods of Thai history emerged during the 17th century with the positioning of the country as a hub for international trade between China, the East Indies and the West.

The first Europeans to arrive were the Portuguese, who traded cannon with the Siamese, who pulled them behind their elephants. In 1605, the Dutch began trading with Ayutthaya, and in 1612, the British. But it was the French who during the reign of Louis XIV made the biggest headway. One incident especially served to increase this.

During the reign of King Narai (1657–1688), a Greek adventurer named Gerakis Constantine Phaulkon arrived in Ayutthaya by boat and worked his way up from a humble trader through the government ranks until he became the King's First

White Elephants

Until the late 19th century, white elephants were considered the ultimate symbol of Siamese royalty and were honoured by beautiful-sounding names, as well as a large government department to look after their wellbeing. When a white elephant was first captured, it would be bathed in tamarind water, fed specially-blessed pieces of sugar cane inscribed with its name, and eulogized by odes composed by the court poets to induce the *Phra Elephant* (Descendent of the Angel) to sleep. Some members of royalty were especially associated with the illustrious animals. King Ramkhamhaeng of Sukhothai was a master of elephant-back combat, defeating in single armed combat a Burmese prince. King Narai of Ayutthaya had several battalions of the noble beasts. King Chulalongkorn was even honoured with the title Lord of the White Elephant. Foreign visitors who arrived during the early centuries were, however, disappointed to discover that the white elephants were not in fact white, but albino with pink and yellow eyes, a light reddish brown skin and white toe nails.

Minister and the second most important man in the land. In this role he acted as the principal go-between in diplomatic exchanges, and encouraged close links especially with the French. In 1680 and 1683, Narai dispatched Siamese missions to Paris and in 1685, the French reciprocated by sending their own ambassador, a man named Chevalier de Chaumont. Phaulkon also encouraged the presence of Jesuit missionaries—he was himself a Catholic convert. A French Catholic school called the College of Nations was even set up to educate the philistine Siamese in the joys of Christianity.

But the dizzy rise of Phaulkon and his unconcealed arrogance sealed the end for foreigners. And in 1688, in a bloody revolt led by General Phetracha and his son Luang Surasak, most foreigners were expelled and Phaulkon was beheaded. Thailand had little contact with the west for over 150 years.

Throughout this period, the kings of Ayutthaya were involved in intermittent wars to annex Lan Na and various principalities in the Malay Peninsula. In their struggles for supremacy, the main opponent was always Burma.

In a campaign of 1549, Queen Suriyothai and her daughter led forays out of the besieged city to demoralize the Burmese. Suriyothai saved her husband's life, but lost her own.

Twenty years later, the news that the Thais had captured auspicious white elephants to train for further wars inspired another Burmese attack. This time the Burmese entered the capital and ruled it as a vassal state until 1593. Then, using 250,000 foot soldiers and 3,000 war elephants, the legendary King Naresuen, defeated the Burmese at Nong Sarai and won back Ayutthaya's independence.

Naresuen went on to regain all Ayutthaya's former territories as well as gaining dominion over Chiang Mai. But Ayutthaya's glorious days were limited. Less than two centuries later, in 1767, another Burmese invasion succeeded in capturing Ayutthaya after a siege of 14 months. The city was pillaged, gold religious images were melted down and almost 400 years of history laid to waste.

Of Men and War

17th century accounts of Siamese warfare, whilst filled with admiration for the Thai soldiers' ability to outmanoeuvre the opposition, cast a new light on their abilities to gain victory. As one Persian account summarizes "They have no intention of killing one another or inflicting any great slaughter. The fixed custom is that when two factions have lined up before one another, a group from each side comes forward, beating kettledrums and playing flutes, and the infantry and the horseman on both sides begin dancing and shouting and raising all the noise they can. Every so often one army advances and the other retreats and in that way the one that has some luck manages to catch the other off guard".

Thus it was with cannon, which the Thais acquired from the Portuguese and dragged behind their elephants, although they never fired them. On certain occasions, the Thai foot soldiers even donned specially coloured uniforms to confuse and dazzle the enemy.

The proof of success? The fact that alone in South-east Asia, Thailand was never colonized.

Taksin

The fall of Ayutthaya marked the biggest tragedy in Thai history, a tragedy that is poignantly remembered to this day. But it was followed by just as quick a turnaround.

During the final stages of the siege, a young general named Phya Taksin gathered a small band of followers and broke free. He raised a new army and, seven months later, expelled the Burmese garrison. But Ayutthaya had been virtually destroyed and a few days later he decided that the capital must be moved. Thonburi, situated on the banks of the Chao Phya River opposite Bangkok was chosen. It was near enough to the sea to facilitate foreign trade, especially the import of arms, yet at a safer distance from the Burmese.

Taksin, as he was popularly known, ruled until 1782. During his reign, Chiang Mai and the rest of northern Thailand were liberated from Burmese rule and Cambodia and most of present day Laos were brought under Thai sovereignty. These victories were largely due to two brothers whom he honoured with the titles Chao Phya Chakri (Most Honourable General) and Chao Phya Sarisih, and to whom he gave command of the army.

Meanwhile Taksin became convinced that he was a reincarnation of Buddha. He began to flog monks and torture officials and members of his family to make them confess to imaginary crimes. In one of a long line of coups in Thailand, ministers and generals forced him to abdicate and he fled to a monastery. Chao Phya Chakri, who was in Cambodia at the time, was appointed king. Taksin was too great a threat to be left alive and was executed in the manner reserved for royalty. After a dazzling performance of dance and music, he was ceremoniously placed in a black velvet sack and his neck was broken with a club made of scented sandalwood. Thus ended the rule of Thonburi and the chapter of early kingdoms.

The Chakri Dynasty

The greatest of all the dynasties, the Chakris were inaugurated on 6 April 1782, with the coronation of Somdetj Phra Buddha Yot Fa Chulakok, King Rama I, the great-great-grandson of the Thai ambassador to the court of Louis XIV.

One of the king's first acts was to move the capital across the Chao Phya River from Thonburi to a small village known as Bangkok (Village of Plums). He had many of the ruined temples from Ayutthaya brought to his new capital, built new canals in order to hold the annual boat races and drew up new laws to rule the country.

Rama I also secured his country's borders. He defeated a number of Burmese expeditions, after which Burma got embroiled in British colonial conflicts and Thailand was left in peace. Under him, Siam included all of present day Laos and parts of Burma, Cambodia and Kedah province in Malaysia. His son Rama II was a gifted poet. He devoted himself to preserving the remains of Thai literature that had survived the fall of Ayutthaya and produced a classic version of the *Ramakien* or *Thai Ramayana*. He also re-established relations with the west and was successful in promoting trade with China.

Perhaps the best known of the early Chakri monarchs is King Mongkut, Rama IV, who reigned from 1851 to 1868. Ironically this notoriety is largely because of the film The King and I, based on the fanciful memoirs of a Victorian governess named Anna Leonowens, who depicted him as a frivolous and cruel despot.

Yet in Thailand Monghut is fondly remembered as an enlightened monarch and a man of great intellect. A Buddhist monk for 27 years, Mongkhut spoke Latin, English and five other languages. During his reign he presided over the opening of new waterways and roads, created new laws to improve the rights of women and children, and introduced a new currency and the first printing press.

Realizing that Thailand's independence could only be maintained by close cooperation with the colonial powers, he cultivated the great western leaders of the time, writing to Queen Victoria as "our dear sister" and offering elephants to Abraham Lincoln to assist him in his efforts during the American Civil War.

It was astronomy that eventually led to his untimely death. Mongkut calculated that there would be an eclipse

If the legendary figures from the Ramayana had been sufficient to frighten their enemies away, Ayutthaya's and Thonburi's kings could have found time to visit the beaches.

of the sun on 18 August 1868 and led an expedition to the marshy south-east. The eclipse took place as predicted. But Mongkut had little time to celebrate. He contracted malaria during the expedition and died two months later.

King Mongkut's portrayal in the book seems fair in one respect. He seems to have been quite a lusty fellow, and made up for his time in the monastery by fathering 83 children by 35 wives. This according to the *Chronicle of the House of Chakri* was only slightly above average for the first five kings of the dynasty.

King Chulalongkorn

The beginnings of what are perceived to be modern Thailand arrived with the coronation in 1868 of the 15 year old Chulalongkorn as Lord of the White Elephant and the fifth King of the Chakri Dynasty.

After completing his education, Chulalongkorn immediately launched a series of revolutionary reforms. He ended the custom of prostration and allowed officials to sit on chairs during royal audiences. He introduced schools, roads, trams, even Siam's first post office, and sent his sons to be educated abroad so as better to serve their country. He also overhauled administration of the Kingdom, and sanctioned the transition in 1892 to a form of cabinet government with 12 ministers, largely his brothers, who were amongst the most educated men in the Kingdom.

It was during Chulalongkorn's reign that Thailand's present borders were defined. In 1863 the French had signed an agreement with the King of Cambodia that effectively made that country into a French protectorate. The Thais, infuriated by the colonial intrusion, called on the foreign powers to intercede, and in the following decades modernized their army, bought machine guns and made several attempts to reinforce their claim. A confrontation took place in 1893. The French sent frigates to the Chao Phrya River, broke through the Siamese defences, blockaded all trade and forced King Chulalongkorn to cede all of Laos to the French empire.

The French were not the only ones with territorial ambitions. In 1886 Britain annexed Upper Burma, leaving Thailand sandwiched. But, whilst border conflicts and gunboat diplomacy forced Thailand to cede areas of their Kingdom, skilful diplomatic manoeuvring and the desire of the western powers to keep Thailand as a buffer zone between them allowed Thailand to be the only country in South-East Asia to avoid being colonized.

Chulalongkorn's contribution to Thailand's independence is recognized even today. On 23rd October every year a national holiday is celebrated in commemoration and students lay wreaths in memory of the king they call *Phra Piya Maharaj* (The Beloved and Great King).

Chulalongkorn's successors, Oxford-educated Rama VI and Eton-educated Rama VII continued to try to modernize by edict. Surnames were introduced, Thai women were encouraged to grow their hair long like western women, and primary school education was made compulsory. Rama VI also introduced football to Thailand. He had his own team and was so keen for it to win that he regularly offered unrefusable royal appointments to the leading players of other teams, which proved very unpopular.

But reforms begun by King Vajiravudh and his successor King Prachathipok (1925–32), created new and powerful groups in the public service and the army. Many were western-educated and they wanted more influence over policy. In 1930 the world recession hit Thailand, to which the government responded by cutting military and civil service salaries. Disaffection came to a head, and on 24 June 1932 a group of army officers and bureaucrats staged a bloodless revolution, and ended the absolute supremacy of the monarchy.

Modern History

Since 1932, date of the constitutional monarchy, the military has never been far from power. Seventeen coups or attempted coups have shaped the face of the Kingdom, and even the periods of democracy have been punctuated by strong military influence and the omnipresent arm of the army.

T hey fought the Khoms, the Burmese, the Khmers, and even the Lao, yet the Siamese preserved some of their greatest energies for painting temple murals.

In 1939, Field Marshal Phibul Songkhram took over the running of the country. He changed the country's name from Siam to Thailand—meaning Land of the Free—to encourage patriotism. At the same time, Phibul embarked on a civilizing campaign: betel nut chewing and the wearing of traditional dress were discouraged; shoes, hats and coats were declared proper dress in public; even serious casualties and pregnant women were not allowed into hospitals without shoes and hats.

Throughout World War II, Phibul cultivated the Japanese as a way to extend Thailand's influence in Asia. One episode particularly dictated Thailand's future. On 25 January 1942, Phibul declared war on Britain and the United States. But the Thai ambassador, Seni Pramoij, refused to pass on the resolution, arguing that it did not reflect the will of the Thai majority. Thus the Thai government cooperated with the Japanese whilst America supplied the Free Thai movement with money to oppose them.

After the war Thailand returned its conquests and Phibul was replaced. But the post-war reconciliation was again shattered on the morning of 8 June 1946 when the Thai public learned that King Ananda Mahidol, who had recently returned from Switzerland after completing his education, had been found dead in his bed shot through the forehead with a pistol. An independent commission first pronounced it accidental death but later investigations revealed foul play. Several members of the government were forced to resign, including the then Prime Minister.

A Gentleman's Coup

The coup of May 1950 ranked as one of the most unusual, even by the standards of the Thais. The great event began when the then Prime Minister, Phibul Songkhram, was taken at gunpoint onto a naval ship called the Ayutthaya moored in the Chao Phya River. The following day, after fruitless negotiations, forces loyal to the Premier decided to break the deadlock by launching a ground and air attack on the boat. But fearing that their eminent hostage might die an undistinguished death, his captors helped Phibul to swim ashore; from there he was able to telephone his headquarters and was picked up by loyal officers and returned to power.

Despite continued turbulence at home and see-sawing politics, which were increasingly becoming a national feature, Thailand continued to support a strongly pro-American policy. It was the Americans who provided Thailand with the funds to strengthen its vigorous anti-communist stance. During the Vietnam War (1962–73), Thailand was used as a base for US operations and Bangkok became the centre for troop rest and recreation. Largely supported by the US, the economy grew.

This brought prosperity to some, but also problems of vice, drugs and inflation which led to violent demonstrations and calls for an end to martial law. In October 1973, students from Thammasat University, with the support of various prominent liberals, took to the streets demanding a new constitution. Despite attempts by the King to mediate, the confrontation turned to bloodshed. Army leaders sent in tanks and helicopters,which left hundreds dead and wounded.

In 1974 a new constitution was proclaimed by a civil government headed by Prof. Sanya Dharmasakti. This helped to bring an end to military rule—but not for long. A period of instability and unrest was followed by another coup, and in 1977 by yet another constitution.

The 1980's ushered in a period of relative stability, first under General Kriangsak and then under General Prem. Only one abortive coup took place, which was overcome in three days without bloodshed—except for one civilian motorcyclist, who was accidentally shot.

In one of the latest periods of democracy (1988–1991), Chatichai Choonhaven led a coalition of parties for three years of unprecedented economic boom. But charges of corruption and allegations of incompetence again provided the military with an excuse to intervene, and in a bloodless coup the Prime Minister was arrested and held by soldiers in an airport hangar.

Soon after this, a transitional government was appointed which paved the way for new elections and spurred hopes that Thailand might finally have put the ghost of intervention behind it. However, in the early hours of Monday 18 May 1992 those hopes were once again shattered when troops opened fire on thousands of peaceful demonstrators who were calling for the resignation of the non-elected Prime Minister, General Suchinda Kraprayoon. Hundreds of pro-democracy protestors were killed or wounded in the ensuing violence, which recalled some of the most turbulent scenes ever witnessed in Thailand.

Following the intervention of King Bhumipol, the reigning monarch, who called for an end to the shooting, Suchinda was forced to tender his resignation; a temporary acting Prime Minister was appointed, thus paving the way for yet another cycle in the endless saga of Thai politics.

The Monarchy

More than any other figure in modern history, the man known as Bhumipol Adulyadej, ninth in line of the Chakri dynasty, has captured the hearts of the Thai people.

Born in Cambridge, Massachusetts on 5 December 1927, he was educated in Switzerland and, like the great Chulalongkorn and Mongkut, is a member of the House of Chakri.

During his youth, few believed he was destined for Siamese royalty. At that time, his uncle King Vajiravudh was on the throne. But when Rama VI died heirless, and Ananda Mahidol, his elder brother was found shot in the palace, Bhumipol, then only 19 years old, was thrust onto the throne.

"We will rule with *dharma* (righteousness) for the benefits and happiness of the Siamese people" the young king told the massive crowds who gathered at his inauguration in 1950.

Over the last 40 years, the king has done more than that: he has become a symbol of hope for the people, visiting all 73 provinces, setting up royal projects in the furthest-flung corners of the Kingdom, working on substitution crops for the hilltribes, or developing new forms of rice to improve the lot of his subjects.

In times of trouble and uncertainty it is the King who is looked to for support and direction. Nowhere more was that power demonstrated than in the 1992 mass protests when, following the shootings, the King called upon the then Prime Minister and the leader of the opposition democratic party to compromise their position and heal the wounds for the good of the nation.

King Bhumipol is also a man of considerable talent: an accomplished jazz musician, photographer, painter and yachtsman, his pictures have been on display at the national exhibition of fine arts; and his musical compositions are played as far afield as Vienna. At one stage he even had a regular radio spot playing with such greats as Benny Goodman and Lionel Hampton. But to the people, King Bhumipol remains above all a symbol of hope and prosperity, and their ultimate guardian.

Chronology

3,500 BC Bronze age civilization.
6–11th century Arrival of the Mons and Khmers.
10th century Southward migration of the Thais.
1238 Foundation of the kingdom of Sukhothai.
1259 Foundation of the kingdom of Lan Na.
1259–1317 Reign of King Mengrai.
1279 Reign of King Ramkhamhaeng.
1297 Capital of Lan Na founded in Chiang Mai.
1350 Foundation of the kingdom of Ayutthaya.
1376 Sukhothai becomes a vassal.

1390–1431 Expansion of Ayutthaya.
1448–86 Rule of King Trailokanat.
1511 Portuguese embassy in Ayutthaya.
1543 Burmese invasion of Ayutthaya.
1548–78 Ayutthaya under Burmese rule.
1574–90 Rule of King Naresuen the Great.
1578 Chiang Mai invaded by the king of Burma.
1605 Dutch begin trading with Ayutthaya.
1612 English begin trading with Ayutthaya.
1657–88 Rule of King Narai.
1680 Siamese ambassadors at court of Louis XIV.
1675–88 Rise of Constantine Phaulkon.
1688 Anti–foreign uprising. French expelled and Phaulkon executed.
1763 Beginning of war with the Burmese.
1767 Ayutthaya falls to the Burmese.
1768 Burmese driven from Ayutthaya by Taksin.
1768–82 Thonburi made capital of Siam.
1774 Burmese driven out of Chiang Mai.
1782 King Taksin executed.
1782–1809 Reign of Rama 1. Capital moved to Bangkok.
1809–24 Reign of Rama II.
1824–51 Reign of Rama III.
1851–68 Reign of Rama IV.
1855 Trade treaty with Britain.
1856 Trade treaty with France.
1862 Trade treaty with Prussia.
1868–1910 Reign of Rama V.

1885 The British conquer Upper Burma.

1893 French blockade the Chao Phya River.

1893 French annexation of Laos.

1910–25 Reign of Rama VI.

1925–35 Reign of Rama VII.

1932 End of Absolute Monarchy.

1935–46 Reign of Rama VIII.

1939 Siam changes its name to Thailand.

1941 Japanese forces occupy Thailand.

1942 Thailand declares war on Britain and the United States.

1946 Rama VIII found shot.

1946 Reign of Rama IX.

1962–75 Vietnam War.

1973 Massive student protests in Bangkok.

1975 Saigon falls to the North Vietnamese.

1976 Social unrest sparks coup.

1988 Return of democratic government under Chatichai Choonhaven.

1991 17th coup topples government.

1992 General Suchinda becomes Prime Minister.

1992 Hundreds killed and injured in pro-democracy uprising.

Chiang Mai's annual flower festival.

Festivals

Nowhere is the Thai love of life better exemplified than through their festivals. These are times when families come together from distant ends of the country, times to honour ancestors and the spirits, and in some isolated northern villages, provide an opportunity for the boys to meet the girls.

Many of Thailand's festivals go back hundreds, if not thousands, of years. Some, like the Visakha Puja recall the birth, enlightenment and death of the Buddha, all falling on the same day. Others, like the end of the rice harvest, or offerings to Crop Grandmother, are smaller, localized affairs.

Probably the most beautiful of all Thai festivals is the ceremony known as *Loi Krathong*. Under the light of the full moon, thousands of little boats in the shape of open lotus blossoms, each lit by a candle and decorated with incense sticks and floral offerings, are set adrift in every river and canal to pay homage to the Mother of Waters.

But there are other wonderful events such as Songkran, the Thai New Year which is one of the 17 occasions in the year on which, according to Siamese texts, the King must take a ceremonial bath of purification; and which is celebrated throughout the Kingdom, especially in Chiang Mai, with the throwing of water over everyone and the sprinkling of sacred images.

Funerals give rise to sumptuous celebrations as well, with offerings of food and flowers, and magnificent funeral pyres, built of wood, cloth and paper in the form of pavilions. The greater the send-off, it is believed, the better the next life will be. Often parties provide food, alcohol, music and gambling, all of which are intended to lure guests and create more merriment.

Elsewhere ordination of novices, or even the top knot ceremony, during

*P*urification ceremony *to cleanse the spirit.*

Ploughing Ceremony

Few people give credit to the foresight and perspicacity of the noble bull. But every year in Thailand its talents are recognized at a ceremony known as *Bidhi Crat Brah Nangala* or the first ploughing. On that auspicious occasion, and to the sound of the *phiphat* orchestra, two massive white bulls anointed with gold leaf are presented with several types of rice seed by the court astrologer. Depending on which type of grain they consume, the court astrologer pronounces a forecast for the rice crop in the year to come. The festival dates back to ancient times, but remains popular especially with farmers who collect the seed afterwards, which mixed with their own seed is said to produce the most potent form of fertilizer.

52

A Chinese Special Rites procession.

which a child has his or her tuft of hair chopped off, is a cause for rejoicing and an opportunity for much merry-making.

Whilst some of these are private occasions to which camera-bearing foreigners will not be welcomed, many are open for all and sundry. Because the dates of many festivals vary from year to year, you should check on arrival in Thailand. The TAT will be able to provide exact details of all the public celebrations on during your stay.

1991 Calendar of Local and National Festivals

January
10–11 Chaiyaphum Elephant Round Up, Chaiyaphum
18–20 Bo Sang Umbrella Fair, Chiang Mai
21–27 Phra Buddha Chinarat Fair, Phitsanulok
23–31 Don Chedi Memorial Fair, Suphan Buri

February
1–3 Flower Festival, Chiang Mai
8–19 Dragon and Lion Parade, Nakhon Sawan

13–17 Bang Sai Arts and Crafts Fair, Ayutthaya
14–20 Straw Bird Procession Fair, Chai Nat
15–17 King Narai Reign Fair, Lopburi
15–24 Phra Nakhon Khiri Fair, Phetchburi
15–30 March Kite Fighting & Traditional Sports Fair, Bangkok
27–28 Hae Pha Khun That, Nakhon Si Thammarat
26–4 March Mar Chao Mae Lim Ko Nieo Fair, Pattani
28 Magha Puja, Nationwide

March

2–3 Barred Dove Festival, Yala
3–10 Phra Buddha Bat Fair, Saraburi

30 Phanom Rung Fair, Buriram

April

3–5 Poi Sang Long, Mae Hong Son
12–14 Songkran, Nationwide
13–15 Chiang Mai Songkran Festival, Chiang Mai
Mid–Apr Wisutkasat Songkran Festival, Bangkok
13 Pattaya Festival, Pattaya

May

10 Royal Ploughing Ceremony, Bangkok
11–12 Rocket Festival, Yasothon
19 Visakha Puja, Nationwide

New year celebrations.

18–20 Lychee Fair, Chiang Rai
28 Hae Pha Khun Tat Fair,
Nakhon Si Thammarat

June
3–9 Fruit Fair, Chanthaburi

July
21 International Marathon, Phuket
25–27 Candle Festival, Ubon
Ratchathani
27 Tak Bat Dok Mai, Saraburi

August
2–4 Longan Fair, Lamphun
10–16 Rambutan Fair, Surat Thani

September
1 Food and Fruits Fair, Nakhon
Pathom
6–8 Phichit Boat Races, Phichit
14–15 International Swan-boat
Races, Bangkok
17–26 Festival of the 10th lunar
month, Nakhon Si Thammarat
20–22 Chinese Lunar Festival,
Songkhla
20–23 Wax Castle and Boat Racing
Festival Sakon, Nakhon
21–22 Langsat Fair, Uttaradit
21–25 Boat Racing and Produce
Festival, Narathiwat

October
7–16 Vegetarian Festival, Phuket
and Trang
8–12 Kluai Khai Banana Festival,
Kamphaeng Phet
12–13 Lanna Boat Races, Nan
20–30 Chak Phra and Thot
Festival, Surat Thani
21–24 Illuminated Boat Procession,
Nakhon Phanom
22 Buffalo Races, Chonburi

24 Tak Bat Thevo, Uthai Thani

November
9–10 Phimai Boat Races, Nakhon
Ratchasima
16–17 Elephant Round Up, Surin
19–21 Loi Krathong and Candle
Festival , Sukhothai
20–22 Yi Peng Loi Krathong ,
Chiang Mai
20–22 Bang Sai Loi Krathong ,
Ayutthaya
22–24 Thailand Long-boat Races,
Phichit
23–3 Dec River Kwai Bridge Week,
Kanchanaburi
24 Bangkok Marathon, Bangkok

December
3 Trooping of the Colour,
Bangkok
9–15 King's Cup Regatta, Phuket
31 New Year's Eve, Nationwide

Official National Holidays

January 1	New Year's Day
February 28	Magha Puja Day
April 6	Chakri Memorial Day
April 13	Songkran Festival
May 5	Coronation Day
May 10	Royal Ploughing Ceremony
May 28	Visakha Puja Day
July 26	Asalha Puja Day
July 27	Khao Phansa Day (Buddhist Lent)
August 12	H.M. The Queen's Birthday
October 23	Chulalongkorn Day
December 5	H.M. The King's Birthday
December 10	Constitution Day
December 31	New Year's Eve

Life of the Buddha

He was born into a life of luxury, a prince in a kingdom. He could have lived free from the cares of mankind, but he sacrificed everything to search the world for truth, and in so doing he came across the Middle Way, the Way of Wisdom. That philosophy or religion is known as Buddhism and has been passed down by word of mouth from India to Sri Lanka and as far afield as Thailand, Cambodia and Burma.

History tells that Siddharta Gautama was born in the 6th century BC in the kingdom of the Sakyas in present-day Nepal. A rich young prince, he had immense amounts of land, a beautiful wife and son. But shocked by the misery of the world, by death, sickness, war and decrepitude, he left his palace, his wife and his child to go in search of the ways of knowledge. Donning a yellow robe, the sign of a religious man, he went into the forest and for six years wandered the valleys of the Ganges, talking with the great philosophers of the time, starving himself and enduring terrible pain. But neither asceticism nor self-deprivation could bring him truth.

Buddha image at Wat Po.

Buddhist monk in meditation.

Siddharta then talked to Brahmans and the famous hermits, Alara and Udaka. But these men too were unable to bring him spiritual comfort or knowledge. Finally, vanquished, he sat under a fig tree to meditate. For seven days he sat, tempted by Mara the god of evil, buffeted by winds and rain, tormented and filled by doubts. Mara turned into a beautiful woman trying to tempt him with lust and desire, but the Buddha remained steadfast. Mara then wrestled with his mind, exhausting him. But still the Buddha could not be moved. Only the animals looked after the Buddha, with the monkeys bringing him honey and the elephants bringing him water.

Finally on the seventh day under a full moon, the evil spirits, realizing that nothing could shake his purpose, left the Buddha. At that exact moment, a great earthquake shook the Kingdom splitting the fig tree—lotus buds sprang up around the Buddha and the Buddha touched the earth, calling on the world to witness his Enlightenment.

Preaching to his Disciples

After his Enlightenment, Gautama, the Buddha, left the bodhi tree, journeying to the furthest valleys and mountains, preaching to rich men and poor men alike. Soon the word spread near and far, and people came from all around to seek the teachings (dharma) of the Buddha and to become disciples.

History tells how one night the Buddha stayed with a powerful hermit named Uruvela who lived at the head of

Flowers for the Buddha.

the Neran-Jara-Nadi River. Whilst he slept, a serpent king, Phya Naga, tried to kill the Buddha, vomiting poisonous smoke and fire. But the Buddha's strength and inner resolve rendered the serpent king powerless.

On another occasion, legend describes how a man named Devaddata, tried to kill the Buddha by letting loose a wild elephant, but a monk named Ananda sacrificed his own life to save the Buddha.

Even kings listened to the Buddha's words, leaving the luxury of their palaces to follow him and to take the spiritual path that would lead them from suffering, to hope and final release.

The Last Days of the Buddha

Forty years after his Enlightenment, the Buddha undertook his last journey to Pavangara, and from there to his last station in Salavan Park near Kusinara. After taking his last meal of pork, he assembled his disciples and lay down on the ground, his head pointed towards the north. Then he lectured his followers on the four noble truths: Dukkha (Suffering is Inevitable); Samudaya (The cause of Suffering is desire); Nirodha (An end of suffering is possible through the extinction of desire); and Magga (The way to end Suffering is to follow the noble eightfold path).

That path involves cultivating right understanding, right intention, right speech, right action, right livelihood, right effort, right mindfulness and right concentration. It may involve living several different lives in different reincarnations.

Yet more than 2,500 years after the Buddha's final life, it remains the core teaching of monks throughout Thailand and a cornerstone and support for millions of Buddhists throughout the developed and developing world.

Just the Essentials

On a first-time visit to Thailand, you may be overwhelmed by the sheer wealth of choices that you have wherever you start. The major landmarks and places to see are proposed here to help you establish your priorities.

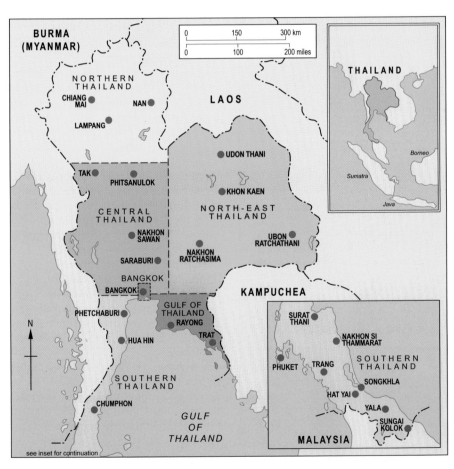

Northern Region
Doi Inthanon: mountain National
Park
Chiang Rai: tribes and trekking
Golden Triangle: legendary border
crossing
Chiang Saen: ruins on the Mekong
River
Mae Sae: northernmost town in
Thailand
Mae Hong Son: city of mists and
spectacular countryside
Mae Salong: picturesque mountain
village
Tha Thon: river journey on the Kok
River
Lampang: horses, carts and temples
Lamphun: charming historic town
Phayao: largest natural lake
Wat Chiang Man: Chiang Mai's oldest
temple
Mae Taem: elephant training centre
Mae Sa: picturesque valley, orchid
farms and snake farms
Doi Suthep: mountainside temple
Nightmarket: vast display of clothes
and handicrafts
Phuping Palace: King's summer
residence
Ban Doi Pui: popular tribal village
Banyen Folk Art Museum: charming
wooden house and antiques
Sankhamhaeng Road: vast
concentration of handicrafts

Gulf of Thailand
Pattaya: sun, sea and sex
Samut Prakarn: world's biggest
crocodile farm
Chantaburi: mountains and gems
Ko Samet: weekend island getaway
Ko Chang: 52-island National Park

North-eastern Region
Khao Yai: National Park and
abundance of birds
Buriram: famous Khmer temples
Korat: silk and pottery
Loei: mountainside National Parks
Nong Khai: Mekong River

Southern Region
Hua Hin: royal resort
Ko Phi Phi: island hopping, fishing
and beaching
Krabi: limestone cliffs and spectacular
coastline
Phuket: international beach resort
Ko Samui: palm-fringed beaches
Phang Nga: famous James Bond
Island
Narathiwat: vast seated buddha
Kaeng Krachin: largely forested
National Park
Phetchburi: old historic town
Ranong: hot springs and lush
countryside
Songkhla: lake and museum
Ko Tarutao: island National Park

Bangkok
Grand Palace: single most impressive
landmark
Wat Phra Kaeo: home of the famous
Emerald Buddha
Wat Arun: beautiful old temple
Pat Pong: world's best-known red light
district
Thonburi: life on the canals
Jim Thompson's: delightful old
residence
Weekend Market: vast outdoor
market
Chinatown: the city's most colourful
and crowded district
National Museum: top history and art
museum

Central Plains
Damnoen Saduak: floating market
Kanchanaburi: bridge over the River
Kwai
Ayutthaya: ancient capital of Siam
Lopburi: old historic city
Sukhothai: beautiful ancient kingdom
Mae Sot: bustling border town

Going Places with Something Special in Mind

For those with specific interests in mind, a better alternative to taking a package tour is to tailor-make your own excursions. Below is a whole series of leisure routes that cater for all kinds of cultural, gastronomic or simply picturesque tastes. Some follow an itinerary. Others show where you can pursue your own interests and should be seen in the context of the main sections.

Northern Hills— Mae Hong Son Circuit

Probably the most beautiful tourist route in the north along a road that twists through mountains and forests with spectacular views along the way. If driving, beware of the hairpin bends.

1 PAI

Charming setting on the Pai River.

*F*rom bustling Bangkok to nomadic tribes may seem a long way, but the ethnic peoples merrily pick flowers just 800 km (500 miles) from the capital.

2 SOPPONG

Departure point for beautiful Cave Lod.

3 MAE HONG SON

Trekking, rafting and elephant rides.

4 MAE SARIANG

Old smuggling town near the Burmese border.

5 BAN OB LUANG

Thailand's version of the Grand Canyon.

6 HOT

Hot springs and pine reafforestation projects.

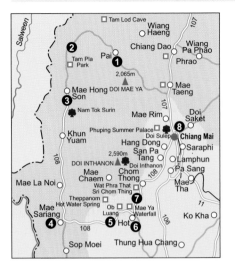

A route through the northern hills.

3 WIANG PA PHAO
Set in a deep valley between hills.

4 MAE SUAI
Bustling northern market town.

5 CHIANG RAI
Sprawling provincial capital founded by King Mengrai.

6 MAE CHAN
Famous for tribal handicrafts and silverware.

7 DOI MAE SALONG
Formerly an opium smuggling town, now better known for its tea.

8 THA THON
Charming town on the Kok River.

9 FANG
Former trading outpost largely destroyed by the Burmese.

7 MAE YA WATERFALL
Lush waterfall, spectacular after the rains.

8 CHIANG MAI
Northern capital and centre for temples and handicrafts.

Scenic Views—From Chiang Mai to Fang

A different and, for the most part, less hostile beauty, yet still there are hills and rice fields, hot springs and impressive limestone cliffs.

1 MAE TAENG
Popular elephant camp and rafting.

2 CHIANG DAO
Spectacular hills and grottoes.

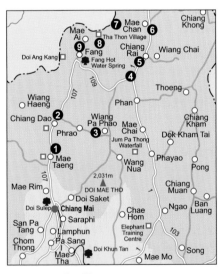

M ore views in the northern hills.

Southern Delights— From Ranong to Krabi

Whilst better known for its beaches than its inland scenery, the South has an abundance of everything. Connoisseurs who can tear themselves away, should try the following.

1 KRA BURI
Narrowest stretch of the peninsula.

2 RANONG
Thermal springs, colourful fishing port and abundant tropical fruits.

3 LAEM SON NATIONAL PARK
Deserted beaches and 20 offshore islands.

4 TAKUA PA
Old tin mining town.

5 KHAO LAK-LUMRU NATIONAL PARK
Quiet undeveloped beaches and rocky coves.

6 PHUKET
Premier international beach resort.

7 PHANG NGA
Catch a boat around staggering limestone cliffs.

8 AO LUK
Than Bokkoroni National Park squeezed between gargantuan rocks.

9 KRABI
Colourful fishing town on the Krabi River.

Southern Beaches— East Coast

This itinerary is for the unashamed beach lover with literally vast amounts of time on his hands. It covers some of the best-known and least-known bathing spots in the region.

1 CHAAM
Popular Thai beach resort.

2 HUA HIN
The royal resort. Beaches play second fiddle.

3 KHAO TAO
Quiet and charming beaches of Hat Sai Noi and Hat Sai Yai.

*P*laces not to miss in southern Thailand.

Kang Kra Chan **1** Chaam
2 Hua Hin
3
Mergui
Sam Roi Yot Mountain Pran Buri **4**
Kui Buri
5 Prachuap Khiri Khan
Huey Yang Waterfall **6**
Thap Sakae
Bang Saphan
Bang Saphan Noi
7 Pathiu
Tha Sae
Kra Buri Pak Nam **8** Chumphon
Ka Poh **9**
Sawi
Ranong Lang Suan
La Mae Ko Phangan
Ko Phangan
Kapoe
1,395m Suan Mok Khapalaram Ko Samui
Ko Samui
Tha Chang
Khuraburi **10** Khanom

Gulf of Thailand

Ko Tao

N

*T*he South's best-loved beaches.

4 SAM ROI YOT
Inland hills, birds and waterside caves.

5 PRACHUAP KHIRI KHAN
Fishing town and popular Thai beach retreat.

6 WANAKON BEACH
Long isolated stretch of beach and pine trees.

7 PATHIU
Beautiful bays with palm-fringed beaches.

8 PAK NAM CHUMPHON
Jump-off point for the nearby island of Mattra surrounded by coral reefs.

9 PAK NAM TAK KO
Visit the beach of Hat Arunothai and the offshore islands.

10 SURAT THANI
Departure point for the idyllic islands of Ko Samui, Ko Phangan and Ko Tao.

Mekong Route

One of the less visited routes with typical Isaan countryside, vast arid stretches of land, the occasional glimpse of the Mekong River and small isolated farming villages.

1 UBON RATCHATANI
Former US airbase, forest temples and provincial hub.

2 KHEMMARAT
Charming market village on the Mekong.

3 PHOPHATEP NATIONAL PARK
Waterfalls and limestone outcroppings.

4 MUKDAHAN
River border trade.

5 THAT PHANOM
Revered Laotian style *chedi*.

6 RENU NAKHON
Famed for its weaving and pretty girls.

7 NAKHON PHANOM
Raw trading town and former US base.

8 BAN PHENG
Small, mainly Laotian community.

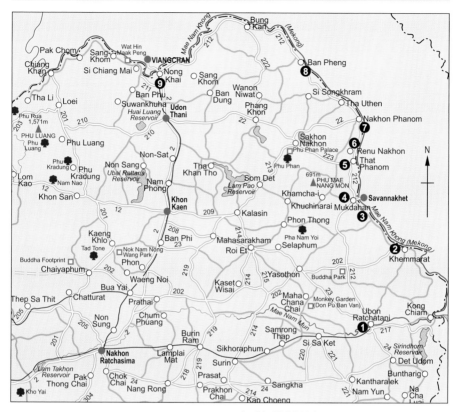

A route along the Mekong river.

9 NONG KHAI
Charming French architecture, lively markets and fine views.

Mekong Route— West of Nong Khai

From Nong Khai the route continues along the banks of the Mekong River with spectacular views over to Laos, with caves, waterfalls and rapids, a gentler, richer countryside.

1 SI CHIANG MAI
Wooden houses, cockfights and charming views.

2 WAT HIN MAAK PENG
Peaceful forest temple.

3 THAN THONG WATERFALLS
Spectacular, but only after the rainy season.

4 SANGKHOM
Waterfalls and Buddha cave of Phatak Sova. Watch out for the gold panners.

5 PAK CHOM
Beautiful countryside and occasional boating opportunities.

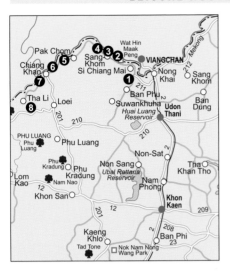

*T*he Mekong Route,
west of Nong Khai.

6 KHUT KHU RAPIDS
Run the rapids, but only in the months just after the rainy season.

7 CHIANG KHAN
Lovely old wooden town set along one of the Mekong.

8 THA LI
Border town near the Heuang River.

The Kwai Valley

This itinerary takes you west from the crowded Bridge of the River Kwai to beautiful National Parks with caves and, further afield, reservoirs and the Burmese border.

1 KANCHANABURI
Historic town.

2 SAI YOK
Caves and waterfall.

3 NAM TOK
Terminus for the famous Death Railway.

4 SAI YOK NATIONAL PARK
Home to the smallest-known bat in the world.

5 TONG PHA PHUM
Old smuggling town on the Khao Laem Reservoir.

6 SANGKLABURI
Charming lake setting and vast wooden bridge.

7 THREE PAGODAS PASS
Rugged border post with Burma.

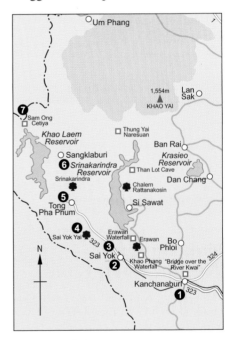

*K*wai Valley.

The Ancient Cities

Historic towns and ancient ruined capitals dot the region known as the Central Plains, home to the first Thai civilizations. For a taste of Siam, go no further.

1 BANG PA IN
Summer residence of former kings.

2 AYUTTHAYA
Ruined ancient capital of Siam.

3 LOPBURI
13th-century Khmer temples and historical museum.

4 CHAI NAT
Old battle ground with the Burmese.

5 KAMPHAENG PHET
Former garrison town of the kingdom of Sukhothai.

6 SUKHOTHAI
Fine ruins and some of the greatest sculptures in Thai history.

7 SI SATCHANALAI
Less visited twin capital of Sukhothai.

Island Hopping

Islands dot the Andaman Sea, some discovered, others still largely off the beaten track and more difficult to get to. Try this for some of the finest gems.

KO PHI PHI
One of the most beautiful islands in South-east Asia.

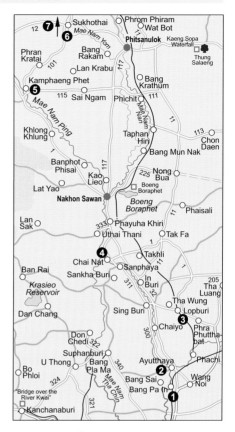

*A*ncient cities in the Central Plains.

KO LANTA
The latest traveller's find with fine white beaches and turquoise seas.

KO HAI
Good reefs for snorkelling.

KO MOOK
Lesser known with palm-fringed beaches and good coral.

KO KRADAN
Fine beaches and luxurious family resorts.

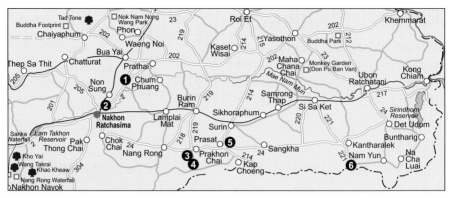

KO TARUTAO
Largest of the 52 islands in the National Park archipelago.

KO ADANG
Smaller, more beautiful, less well known.

Ancient Khmer Ruins

The Khmers left their landmarks not only in the Thai language and script, but in some of the greatest ruins scattered over vast areas of the North-east.

1 PHIMAI
Magnificent 11th-century temple built in the style of Angkor Wat.

2 PHANOM WAN
Smaller than Phimai, but with a wild grandeur.

3 PHANOM RUNG
Sacred mountaintop shrine built by King Siriya Voraman VII of Cambodia.

4 MUANG THAM
Charming 10th-century temple built around lotus pond.

Ancient Khmer ruins.

5 PRASAT BAN PHLUANG
Fine sandstone lintels.

6 KHAO PHRA VIHARN
The most impressive of all, but still largely inaccessible.

Emerald Triangle

Some of the most beautiful and isolated scenery in the north-east, but a journey only for the adventurous—and preferably those who speak reasonable amounts of Thai.

1 KANTHARALAK
Raw nightclubs and markets.

2 NAM YUN
Archetypal one-street Isaan town.

3 NA CHA LUAI
Charming village set in delightful surroundings.

4 KENG LUANG
Jump-off point for beautiful Phuchong Nayoi National Park.

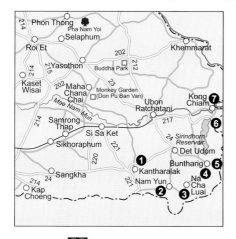

*T*he Emerald Triangle in the north-east.

5 BUNTHARIG
Typical Isaan town near the Srindhorn Reservoir.

6 CHONG MECK
Lhao border market. Try a bottle of 1983-vintage Bulgarian wine.

7 KONG CHIAM
Perfect setting on the confluence of the Moon and Mekong River.

Historic Towns of the South

Thailand's fantastic history encompasses the Arabs, the Khmers, the Mons, the Burmese and even the Portuguese. The following southern towns all have something a little special from another age.

1 PHETCHBURI
Old Mon settlement. Khmer temples.

*H*istoric towns of the south of Thailand.

2 CHAIYA

With the revered Phra Boromathat, thought to be more than 1,200 years old.

3 NAKHON SI THAMMARAT

A former outpost of the great Sri Vijaya empire.

4 SONGKHLA

Museum and old fortifications.

5 PATTANI

Once the home of Arab merchants and of a people who were renowned for their lasciviousness.

6 NARATHIWAT

Old provincial town with colourful markets.

7 PHUKET

Charming Portuguese-style houses.

The Muslim South

The area beyond Hat Yai is better known for its mosques and Muslims than its temples and Thais. There is, however, a little bit of everything.

1 HAT YAI

Swinging southern capital and entertainment centre for Malaysians.

2 CHANA

Beautiful bird cages and cooing doves.

3 PATTANI

Famous mosque.

The Muslim south.

4 NARATHIWAT

Largest seated Buddha in Thailand and beaches.

5 TAK BAI

Border town with Malaysia.

Southern Fishing Ports

Colourful fishing boats line the piers of almost all the main coastal towns that lie along the southern coast. The following are especially worth looking at.

1 CHAAM

Quiet and picturesque, set against gently rising hills.

2 HUA HIN

Colourful, especially at dawn and dusk.

3 PRACHUAP KHIRI KHAN

Sleepy provincial port.

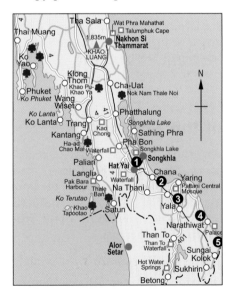

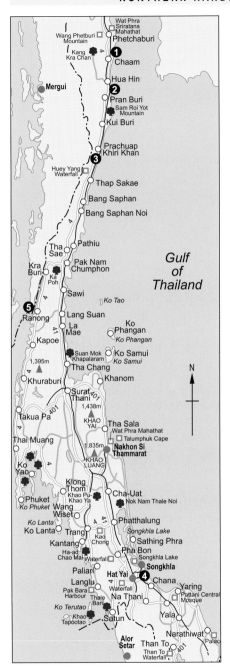

The south's prettiest fishing ports.

4 SONGKHLA
Largest fishing port in Thailand.

5 RANONG
Countless fishing boats and long-tailed boats leaving for Burma.

Ancient Houses

Many of Thailand's charming old residences have been swept aside by progress, but there are still a few well worth visiting.

BANGKOK
Beautiful old wooden houses at Jim Thompson's, Kamthieng House and Suan Pakkard.

CHIANG MAI—BANYEN
A charming old Lan Na style residence.

LOPBURI
Former home of Chevalier de Chaumont, the first French ambassador to Thailand.

SONGKHLA
Fine old wooden houses and the residence of the former governor of Songkhla.

AYUTTHAYA
Beautiful Chan Kasem Palace set in delightful gardens.

Northern Handicraft Centres

The handicrafts in this cheerful region are not surprisingly rated as some of the finest in the country.

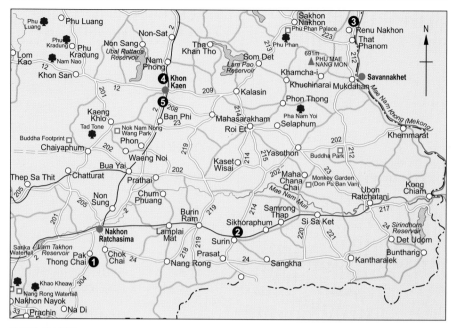

BOR SANG
Colourful umbrellas.

LAMPANG
Silverware and *celadon*.

SANKHAMHAENG
Everything a handicrafts' connoisseur could dream of.

CHIANG MAI
Northern handicraft's centre.

MAE SAI
Delightful *kalaga* tapestries, Burmese puppets and lacquerware.

North-eastern Silk Towns

Not all the silk in Thailand now comes from the country. Some is even said to be imported. But the following north-

North-eastern silk towns.

eastern towns are all famed for producing or marketing the threads.

1 PAK THONG CHAI
One of the region's best-known silk producers.

2 KHAWOWSINRIN
Silk, silver trinkets and Khmer bracelets.

3 RENU NAKHON
Colourful selection of *mutmee* and *axe* pillows.

4 KHON KAEN
Famous giant silk fair in December.

5 BAN CHONNABOT
Watch the process of spinning and weaving.

National Museums

The Thais' natural pride in their past is not always reflected in their preservation of their cultural heritage. The following museums, however, all have items of cultural interest.

1 BANGKOK
One of the most comprehensive museums in south-east Asia.

2 AYUTTHAYA
13th- and 14th-century stone and bronze buddha images.

3 LOPBURI
Lopburi-style sculpture and pavilions from the Ayutthaya period.

4 KORAT
Collection of Khmer artefacts and door lintels.

5 SUKHOTHAI
There is a famous Ramkamhaeng inscription and 14th-century walking Buddha here.

6 CHIANG MAI
Buddha's footprints, folk and hilltribe arts.

7 NAKHON SI THAMMARAT
Southern sculptures and traditional shadow puppets.

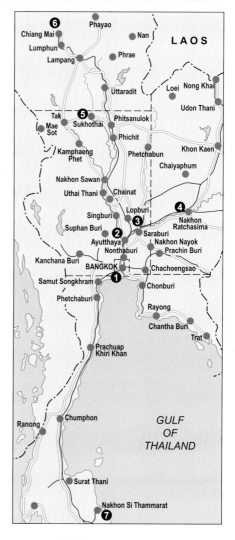

The best museums in the country.

Ancient Civilizations

One of the oldest civilizations in the world. So claim some anthropologists. Budding archaeologists can examine the following.

1 BAN CHIANG
Pots, skulls and bronze dating back thousands of years.

2 BAN KO NOI
Kilns dating back to AD 900.

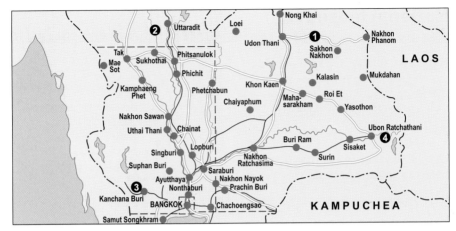

*A*rchaeological sites.

3 BAN KAO
Neolithic remains said to date back 4,000 years.

4 PHA TAEM
2,000- to 4,000-year-old cave paintings.

Northern Temples

The beautiful temples of the north are legendary. The following are all prized either for their northern-style *wats* or for the tales that go with them.

1 LAMPANG
Famed above all for its Wat Phra Kaeo Don Tao.

2 LAMPHUN
Beautiful 11th-century Wat Phra That Haripunchai.

3 CHIANG MAI
Some 300 temples within reach of the town.

4 NAN
Burmese and Laotian style *wats*.

5 CHIANG SAEN
Ancient ruined temples dating from the 13th century.

*S*tar northern temples.

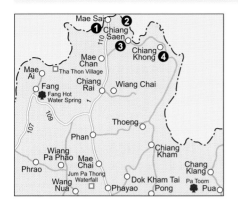

A route through the
Golden Triangle.

Golden Triangle

The most famous of Thailand's tourist
routes through an area of spectacular
scenery, once renowned as an opium
trafficking centre, now better known
for its hotels and river trips.

1 MAE SAI
Busy trading town with large Burmese
minority.

2 BAN SOP RUAP
Official Golden Triangle. Expect
tourists by the thousands.

3 CHIANG SAEN
Historic town on the Mekong.

4 CHIANG KHONG
Picturesque, riverine and away from
the crowds.

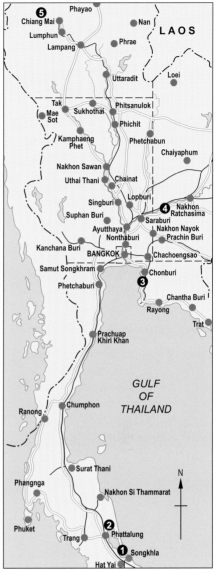

*S*ome good
birdwatching sites.

Birdwatching

Once they were everywhere. Now birds
are becoming a rare commodity. But
there are places to see them, either in
National Parks or for those short of
time, in local zoos.

1 KHU KHUT, SONGKHLA
More than 100 species of waterbird.
Best between December and May.

2 THALE NOI, PHATTALUNG
Rich birdlife in a beautiful lake setting.

3 KHAO KHIAO OPEN ZOO
Thailand's most spectacular aviary.

4 KHAO YAI
Countless hornbills along with orange-breasted and red-headed trogons.

5 DOI INTHANON
Famed for its ashy-throated warbler and yellow-bellied flowerpecker.

*I*sland National Parks.

Island National Parks

These are some of the finest pieces of marine landscape that Thailand has to offer, and are still fortunately under the protection of the National Parks Commission.

1 SURIN ISLANDS
Islands, diving and turquoise seas.

2 SIMILAN ISLANDS
Celebrated above all for diving.

3 TARUTAO ISLANDS
52-island National Park extending towards Malaysian border.

4 ANG THONG MARINE PARK
Strangely shaped islands, largely forested.

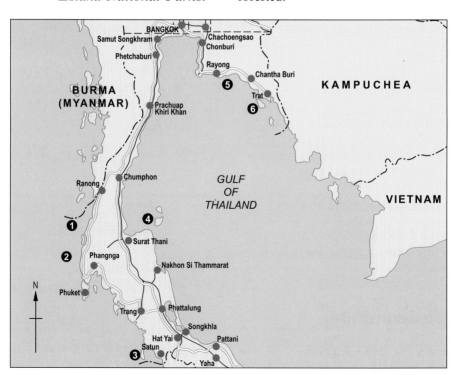

5 KO SAMET
Beautiful, but crowded, especially at weekends.

6 KO CHANG ISLANDS
Wilder, less developed with forest and waterfalls.

Inland National Parks

The trademarks of Thailand's National Parks are beautiful scenery, but not always abundant wildlife. Some, however, do reward those prepared to take time and make the effort.

1 KHAO YAI
One of the biggest concentrations of wildlife in the country.

2 KAENG KRACHIN
Largest National Park with opportunities for trekking.

3 PHU KRADUNG
Vast tabletop plateau with wildflowers and spectacular sunsets.

4 KHAO SOK NATIONAL PARK
Heavily forested and home of the famous jungle trekking lodge.

5 THUNG SALAENG LUANG NATIONAL PARK
Covers 789,000 *rais* of lush green forests and mountains.

The Gulf Coast Route

Early travellers like Henri Mouhot found the Gulf region one of the wildest and lushest in the country.

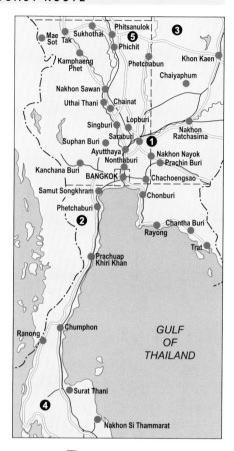

*I*nland National Parks.

These days it is still picturesque. But it's also fast developing as a sort of Thai Riviera.

1 CHONBURI
Busy commercial town.

2 ANG SILA
Fishing village famed for its granite pestles.

3 BANG SAEN
Popular Thai beach resort and water fun park.

77

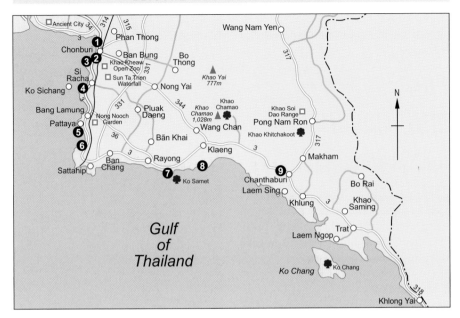

*A*long *the Gulf coast.*

4 SI RACHA
Famous for its health spa and its fiery hot sauce made from crushed shellfish.

5 PATTAYA
The most extreme beach destination in south-east Asia.

6 BANG SARAY
Charming fishing village.

7 BAN PHE
Jump-off point for beautiful Ko Samet.

8 BAN KLAENG
Situated at the end of a beautiful tree-lined road.

9 CHANTHABURI
Gem town set in lush countryside.

The Rice-producing Heartlands

Of the 22 million tons of rice that Thailand produces annually, much comes from the Central Plains. The following lie in the very heart of it, but all have a few other sights worth seeing.

1 SARABURI
Within easy reach of the shrine of the Buddha's holy footprint.

2 SUPHANBURI
Ancient Dvaravati town dating from AD 877.

3 DON CHEDI
Pagoda commemorating the victory of King Naresuan over the Burmese.

4 NAKHON SAWAN
Sprawling rice trading town.

Festivals

November and December are the best months for festivals. With a bit of planning, it may just be possible to fit in the following.

SURIN
Colourful elephant round up.

SUKHOTHAI
The most beautiful place to celebrate Loi Krathong.

CHIANG MAI
Loi Krathong, celebrated with balloons and processions.

KANCHANABURI
Sight and sound show at the bridge over the River Kwai.

BANGKOK
Trooping of the colour to celebrate the King's birthday.

Northern Villages

In the north, villages are more rugged, built at high altitude, with a sense of wildness and a special charm of their own. The following especially have something to captivate.

1 DOI MAE SALONG
Spectacular mountainside setting.

2 PAI
Set in idyllic surroundings within a deep valley .

3 MAE AW
Rugged KMT village high up in the hills.

4 DOI PUI
Picturesque Meo village, but crowded with tourists.

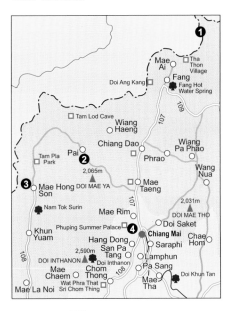

Places to visit in the rice-producing Central Plains.

Charming villages of the north.

Around Phuket

This is a picturesque route that combines some of the most developed beaches in the country with spectacular hilltop views and lush interior landscape.

1 PATONG
The queen of Phuket's beach life.

2 KARON BEACH
Long curving bay stretching for miles.

3 KATA BEACH
Another pleasant and equally beautiful stretch of sand.

4 NAI HARN
Small bay enclosed by headlands.

5 PROMTHEP CAPE
Fine views of the Andaman, especially at sunset.

6 RAWAI
Sleepier, less touristed, famed for its sea gypsies.

7 AO CHALONG
Yachties delight.

8 PHUKET TOWN
Portuguese architecture and brash concrete shops.

Around Ko Samui

The sights on this idyllic island have the reputation not perhaps for their wildness, but for their lush coconut plantations and waterfalls—the perfect complement to days on the beach.

1 NAI THON
Main town and arrival point.

2 MAENAM BEACH
Fishermen and palm trees and memories of days gone by.

3 BIG BUDDHA BEACH
12-metre statue of the sitting Buddha.

4 CHOENG MON
One of the most beautiful beaches reached by a bumpy dirt road.

5 CHAWENG
Most popular and upmarket strip of beach.

6 LAMAI
Strangely shaped "grandfather" rocks.

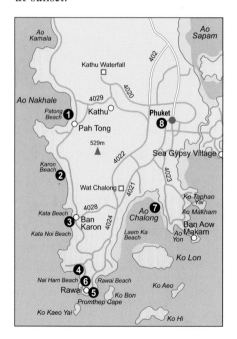

A route around Phuket.

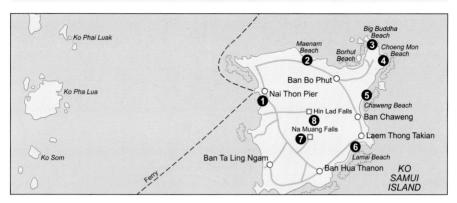

7 NA MUANG WATERFALL
Best seen soon after the rainy season.

8 HIN LAD WATERFALL
Smaller, but with pleasant walks.

What to see on Ko Samui.

Gastronomic Towns

Good food in Thailand can be found almost everywhere. But the following towns claim to have something that they are particularly proud of or in other cases are renowned for.

CHIANG MAI
Khao soi (noodles) and *gaeng hang le* (a thick pork curry).

PATTANI, YALA AND NARATIWAT
Ferociously hot *kaeng tai pla* (fish head kidney curry) and *kaeng lueang* (yellow curry with fish).

SURIN
Larb moo (spicy minced pork) and *somtam* (spicy grated mango salad).

PHUKET
Phuket lobster and every conceivable sort of seafood.

Gardens

Lush and tropical the countryside may be, but the flowers are not always easy to come across. The following all have fine gardens, especially in the months from November to February.

BANGKOK
Rama IX Park contains a large botanical garden and flower garden.

SUAN PAKKARD PALACE (BANGKOK)
set in peaceful gardens with resident pelican.

CHIANG MAI
Phuping Palace set in beautiful grounds.

MAE SA
A veritable hub of orchid farms, gardens and quaint hillside scenery.

Teaming Metropolis and City of Angelic Extremes

Picture seven million people, one million cars, and a ton of lead. Add 400 temples, 11,000 restaurants, markets, high-rises and sleepy canals. Throw in some calm and chaos for good measure, hoards of smiling people, kebab stalls and flowers. Spice in a few more contradictions. And you get Bangkok, Great City of Angels.

It was not always thus. When King Rama I, first monarch of the great Chakri dynasty moved his capital over the banks of the Chao Phya River in 1782, he chose a drab malarial village inhabited by a few Chinese traders. But the King, with the pre-eminence that has given him a lasting place in Thai history, built palaces filled with statues that were brought from Ayutthaya on the back of elephants, laid out canals, and turned it into a city fit for kings.

King Rama I may have started the ball rolling, but his royal successors have also done their bit to make this a city of temples.

By the mid-19th century, reports from westerners described magnificent waterways and beautiful golden barges, barely spoilt by the "almost naked people" and the pariah dogs. But Bangkok's days of somnolence were numbered. During the reign of King Mongkhut (1851–68), new roads were built and in the reign of King Chulalongkorn (1868–1910), trams, hospitals and schools were introduced. Then came the Americans in the mid-1960s, who pumped in millions of dollars as part of their aid support during the Vietnam war. Since then, the city has been transformed into a bristling capital of high-rises and traffic and the administrative centre of the Kingdom.

The Bangkok of today is a mix of everything with its dazzling Grand

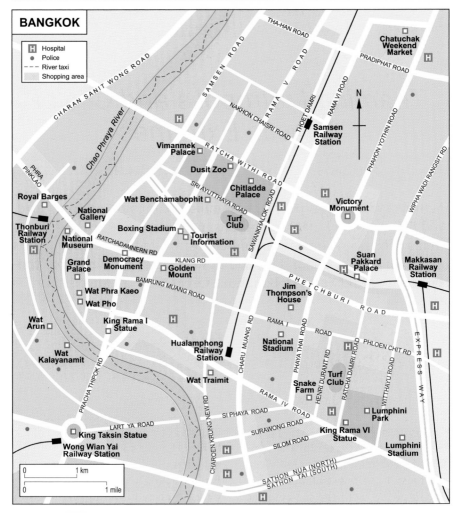

BANGKOK

- H Hospital
- • Police
- -- - River taxi
- Shopping area

Town plan of Bangkok.

Palace—which should not be missed—its 400 temples, and waterways, red light district, markets and museums. More than 10 per cent of the entire population now live here, factory workers and migrants from the northeast residing in the squats of Din Daeng and Klongtoey, and the King himself in Chitralada Palace.

Suitably for a city of such extremes, it also boasts the longest name of any city in the *Guinness Book of Records*. The city's title in full means "Great City of Angels, the Supreme Repository of Divine Jewels, the Great Land Unconquerable, the Grand and Prominent Realm, the Royal and Delightful Capital City Full of Nine Noble Gems, the Highest Royal Dwelling and Grand Palace, the Divine Shelter and Dwelling of the Reincarnated Spirits".

Every corner, every step in this gargantuan city will bring a different impression. Just wander off one of the main streets down the *sois* (lanes) or country lanes, down past the diminutive Chinese woman washing plates, or the market overflowing with fresh papaya, mango and durian. Savour the scent of lotus flowers, freshly cut and sold in garlands, the subtle nuances and the excitement, which combine to make Bangkok a city of endless fascination.

Finally, the more time you invest in the city, the bigger will be the rewards. Bangkok cannot be "done" in a day. It is only through absorbing the calm and the chaos that the real spirit of the place will shine through. And once it does, nowhere will be the same.

Around the City

If you are arriving in Bangkok for the first time, don't expect to find a centre of town. There isn't one. The city's development has been haphazard with temples, hotels and shopping centres spread liberally over an area the size of London or Paris.

There are, however, several major districts connected by a network of busy main roads and winding side streets known as *sois*. All of these areas offer various attractions, but like everything in Bangkok, there is a downside. Getting from one to the other, especially during the rush hours—worst in the early morning and evening, but generally bad all day—can be hot, painful work. So if there is one particular area you are interested in, it is best to stay there.

From snakes' blood to fried grasshoppers and ice cream, Bangkok's band of hearty vendors merrily provide sustenance to appreciating locals.

Before leaving your hotel, make sure that you buy yourself a city map with all the bus routes marked—one of the best is *Tour and Guide Map* published by S.K. Thaveepholcharoen—and if possible get someone to write instructions in Thai. It is also worth dropping by the Tourist Office (TAT) at 4 Ratchadamoen Nok Avenue,Tel: 282 1143, to pick up the latest updates and lists of any festivities.

Finally, forget norms of logic and order. Bangkok does not have any of them. One day there may be glistening main highways, clinically clean subways, even the long promised skytrain.

85

If the founding kings had countenanced Bangkok's soaring condominiums, even the great Chakris might have taken a less progressive line.

Until then enjoy the freneticism and unpredictability that make Bangkok one of the most invigorating cities in the world.

To give you an idea of the city we describe the six main districts. In the later section we then list the various sites broken down into temples, churches, other historic monuments, waterways, zoos, markets, hotels, restaurants and nightlife.

Silom-Surawong

Running east from Charoen Krung New Road on the river to busy Rama IV Road is Bangkok's Oxford Street and Monmartre rolled into one.

On Silom you will find delightful clusters of street stalls, overshadowed by vast office blocks, a beautiful old cemetery, and almost directly opposite the headquarters of Bangkok Bank, Patpong Road, the most well-known red light district in the city—and probably in the world.

At the east end of Silom, over the traffic-ridden, exhaust filled Rama IV Road intersection is the city's principal patch of greenery. Lumpini Park has a lake with paddle boats for hire and some lush green grass, the perfect retreat from the bustling city.

Running parallel to Silom is **Surawong Road**, home to Jim Thompson's Silk Factory, one of the most famous institutions in the city, and to a host of other silk shops, restaurants and hotels.

To get to the bottom of Silom, ask any taxi or *tuk tuk* driver to take you

86

to "Silom soi 23"; or if that fails, the Holiday Inn Hotel. But be warned though. To walk from one end to the other is a considerable distance.

Siam-Pratunam
North of Silom/Surawong along the busy Ratchadamri Road is another area renowned for its shopping.

Siam-Pratunam contains more than ten shopping centres and rows of boutiques selling the latest in Bangkok fashionware. The largest and most fashionable stores are to be found at Peninsula Place on Ratchadamri Road, at the Amarin Plaza and Sogo Department store—and best of all at the **Siam Shopping Centre** on Rama 1. Plans are underway for a 63-storey World Trade Centre complex opposite Ratchadamri Arcade.

At the junction of Phaythai Road with Rama 1—which connects up with Ploenchit Road—is Siam Square, and across the road the Siam Centre with boutiques and cinemas. This is a traditional gathering spot for the young affluent Thais who come for its cinemas and open air markets as well as its pizza huts and ubiquitous McDonalds' hamburgers.

To get there all you need do is ask for Siam Centre. Every taxi driver and *tuk tuk* driver will have heard of it.

Sukhumvit Road
Further to the east, Ploenchit Road becomes Sukhumvit Road, the longest and one of the most disparate roads in the capital. One minute you can be walking down one of the *sub-sois* (small lanes) between Sois 39 and 49, past lush garden mansions where residents sport parrots and sit on wooden

verandas. The next you will come to a half-finished condominium surrounded by towering cranes and workmen.

The roads leading off Sukhumvit do not have names but are denoted in *sois*, starting with Soi 1 at the western end and moving to Soi 103 on the outer fringes towards the Bang Na Trat Highway.

To see the liveliest restaurants go to Soi Langsuan, and for more dubious strips of bars and nightclubs, Soi 21 (Soi Nana) and Soi 23 (Soi Cowboy). The main shopping district is close to the Ambassador and the Landmark

*F*ive hundred different kinds of flower and plant have found their way into Bangkok. Most of them can be seen in Pak Klong market, along with live frogs and pigs' innards.

Hotels, with silk shops and tailors; whilst around the lower numbered sois are to be found most of the hotels and guesthouses.

To the north of Sukhumvit Road is New Phetchburi Road, where building continues with added ferocity, and there is a profusion of executive massage parlours—marble fronted and four-storeys high. There are fewer tourists here, and probably fewer attractions; but there are several big hotels as well as Nasa, the largest discotheque in Thailand.

Before leaving for Sukhumvit work out which end you want to be, a particular landmark like the Central Department Store (pronounced Centan) and preferably the *soi* number too. Otherwise you could end up heading out towards the Cambodian border.

Chinatown

Squashed between Charoen Krung New Road and Yaowaraj Road on the western side of the city lies Bangkok's most colourful and crowded district. In Chinatown there are all the gold shops, the antiques and the excitement of Hong Kong tied with the smiles that are so inextricably Thai.

The best way to explore the area is on foot, along Soi Wanit 1, past the piles of dried fish in bamboo panniers at **Talaht Khao** (old market) and to the area around Ratchawong Road with its labyrinthine streets and stalls selling bird's-nest and shark-fin soup.

Or cross Songwat and head north on busy Soi Issaranuphap with its old colonial houses and pervasive smell of spices and herbs.

To the west of Chinatown at the foot of the Memorial Bridge is **Pak Klong Market**, a gigantic wholesale market selling every shade of orchid, fish and fruit. Get there at dawn to see it at its best; and afterwards visit the **Thieves' Market** in Nakhon Kasem, home to Chinese objets d'art, musical instruments, and to an abundance of fake antiques.

Chinatown can be reached either by bus or by catching a Chao Phya Express Boat and getting off at the Tha Ratchawong Pier. Follow Ratchawong Road from here, turn right onto Soi Wanit and you will be in the thick of things. Once you are there, it's too busy for transport.

Royal Bangkok

Lying further west beyond Chinatown, in a curve of the Chao Phya River is the old heart of the city and the district famed for some of Thailand's greatest temples.

The **Grand Palace**, **Wat Po** and **Wat Phra Kaeo** lie within a stone's throw of one another, surrounded by an arc of

---

New Road
Known as the first road in Thailand, Charoen Krung was built following complaints by foreign residents, who suffered greatly from the smell of rotting refuse and the lack of sanitation, and who wished for roads so that they could promenade and take the air. King Mongkut agreed to their request, and by his death in 1868 there was a network of streets running through the southern part of the city. Not that they stayed in a state fit for promenading. By the time Carl Bock arrived in Bangkok in 1881, he found the Charoen Krung Road to be habitually flooded and in "a chronic state of filth".

water that was dug under the orders of Rama 1 to allow the annual boat races to be held. This is the area to come to for glimpses of *The King and I* with its bejewelled temples and the glorious feel of ancient Siam—or just to wander in

Nine kings and several million people made merit to produce the Grand Palace, and every year they add more gold to make sure that it keeps its shine.

an area still largely untrammelled by the building boom.

Almost opposite the entrance to the Grand Palace is a vast area of green known as **Sanam Luang** (the Royal Field), where in former times the royal white elephants were put out to graze, and where these days spectacular kite fighting takes place at weekends from February to May. Further south, connected by Ratchadamnoen Avenue, lies the Dusit area, largely developed by King Chulalongkorn, Rama V, after his visits to Europe and containing several royal residences, the **National Assembly** and even **the Zoo**.

To explore the area take a tour, or limit yourself to a couple of sights—for example the Grand Palace and Wat Po. Trying to see the whole area in an afternoon would be like trying to run a marathon in an hour. You'd reduce yourself to a heap of exhaustion.

Regal Delights

During the 19th century, the inner walls of the Grand Palace played host to more than just the Royal Family. According to Malcolm Smith, an Englishman who was the Royal Physician in the late 19th century, they constituted the inside quarters or harem containing the king's concubines, all of whom were women of considerable beauty and good family. At its peak, during the reign of Rama V, the inner palace was said to have up to 3,000 residents including many wives of the former ruler, and occasionally even their sisters and mothers, who were thought of as too noble to give away. By the reign of Rama VI, the population, however, began to fall, and now the inner quarters are inhabited only by members of the Phra Tamnak Suan Kularb school, working to preserve court arts.

Thonburi

Beyond the Chao Phaya River, on the west bank, the mood changes: highrises are replaced by smaller, less prosperous dwellings, shady alleys, and the steady chatter of boats ferrying people along the tiny klongs (canals) that bisect the city like arteries.

This area is known as Thonburi, once capital of Siam, now something of a backwater, home to river dwellers and to colourful markets. Main roads carve through the area and the Southern Highway leads out of it—but the canals remain, a reminder of the days when Bangkok was known as Venice of the East.

Although largely overlooked, the area contains several delightful temples such as **Wat Kalayanimit** and the famed turtle temple **Wat Prayoonwong**, as well as the charming old **Santa Cruz Church**. Here too are the narrow alleyways where Europeans such as Robert Hunter and his wife, who was the great-granddaughter of Constantine Phaulkon, resided at the beginning of the century.

Opposite the Thonburi Railway Station is one of the city's most colourful markets, filled with stalls selling fruit and vegetables.

Trips to Thonburi can be organized by boat from the Tha Chang Pier near the Grand Palace or by taking a tour to the famous Floating Market.

A better way, if you have the time, is to cross over Memorial Bridge and to wander down the small streets, with their simple river dwellings.

Touring the Temples

At the end of almost any street, on any corner, you will come across one of

Bangkok's temples. Some are known as Royal Wats, and were built and maintained by kings, while others were built by ordinary citizens or monks as a means of earning merit. One of the most prolific temple builders was King Rama III, who left behind him nine entirely new structures and repaired at least 60 more. King Mongkut, Rama IV, built another five, as well as restoring 35.

Although they are scattered all over the city, several temples are close together. Some like Wat Phra Kaeo are so dazzling there is almost too much to absorb in one visit. Others can be seen from the comfort of the river or glimpsed among sprawling new building sites which have become Bangkok's monuments to capitalism. Almost every hotel and travel agent will organize morning and afternoon tours.

Grand Palace

The most famous landmark in Bangkok and without doubt one of the great sights in the East, is the Grand Palace, situated near the river, a short walk from Tha Chang Pier.

The Grand Palace was begun in 1782 during the reign of King Rama I, and constructed behind a vast walled compound as the symbolic heart of the new capital.

Since then each of the Chakri monarchs has done his bit to add to the splendour, transforming the 2.5 sq km (1 sq mile) area into a glittering fairy world of jewel-encrusted monuments and spires.

The centrepiece is the **Chakri Maha Prasad**, the last of the buildings to be constructed, and completed in 1882 by King Rama V. It was designed by a British architect in the style of the Italian Renaissance, with a central balcony and wide approach stairway, topped by a traditional Thai roof that rises in levels to three seven-tiered spires. A golden urn beneath the towering central spire contains the ashes of the eight Chakri kings, and nearby lie the ashes of some of the other principal members of the royal house. The palace is seldom used, though, except when His Majesty, the King, receives ambassadors from a spectacular *niello* throne.

West of the Chakri Maha Prasat is the delightful **Dusit Maha Prasat** built in 1789 on the site of an earlier building struck by lightening. It comprises a cruciform building with a gilded nine-tier roof supported by four *garudas* (large mythical birds) clasping dragon-headed serpents. The building was originally used as a coronation room and for the revision of the Buddhist scriptures, and these days is still occasionally used for royal functions.

Next door to the Dusit Maha Prasat, you will see an elegant white marble pavilion known as the **Arport Phimok Prasat** (Disrobing Pavilion) where the king alighted from his carriage and stationed his ceremonial hat before entering the throne hall. So impressed was King Chulalongkorn by this beautiful edifice that he built a similar one for his summer residence at Bang Pa-In near Ayutthaya.

East of the Chakri Maha Prasat is the famous **Amarin Winichai Hall**, one of the earliest buildings, constructed during the reign of Rama 1 and containing two thrones. The upper throne, shaped like a boat, is now used as an altar; the lower throne is covered by a magnificent nine-tiered white canopy. In the past this was used as a formal audience hall. These days it is used for birthday rites of the Royal Family.

Countless other buildings, audience halls and pavilions lie in the vicinity, as well as the hidden and mysterious "inside" quarters once inhabited by the harem, currently closed to the public.

Until the death of King Ananada Mahidol, who was mysteriously found shot in the palace in 1946, all the great Chakri monarchs resided here. King Bhumipol Adulyadej, the current monarch has since moved his residence to the Chitralada Palace which is closed to the public, but the Grand Palace remains the pre-eminent symbol of the monarchy in Thailand and one of the most colourful displays of Thai architecture in the Kingdom.

On the way out, visit the Decorations and Coins Museum, situated near the ticket office and containing decorations, medals and gold coins dating back from the 11th century.

Y akshas nagas *and* kinari *are just some of the strange mythical creatures that people the inner temples of Wat Phra Kaeo.*

Wat Phra Kaeo (Temple of the Emerald Buddha)

Occupying its own compound within the Grand Palace—and included in the price of the entry ticket—is Wat Phra Kaeo which contains Thai Buddhism's most sacred object. The Emerald Buddha measures just 75 cm (30 ins) tall and 45 cm (17 ins) wide, and has been the cause of numerous wars with neighbouring Laos, from where it was eventually retrieved by General Chakri, Rama I, in the mid-18th century.

Nobody knows how old it is, or precisely where it came from. But Thais believe that as long as the Emerald Buddha remains with them, they will retain their independence.

The image is to be found in the main chapel (*bot*) seated in meditation on a raised gilt throne, flanked on pedestals by two standing Buddha images cast by Rama III and covered with gold weighing 38 kg (84 lb).

Three times a year, the King changes the clothes of the Emerald Buddha: in the rainy season the Buddha is dressed in a robe gilded with gold and studded with sapphires; in the summer, a gold and diamond robe leaves the right shoulder bare; in the

92

winter, a woven saffron robe covers the entire body and a headpiece is embedded with diamonds.

The whole inner compound of Wat Phra Kaeo is decked with finery, unrivalled even by the standards of Bangkok's other great temples. The Emerald Buddha is protected by a nine-tiered umbrella symbolizing royalty. On the inner walls are murals depicting events from the great epic the *Ramayana* and other mythological scenes, as well as episodes from the *Jatakas,* which relate tales of the Buddha's former lives.

Outside the temple, the walls are covered with millions of mirror fragments, with doors and windows of mother of pearl and the entrance guarded by Khmer-style bronze lions believed to have been brought from Cambodia by King Rama 1.

Surrounding the main chapel stand 12 open marble-floored pavilions and the **Royal Pantheon** (*Phra Thepidon*), which contains the life-size statues of the first eight kings of the Chakri dynasty, guarded by *kinarees* (mythical bird women). And further around countless *chedis,* chapels and even a library known as the Ho Phra Montien Tham containing scriptures in mother of pearl-inlaid cabinets.

The Grand Palace and Wat Phra Kaeo complex are open daily from 8.30 a.m.–3.30 p.m. Dress appropriately since visitors wearing shorts and vests may be politely turned away.

Wat Mahathat

Walk north of the Grand Palace and you will reach Wat Mahathat, temple of the great relic and one of the oldest wats in the city dating back to the reign of Rama 1 (1782–1809). The temple is a major Buddhist centre of learning, containing not only one of Bangkok's two Buddhist universities, but also the national headquarters for the Mahanikai monastic sect. Those interested in learning about Buddhist meditation can speak to the monks in section five, where meditation instruction is available in English. Wat Mahathat is open daily from 9 a.m.–5 p.m.

Wat Po

To the west of the Grand Palace, nestling behind dozens of astrologers and drink stores, is one of the oldest and largest temples in the city. Wat Po was founded in the 18th century—built on the site on an even older temple— and contains a vast collection of Buddha images, of chapels (*viharns*) and pagodas, facilities for teaching medicine and archaeology and tablets of stone detailing the art of massage.

The largest concentration of buildings lies within the northern compound —opposite the living quarters of the monks—and contains a *bot* enclosed by a gallery of Buddha images and four *viharns,* four large *chedis* commemorating the first four Chakri kings, 91 smaller *chedis,* an old library, a *serman* hall and a large *viharn,* which houses a school building for Buddhist philosophy. These buildings were all built by various kings of the early Chakri dynasty.

Set around it are a maze of pavilions, rock gardens—which once contained crocodiles—bell towers and other temples containing the famous Buddha Phra Jinaraja and a hair relic of the Buddha.

*O*ne hundred and eight auspicious signs went into the feet alone of Wat Po's giant reclining Buddha. The whole body measures an astronomical 46m (150 ft) and is covered in gold leaf.

The centrepiece, however, is the gigantic reclining Buddha. The figure, modelled from plaster and finished in gold leaf, measures 46 m (150 ft) long and 15 m (50 ft) high and is inlaid with mother of pearl. On the feet are 108 auspicious characteristics of the Buddha, and around the walls, murals depict the Buddha's former lives.

The reclining Buddha symbolizes the passing from this life into nirvana, and was cast during the reign of Rama III. Many of the other Buddha images in Wat Po, are said to have been brought to Bangkok after the fall of Ayutthaya on the back of elephants.The building housing the reclining Buddha is open daily from 8 a.m.–5 p.m.

Wat Arun
Almost directly opposite Wat Po, situated on the west bank of the Chao Phya River, you will glimpse the primordial mound of Wat Arun, popularly known as the Temple of Dawn, and at 79 m (260 ft) high it was for many years the tallest pagoda in the city.

Built during the first half of the 19th century by Rama II and Rama III, it is decorated with millions of pieces of porcelain set in the shape of flowers, some of which were donated by Chinese immigrants who lived in the surrounding area. From halfway up some precarious and slippery stairs you get an unimpeded view of rice barges battling their way up the Chao Phya River. Paradoxically, it is at sunset that the temple is seen at its most beautiful, viewed from the opposite bank.

To get to Wat Arun, cross the river by boat from That Tien Pier near Wat Po. The *wat* is open daily from 8.30 a.m.–5 p.m.

Wat Bovonives

With a name like Wat Bovonives (The Most Excellent Resting Place) it is hardly surprising that this temple is

W̶hen Rama I christened his new city he was filled with such ardour he called it the "City of Angels and Supreme Repository of Divine Jewels". Judging by the number of Buddhas in Wat Arun the good monarch may have been conservative.

inextricably tied to royalty. Prince Mongkut, subsequently Rama IV, served 14 years as an abbot of this wat before he became King. His successors, King Rama VI and King Rama VII also spent time living here, as did the present Monarch King Bhumipol Adulyadej, Rama IX, who became a monk for two weeks in 1956.

Besides a much venerated 4 m (13 ft) bronze statue of Buddha, many of the walls and pillars are covered in sombre murals showing the shortcomings of the people before the Buddhist influence cleansed them. There is also an English language Buddhist bookshop across the street from the main entrance of the *wat*.

The *wat* is on Phra Sumane Road and opens daily 8.30 a.m–6.30 p.m.

Wat Sakhet
(The Golden Mount)

Wat Sakhet, the 19th-century temple that lies east of Klong Lawd, is not one of the most magnificent edifices to look at. But it certainly makes up for what it lacks in architectural appeal with its charming unobstructed views, its faintly rural appearance and its notoriously friendly monks. To get the best views, climb the steps leading up the 78 m (260 ft) artificial hill known as the Golden Mount.

History relates that the mount was originally intended to house a large *chedi,* but collapsed during the reign of King Rama III. His successor King Rama IV opted for a less ambitious scheme, building a small gilded chedi on the remains, which houses relics of the Buddha.

Every November, a giant fair is held around Wat Sakhet with candlelit processions, food stalls and side-shows with pop singers dressed as monkeys.

To get to Wat Sakhet head for the intersection of Mahachai Road and Ratchadamnoen Avenue, close to Democracy Monument and look upwards. You won't be able to miss it.

Wat Suthat

Continue south-west of the Golden Mount and you will come to beautiful Wat Suthat which has a 14th-century Buddha from Sukhothai, decorated pavilions and intricately painted murals dating from the reign of King Rama III. Outside the *wat* is an incongruous looking, red painted, gigantic and precarious looking swing known as sao ching cha. The swing was traditionally used in a Brahman festival held to honour Siva and Vishnu who were believed to descend to earth once a year. Teams of Brahmins, specially chosen to honour the deities, would swing higher and higher

---

A Man of his Age

Somerset Maugham, gentleman, traveller and man of letters recalled with joy his impressions of the Siamese temples which "glitter with gold and whitewash, yet are not garish". Maugham arrived in the East in the 1920s and went on to travel at leisure around large areas of Siam and Cambodia. Life, however, was not all easy. Despite manservants and the goodness offered to him by many notable gentleman, he caught malaria whilst staying at the Oriental Hotel and nearly died there. He leaves behind him such works as *Gentleman in a Parlour* and a fairy tale known as *Princess September,* supposedly written during his convalescence.

as they tried to grasp a bag of gold coins in their teeth. A number of them fell off, and in 1935 the ceremony was abolished. The swing, minus its seat, however is still worth a visit and can be seen at the end of Bamrung Muang Road.

Wat Suthat is open every day from 9 a.m. to 5 p.m.

Wat Traimit

For a glimpse of the biggest gold image in Thailand—and quite possibly one of the largest in the world—head to the end of Yaowarat Road near Bangkok's Chinatown.

The golden Buddha weighs in at 5.5 tons of solid gold and was discovered by chance when workmen extending the port of Bangkok dropped the stucco-covered statue from a crane, revealing a vast gold image inside. The statue probably dates from the Sukhothai period (1250–1376), but during the great siege of Ayutthaya in the 18th century was disguised by monks to keep it out of Burmese hands. The Buddha can now be seen in Wat Traimit on the corner of Charoen Krung Road and Yaowaraj Road. The temple is open daily from 9 a.m.–5 p.m.

Wat Benchamabophit

North from the Grand Palace—but still easily reached by a short *tuk tuk* or taxi ride—is Wat Benchamabophit (Marble Temple), probably the finest example of recent temple architecture in Bangkok.

Built around the turn of the century on the site of an earlier temple, it contains four porches, made of marble brought from Italy, and multiple roofs,

*E*ven the doors of Bangkok's temples are amazing works of art.

covered with coloured glazed tiles from China.

Enter the cloisters and you will find bronze statues of famous images from all over the Kingdom, as well as elaborately adorned gables and figures of Vishnu riding an elephant. Outside and past the canal are the monks' quarters set amongst green lawns; a haven of calm amongst the bustle of inner Bangkok.

Get there at dawn to see the monks gathering outside the gates of the temple to collect alms—fruit and rice given by passersby. Afterwards you can make merit by freeing birds from cages or turtles from buckets. A camera—and if you arrive early enough, a tripod—is a must. Wat Benchamabophit is located on Sri Ayutthaya Road close to the Rama V Road intersection.

Wat Thong Noppakhun

On the Thonburi side of the River (some distance away from the other temples) is one of the most intriguing of all Bangkok's monuments. Wat Thong Noppakhun shot to fame during the reign of King Mongkhut, Rama IV, when an artist named Phra Kru Kasin Sangvorn painted murals depicting urinating angels and others showing their bare buttocks. So shocked was the good monarch, who was renowned as a bastion of Buddhist conservatism, that he demanded that the offending murals be re-painted. These re-touched versions can still be seen at the temple, situated on the west bank of the river opposite Tha Ratchawong Pier.

Others

For those not already surfeited, there remain an abundance of other temples, less visited, yet each bearing its own colourful characteristic. If you have the time or find yourself in the vicinity, we recommend **Wat Kalayanimit**, **Wat Prayoonwong** and **Wat Rajanadda**.

Wat Kalayanimit is spectacularly set on the west bank of the Chao Phya River opposite Pak Klong Market and reputedly houses the largest bronze bell in Thailand as well as a fine collection of Buddha statues including the famous Luang Paw Toh.

Wat Prayoonwong is situated a short walk from Wat Kalayanimit on Thetsaban Sai 1. It is known as the Turtle Temple and is famed for its thousands of amphibians. Buy a plate of cut-up fruits and make merit by

feeding the fat illustrious turtles with slices of watermelon, papaya and banana—papaya is said to be their favourite. Wat Rajanadda is situated off Mahachai Road and is famous for its Burmese-style architecture and amulet market selling images of the Buddha used to ward off evil spirits.

Around and about are literally hundreds of other temples, almost all of them still in use. To find them, simply walk off any of the main streets. At some stage you're bound to bump into one.

Churches

To see some of the countless churches in this cosmopolitan city you won't have to go far. Portuguese traders, Vietnamese refugees and French missionaries built many during the 19th century although the majority have since been renovated. We recommend **Assumption Cathedral**, **Francis Xavier Church** and **Santa Cruz Church**.

On Oriental Lane near the Oriental Hotel, you will find the impressive Assumption Cathedral with the main altar made of marble imported from France. It was built by Father Colombet in 1910 and contains beautiful paintings of the Virgin Mary.

Off Samsen Road near Krung Thon Bridge is the 130-year-old Francis Xavier Church, originally constructed by Christian Vietnamese refugees who fled Cambodia after a revolt.

Cross over to the Thonburi side—either by the *baht* ferry or the nearby Memorial Bridge—turn down Thetsaban Sai 1, and to the right you will glimpse the beautiful Santa Cruz Church, originally constructed after the fall of Ayutthaya, but rebuilt in 1913.

Other charming little churches include the Church of the Immaculate Conception, off Krung Thon Bridge, and the Holy Rosary Church, a short distance from the Royal Orchid Hotel.

Historical Buildings and Shrines

Besides its temples, Bangkok is also rich in historical buildings, shrines and museums. Many of them were built to house members of the Royal Family and have since been opened to the public. Others recall the days when Bangkok was called the "Venice of the East" with wooden houses set on stilts in canals.

Most of them can be seen by public transport, but note the opening hours as some can be closed on Mondays; others are closed on Sundays.

Lak Muang

The entire spirit population responsible for the foundation of Bangkok are said to inhabit this intriguing shrine, founded by Rama 1, and situated within walking distance of the Grand Palace. It is made up of a colourful multiroofed pagoda covered with gold leaf and flower garlands and dedicated to Phra Lak Muang or the guardian of the city.

Phra Lak Muang, along with the various other spirits, is believed to inhabit a 5 m (16.5 ft) column, originally taken from a laburnum tree. Every day crowds of locals gather to ask him to grant them wishes and donate flowers or entertain him with a dancer—conveniently rented nearby.

The best time to visit Lak Muang is before 11 a.m., after which time the spirits are believed to retire to heaven for the rest of the day. Lak Muang is located at the south-east corner of the Phramane Grounds, just opposite the corner of Sanam Luang, near the Grand Palace.

The National Museum

This museum is worth a visit even for those with little interest in history. It lies near Lak Muang and across the road from Sanam Luang and houses probably more valuable artefacts than any other collection in South-east Asia.

If you are short of time though, you will be faced with an undignified number of choices. The Museum covers every period of Thai history, from the very earliest discoveries at Ban Chiang—dating back more than 5,000 years—to coins, Buddha images and royal seals and insignia.

The best way to get a sense of the place is to take a tour. Alternatively, purchase a map, decide your main area of interest and head to the relevant hall. The museum is divided into countless sections, the most important of which are History and Prehistory, Thrones, Royal Barges, Buddhism in Asia and Art—all labelled with short write-ups in English.

If that's not enough to whet your appetite, there is also a Weapons Room with trappings from the days of elephant wars, a Coronation Room and a hall filled with royal funeral chariots, the largest of which is 12 m (40 ft) high, weights 20 tons and took 290 men to move. After inspecting the various artefacts, examine the museum buildings, particularly the residential

A Gruesome Celebrity

Thailand's most notorious murderer of the 1950s, a man named See-ouey, gained celebrity status when he strangled seven children over a 10-year period, eating their hearts and livers raw in the belief that he would possess their spirit and strength. Since then he has become the subject of two films and several books. His shrivelled exhibit can still be seen in Bangkok's Sirraraj Hospital's Forensic Museum where he lies pickled in formaldehyde and propped up in a glass case for all to see. Just in case mould should grow on the body, every couple of years a coat of oil is applied to keep the corpse intact. In the same museum pickled hearts with bullet holes are on display, as are pieces of scalp from people who have been electrocuted due to electrical faults. The aim of the museum is educational, say officials

quarters of King Pin Kla, second king of Rama IV or surrogate monarch, the **Isarawinitchai Hall**, formerly the Audience Hall of the Palace of the Front, and the Tamnak Deang, a splendid wooden structure dating from the reign of Rama I.

Guided tours of the museum in English begin at 9.30 a.m. on Tuesdays, Wednesdays and Thursdays. For other languages enquire at the tourist office. The museum is open from 9 a.m.–4 p.m. every day except Mondays and Fridays, and is situated on Na Phra That Road.

The National Arts Theatre and Art Gallery

Anyone interested in Thai classical drama, should drop by the National Theatre on Na Prathat Road, if only to see where the delicate ballerinas that abound in the restaurants are trained. Those who are fortunate may even find a scheduled performance coinciding with their stay. For those who don't, special public exhibitions of Thai classical dance drama are held on the last Friday of every month at 5 p.m. Contact the National Theatre, Tel: 221 5861, for details.

Opposite the theatre is the National Arts Gallery, which displays a collection of traditional and contemporary art. It's open daily, except Mondays and Fridays from 9 a.m.–12 p.m. and from 1 p.m.–4 p.m.

Suan Pakkard Palace

This splendid collection of wooden buildings was left courtesy of the late Prince Chumpot of Svarga, who was also an avid collector of old furniture, Khmer stone heads, musical instruments and porcelain antiques. The residence now belongs to Princess Chumpot and is known endearingly as the Lettuce Palace—though no one quite seems to know why. The palace consists of five traditional wooden houses set in lush gardens full of sprouting plants and bushes, with a small pond and resident pelican. The most exquisite museum piece is the lacquerwork pavilion brought from a *wat* near Ayutthaya and restored by the Prince. The house and gardens are situated on Sri Ayutthaya Road near the Phaya Thai intersection and are easily combined with the nearby **Pratunam Market**. It is open from Monday–Saturday 9 a.m.–4 p.m.

Jim Thompson's House

For a glimpse of old Bangkok, when wooden houses dotted the banks of the

*C*IA *agent, silk king and enigma he may have been, but he was a connoisseur. Jim Thompson's former residence has everything from Buddha statues to tropical plants and even a* klong *to recommend it.*

klongs (canals), you won't want to miss this charming old edifice that was home to the famous Jim Thompson. Although Thompson, a silk entrepreneur—and reputedly a spy—disappeared in the Cameroon Highlands of West Malaysia in 1967, he left behind him this delightful residence set at the end of a small *soi* next to Klong San Saep, a rather smelly canal. The building consists of six houses made of teak, a luxuriant garden and a fine collection of art, pots, antiques and silk cushions, which few museums can match. The house is open from Monday–Saturday, 9 a.m.–4.30 p.m., and is located just off Rama I Road, opposite the National Stadium.

Ban Kamthieng

Head 4 km (2.5 miles) west from Jim Thompson's house to reach another of the great old Bangkok residences, even more incongruously set against a skyline of high-rises. Ban Kamthieng (Kamthieng House) originally did not

It was once home to King Chula-longkorn and although he didn't stay here long—he moved house after just two years. It provides another refreshing glimpse of the old city. Thirty of the 81 rooms are open to the public, and contain a treasure-trove of delicate silver betel nut boxes, porcelain, mounted elephant tusks—and even a shower in the royal bathroom, believed to be the first installed in Thailand.

The palace is surrounded on all sides by water with Klong Rong Mai Hom (Fragrant Wood Canal) to the east, Klong Khab Phaen Krachok (Sheet of Glass Canal) to the north, Klong Rang Ngoen (Silver Canal) to the west and Ang Yok (Jade Basin), a green pond to the south. Vimanmek is open daily from 9.30 a.m.–3 p.m. and is situated off U-Thong Nai Road next to the National Assembly across from the Dusit Zoo.

Bangkok's ancient buildings have a lot to offer, as the magnificent teak edifice of Vimanmek Palace will prove.

come from Bangkok at all, but was taken from Chiang Mai and reconstructed to show the typical northern style house with its *ham yong* (sacred testicles), variety of items used by Thai farmers and beautiful gardens. The house is open from Monday-Saturday 9 a.m.–12 p.m. and 1 p.m.–5 p.m., and is situated on 131 Soi Asoke (Soi 21).

Vimanmek Palace

This delightful teak wood building, designed by a famous architect known as Prince Naris, is also the world's largest.

Erawan Shrine

Of all the shrines scattered around Bangkok, the one known as the Erawan is the most famous—and according to most accounts, the most effective. It is located at the intersection of Rama 1 with Ratchadamri Road. The shrine, which is named after the sacred three-headed elephant of Buddhist iconography, was erected by the owners of the former Erawan Hotel following several disasters, which culminated in the sinking at sea of a ship bringing marble to the Hotel.

Since the shrine was completed, there have been no further incidents. But to make sure it remains that way, every day thousands of devotees swarm there with offerings of flowers, wooden elephants, garlands and food, whilst a troupe of weary classical Thai dancers perform for a fee to make sure the spirits do not get bored. The shrine is situated next to the Hyatt Hotel, which given its auspicious position, is not surprisingly one of the finest. Bring a camera, buy a joss stick and flowers, and if things are really going wrong, hire the troupe of dancers. They are said to be not 100 per cent effective, but have a fairly high success record.

Royal Barges

The Royal Barges are fantastically ornamented boats used by the king for ceremonial processions on the Chao Phya River. The largest—known as *Suphanahong* after a mythical swan—measures 50 m (164 ft) long and requires as many as 54 men to row it. Others include the Anantanagaraj, with its beautifully carved seven-headed naga serpent bow.

Although no longer in the water, you can still visit them in sheds on the Thonburi side of the river near the Phra Pin Khao Bridge. The barge shed is open daily from 8.30 a.m.–4.30 p.m. To get there take a ferry to the Thonburi train station, then walk down the street that runs parallel to the tracks for 200 m (656 ft) until you come to a bridge over the canal which leads to the sheds. Better still, get there with one of the boats that travel up the Klong Bangkok Noi.

Touring the Klongs

Taking a boat on a *klong* (canal) is one of the most enjoyable and fastest ways of getting around the city. These boats can be caught from any number of piers, come in all shapes, sizes and price ranges, and provide a rare glimpse of the days when Bangkok was known as the Venice of the East.

The most regular form of river transport is the Chao Phya Express Boat, running from Wat Rajsingkon Pier near Krung Thep Bridge in the south of Bangkok to Nonthaburi in

When you live in the hottest city in the world there is only one thing to do—buy a big hat and work on the Chao Phraya River.

the north. Boats leave every 15 minutes starting at 6.30 a.m. and finishing at 6 p.m., stopping at the Oriental Pier, Tha Thien, departure point for Wat Po and Wat Arun; Tha Chang, departure point for the Grand Palace; and many other central tourist spots. To get on one, all you have to do is wait on the pier and when the boat arrives literally leap on board since they stop for only a few seconds.

There are also short-haul steamers that merely cross from one side of the river to the other costing just Bt1.

A River Excursion

For a three- to four-hour round trip of the river costing little more than Bt20, catch one of the Chao Phya Express Boats from the Oriental Pier (Soi Oriental) heading west—to the right.

Look out for the first magnificent building before you even get on the boat. The **East Asiatic Company Building**, built in 1901, lies almost directly opposite the pier. It was founded by an eminent Danish sailor who went on to become Thai consulate general.

Passing the **Oriental Hotel**—itself something of a historical piece—keep an eye open for the French embassy

Venice of the East was the title that early travellers gave Bangkok. With the city sinking several centimetres a year some say it is well on the way to becoming a city of canals once more.

on your right, with its louvred shutters and charming European air; it was built in the mid-19th century.

The next monument of interest lies on the left bank beyond the first bridge, Phra Pokklao Bridge, in the form of a diminutive church, named Santa Cruz, built on the sight of a former Portuguese church. A little further on the the same side is Wat Kalayanamit, home to the biggest bell in the country.

From Wat Kalayanamit, the boat continues past the towering spire of Wat Arun on the left and, shortly afterwards, the glittering spires of the Grand Palace on the right. Further on, you will see 19th-century **Siriraj Hospital** on the left, which contains a pickled Chinese murderer named Si-oui and various other gruesome specimens.

Beyond the next bridge, Pha Pinklao, there are several distinguished looking buildings on the right bank including the **Bank of Thailand**, just before the belching smoke stack of the Bangyikhan Distillery, and beyond Wat Ratchathiwas, built by Rama V, and the 19th-century Church of the Immaculate Conception.

Passing under another bridge, Krung Thon Bridge, the boat weaves its way past the Boon Rawd brewery, on the right bank, and the peculiarly shaped **Wat Anamnikayaram**, originally constructed by a group of Vietnamese, but rebuilt after a fire, on the right bank just before Rama VI Bridge.

By continuing to the last river pier, you will reach the small suburb of **Nonthaburi,** the ideal spot to stretch your legs and explore the fruit and fish markets before taking the return boat.

Be warned though—often the boats can be crowded and you may find yourself standing for the entire journey. The last boat departs from Nonthaburi for the return trip at around 5.30 p.m.

Long-Tailed Boats

For those who wish to explore the river, but prefer a greater level of comfort, a better alternative may be the form of river transport known as the *hong yao* or long-tailed boat. This species of transport cruises the canals powered by giant 3 m (10 ft) propeller shafts that make the noise of a jumbo jet set for take-off.

Some boats are public services and can be taken from the Tha Tien Pier near Wat Po, to Klong Mon, or from Memorial Bridge Pier to Klong Bang Waek costing as little as Bt4.

Others can be chartered from the Oriental Pier, the Grand Palace Pier *(Tha Chang)* and almost all the other

---

Watery Memoirs

When Sir John Bowring came to Bangkok in 1855 to negotiate an historic treaty with King Rama IV, he was struck by the immense beauty of the Chao Phya River with its magnificent royal barges, the bright and beautiful green foliage, the birds winging their way over head and the fish gliding over the mud banks. Less than a decade later, King Mongkhut, Rama IV, in what must have been the first bid to stall pollution, outlawed the throwing of dead animals into the river. The ruling appears to have had some effect. For in the 1920s, the great author Somerset Maugham was able to report that the river is "broad and handsome".

big ferry piers, costing upwards of Bt350 an hour and taking up to 20 passengers. They will in theory take you anywhere, although the most common trip is to the **Floating Market in Thonburi**.

Hundreds of different travel agents also operate riverine tours. These leave regularly from the Grand Palace Pier or can be arranged through any of the big hotels. Normally the tour will take you down the well-trodden, camera-wielding tourist spots, past the occasional diminutive paddlers with their wide brimmed hats, and afterwards to the Snake Farm, Wat Arun and the Royal Barges. The best time to go is early in the morning when there is still a breeze and when the inhabitants of the *klongs* can be seen washing and brushing their teeth in the glutinous brown waters.

Some visitors now complain that the trip has become almost like a zoo with traffic jams of picture-hungry *farangs* far outnumbering the odd boat woman selling cabbages. But for those wanting a glimpse of a lifestyle that was once all-Bangkok it remains a delightful and fascinating trip, which can provide the necessary vigour to carry you through another day in the bustling metropolis.

Further afield there is a more authentic floating market. This is situated at **Damnoen Saduak** and can be reached by car, bus or organized tour.

If you are seriously interested in spending time on the canals, look no further than William Warren's excellent book called *Bangkok's Waterways*. The book is published by Asia Books and can be purchased at almost any major Bangkok bookstore.

Reptiles and Parks

Anyone interested in zoos or reptiles, should have a field day in Bangkok. Not only is there a **Snake Farm** at the Pasteur Institute on Henri Durant Road just off Rama IV Road, but there are reptiles on display at the Floating Market in Thonburi, at the **Crocodile Farm** at Samut Prakarn and at the **Rose Garden**.

The best and easiest place to visit however is the **Dusit Zoo**, situated near the Chitralada Palace on Sri Ayutthaya Road. This has a pretty park and a good collection of native birds and animals, crocodiles and tigers. There are a lake for the children, open air restaurants and a rather murky pond where enormous turtles can occasionally be seen trying to consume coke bottles. The zoo is open daily from 8 a.m.–6 p.m.

Elsewhere, Bangkok has a couple of parks. These are generally some way out of town but are easily accessible by bus. The exception is **Lumpini Park**: a relative haven of calm bordered on one side by Rama IV Road and on the other by Ratchadamri Road. At weekends, crowds of Thais pack the fringes of the park, sitting on mats, picnicking, drinking Mekong whisky and excelling in the art of *Sanuk* (good time). For those who have come unprepared, there are plenty of stalls selling dishes of kebabs and noodles, whilst on the northern exit onto Soi Sarasin there is a restaurant and bar called *Pop*, where you can sit and watch the sun go down over busy Bangkok. To get there ask for "Suwan Lumpini" or alight at the Dusit Thani Hotel, which stands opposite the Park on Rama IV Road.

Bangkok's other major park is situated at Phra Kanong on the outskirts of town beyond Soi Udom Suk—Sukhumvit Soi 103—and is known as the **King Rama IX Royal Park**. It was built to commemorate His Majesty the King's 60th birthday and boasts a great variety of plants and landscapes, as well as aquatic animals and birds and the largest collection of cacti in the country.

Markets

Markets can be found everywhere in Bangkok, nestling beneath high-rises and squeezed between side streets, selling fried grasshoppers and *Khao phat gai* (steaming mounds of glutinous rice). Markets are where the ordinary Thai does his shopping and where the *joie de vivre* of the people is at its height, and nowhere are there more of them than in Bangkok itself.

Perhaps the most famous market in Thailand is the **Weekend Market**, at Chatuchak Park, on Paholyothin Road. On Saturdays and Sundays, the vast area near the Northern Bus Terminal is transformed into a seething mass of 5,000 stall owners selling almost everything from live pigs and parrots to clothes, pots and herbal remedies for acne or infertility. There are also the most delicious snacks, sweet biscuits and barbecued chickens' feet. Often the people selling are as colourful as the goods sold, so if you're a photographer, bring lots of film, preferably ASA 200 or 400, as well as a flash.

It's best to arrive early. Stalls start going up at around 6.30 a.m. and by 10 a.m. the place is so crowded that it is almost impossible to move. Buses to the Weekend Market leave from Victory Monument, which can be reached easily from anywhere in the city. Note that parts of the market are only open on Saturdays and Sundays.

Over in the west on the curve of the river near the Grand Palace is the **Pak Klong Market**. The best time to visit the market is at dawn when the first flowers are being put out and piles of fresh produce spill out of their wicker baskets. Pak Klong is Bangkok's main wholesale market, the place where restaurateurs and greengrocers buy their produce, and where the fruit and vegetables of the Central Plains are sold. It was once the main market for the people of the city and remains the most colourful. It is located at the foot of the Memorial Bridge and can be reached by river taxi, getting off at Tha Rachini Pier.

For ready-to-wear clothing, made-to-measure garments and all derivatives of cloth, a good place to try is **Pratunamt**, situated near the Indra Hotel. Here diminutive seamstresses will stitch you up anything in a matter of minutes, while their no less enthusiastic counterparts sell T-shirts, skimpy bikinis and trendy padded-shoulder jackets. Here too you'll find some of the best and cheapest fresh seafood sold from open air restaurants, from where you can stare out at the teeming stalls beyond. The market can be reached by buses running north up Ratchadamri Road.

Few tourists visit **Klongtoey Market**. It's too close to the shanty towns, too far from the Grand Palace and too unfashionable compared with Sukhumvit.

*T*he spiciest
concoctions in Bangkok are to
be found in its markets.

Their reticence should prove your advantage. Klongtoey may not be the smartest, nor the biggest, but it is certainly the cheapest. To get there take bus number 4, 13 or 47 and ask for "Talaht Klongtoey". The market starts on the crossroads of Rama IV Road with Soonthorn Kosa Road, and extends all the way up to the railway crossing.

Remember that in all markets and almost all shops, bargaining is the normal practice. To start with the stall owner will probably quote a price that is at least 30 per cent too high. In your best Thai say *"peng maak maak"* (too expensive) and answer with a price slightly lower than the one you intend to pay. The process will continue until a price can be agreed upon—or until either you or the stall owner refuse to budge. If one stall will not bargain try another. And if you can't speak Thai, use fingers to denote every Bt10 you are prepared to pay.

...and Shopping Centres

If markets are the old face of Bangkok, then supermarkets and shopping centres are the new with air-conditioned department stores selling almost all of the products you'd expect to find in Singapore or Paris.

The biggest, most crowded and probably the cheapest of them is the **Marbun Krong Centre** on Phayathai Road, just off Siam Square, a teeming megastore with clothes, jewellery and even a *Dunkin Doughnut* thrown in for good measure. Other department stores include Robinsons on Silom

*F*rom fans to films and
birds to balloons Bangkok's
merchants can provide almost
everything and more.

Road, Central Department Store on Ploenchit Road and Silom Road, or the Japanese Sogo at the Erawan Shrine corner of Ploenchit Road and Ratchadamri Road.

There are also numerous boutiques providing much of the designer fashion, which is sold not only in Bangkok, but in some of the major centres around the world. One of the most impressive displays is at Siam Shopping Centre on Rama I Road with four floors of high-fashion clothing. Other haute couture boutiques are to be found between Soi 31 and Soi 37 Sukhumvit Road, as well as on floor 1 and 2 of the Baiyoke Building behind the Indra Regent Hotel.

If there's nothing that takes your fancy off the peg, these shops will run you up a suit, a dress or tailor-made pyjamas, sometimes in as little as an afternoon. Try to bring along a magazine picture or an item of clothing to model it on and make sure you get them to use good quality cloth. Cheap suits with shiny surfaces make some of London's mass-produced efforts look like works of art.

As a general rule, Chinatown is known for its gold jewellery, Silom Road for its silk, Sukhumvit Road for its leather goods and tailors, Siam Square for its high-fashion boutiques, Banglampoo for its hippy hilltribe wear and faded waistcoats. But as with every rule in Bangkok, there are hundreds of exceptions, with good silk to be found in Siam Square and conversely good leather goods to be found in the Silom/Surawong district.

There is however consensus about one thing and that is **Jim Thompson's Silk Factory**, which is undoubtedly the best known, most prized silk emporium in Bangkok, and probably in the world. Inside the two-storey house, which is situated on Surawong Road next to the intersection with Rama IV Road, is a selection of some of the finest handmade items that Thailand has to offer, ranging from silk table mats to handbags, ready-made clothing and even silk for wedding dresses. Prices are not cheap, but quality is guaranteed. Next door to Jim Thompson on Surawong Road and further down Rama IV Road, there are a host of other silk shops which are cheaper, but which lack that *je ne sais quoi* that comes with Mr Thompson's credentials.

Silom Village on Silom Road caters for a different kind of shopper—those with a little more time and a taste for good food. The village, which has the official TAT approval, is made up of a number of shops selling silk, leatherware and lacquerware and in the centre has a breezy spot with a restaurant.

Farang Talk

The *Encyclopaedia of Thai/Anglo Expressions* defines a *farang* either as a foreigner of Caucasian descent or as a type of guava fruit. The word is originally said to have come from *ferenghi,* the Indian word for French, and was used by the Siamese to describe traders from that country during the reign of Louis XIV. Since then it has become a common term for every white skinned person. Discriminatory it may be, but derogatory it is not. Indeed, wherever you go and whoever you are, you can't escape the term. And when you are not called *farang,* the authorities use another word to officially describe foreigners—aliens.

The restaurant frequently has traditional Thai music, so that you can take a breather from your purchasing, dine on fresh lobster and then return to the boutiques with added fervour.

From the bottom of Silom Road, it is just a short distance to the **River City Centre** next to the Royal Orchid Sheraton Hotel off Charoen Krung Road. This was one of the first shopping centres to be built on the river and remains the most popular. Its four floors contain a collection of shops and restaurants selling clothes, leatherware, and jewellery with the third and fourth floors being entirely devoted to antiques. Shoe connoisseurs also claim that River City is the best spot in the city to purchase a good pair of leather brogues.

For handicrafts, a chain of outlets called **Chitralada** is well worth visiting. The chain was set up, with the support of Her Majesty Queen Sirikit, to exhibit rare crafts, especially from the hilltribes in the North. Chitralada Stores can be found at Don Muang Airport and at the Oriental Plaza and the Hilton Hotel.

Some of the more reliable gem shops in Bangkok are the Thai Lapidary, 277/122 Rama I Road, Tel: 214 2641; Uthai Gems, 23/7 Soi Ruam Rudee, Tel: 252 4635; and New Universal, 1144–46 Charoen Krung New Road, Tel: 234 3514. The TAT also issues a list of recommended dealers. You should, however, always check the authenticity of major purchases by getting them valued at the **Asian Institute of Gemology** on 987 Rama Jewellery Building, 4th Floor, Silom Road. Most reputable dealers will now provide you with a written agreement to give a full refund for any gems returned within 90 days of purchase, although nowadays, even these cannot be totally relied upon.

Finally, if authenticity is not what you're after, and cheap shirts and watches are, there is nowhere to beat **Patpong Road**. Gucci watches sell for as low as Bt350 with Lacoste T-shirts for Bt100. You can even get cheap fake tapes and videos, though reproduction can be fuzzy, with the life of the tape often little longer than your memories of Patpong.

If time is running short and you are after something official, try one of the hotel shopping arcades where there is normally a stash of Bangkok's most popular buys. The prices here are generally only marginally higher than the outside stores. The TAT publishes a small brochure on shopping. There is also a book called *Shopping in Exotic Thailand* written by Ronald and Caryl Krannich and published by Impact Publications, which lists a number of the best places to find quality goods.

Outside the main department stores, remember to bargain. And avoid the ubiquitous touts or people selling themselves as unofficial guides, who are officially outlawed by the TAT. They are cool, smooth-talking and helpful, but as a rule they are more trouble and cost than they're worth.

Thai Massage

Whether you've spent a hard day in the shops or a hot day in the traffic, there is probably no better way to round it off than with a touch of Thailand's most famous physical cure.

Paen boran (Thai massage) was imported by the Indian Brahmins hundreds of years ago. Like acupuncture it is based on energy lines and pressure points. Generally someone either walks up and down your back, or squeezes, kneads and gently pummels your arms, legs and head. The aim of all this is to unblock the flow of energy, which in turn contributes to improved health, thereby providing opportunity for even greater *sanuk*.

The spiritual home of Thai massage is *Wat Po*. It was here that King Nangkloa, Rama III, inscribed details of the art on marble tablets to prevent the tradition from being lost. Most experienced practitioners still do their training here. A massage costs as little as Bt120 and lasts for an hour. Wat Po even offers two or three-week training courses for those captivated with the art.

Outside Wat Po, there are a couple of other traditional establishments. **Marble House**, at 37/18 Soi Surawong Plaza, Tel: 235 3519 is renowned for its facilities and experienced masseurs and is under the patronage of Queen Sirikit. **Buathip Massage Parlour**, a sister branch, at 4/13 Sukhumvit Soi 5, opposite the Landmark Hotel is similarly esteemed. Elsewhere certain modern accompaniments have been introduced. Try them at your pleasure or peril!

Places to Stay

Bangkok's hotels have justifiably earned themselves a reputation as being amongst the finest in the world. The rush of new five-star luxury names

is likely to ensure that it remains that way, with charm, comfort and attention to detail enough to ensure that the city remains at the top of most travel agent's lists.

There is no one area that is necessarily better than others. Being close to the river offers the best views in the city, but some of the worst traffic. Being on Sukhumvit Road, puts you close to good shopping, but a long way from the Grand Palace and the old part of town. Whilst being in Banglampoo puts you in the heart of the old town, but has the feel of a world backpackers' ghetto.

Remember to book early as occupancy rates in the peak season—November–February—can sometimes run as high as 80 to 90 per cent. If you

Claims to Fame
Amongst the great men once counted as guests of the late 19th-century riverine hostelry known as the Oriental Hotel are Joseph Conrad, the Polish sailor and author of *Victory* fame; Somerset Maugham author of *Gentleman in a Parlour,* as well as James Michener, Noel Coward and even the recently-deceased Graham Greene. Others of no less reputation stayed here including Ronald Reagan, pop singer Bob Seager, and Count Zalata of the Ukraine, who fled his homeland after being accused of raping 72 peasant girls. Still it is the literary names that are remembered best: each of them has a suite bearing his distinguished name, as well as a regular write-up on the dinner menu served on the terrace. Conrad appears to have been an enthusiast of seafood salad. The name of Count Zalata is, however, conspicuous by its absence, even from the dessert menu.

A touch of legend accompanied by dinner. A Bangkok restaurant hosts dances from the great Thai epic the Ramayana.

arrive without a reservation, get one of the travel agents to make a booking. Often they get big discounts.

Places to Eat

The problem facing the aspiring gourmet is not so much finding a good eating haunt, but deciding which one to opt for.

Bangkok has some 11,000 restaurants, a higher concentration than almost any other capital city in the world. They range from romantic dinner cruises along the Chao Phya River and landscaped garden restaurants with pavilions strung with lights and lotus ponds, to countless places offering not only the spicy cooking of Thailand, but also the best of Japan, France, Italy, Germany, China and a dozen others. Standards are almost universally high—and prices almost inevitably low, with even the top restaurants generally costing less than Bt800 per head, without wine.

Some restaurants now offer cooking courses for those really taken by the food: The Oriental, Tel: 437 6211, has a five-day course; the Bussaracum, Tel: 235 5160, a ten-day course.

For a selection of some of those eating establishments that have made Thailand's capital a gastronomic delight, see RESTAURANTS. Alternatively, just look for places frequented by locals and take your pick. You're unlikely to be disappointed. Restaurants generally open at 6.30 p.m. and close at 10 p.m.

Floating Restaurants and Classical Dancing

Several boats ply the Chao Phya River nightly offering evening cruises and dinner. They generally cost in the region of Bt500 per person, not including alcohol. Most require advance phone reservations. Try the following: Oriental Hotel, Tel: 236 0400/9, leaves from Oriental pier Wednesdays only; Loy Nava, Tel: 437 4932/7329, leaves from River City Pier daily; Dinner City Cruise, Tel: 234 5599, leaves from River City Pier daily.

Several restaurants also put on classical dance performances so that you can dine traditional style and enjoy scenes from the Thai epic, the *Ramayana*. Probably the best and the most expensive is the **Sala Rim Naam**, Tel: 437 9417, situated opposite the Oriental Hotel on Charoen Nakhon Road, with nightly performances between 8.30 p.m. and 9.30 p.m. **Sawasdee Restaurant**, off Sathorn Road, does a display of classical dancing accompanied by tape recorded descriptions of the dances in English, French, German, Japanese and Spanish. But it is generally attended by coachloads of tourists and the food is bland. Other restaurants with Thai classical dance can be found at the **Baan Thai**, 7 Sukhumvit Soi 32, Tel: 252 6312, at **Maneeya's Lotus Room**, on Ploenchit Road, Tel: 252 6312 and at **Ruen Thep**, Silom Village Trade Centre, Silom Road, Tel: 233 9447.

At Night

Bangkok's nightlife is without parallel. It is noisy and colourful and riotous. Whatever you want, something will fit the bill and if doesn't, then you have gone to the wrong place.

The most famous nightspot in Bangkok and the place that gets more tourists every year than even the Grand Palace is the area known as **Patpong**. It's made up of three parallel *sois* that run between Silom Road and Surawong Road and from 6 p.m. until 2 a.m. and often, even in the afternoons, it is a mass of neon lights, girls, trendy touts and menus.

Inside the bars Thai girls, flimsily dressed with numbers pinned to their

---

A Matter of Foresight

When a young Chinese businessman of the name Pong Pat bought up a large chunk of rice-terrace on the outskirts of the city, hardened Bangkokeans thought he was mad. But the far-sighted gentleman had other ideas. First he attracted small-time tenants to start up shops and tailoring, then he encouraged restaurants and airline offices. Finally, he attracted people who started the bars that have made Patpong the best known red light district in the world: and the successors of Patpong one of the richest families.

bikinis, gyrate to the sounds of *One Night in Bangkok*, whilst throngs of tourists and businessmen sip Kloster beer, watching videos, nibbling pizzas, even playing darts. Upstairs are shows where the girls perform rather dubious gymnastic feats.

Outside, packed into a tiny area is one of the city's liveliest night markets, and possibly one of its greatest fire hazards, lines and lines of stalls selling counterfeit cassettes, handbags and T-shirts; as well as foreign exchange offices, an all-night supermarket and, at one end, a Thai boxing ring.

Most bars do not charge entry though you should always check —phenomenal cover charges are not unknown. The girls make their money by persuading men or women to buy them cokes, of which they get to keep Bt20, or by negotiating other nocturnal activities. When the bars close, they move on to discos, open until 5 a.m., and when the discos close, to coffee bars, massage parlours or home, in the squats of Lumpini, Klongtoey or Din Daeng.

A Touch of the Red Light
The decree of 1960 makes the matter clear. Brothels, it writes are banned. Police Lieutenant General Wirot Pao-in, the Metropolitan Bureau Police Commissioner was no less adamant. In 1991 he announced to the world "there are no brothels in Bangkok". That has not stopped a number of nightlife establishments from employing an estimated 500,000–700,000 call-girls throughout the Kingdom. The word now is that prostitution may be made legal; but brothels, if there were ever such a thing, would certainly not be.

Estimates of the number of prostitutes in Thailand range from 150,000–500,000. Most of them are devout Buddhists, who regularly make offerings to monks, and send money home to their families in the poorer areas of the North and the North-east. Despite efforts to clean up Bangkok's image and the threat of AIDS, the industry continues to boom—a poignant reminder of the intriguing complexity of Thai ways.

Besides Patpong, there are several other red light districts in the city. Between Sukhumvit Soi 21 and Soi 23, you will find **Soi Cowboy**, a more recent addition, that has all the bars and girls, but less of the markets and watches. On Soi 4 (**Soi Nana**) there's a complex of bars with live music and everything else that the Thais think the tourist may desire. And elsewhere, literally hundreds of other such establishments frequented by the local community.

For a historical review of Patpong, packed with anecdotes about Margaret Thatcher's daughter at a live show, or the KGB agents caught with their pants down, buy the book called *Patpong* by Alan Dawson. It is printed by Thai Watana Panich Press and can be purchased from a number of bookstores in Bangkok.

Music Clubs, Pubs and Discos

At night, even the humble little *sois* come alive with a profusion of sounds, of jazz, rock and roll and even reggae.

Some of the best establishments can be found along **Soi Sarasin** near Soi Langsuan, the classy strip which runs behind Lumpini Park. **Brown Sugar** is a popular haven for young trendies

*L*ewd sordid even scintillating, Bangkok's famous red light district on Patpong Road lures more tourists than even the Grand Palace.

tapping their feet to jazz or sitting at tables outside. Next door is **Wild West** and further down the road a line of small bars with bands where the locals *pai thiau*, drinking expensive brands of whisky.

At 145 Gaysorn Road, off Suk-humvit, is the **Blue Moon** with three floors for eating and drinking and reg-ular bands playing some of the best music in Bangkok.

At the other end of town, close by Victory Monument is **Saxophone**, a 1960s-style bar with reggae and rock 'n' roll and endless crowds in faded jeans and an electric atmosphere.

One of the most famous haunts for the British expat brigade is **Bobby's Arms**, Bangkok's popular English pub where they meet for darts and the fa-mous roast beef and pies and draught beer. On Wednesdays, Fridays and Saturdays there is country and western folk music. On Sundays there is Dixieland jazz.

Occasionally even big international stars take in Bangkok on their world circuits. David Bowie did his bit in the mid-1980s with his famous rendering of *China Girl*. Shaking Stephens was a more recent visitor. However for the most part it's Thais and Filipinos that you will find jamming for the joy of it.

For the more energetic, there are also numerous discotheques with all the high-tech gadgetry from abroad imported, installed and enthusiastically gyrated-to by the capital's new breed of yuppies.

One of the best known is the **Nasa Discotheque** at 999 Ramkamhaeng Road, a giant club with a space ship that takes off at midnight, and which can pack in capacity crowds of up to 4,000. Smaller and quieter is **Bubbles Discotheque** at the Dusit Thani Hotel off Rama IV Road, which still gets its fair share of trendies with sunglasses and padded shoulders.

There are a number of others too, including, Diana's at the Oriental off Charoen Krung Road, Talk of the Town at the Shangri-La Hotel and the upmarket and trendy Paradise on Arun Amarin Road. Admission is gen-erally around Bt 200, including two free drinks, but prices are higher at weekends.

On Patpong Road, there is also the lively **Rome Club**. It's a gay club with a transvestite floor show of international fame, but is universally popular and always packed.

Other Entertainment

For those in search of quieter entertainment, Bangkok has a many alternatives. Good cinemas that show English films, with Thai subtitles, are in abundance around Siam Square as well as on Rama IV Road. Some cinemas exclusively show Thai films with no subtitles. These are normally characterized by blood and guts with one plot very similar to another, but are supremely popular and can provide an interesting insight into the Thai character. Check out the programme in the free handout entertainment weeklies or the Sunday editions of the Bangkok Post and Nation. The British Council, Alliance Française, Goethe Institute and AUA also show films from their respective countries.

On Ratchada Pisek, there's a **Cultural Centre** where occasionally the *Ramayana* or other Thai dramas are staged. Sometimes Bangkok's own orchestra plays under patronage of His Royal Highness, the Crown Prince.

For sports lovers there's live action with Thai boxing held at **Ratchadamnoen Stadium**, Sunday, Monday, Wednesday and Thursday from 6 p.m., Tel: 281 4205, or **Lumpini Stadium,** Tuesday, Friday and Saturday from 6 p.m., Tel: 251 4303.

Day Trips and Tours

For every thousand new tourists that come to Bangkok, a new travel agent generally pops up somewhere in the city. Most big hotels now have an official travel desk to arrange tours almost anywhere in the Kingdom and are generally reliable, but at all times beware of touts and guides who approach you on the street.

Most popular of the day tours are the *klongs* (canals), the Grand Palace, the Thonburi Floating Market—and further afield the crocodile farm, the floating market at Damnoen Saduak and Ayutthaya. These tours generally leave early in the morning and will more often than not pick you up from your hotel in an air-conditioned bus and will arrange lunch.

The alternative is to do it yourself. This method is generally cheaper, almost always more time consuming, but will allow you to absorb something of the local colour.

We list four of the easiest—and most popular day trips: namely the Ancient City, the Crocodile Farm, the Damnoen Saduak Floating Market and the Rose Garden. Other destinations like Nakhon Pathom, Bang Pa-In and Ayutthaya can also be reached in a day, but are better suited as stepping-stones up north. We include them in the section on the Central Region.

Ancient City

Legend has it that those who pass through the **Triumphal Archway** at **Meung Boran** will enjoy prosperity and everlasting happiness. But there are other reasons for coming to the Ancient City, which is the largest outdoor museum in the world. Here there are miniature copies of some of Thailand's most famous monuments, including Wat Mahathat in Sukhothai and Wat Phra Si Sanphet in Ayutthaya.

The day's outing should prove attractive both to budding students of Thai architecture and to those who want to avoid traipsing around too many historic sights. Within the 80 hectare (200 acre) area there are 89 monuments, some of them original, others painstakingly reconstructed. There are also stone carvings and gardens filled with sculptures. The owner is Bangkok's largest Mercedes dealer, who has an avid interest in Thai art.

Ancient City is 33 km (20 miles) from Bangkok on the road to Chonburi, the Sukhumvit Highway, and can be reached by bus number 25 to

Unlucky crocodiles at Samut Prakarn end their days as handbags. This farm prides itself as one of the largest suppliers in Thailand.

Samut Prakarn. Alternatively, tours can be arranged by several agents including the Ancient City Co, Democracy Monument, Ratchadamnoen Avenue, Tel: 323 9252/3.

Crocodile Farm

Easily combined with a trip to the Ancient City is the Crocodile Farm, Tel: 387 0020, at Samut Prakarn, which has

T hailand's last great waterway market still brims with fruits, hats, chillis and, most of all, authenticity.

more than 30,000 crocodiles, and many species of birds as well as elephants, monkeys and snakes. The crocodiles are bred for handbags, but are also adept performers. Every day at 10 a.m. and 3.30 p.m. a crocodile wrestling show is held and at 5 p.m. the scaly reptiles are given their dinner.

To get to the Crocodile Farm catch bus number 25 to Samut Prakarn or take one of the tour packages. The Farm opens daily 8 a.m.–6 p.m.

Damnoen Saduak

Undoubtedly the greatest of all the day trips from Bangkok is to the small village of Damnoen Saduak, which plays host to the world famous **Floating Market**.

Less than 50 years ago, these markets were seen all over Thailand. Today, this is one of the few remaining river markets where you can still see the locals in wide-brimmed hats paddling themselves around in delightful little sampans selling great spiky durians, bananas, papaya and almost every kind of fruit and vegetable you could dream of.

The best time to arrive is at dawn, although most tours do not get there until 11 a.m., when both the volume of paddlers and of trade are at their height. From the banks of the *klong,* walk along a network of paths and bridges—best for taking photographs —or hire one of the boats that will take you on a circuit of the canals.

On shore is a no less active market with truckloads of garlic and chillies, and hoards of smiling children selling kebabs and less identifiable culinary extravaganzas. Only on the far side is the extent of the tourist invasion evident, with a vast complex of shops offering every form of tourist trinket. Generally they are expensive, though, and for the most part you would do better purchasing the goods in Bangkok.

Damnoen Saduak is about 80 km (50 miles) south-west of Bangkok and is most easily reached by tour. Alternatively, buses leave from the Southern Bus Terminal on Charoen Sanitwong Road to Nakhon Pathom, from where you must catch a minibus to the the town of Damnoen Saduak.

Rose Garden Resort

If you've got a day to spare, want to escape the city and don't mind milling crowds of other tourists, then the **Rose Garden Resort**, 32 km (20 miles) west of Bangkok, is well worth a visit. The extensive grounds situated on the banks of the Thachin River include a hotel, Thai-style bungalow accommodation, boating lake, swimming pool, bicycle hire, restaurants and shops. A cultural performance is held daily at 3 p.m. featuring folk and classical dances, sword fights, Thai boxing, an elephant show and even a traditional Thai wedding.

The trip can easily be combined with a visit to Damnoen Saduak. Alternatively contact the Rose Garden Office, Tel: 253 0295-7.

Transport

From dawn to dusk the picture rarely changes. Roaring taxis, clapped out *tuk tuks*, manic motorbikes and belligerent buses all stuck in traffic jams and merrily churning out vast quantities of pure, unadulterated toxins for pedestrians to savour.

As a general rule, traffic is at its worst from 8 a.m.–10 a.m.. and from 4 p.m.–7 p.m., when the majority of the city's daily ton of lead is deposited into the air. For the remainder, traffic oscillates between bad and appalling, depending on the state of the weather, if there's a boxing match and, as always, whether you're in a hurry. Only on Sundays does the mayhem lessen, and the roads take on an appearance of normality.

If you are uncertain about which mode to go for, take a taxi and a book to read. If you are going by bus, buy a map. And if you want to get somewhere in a hurry forget it. Time is a flexible commodity in Thailand and being late is an inextricable part of the *mai pen rai* (no worries) mentality.

To and from the Airport

Bangkok's International Airport, Don Muang is located 30 km (19 miles) from the heart of the business centre and can be reached in anything between 40 minutes and 2 hours, depending on the state of the traffic. Buses to the centre leave frequently.

The number A4 bus passes all the big hotels. Thai International also has an air-conditioned bus, which leaves every half hour from 6 a.m.–9 p.m. from the Asia Hotel at 296 Phayathai Road.

Loads of Lead
Statistically speaking, Bangkok is no ordinary city. In a report by UN-ESCO, Bangkok is said to pump out a ton of lead into the atmosphere a day. Every year workers spend an average 54 days in a traffic jam costing more than Bt14,000 million in fuel bills. Some 50 per cent of all traffic police have respiratory diseases. And the culprit ? Those lovely *tuk tuks*, buses and motorbikes that we all ride around in.

From over the footbridge, trains also depart for Hualamphong Station on Rama IV Road in the centre of town. But they are irregular, crowded and extremely slow.

If you don't know Bangkok, probably the best and safest ways to get into the city is to take one of the Airport Limousines run by Thai International. Officials in coloured blazers will point you to the booths as you come out of customs. The cost of the limousine is Bt350, but the advantage is that the drivers are likely to speak English and have a better knowledge of the area.

Recently there have been several muggings and a spate of thefts. Beware unlabelled taxis or people who offer you a lift into town.

Tuk Tuks

If every city has a special means of transport, then in Bangkok it is undoubtedly the *tuk tuk*, which is a clapped out three-wheel motorbike that compensates for what it lacks in appearance with its contribution to noise, pollution levels and hospital beds.

Officially they take only three passengers, unofficially up to eight. The minimum price for a short distance is around Bt 30 and for a longer journey around Bt 90.

For extended journeys, *tuk tuks* are generally more expensive than taxis and at rush hour, you'd need a gas mask. Remember to bargain and agree a price before you leave.

Tribute to a *Tuk Tuk*
In one of the most momentous events of the 1970s the government announced its decision to ban the three-wheeled *tuk tuk* from the streets of the capital. Enraged *tuk tuk* drivers marched to the National Assembly, blockaded the streets and petitioned the King. With the characteristic goodheartedness for which he is renown, the King intervened, and *tuk tuks* were assured of their future. To show their gratitude, every year *tuk tuk* drivers donate a pint of blood to the local hospital.

Bus

Bangkok has a rumbustuous fleet of old-world buses that would be the pride of many a western museum. In working condition, they are a miracle. These buses are cheap, run frequently and cover just about anywhere in the city.

Most comfortable are the air-conditioned buses, which have automatic doors, and will charge you a fare from Bt5–Bt15. Other buses have a flat rate

Life in the fast lane has always been a feature of Bangkok, both night and day.

fare of Bt2 or Bt3 and often no windows. A city bus map is essential. This can be purchased from any big hotel or bookstore.

Taxis

Taxis are the most comfortable form of transport. In addition their drivers are the most likely to speak a little English, and they offer the most protection from the fumes which pervade the city outside.

To get one, flag it down, state your destination, or get it written in Thai, bargain profusely and agree a price before you get in.

Taxis do not use meters, so if the quoted fare sounds too much, wait until another one comes and start all over again.

Fares to most places within the city range from about Bt50–Bt120, and depend on the distance and the state of the traffic. The drivers do not expect to be tipped.

The Most Fertile Area on Earth with Temples of Abundance

When the people of the Central Plains celebrate the coming of the rains, it is with untold enthusiasm. Blessed with fine weather, with rich land and abundant rivers, they have much to be grateful for. Visitors who come here will discover not only the ruined ancient cities of Sukhothai, Kamphaeng Phet and Ayutthaya, but national parks and glittering temples, and a world still largely tuned to the cycle of rice and farming.

They begin almost before you are out of the capital. Mile after mile of rice fields stretching to an endless horizon. Here and there you glimpse groups of farmers up to their knees in black glutinous mud, the mud which grows the rice and has made this one of the most fertile areas on earth.

The Central Plains is Thailand's rice bowl, home to some 30 per cent of the population and to the great Chao

*W*hen the harvest is good and the rains have come, even the local farmers find time for a party.

Phya River, which runs down from Nakhon Sawan for 364 km (225 miles) before emptying out into the Gulf of Thailand. Geographically it is delineated by the rugged western mountains bordering Burma and to the north by Phitsanulok, stretching east towards the Cambodian border and the Gulf of Thailand and south to the sprawling city of Bangkok.

Rivers are the life-blood of the region, and along the banks of the Chao Phya and a dense network of interconnecting canals, barges laden with produce journey slowly down the river, bringing rice and fruit to and from Bangkok.

Further to the west lie giant reservoirs and National Parks, the province of Kanchanaburi with its gems and its

CENTRAL THAILAND

Map of the Central Region.

caves, and beyond the rugged border with Burma, a thread of mountains and tiny villages, largely unexplored.

Centuries ago, this agricultural heartland was home to some of the Kingdom's greatest civilizations: to the ancient capital of Ayutthaya; to the city of Lopburi; and to Nakhon Pathom where Buddhism was first introduced to Thailand some 2,300 years ago. Their ruins can still be seen, some restored to their ancient glory, others still wrapped in shrubbery and the mists of time.

New cities have sprung up beside the old, tractors and trains beside the water buffalo and ox carts. But despite the changes, the Central Plains remains in many ways a world apart: a world that revolves largely around the rains and the village *wat*, and whose natural attractions of lush forests and valleys provide an enchanting contrast to the teeming metropolis.

Trips to the Central Region can be made as a short break from Bangkok. But the area also makes a good stepping-stone on the way to or from the Northern region. Good main roads lead both west, towards Kanchanaburi, and north, towards Phitsanulok, with numerous tarmacked roads as alternatives. Trains also run from Bangkok to Ayutthaya, Ban Pa-In, Nakhon Pathom, Kanchanaburi, Lopburi, Nakhon Sawan and Phitsanulok. There are also flights connecting the capital with Mae Sot, Tak and Phitsanulok.

Ayutthaya

To reach the first of the ancient capitals in the Central Plains you must head north from Bangkok to the spot where the great Chao Phya (Mother of Rivers) joins the rivers Lopburi and Nam Pasak forming an island.

When the mighty U-Thong founded his kingdom, it was this spot that he chose, well protected from the Burmese by three rivers and a canal and yet perfectly positioned for trading with Europe and the East Indies.

According to the Royal Chronicles, Ayutthaya was founded in the Year of the Tiger on the sixth day of the waxing moon at three *nalika* nine *bat* after the break of dawn (Friday 4th March 1350). For the next 400 years it ruled over a kingdom that extended north to Vientiane in Laos and west to Pegu in Burma, that was bisected by great waterways and was filled with golden temples.

But in 1767, the Burmese laid siege to the city, finally breaking down the battlements, killing or taking into slavery all but 10,000 of the inhabitants and razing one of the greatest Kingdoms in Siamese history. Such was the enormity of the event that, according to historical records, tears from the principal Buddha statue in Wat Panangcheung ran down its chest. The heart of Phra Boromtrailokanat, the Buddha statue in Wat Phra Si Sanphet broke and fell in its lap. And a raven committed suicide by piercing its body over the pinnacle of the *chedi* at Wat Rajaburana.

Today, little is left of Ayutthaya but leafy temples and faded dreams, but even these have a grandeur about them, a subtle power which testifies to its glorious past.

Getting Around

Because the area covered by the ruins is so vast and the distance between the sights so great—there are 375 temples, 29 fortresses and 94 city gates—something beyond one's own two feet is called for. Probably the best way to get around is to hire a *samlor* (tricycle). These can be hired for a morning or the whole day and will take you to all the major sights. For the fit, you can even hire bicycles, although on a hot day, roving cyclists can be reduced to wet rags.

One other alternative: take a short boat trip around the river. The one-hour circuit takes in Wat Phanam Choeng, Wat Phuttaisawan, Wat Kasatrathira, Wat Chaiwattanaram and the spot where Queen Sunanda and her children drowned. Boats leave from the landing near the Chandra Kasem Palace. You should be prepared to bargain hard.

The Temples

Most tours begin at the magnificent **Wat Phra Si Sanphet** on Si Sanphet Road, originally part of an extensive group of buildings comprising the King's Palace. The temple was built in 1448 and at one stage contained a 16 m (50 ft) Buddha image covered in gold and weighing 170 kg (375 lbs) But in 1767, the Burmese set fire to it in order to melt off the gold, completely destroying both the image and the temple. You can still see the restored

The most beautiful city in Asia, said early ambassadors. Some modern-day sightseers say Ayutthaya is better in ruins with its weathered statues.

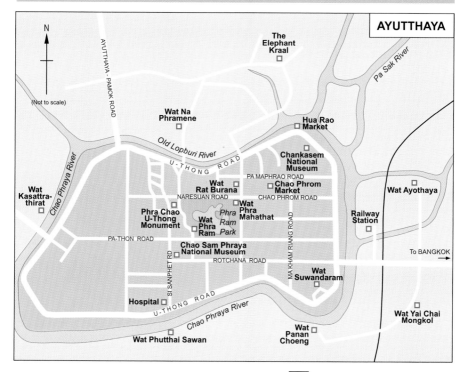

own plan of Ayutthaya.

chedis though, which contain the ashes of King Borom Trai Lokanat and his two sons.

If you leave the temple and turn right you will reach the **Viharn Phra Mongkol Borit**. This contains the biggest bronze Buddha statue in Thailand. It is said to be four or five centuries old, but lost one of its original arms when the roof of the temple collapsed.

Wat Phra Ram, situated a short distance to the south-east, has a different attraction. It was built in 1369 by King Ramesuan, the second king of Ayutthaya, on the site where the remains of his father were cremated. It contains several elephant gates and a large central *prang* surrounded by a gallery of stucco nagas, garudas and statues of the Buddha.

Cross the lake from Wat Phra Ram to see **Wat Mahathat** where many treasures of gold, crystal and precious stones were unearthed from the 14th century, as well as a relic of the Lord Buddha contained within a golden casket. The temple was formerly built by King Ramesuan in 1384, but was restored in 1956. To see the valuable objects though, you'll have to visit the National Museum in Bangkok.

Next door is **Wat Rachaburana**, built in the 15th century in memory of Prince Ay and Prince Yi, two brothers who slew each other in a tragic battle on elephant back. Rare frescoes remain in the crypt, but the more valuable golden images were carried off by thieves many years ago.

Continue east beyond the railway station on the banks of the Pasak River to get to **Wat Chaimongkhol**, originally built by King U-Thong in 1357 for monks who had studied in Ceylon. A massive pagoda was subsequently built to commemorate King Naresuan's victory in single-handed elephant combat over the Crown Prince of Burma.

A good place to finish your tour is at **Wat Chaiwattanaram** situated off U-Thong Road on a bend of the river. It was built in 1630 by King Prasartthong in memory of his late mother, who once resided in the vicinity. The temple is built in Khmer style, with the central pagoda representing Khao Phra Sumeru, the abode of the God of Siva. Being a pious Buddhist, the king also had a large *ubosot* constructed. The result is one of the most beautiful and romantic of the ruins, best seen at sunset.

Museums and Elephants

A couple of delightful museums lie within easy reach of the ruins. On Rojana Road, opposite the city wall is the **Chao Sam Phraya**, open Wednesday–Sunday 9 a.m.–4 p.m., which contains stone and bronze Buddha images dating from the 13th and 14th century, and a collection of 17th- and 18th-century door panels.

In the north-east of town off U-Thong Road you will find the **Chandra Kasem Museum**, open Wednesday–Sunday, an old palace built during the reign of King Maha Thammaraja, the 17th monarch of Ayutthaya. It was subsequently destroyed by the Burmese and only reconstructed in the 19th century by King Mongkhut.

For those with the time, drop by the **Elephant Kraal**, situated a few km out of town where the great Norwegian naturalist, Carl Bock, described 200 elephants being driven in by an army of hunters under the command of Chow Fa Maha Mala. The elephants were lured into the stockade through a one-way entrance and, once there, were put into the king's service, either as fighters or, if of the rare white variety, as idols and symbols of power. The last capture was in 1903 during the reign of King Chulalongkorn.

Besides its temples and Elephant Kraal, Ayutthaya has few attractions, except reportedly, as a major provider of gangsters, who as a sideline have a monopoly on *tuk tuks*. There are a few rice and tapioca mills and a modern commercial centre, but little else to delay one's departure.

Side Trip to Bang Pa-In

Twenty km (12 miles) to the south of Ayutthaya and easily reached by minibus from Chao Prom Market, or included in most day tours, is the **Royal Palace of Bang Pa-In**. It was originally built by King Prasat Thong of Ayutthaya during the 17th century and used as a country residence by a succession of monarchs. But it fell into disuse and was only revived in the late 19th century during the reign of King Mongkut, Rama IV, and King Chulalongkorn, Rama V.

Today, most of the original buildings have gone, replaced by architecture more reminiscent of the Palais de Versailles than of Siam. Apart from the beautiful pavilion called the **Aisawan Tippaya Asna** (The Divine Seat of Personal Freedom) situated in the middle of the lake, only the names remain truly Thai, with the royal residence known as **Warophat Phiman** (Excellent and Shining Abode), the two-storey **Saphakhan Ratchaprayun** (Assembly Hall for Royal Relatives) and the **Ho Withun Thasana** (The Sage's Lookout). It is a good place in which to wander, with leafy gardens and shady trees providing respite from the heat and the crowds.

Outside the Palace, there are pleasant walks along the river, and for the energetic, a good 20-minute stroll towards Bang Pa-In station where trains leave regularly for Bangkok and the North.

Bang Pa-In is open every day except Monday and Friday, 8 a.m.–3 p.m.

Death of a Queen
One of the great tragedies to befall King Chulalongkorn in 1881 drew the attention of the world to certain incongruities that had laid untouched within the Book of Palace Law for centuries. The one responsible for the disaster read as follows: "If a royal barge founders, the boatmen must swim away; if they remain near the boat they are to be executed. If they lay hold of him (the King), to rescue him, they are to be executed. If the barge founders and someone throws the coconuts so that they float towards the shore, his throat is to be cut and his home confiscated". Thus Queen Sunanda, Chulalongkorn's half-sister and favourite wife, drowned in front of crowds of onlookers at Bang Pa-In, who were unable to come to her rescue. Although Chulalongkorn had 91 other wives, he was so moved by the incident that he had a statue built in her remembrance at Pliu waterfall near Chantaburi.

Nakhon Pathom

The giant *chedi* at Nakhon Pathom is worth a visit if only for its size. It stands 127 m (416 ft) high, taller even than the famous Schwadagon Pagoda in Burma, and supposedly marks the spot where Buddhism was first brought to Thailand in the 3rd century BC, by missionaries sent out by the Emperor Asoke of India.

The original *chedi* was badly damaged by the Burmese in 1057 and was subsequently rebuilt and restored in the 19th century by King Mongkhut, Rama IV, and King Chulalongkorn, Rama V, to house certain relics of the Buddha. It nearly fell down again during the 1970s, but prompt action by the Fine Arts Department with a Bt35 million grant from the government saved the day and today the *chedi* can be seen in all its glory. At each compass point in the outer courtyard is a *viharn* (hall), housing Buddha images in various attitudes: one standing; one reclining; one protected by the sacred serpent or *naga;* and the last overlooked by a mural of a bo tree.

To go with its *chedi,* the town has a remarkably pompous history. Indeed the name Nakhon Pathom means First City and there is considerable evidence to suggest that it was capital of the ancient kingdom of Surarnabhumi dating back as far as 150 BC. There are few reminders of the early age, and apart from another striking *chedi* 3 km (2 miles) to the east at **Wat Phra Pathon Chedi**, little else of historical interest.

Trips to Nakhon Pathom are usually combined with a visit to the floating market at Damnoen Saduak or used as a stepping-stone to Kanchanaburi.

Thousands of Allied POWs died during the construction of the infamous "Death Railway" in Kanchanaburi.

Kanchanaburi

Seventy kilometres (45 miles) to the north-west of Nak-hon Pathom, in a gentle valley at the confluence of the River Kwai Yai (Big Buffalo) and the Kwai Noi (Small Buffalo), is the charming town of Kanchanaburi.

Easily reached from Bangkok, yet surrounded by distant mountains and sugar cane plantations, it is the most ideal location for spending a few days or for using as a base to explore the region. But Kanchanaburi is also known as the place where the notorious **Bridge over the River Kwai** was built. During World War II, thousands of British, Australian, Dutch and American prisoners of war were brought here by the Japanese to construct a bridge and railway line to connect Japanese-

occupied Singapore with Rangoon. Many of them died of diseases, others of torture and malnutrition.

In 1945, the bridge was bombed and destroyed and for the remainder of the war the line was never used. A reconstruction of the bridge, with some of its original girders, can still, however, be seen 5 km (3 miles) to the north of town, and every day at 10.35 a.m., a train passes over on the way to Nam Tok, a small town which marks the end of the line.

Around Town

An abundance of other historic monuments lie within easy reach of town as memories of that tragic past. At the **Kanchanaburi War Cemetery** on Saeng Chuto Road lie the gravestones of 6,982 servicemen, beautifully kept up by the Commonwealth War Graves Commission. To the south-west, on the opposite bank of the river, best reached by boat, is the smaller and quieter **Chong Khai Cemetery** containing a further 1,750 gravestones.

At the **Jeath Museum**, which is open daily 8.30 a.m.–4.30 p.m., and is sited

---

Fact and Fiction

Pierre Boulle's internationally acclaimed novel *Bridge over the River Kwai* and the film based on it recounted the agony of the prisoners of war who built the now infamous bridge. But it contains several inaccuracies. The Bridge was concrete, not wooden, and it was blown up by British bombers from Cyprus and not by dynamite. Still the horrors are well documented. Besides 16,000 prisoners of war, more than 60,000 civilians died— some 38 people for every kilometre of railway built.

at the entrance to Wat Chaichumphon on Paak Phraek Road, a replica prisoner of war hut with photographs and paintings document the atrocities inflicted on the prisoners.

To see the sights, hire a tricycle, or better still, one of the noisy long-tailed boats, which leave from the pier next to the bridge. These boats will take you on a circuit of the cave at **Wat Tham Khao**, the smaller **Commonwealth Cemetery** and the Jeath Museum. The tour takes an hour and costs Bt350. Several guesthouses organize two- to three-day trips going as far as **Sai Yok National Park**, although you will need quantities of mosquito cream and an extreme diffidence of hard cane floors to enjoy them.

Lit up by stunning colours, the light and sound festival at the Kwai Bridge still carries a morbid message. More than 75,000 people died building the railroad.

In the evening, wander down **Song Kwai Road** where excellent river fish are served. Especially famous is the *pla yisok* fish, distinguished by its unusually large dorsal fin and served with *nam phrik phao* (salt-garlic fish sauce) or *priaw wan* (sweet and sour). Alternatively, try the small open air food store next to the River Kwae Hotel. Delicacies include spicy wild boar stew, venison, monitor lizard and frogs.

*V*egetables of every sort are the spice of life in the Central Plains. Here, workers load up garlic.

Ban Khao and Prasat Muang Singh

Visitors with an interest in history, will not want to miss out on the famous archaeological museum of Ban Khao, situated 34 km (21 miles) to the west of town. The museum, open Wednesday–Sunday 8 a.m.–4.30 p.m., contains Neolithic remains, which are said to date back an astounding 4,000 years. The remains were uncovered by a Dutch prisoner of war, during construction of the "Death Railway"; and subsequent excavations made by a joint Thai/ Danish group of archaeologists revealed human skeletons, pots and jewellery made from animal bones, many of which have since been moved to the National Museum in Bangkok.

Continue 8 km (5 miles) north from Ban Khao to the beautifully restored **Prasat Muang Singh** (Lion City), a sprawling 12th-century Khmer temple fortress located on a bend of the Kwai Noi River. The temple has been declared an Historical Park—open daily from 8 a.m.–4 p.m.—with shrines encircled by ramparts said to represent the westernmost point of Khmer influence in the region. To see the various sculptures dating back from the 13th century, though, you will have to visit the nearby museum.

For details of tours, drop in at the TAT Office on Saengchuto Road, Tel: 511 200.

Erawan National Park

Magnificent Erawan National Park cannot be seen properly in a day, but for longer jaunts can make a perfect break.

It lies 65 km (40 miles) north-west of Kanchanaburi, and is famed for its seven-tier waterfall and an abundance of red junglefowl, kingfishers, hornbills and babblers. To get there catch a bus from the terminal off Saengchuto Road or follow Highway 3199 towards the Sri Nakharin Dam.

Don't expect a Niagara Falls. From February to June, little more than a sprinkle of water drips down, but after the rains, and especially between September and November, a vast torrent pours down the mountainside.

At weekends and on national holidays, the park is packed with crowds of Thais with bottles of Mekong whisky, Garfield T-shirts and guitars. At any other time, it's a calm spot with good walks and plenty of places to swim. Accommodation can be found at the Park Headquarters, although you should make reservations in advance at the National Parks Division in Bangkok, Tel: 579 4842.

Sai Yok National Park

The second of Kanchanaburi's great National Parks lies 105 km (65 miles) to the north-west of town and is best known for its three waterfalls and seven caves, one of which plays host to an extremely rare type of bat. The tiny winged creature is known locally as khun kitti bat (*Craseonycteris thonglongyai*) and can be found 1.5 km (1 mile) from the Visitors Centre in the Bat Cave. Its body is just 2.5–3 cm (1 in) long with a wingspan of 10 cm (4 ins), and it weighs only 1.5–2 g (0.05 oz). It was discovered in 1973 by the late Prof. Thong Long Ya Kitti.

Though crowds of waterfall fanatics descend at weekends, Sai Yok is quiet during the week and offers good opportunities for walking and swimming. Accommodation is available in rafts on the river. For further information contact the National Parks Division in Bangkok, Tel: 579 4842. Buses leave from the terminal off Saengchuto Road.

Along the Western Border

Some of the wildest and most spectacular landscape in the Central Region lies to the west of **Sai Yok**, with roads running along the side of the giant **Khao Laem Dam**, mountain villages perched over the western border, and large numbers of Burmese, and Mon and Karen people, who have fled from Burma over to Thailand to seek a safe haven.

The biggest towns along the route are easily accessible by regular buses leaving from Kanchanaburi for **Tong Pha Phum** and **Sangkhlaburi**. To get to others like Pilok or Three Pagodas Pass, there are *songthaews,* but only at irregular and unfixed intervals. And in the main towns there is reasonable if basic accommodation.

Before leaving you should check with the local authorities in Kanchanaburi about local conditions, for although there is rarely any danger, occasionally border areas can be closed.

If you follow Highway 323 beyond Sai Yok National Park, the first major town you get to is the rugged border smuggling town of Tong Pha Phum near the Khao Laem Dam.

It is an old town largely made up of wooden houses perched on the hillside, and was for many years the last outpost of civilization in this part of the Kingdom. In 1982, large areas of the valley were flooded by the **Khao Laem Reservoir**, now a major source of hydroelectricity; and for much of the year the tops of the submerged trees can be seen shrouded in early morning mist.

You can hire boats from the edge of the lake, about 5 km (3 miles) further up on Highway 3272, for as little as an hour. Often it is possible to continue by boat all the way to Sangklaburi, a five-hour journey away. But the biggest attraction lies 65 km (40 miles) beyond Tong Pha Phum high up in the hills overlooking the border with Burma. To get to **Pilok,** you must take Highway 3272, which leads around the dam for about 26 km (16 miles) before forking to the left and winding its way up up the mountain through wooded hills and bamboo. It's a dirt track, steep in places, but easily passable by motorbike or four-wheel drive and it offers some of the finest views anywhere in Thailand.

Pilok means mine, and the sprawling town of wooden houses and corrugated roofs is the traditional jade and gem smuggling centre between Burma and Thailand. Even today, some of the shops offer sapphires brought over from the border, as well as more basic local fare like barbecued chicken's feet.

If you drive or walk uphill a further 500 m (550 yds) beyond the town, you will get to the westernmost border crossing with Burma. The spot is marked by a solitary Thai flag. Beyond lies a landscape of thick jungle and mist and rolling hills controlled by the Karen Resistance Army. Currently there is nowhere to stay in Pilok, so you have no choice but to return to Tong Pa Phum where basic accommodation can be found at Boonyong Bungalows and further up the main road, Tong Pha Phum Bungalows.

Early morning mist over the Khao Laem Reservoir reveals magnificent views of the rugged hills of Burma.

Sangkhlaburi

North of Tong Pha Phum, the road cuts through limestone cliffs and forest, winding its way along the side of the Khao Laem Reservoir and descending after 74 km (46 miles) into the town of Sangkhlaburi.

The original town of Sangkhlaburi was located 20 km (12 miles) away in what is now the middle of the lake. The town that has replaced it is an incongruous mixture of modern architecture and old wooden huts straddling the *Sam Prasom* (Three Confluences).

On one side of the lake is a concrete administrative zone, with buildings arranged in neat squares and a permanently unfinished appearance; and on the other side, reached by the longest wooden bridge in the Kingdom, the part known as **Mon** town. This is a fascinating but decrepit place inhabited by Burmese and Karen, many of whom have attained permanent resident status in Thailand; and by the Mons, known as the forgotten people, or Palestinians of South-east Asia.

From near the bridge, boats can be rented to take you out to see the original town which lies submerged beneath the surface of the lake. In Mon town there is also a temple with its base made entirely out of wood salvaged from the flooded town. The abbot, named Sante, speaks fluent English and likes to show pictures and describe the history of the old town to visitors, although these days he is in such demand you may have to make an appointment.

Beside the temple is a market selling silver jewellery, sarongs, hats, Burmese lacquerware and feather dusters. You can easily spend half a day wandering around the Mon part of town and for a moment forget you are in Thailand. People dress the Burmese way, they speak Burmese. It is like two worlds in one city, linked by a bridge.

Side Trip to Three Pagodas Pass

Only ten years ago, it would have taken two days on an ox cart to reach Three Pagodas Pass from the old town of Sangkhlaburi. Today it can be done in two hours—an hour each way—along a good dirt track, which leads for 19 km (12 miles) through the mountains.

The pass is marked by three small white pagodas and a couple of Thai and Burmese flags. The pagodas are said to have been built by the Burmese as an assembly point from where their armies with elephants would attack Ayutthaya. Today, the white pagodas mark the official border crossing between Thailand and Burma, although much of surrounding territory remains in the hands of the MFLA, the Mon Freedom Liberation Army, engaged in a battle of independence with the Burmese government.

Periodically, Burmese government troops attack the rebel villages and the civilian population takes sanctuary on the Thai side.

These days, however, fighting is rare and generally visitors can continue into Burma for the day, although you must sign a book and be back at the checkpoint by 4.30 p.m. Burmese time.

On the far side of the border, a new town is rapidly springing up with markets selling cane wood, Coca Cola and Thai cigarettes, as well as ominous looking Burmese delicacies like raw crushed chilli with ground beetle, bird embryo kebabs and doughnuts.

From the village, there is a dirt track stretching into the distance, a narrow line of dust and bumps through miles of uninhabited scrubland.

Currently, there is nowhere to stay in Three Pagodas, so if you are going back to Sangkhlaburi, you should make sure you leave well before the sun goes down as it is not advisable to drive after dark. Before leaving, check on local conditions, as occasionally the pass can be closed for security reasons.

From Kanchanaburi to Saraburi

Endless rice fields line the roads north-east of Kanchanaburi, dotted here and there by small villages and by the colourful roofs of temples and *wats*.

Two or three times a year, the area is covered with ripe rice plants, a sea of gold. Around April, in July and sometimes in January, the villagers are out planting rice seedlings into ankle-deep water, kept at the required level by an intricate system of dams and canals. The rice ripens three months later, is harvested mainly by hand and the grains are sent to the mills.

Whether you are heading north or into the heart of the Central Plains, there are several interesting towns on the way. At **Don Chedi**, 31 km (19 miles) north of Suphanburi, a large pagoda commemorates the victory of King Naresuan the Great over King Maha Uparacha of Burma in single-handed elephant combat. The temple was only discovered in 1913, but has since been renovated. A new pagoda now covers the original, and in front of it is a statue of King Naresuan mounting the elephant's neck.

Forty km (25 miles) further to the east is the settlement of **Ang Thong** and nearby the reclining Buddha of Wat Khun in **Pramun.** But the most intriguing town in the area lies a further 105 km (65 miles)to the east near the the town of Saraburi at the village of **Phra Buddha Bat**, shrine of the Buddha's Holy Footprint.

According to legend, the footprint was discovered during the rule of King Songtam in the 17th century, when Sri Lankan monks informed the Monarch that a great relic of the Buddha existed in his Kingdom. A nationwide search was ordered. The Buddha's footprint was finally brought to light by a deer-hunter named Boon, who found that a pool of water in the shape of an enlarged human foot had medicinal powers and was able to revitalize a deer that he had shot. The King was overjoyed and accompanied by elephants and horses visited the spot and ordered that a temple be built.

Every year since then pilgrims from all over the Kingdom have flocked to

---

Harvesting the Rice

In the countryside, where some 70 per cent of the population spend their lives, the day can begin as early as 5 a.m. Breakfast may consist of curried pig's bladder, vegetables and rice. Then the whole family gathers in the rice fields, tilling the soil or sowing the rice, often working until nightfall; then taking the water buffalo home, cooking and sleeping. It's an endless cycle dictated by the rains and by the sun, oblivious to events in the outside world. When harvest is finished planting begins anew, and the rains once more begin. Thus it has been for centuries. Thus it will remain.

the shrine, especially in the months of January or February, when a giant fair is held.

Traditionally it was said that visiting the shrine three times in a lifetime would secure a seat in heaven. Kings even went there to make three rounds of the temple and to dance on an elephant's back in the belief that this would ensure a long reign.

Today around the original footprint, covered in gold leaf and coins donated by the faithful, numerous temples and shrines have sprung up catering to specific requests of the people. If you can lift a ten kg (22 lb) bronze elephant, using only your little finger, any wish that you make is supposed to come true. If you can ring 93 bells and count

M ore than 60 per cent of the population work the fields, producing more than 22 million tons annually of the grain known as khao suay *or, quite simply, "beautiful rice".*

them at the same time, you may even live to become 93 years old.

Lopburi

Temples and monkeys are the chief attractions of the old town of Lopburi, sitting astride the Lopburi River 50 km (30 miles) north of Saraburi. From the 6th –11th centuries, it was inhabited by people of the Dvaravati Period, an early India-influenced civilization of which little is known. And for the following 400 years by the Khmers. But it was in the 17th century under the rule of King Narai that Lopburi was to reach its nadir, when it became a second capital of the kingdom of Ayutthaya.

One of the best known of all Ayutthaya's monarchs, Narai took great pains to cultivate the Europeans and invited French Jesuit missionaries to help build his various temples and palaces. Under Narai, Constantine Phaulkon, a Greek with French sympathies even became Prime Minister. But his influence and that of the French was resented, and he was beheaded in 1668, whilst the king lay on his deathbed.

Today, Lopburi's Khmer temples and French-influenced palaces provide a colourful backdrop for a thriving provincial town. Almost all the major sights are within easy walking distance of the railway station, where an old steam train manufactured in 1913 is prominently displayed.

Sights

The best place to start a tour is at the **Narai Ratchanivet Palace**, open Wednesday–Sunday 9 a.m.–12 noon, and 1 p.m.–4 p.m., and which is situated between Ratchadamnoen Road and Pratoo Chai Road. This magnificent building was constructed in 1665 with the help of French architects, taking more than 12 years to complete. Inside is the **National Museum,** which houses exquisite examples of the Khmer art that has become a hallmark of the period.

If you wander through the various buildings, you will find a banquet hall, an audience hall for high-ranking foreign visitors, and the old treasure houses; as well as stables where the King was wont to keep his elephants and horses.

Afterwards, you can visit **Vichayen House**, originally the residence of Chevalier de Chaumont, the first French ambassador to Thailand. Later it was inhabited by Constantine Phaulkon himself until his death in 1668.

One other sight not to miss is the 12th century **Wat Phra Si Ratana Mahathat** with its fine Khmer-style architecture, and the later addition of chapels and *chedis* built in Sukhothai and early Ayutthaya style.

The Lopburi Monkey

Besides its temples, Lopburi has another claim to fame: monkeys—literally hundreds of them. Some of them live in the **Kala Shrine** next to the railway track; others in the nearby **Phraprang Sam Yod**, an impressive 13th-century temple where they can be found hanging from its three distinguished *prangs* and begging food and fruit from visitors. So legendary have the Lopburi monkeys become that the city hosts a huge banquet for them every year in the hope that this will bring good luck. You would be well advised, however, to hold on to your camera or anything else of value. It has become common for someone crazy or acquisitive in Thailand to be called a Lopburi monkey.

In the evening, if you have the time, wander down by the river in the old part of town where there are old

Temples and monkeys may be the tourist highlights, but much of Lopburi's workforce makes its money by weaving baskets.

wooden houses and little market stalls selling local wickerware and flowers. Afterwards you can visit the **White Horse Garden** on Phra Yam Jamkat Road, which serves some of the best food in town.

Occasionally you may see ranks of soldiers marching in town or leaping out of planes on the end of parachutes, for Lopburi is one of the biggest military bases in the Central Region. But there is little trouble in town, the people are friendly, and the place worth a lot more attention than it currently gets.

Kamphaeng Phet and the Ancient Ruins

The largest concentration of historic monuments in Thailand, and some of the most beautiful examples of early temple architecture are to be found in the area north of Lopburi and beyond the big, busy town of **Nakhon Sawan.**

During the 13th and 14th centuries this fertile land was known as the Kingdom of Sukhothai, and was inhabited by groups of Thais who had displaced the Khmers on their migration south. They built themselves great cities with temples dedicated to Buddha and with complicated irrigation systems.

For more than 100 years the Kingdom of Sukhothai and the sister towns of Kamphaeng Phet and Si Satchanalai thrived as centres of civilization, until their power waned and the focus of history moved to the emergent kingdom of Ayutthaya.

If you are driving north, **Kamphaeng Phet** (City of Diamond Ramparts) is the first of the ancient cities you will reach along Highway 3. It was a former garrison town of Sukhothai, marking the southernmost point of the Kingdom and contains some of the least visited temples in the Central Plains.

The main ruins lie within the old city wall on the east bank of the river, with the finest temples to be found in the **Historical Park**. The most important is **Wat Phra Kaeo**, said by early chronicles to have housed the Emerald Buddha, now made up of weathered carvings and dominated by a Sri Lankan style pagoda. Opposite a ruined circular *chedi* is one of the most peaceful Buddha images in the Kingdom, with the figure reclining on a pillow of stone, the position waiting for nirvana.

A few hundred metres or yards south is **Wat Phra That**, the town's second most important temple, built some time during the 14th century and containing the remains of a *viharn* and several ruined *chedi*. Nearby are several other temples and a **National Museum**, open Wednesday–Sunday, which displays fine pieces of sculpture from the Lopburi period, and a variety of terracotta ornaments and Buddha images from the ruined temples of Kamphaeng Phet.

Beyond the city walls are countless other temples such as the beautiful **Wat Chang Rob** with its 68 crowned elephants and stucco demon figures, and further on, a vast complex of ruins reached by interconnecting roads.

Currently work is still underway as part of a massive programme to restore the place and make it another tourist show piece. But whilst some of the rehabilitation has now been finished, there are still plenty of untouched ruins, and until the restoration programme is completed, it is likely to remain a beautifully quiet and untrammelled place set amongst trees where you can even hear the sounds of birds.

If you have not got transport, the only sensible option is to go on one of the tours organized by the larger hotels and travel agents as the ruins are spread over a vast area and are a considerable distance from town.

Kamphaeng Phet is also renowned for its bananas, especially the famous *kluai khai*, a sweet banana found in abundance in the surrounding areas. Revenues from the bananas exceed Bt160 million every year, and in the tenth lunar month, normally September, the city holds a festival with dances and cultural performances and even a Miss Banana pageant.

Sukhothai

Even those with little interest in ruins cannot fail to be moved by the sights of Sukhothai, the second of the great ancient cities in the northern central plains, and probably the most beautiful.

According to legend, the city was founded in 1238 by a freedom fighter named Phor Kun Sri Intharathitya (Father of Dignitaries). He became the first king, and his second son Phor Khun Ramkhamhaeng, known as The Great for his bravery, became the most famous monarch in the history of Sukhothai.

For 127 years, Sukhothai ruled over an area stretching north to Vientiane, east and south towards the Malay Peninsula. Ramkamhaeng is credited with inventing the Thai script, introducing a free trade system and personally dispensing justice. Recent earthenware pots from the Sukhothai period were discovered as far afield as Sumatra and Borneo. Tests have revealed that they carried palm oil and palm wine and that an extensive trade existed with the area that is now Indonesia. After the reign of Ramkhamhaeng, Sukhothai's power waned and in 1365, it became a vassal of Ayutthaya and was abandoned for several centuries.

Today under a US$10 million renovation programme from the Thai government and Unesco, some 200 temples, images, moats and kilns have been restored. These lie within the historical park, 13 km (8 miles) west of the new town of Sukhothai. *Songthaews* regularly run the route from the market, and you should ask for "*meun khao*".

Most people take guided tours. A better way to explore them is by bicycle; or for the less energetic, on a new and incongruous electric tram.

Touring the Ruins

To flavour of the ruins, begin at the **National Museum** near the Kamphang Hek Gate, open Wednesday –Sunday, 9 a.m.–4 p.m. It contains a delightful collection of sculptures and Buddha images unearthed in Sukhothai and the nearby provinces, as well as a magnificent 14th-century example of the walking Buddha, the image which archaeologists claim to be the finest of all Buddhas in Thailand. A replica of King Ramkamhaengs' famous inscription "there is water in the fields…" is also to be found here.

From the museum, it's just a short walk past the moat to **Wat Mahathat**, temple of the **Great Relic**, the biggest and finest temple in Sukhothai. The temple dates from the 14th century and contains a graceful inner *chedi* surrounded by four *viharns* and rows of

standing Buddha images known as Phra Attharot. During the reign of King Ramkamhaeng, it is said that a bell was hung outside the nearby palace and citizens would ring it to get the attention of the good monarch who would emerge to settle disputes and extend justice.

South-east of Wat Mahathat is the temple of **Wat Sri Sawai** built in the 12th century and bearing three majestic *prangs.* It's a Khmer-style building and must have predated the city, although Ramkhamhaeng himself is said to have helped convert it into a Buddhist temple.

Afterwards, visit beautiful **Wat Sra Si** (Temple of the Splendid Pond) with its slender bell-shaped *chedi* and graceful image of the Walking Buddha; and **Wat Trapang Ngoen** situated around a large lake and, during the rainy season, occasionally flooded.

Outside the walled city, and 500 m (547 yds) beyond the San Luang Gate, you will find the second largest area of ruins. The 12th-century **Wat Phra Phai Luang** (Temple of the Great Wind), is said to have been a Khmer-Hindu shrine, and features three *prangs,* one of which is decorated with stucco seated Buddha images; the other two formerly containing phallic emblems of the Hindu god Shiva.

Further west is **Wat Sri Chum**—one temple not to be missed—with a monolithic sized Buddha that measures 11.3 m (37 ft) from knee to knee with each finger as large as a man's body. Inside is a secret passage decorated with engraved slabs said to have been the work of Ceylonese artists.

Those that like their ruins unspoilt can continue 2 km (1 mile) west of the

*H*eralded as the finest of all the Buddhas the Sukhothai image treads between heaven and earth, fluid in movement, serene and enlightened. This one outside Wat Sri Si has everything that it takes.

city to the temple of **Wat Sapan Hin**, known as the Temple of the Stone Bridge after the slate pathway leading up the hill. Once home to armed bandits, it's now a popular place from where to watch the setting sun and to feel, if only for a moment, the silent power of times gone by.

The best time to visit Sukhothai is during the full moon of the 12th lunar month—normally mid-November—when. Thailand's loveliest festival known as *Loy Krathong* is held. The festival is believed to have originated some 700 years ago after one of the king's concubines fashioned a lantern from carved fruit bearing a lighted candle and sent it floating down the river. Today thousands of people gather by the lake to launch boats made from banana leaves and to enjoy colourful processions and a firework display.

The majority of sightseers come to Sukhothai on day trips from nearby Phitsanulok. A better idea is to stay in the very reasonable accommodation either near the historical park or along the road in the new town. The advantage of spending the night here is to get a full day's viewing and a

chance to wander in the early morning or late evening when the crowds have gone.

Side Trip to Si Satchanalai

Although most visitors exhaust their temple fervour at Sukhothai, a rewarding side trip can be made to Si Satchanalai which lies 55 km (35 miles) to the north off Highway 101.

If you are driving take a turning to the left 11 km (7 miles) before you get

Another beautiful sunset over the ancient temples of Sukhothai.

to the new town or if you are on the bus ask the bus conductor to drop you off at "*meun khao*".

According to the *Northern Chronicles*, the name of Si Satchanali derived from an ascetic named Rsi Satchanalai who advised that the town be built to worship the gods of fire. It was constructed on top of an old settlement thought to predate Sukhothai, and is believed by historians to be the twin capital of Sukhothai.

But after King Naresuan of Ayutthaya attacked the town and took the inhabitants to Phitsanulok, it was abandoned until the beginning of this century when a British consul general named Reginald Le May once again put the place on the map. Now a bridge has been built over the River Yom and the Fine Arts Department has been busily renovating the main area, which has been made another Historical Park.

Three temples are especially worth visiting. To the north of the park at the top of a steep flight of steps are the ruins of **Wat Khao Suwankhiri**, which is worth the climb just for the fine views. If you head east and you will reach **Wat Khao Phanom Ploeng** with a large seated Buddha and the columns that supported the roof of a once great *viharn*. The most impressive temple, though, is **Wat Chang Lom** (which translates literally as the Elephant Temple). According to King Ramkamhaeng's famous inscriptions, this marked the spot where in AD 1287, the relics of the Buddha, after being dug up, were honoured for one month and six days and then re-enshrined. The *chedi* is surrounded by 39 standing elephants and a stairway imitating

*T*he local band gets *people up and running, but the village elders call the tune.*

a ladder to heaven. In front of the temple the locals have stationed a real elephant—and it is often possible to get rides around the park. Barring that, you can hire bicycles from the main road.

From the Historical Park, continue to **Ban Khao Noi**, a tiny village which lies 4 km (2.5 miles) to the north. Since archaeologists started digging in the area in 1980, more than 200 kilns have been uncovered along with 27 iron furnaces. The results may prove that pottery first began in Thailand, some 400 years before the Chinese acquired the techniques.

Phitsanulok

Phitsanulok, the provincial capital and economic centre of the northern Central Plains, lies 70 km (43 miles) east of Sukhothai on the gentle banks of the Nan River. It is a town of little charm, mainly used as a transportation hub, but it does offer the comforts of good hotels and nightclubs and it even has its own piece of history.

Phitsanulok was the birthplace of King Naresuan the Great of Ayutthaya and his brother, Prince Ekatosarot, and was a major place of recruitment when Ayutthaya waged war with Burma.

Briefly, during the reign of King Borom Trailoknart, it was even the capital of Thailand. In 1960, however, a fire destroyed much of the old town and most of its history along with it.

One monument, which survived the fire was the venerable temple of **Wat Phra Sri Rattana Mahathat** on the east bank of the Nan river opposite the City Hall.

The *wat* known to the locals as *Luang Paw Yai* (Big Temple) contains the **Chinnarat Buddha**, one of Thailand's most revered images covered in gold leaf donated by King Ekatosarot himself. It was built in 1357 with fine mother of pearl-inlaid chapel doors donated by another Monarch, King Boromkot and a *prang* with several large Buddha relics.

Besides its temples, there is a **Folk Museum** and a Buddha-casting factory where you can see bronze Buddha images of all sizes being cast. There are also some nice old raft houses on the banks of the Nan River and a couple of floating restaurants.

Evening entertainment generally consists of tricycle night tours of the old city, stopping at the old city walls and the riverside food bazaar famed for its vegetable-throwing chef. Afterwards, with little prompting, the same

*W*hen it is hot and customers are sparse, Phitsanulok's samlor drivers take an afternoon rest.

tricycle driver will show you the city's nightlife, for which, at every club or massage parlour, he gets commission.

The local tourist office also suggests a walking tour. It takes you from Wat Phra Si Rattana Mahathat to Wat Nag Phya, and then along the Nan River footpath to the riverside bazaar. From there you can walk to the municipal market where you can treat yourself to delicious barbecued kebabs, tropical fruits and exquisite and extremely sweet Thai deserts.

Around Phitsanulok, there are a number of waterfalls and National Parks—details can be provided by the Tourist Office (TAT) at 209/7–8 Surasi Trade Centre, Borom Trailoknart Road, Tel: 252 742.

From Phitsanulok, it is possible to cross into the North-east Region along a beautiful winding road through Nan Nao National Park and then across to Loei.

Tak and Mae Sot

West of Phitsanulok and the ancient cities, along the rugged Burmese border, lie the towns of Tak and Mai Sot, bustling trading centres and suppliers to neighbouring Burma.

To get to Tak you have to take Highway 12 from Sukhothai or Highway 104 from Kamphaeng Phet. Tak is a ramshackle place which sits on the bank the Ping River. Besides a narrow suspension bridge that spans the river and a colourful market place, it is little more than a stopping point en route for Mae Sot. There are, however, a couple of good hotels as well as cheap and basic alternatives.

From Tak there are two ways of reaching Mae Sot. To do the first you have to backtrack to the beautiful little town of **Baan Tak** nestling 23 km (14 miles) upriver, from where you cross the bridge and follow a steep but tarmacked, road—Highway 1175—through the mountains, which connects up with main road.

Alternatively you can follow the shorter and easier Highway 105 that the buses take through rugged hills and forested mountains. Either way it is a pleasant journey that will take a couple of hours.

Mae Sot itself is a fascinating jumble of beautiful old wooden houses, concrete shop fronts and temples, all in a permanent state of disrepair.

The people here are Burmese, Indian, Muslim and Thais, and all of them seemingly connected in one way with commerce. For trade is the lifeblood of the town and everyone appears to be buying or selling some form of commodity.

The best place to see the frenetic trading is, however, at the border town of **Mae Tao** on the Moie River, a further 7 km (4 miles) to the west and easily reached by *songthaew*.

This is the place to watch the Burmese buying tyres, powdered milk and washing powder, and the Thais scurrying back clad in Burmese hats and carrying bottles of Johnny Walker and illegal Burmese cheroots. During the dry season, the locals paddle across the Moie River, which lies just 50 m (55 yds) away from the Burmese town of **Myrawaddy**. Such freedom is not, however, extended to foreigners, who are limited to wooden benches on the water's edge.

In the nearby market you can buy Burmese jade and rubies, as well as illegal Burmese and Karen whisky, a pink concoction that tastes like paraffin and gives a kick like a motor engine.

Government officials estimate official daily trading with Burma at Bt10 million, most of it consumer goods and motor oil. But with gems and live animals, cheroots and timber, the figures are probably considerably higher. Only sometimes does the trading stop. Every so often fighting on the Burmese side closes the border and huddles of people sit around waiting for the distant shelling to stop and activity to return to normal.

Besides visiting nearby Mae Tao, there is little to do in Mae Sot except watch. There is a beer garden, a couple of guesthouses and Chinese hotels. There is also a lively market selling noodles, pakhora and kebabs and one restaurant, with a menu in English. By 10 p.m., however, the stores and restaurants close up, the traders go home, and the place has a ghostly emptiness about it.

Side Trip to Umphang

From Mae Sot, the adventurous can continue south to Umphang, a further 163 km (101 miles) away on Highway 1090, once known as the Death Road, after the communist insurgents, who were forever trying to blow it up. These days the communists have gone, and most of the trees too, but it is a steep road with little habitation along the way and you would be ill-advised to drive it alone.

Umphang is a tiny place with just one guesthouse. From here a road runs

*G*entle scenes on Mae Sot's Moie River belie the truth. Shelling has historically been the region's biggest commodity.

south past the **Lor Jor Waterfalls** and the **Ze Pe La Waterfalls** for 47 km (30 miles).

Beyond lies one of the last unspoilt forest areas in South-east Asia, a vast and largely unexploited region stretching all the way south to Sangkhlaburi and east to Uthai Thani. It is largely funded by the World Wildlife Fund and covers some 6,000–7,000 sq km. (2,300–2,700 sq miles) Zoologists claim there are as many as 300 tigers living here, as well as elephants, monkeys and gibbons. Treks can occasionally be organized from the guesthouse to the **Huai Mae Lamung Rapids** and to a nearby Lisu village. Currently however the area is mainly used as a centre for students studying forest ecology. There are footpaths and tracks, but few roads and you have little choice but to backtrack to Mae Sot.

The Spirits

They live precariously in little houses on the top of posts, in grand government buildings and even in people's heads. They are officious, gentle and down-right mischievous and, along with Buddhism, they provide the key to a person's future.

Because of the *phi* or spirits, Thais never have their hair cut on Wednesday. And because of them, they never move house on a Saturday. Even royalty is not above them. The kings of old, before having their hair cut, would traditionally recite certain propitiatory verses which were especially composed to please the spirits and to avert offence to the *Khwan* (Spirit of the Head).

Often the local *phi* have idiosyncratic tastes. Spirits who live in trees are placated by having their trunks swathed in brightly coloured silk. Others may be offered headbones of swordfish or hard boiled eggs or wooden elephants. One particular spirit in Bangkok is believed to have a penchant for pigs' heads.

Every city in Siam that ever attained any degree of independence is said to have boasted its guardian spirits. The inhabitants of Ayutthaya believed that spirits lived in the barrel of their guns influencing the outcome of a battle. Mountain spirits were especially potent. One certain Brana Khabun was called the Greatest Spirit of the Realm by King Ramkamhaeng of Sukhothai.

Today, in many fishing villages around the coast, brightly coloured phalluses are erected outside the shrine of Chao Mae Chiwit (Lady Mother of Life) to fertilize the sea and ensure good catches. On dangerous corners on roads and highways you will often see spirit houses, draped with flowers and surrounded by little offerings, to ensure the safety of drivers.

Seasonal Worship

At different times of the year, special ceremonies will be held to appease the spirits. At harvest time and New Year, in the northern hills, the Karen tribes make special offerings of chicken and pigs to the Lord of Land and Water, who owns all the jungle, water and fields around. A mighty spirit, known as Crop Grandmother, is said to preside over the harvest and ensure plentiful supplies of food for the coming year.

In many other parts of the country if a member of the family is sick, a spirit man or *prahm* will be consulted to lure back the soul, which may temporarily leave the body. A particularly bad sign may be a gecko croaking from behind or a vulture spotted flying over someone's property.

Often a ritual ceremony will be performed in which boiled chickens, sweetmeats and betel nuts are offered up in exchange for the return of the

Making a wish to the spirits.

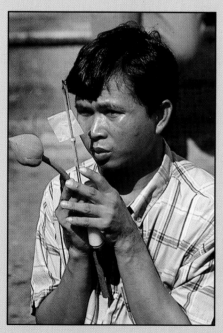

khwan. In especially bad cases, token gifts fashioned out of leaf-cuttings as well as flowers and incense are also used to win back the errant spirit.

Perched decoratively atop a post resides the phi *the most important resident in the house Ignore him at your own peril.*

An upmarket spirit shrine in Bangkok.

Lord of the House

On the verandah of almost every house or in a shady corner of the garden you can see the gaily painted wooden doll's house known as the *Phra Phum*, or the Lord of a House. This must face either north or south—preferably north—to make sure that the spirit will come and live here, and will contain a single room, outside which three joss sticks are placed along with a glass of fresh water and a bowl of rice.

Often the spirits are provided with other types of food, gifts and flowers, especially when the birth of a child or the marriage of a daughter is pending. To make sure that the spirit does not get lonely, a symbolic picture is intricately carved on a small piece of wood placed inside the little house and, sometimes so they will not get bored, the spirit houses are decorated with nude dancers.

Indeed if Thailand is blessed with fine weather, with abundant crops and with one of the fastest economic growth rates in the world, there is one benevolent influence more than any other to be grateful to—the spirits: And no Thai can afford to ignore them.

Offerings to the spirits include the 'phi's favourite', boiled eggs.

Childish Fancy
It pays to call your child fat, pig or ugly. In Thailand anyway. Those that do not may find their loving offspring possessed by some evil spirits. These spirits generally prefer sweet, honorific sounding names, which is why you never hear of a child called suay (beautiful). So next time someone calls your child ugly, treat it as a form of long-term commitment to their wellbeing.

Northern Wisdom
One of the great pieces of wisdom handed down from the people of the north was that a house should have facilities both for man and spirit. As such it should be built on a raised platform with outward slanting walls, and have one large single room as sleeping quarters. But most important of all, it should contain a pair of ham yon or sacred testicles, wherein live the spirits of fertility. So powerful are these spirits that when new inhabitants move in, the ham yon are symbolically castrated by being shaken against the wall to remove the potency of the former residents.

Flying High
Patriarchal help is applied even to Thailand's foremost airline. Before any Thai International jet makes its maiden journey, the most senior member of the Buddhist order, the veritable Patriarch himself, blesses the plane on the runway of Don Muang's International Airport. It is possibly no coincidence that Thai International has reported 27 consecutive years of profit, and has on several occasions been nominated as one of the finest Asian airlines. In 1991 it was even able to report a handy Bt5 billion net earnings.

Centuries Old Kingdom at the Foot of the Golden Triangle

When King Mengrai established the Kingdom of Lan Na, he chose a region of lush hills, river valleys and caves. That was more than 700 years ago, but visitors can still experience colourful hilltribes, lush national parks, the legendary Golden Triangle—and just to add to it, some of the best handicrafts and most comfortable hotels in the country.

Rising up from the foothills of the Himalayas, the Northern Region sweeps down from the borders with Laos and Burma, descending into the deep valleys and finally opening out into the great plains of the Central Region. Bisected for a short stretch by the great Mekong River, by the Ping and the Teng, it is at its northern point less than 100 km from China as the crow flies.

Until the 13th century, the north was divided into small principalities. But under legendary King Mengrai,

*K*aren tribesmen have been around almost three centuries.

they joined together to form the powerful kingdom of Lan Na, land of a million rice fields.

For 250 years, the kingdom flourished under a succession of kings until 1556 when the Burmese overran the capital of Chiang Mai and put the inhabitants to flight. Lan Na remained under Burmese sway except for brief periods until 1775, when King Taksin defeated the Burmese and the kingdom came under Siamese rule. But even as recently as 60 years ago, the north continued to have a measure of autonomy.

History has instilled a fierce pride amongst northerners. The people speak their own dialect, influenced by Burmese and Lhao—and have their own culinary specialities. Indeed they do not call themselves Thais, but *khon*

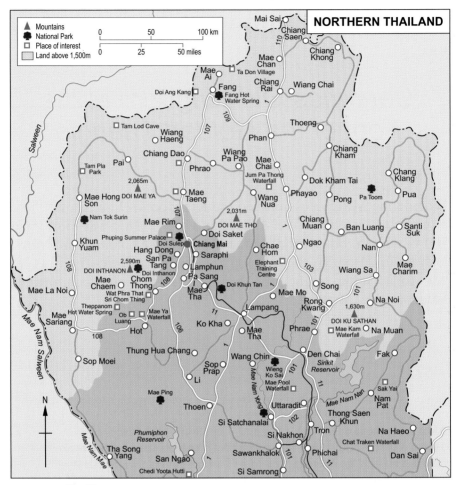

*M*ap of
Northern Thailand.

meung (People of the Province)—and their festivities emphasize a people proud, free and independent. The north too is the home of hilltribes or *chai doi,* colourful ethnic groups who have moved down from China and Tibet, eking a living from the land, cultivating opium and arable crops. Many of them live along the rugged terrain close to Burma, others around the infamous area known as the Golden Triangle, the spot where the borders of Thailand, Burma and Laos meet which is the second largest opium-producing region in the world.

Today, despite the rapid growth in tourism and the gradual erosion of traditional values, it is possible to share at least some of the excitement and to go rafting, elephant riding or trekking; or just to enjoy the scenery from the comfort of a five-star hotel. Many tourists use Chiang Mai, the biggest town in the North, as a base to explore the region. But the surrounding area is rich in historical and natural interest, with charming towns like Chiang Saen and Nan, the wildness of Mae Hong Son or the still unspoilt beauty of the Mekong River.

Good roads connect almost all the major towns, leaving the dirt tracks for the adventurous and for those who want to discover a different side of Thailand on their own. The North also boasts an extremely high standard of hotels and has the advantage of a relatively large English-speaking community.

For those with cars or motorbikes, one of the best routes will take you north from Lampang to Chiang Mai and then west to Mae Hong Son before continuing to Chiang Rai and the Golden Triangle. Vehicles can be hired in any of the larger towns by the day or week.

Alternatively, the North also has an excellent network of buses and tours enabling visitors to travel to almost any destination without their own transport.

The North can be easily reached from Bangkok by plane, train, bus or car; there are airports at Chiang Mai, Nan, Chiang Rai and Mae Hong Son. It can also be used as a stepping-stone to the North-east, via the towns of Phitsanulok and Loei.

Lampang

The first major town in the Northern Region lies in a deep fertile valley of the Yom River, 174 km (108 miles) north of Tak. Lampang was the scene of regular battles. It was once a major provincial city in the Haripunjaya Empire, an ancient kingdom centred around Lamphun. But in 1281, King Mengrai laid siege to the town, tearing down the battlements and including it in the Lanna empire. During the 16th century, Lampang was attacked and occupied by the Burmese. Only in 1775 was it finally liberated by King Taksin and incorporated into the Kingdom of Thailand.

Something of Lampang's colourful history remains in its ancient *wats,* many of them influenced by Burma, others by Lanna. **Wat Sri Rong Muang** on Tha Krao Noi Road and **Wat Sri Chum** on Sri Chum Road both contain good examples of the Burmese style carvings, hallmarks of much of the North, whilst **Wat Pongsanuk Thai** on Pongsanuk Road has tiered roofs and a Lanna style *chedi.*

The most revered of all the temples in Lampang, however, is **Wat Phra Kaeo Don Tao** situated on the far side of the river, 1 km (0.6 mile) north-east

An Opium Edict

"Persons who smoke and eat opium have become very abundant and increasing" lamented an early 19th-century royal report. As a result the King of Siam published an edict against the introduction and sale of opium within his dominions. It read "His Majesty perceived that opium is an evil thing and contraband in every reign (land) from time immemorial till now. He therefore formally condescended graciously to the tuft of hair of the head, and pronounced a divine word, a commandment, not allowing any person whatever to buy and sell opium, prepared or raw. Anyone who did so would be fined 10 times the value of the opium".

*T*hree naga *snakes guard the outside of one of Chiang Mai's temples. Had they been crafted a little earlier they might have saved the city from being taken over by the warring Burmese in 1558.*

of the Rasada Phisek Bridge. The temple at one stage is said to have housed the famous Emerald Buddha. Under the influence of the zealous northern monk Kruba Srivijaya it has been extensively renovated with the additions of a *viharn* with ceilings of sculptured wood and fragments of mother of pearl.

For those less interested in temples and more interested in scenery, pleasant walks can be taken around Wat Phra Kaeo and along the river where few tourists stray, and down the narrow roads with their rickety wooden houses. Less than a century ago, when Lampang had a population of 20,000 and more than 4,000 elephants, the river was used to float teak down to the Central Plains where the timber would be taken to the saw mills.

These days there are only a few farmers herding cattle on the river banks and you can wander along the narrow roads that parallel the river for some considerable distance. Rarely is there any need to backtrack, for there are numerous bridges and always the odd boatman who for a couple of Baht will take you over to the other side.

In the eastern part of town, beyond the Thip Chang Hotel, is old **Lampang Chinatown** with its narrow alleys which are home to fine silversmiths. Open shophouses allow you to watch bowls and bells being made much as they have been for centuries. The town is also renowned for its blue and white ceramics, woodcarvings and handmade furniture, which can be found not only in the small shops near the old part of town, but in big modern warehouses along Paholyothin Road.

Although Lampang has buses and even the occasional *tuk tuk*, the best way to explore the area is by horse-drawn carriage, the traditional mode of public transportation still widely used in town. These are located mainly along Paholyothin Road and near the railway station, but around lunchtime you may find it hard to get one as they are busy ferrying children back from school.

Few visitors stay overnight, preferring to continue to Chiang Mai situated 100 km (60 miles) to the north-west. But if you do, Lampang has some fine restaurants along the river.

Chiang Mai

This delightful city is undoubtedly the most popular in the north. Former capital of Lan Na, business hub and boom town, it contains an abundance of tourist sights—including elephants, orchid farms and temples—although the growth of hotels and influx of visitors has long put paid to its sleepy reputation as Rose of the North.

It was the great King Mengrai who founded the city. In 1296, he spotted two white barking deer, two white sambar deer and five mice, and decided that this was sufficiently auspicious to found his capital there. With the help of 90,000 men, supposedly working 24-hour shifts, moats were built and the city surrounded by walls to protect the hundreds of temples within.

In 1558, however, arguments over a Buddha image brought to a head long-standing conflicts with Burma; the King of Pegu invaded and the city was left almost deserted until 1774 when it was incorporated into Siam.

Many of the historical monuments have long since gone, victims of the Burmese and of a massive and largely uncontrolled building boom. Still there is no shortage of temples; they are spread on both sides of the Ping River, a monument to its founder, who was struck by lightning in 1317.

Chiang Mai also has the advantages of a cooler climate—between November and January bring a sweater—and the biggest concentration of surrounding sights in the Kingdom. Whether it's trekking or hilltribes, fine handicrafts or orchids, you'll find something to your taste; whilst for a touch of old Lanna, just visit the old markets or wander down the small side streets.

For those fortunate enough to be in the vicinity during February, April and November, you will see some of the most joyous festivals in all Thailand.

flower festival with colourful floral floats and parades. Whilst on the full moon day of the 12th lunar month, generally mid-November, it holds Yee Peng, the loveliest festival of all when, under the full moon, people float banana-leaf boats bearing a lighted candle to float away the past year's sins.

At other times of year too, Chiang Mai always appears to have some form or celebration or colourful procession to be seen; a Chinese funeral, or a ceremony to appease the capricious local spirits who may have brought mishap on local members of the community.

Orientation

Geographically Chiang Mai is divided in two. The older part of town originally constructed by King Mengrai in 1296 is enclosed by a square moat and surrounded by four walls. Some of the original walls have fallen down and been rebuilt. But the five city gates are still very much in evidence. They are the **Elephant Gate**, the **Chiang Mai Gate**, the **Tapei Gate**, the **Suang Prang Gate** and, finally, the **Suan Dok Gate** to the west.

As the town has expanded, however, the centre has shifted, with the main part of town now spread along Tapae Road towards the west bank of the Ping River.

Although many visitors prefer to explore the town by bicycle, or foot, the most common form of transport is a contraption known as the *songthaew*. This is a converted jeep, normally coloured red, with seats in the back, which drives around town, picking up as many passengers as it can squeeze in. To catch one you just have to flag

N *ortheners have every right to celebrate. After all, when King Mengrai ruled over the Kingdom of Lan Na, Bangkok was still a malaria swamp.*

None is more so than Songkran, held at the beginning of April, with four days of processions, of anointing monks and of water-throwing. In the first week of February, to coincide with the period when the city's flowers are in full bloom, Chiang Mai holds a

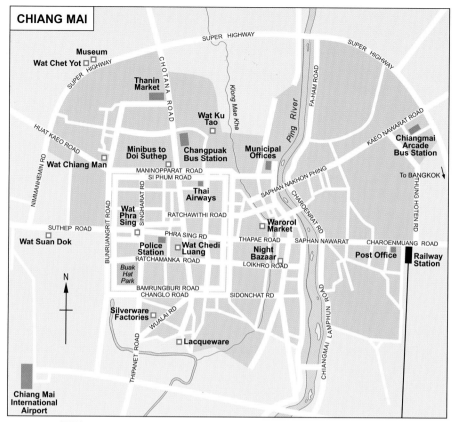

CHIANG MAI

Museum
Wat Chet Yot
SUPER HIGHWAY
SUPER HIGHWAY
SUPER HIGHWAY
Thanin Market
CHOTANA ROAD
Klong Mae Kha
Ping River
FA-HAM ROAD
KAEO NAWARAT ROAD
Chiangmai Arcade Bus Station
Wat Ku Tao
HUAT KAEO ROAD
NIMMANHEMIN RD
Wat Chiang Man
Minibus to Doi Suthep
Changpuak Bus Station
Municipal Offices
To BANGKOK
HUNG HOTEN RD
MANINOPPARAT ROAD
SI PHUM ROAD
SAPHAN NAKHON PHING
CHAROENRAT RD
SUTHEP ROAD
Wat Phra Sing
Thai Airways
RATCHAWITHI ROAD
Warorol Market
SINGHARAT ROAD
BUNRUANGRIT ROAD
Wat Suan Dok
PHRA SING RD
THAPAE ROAD
SAPHAN NAWARAT
CHAROENMUANG ROAD
Police Station
Wat Chedi Luang
Night Bazaar
Post Office
Railway Station
RATCHAMANKA ROAD
LOIKHRO ROAD
Buak Hat Park
N
BAMRUNGBURI ROAD
CHANGLO ROAD
SIDONCHAT RD
Silverware Factories
WUALAI RD
THIPANET ROAD
CHIANGMAI LAMPHUN ROAD
Lacqueware
Chiang Mai International Airport

*T*own plan of Chiang Mai.

even give you an up to date map as well as information about upcoming festivals.

Exploring the City

To get a sense of this city, start off with a morning's tour of some of the major temples. In all there are more than 300 around Chiang Mai, but we limit you to a few of the best. Enthusiastic walkers can do the first part of the trip on foot, but just in case, there is never a shortage of *tuk tuks* or *songthaews* circulating around the city.

A good starting point is **Wat Chiang Man** on Ratchaphanikai Road in the north-eastern corner of the old city.

it down, check it is going to your destination and jump in. Fares are cheap, but always check before getting in, as sometimes if there are no other passengers, you may be charged for rental of the whole vehicle.

Before setting out, you would be well advised to drop by the Tourist Office at 105/1 Chiang Mai-Lamphun Road. They will provide you with advice on trekking and tours. They may

This is the oldest temple in Chiang Mai, built in 1296 and containing a precious crystal Buddha brought from the kingdom of Haripunjaya and said to have the power to bring rain. It's surrounded by lush gardens and by a pond containing turtles and, at the rear of the temple, by a *chedi* surrounded by sculptured elephants.

From Wat Chiang Man its a pleasant *tuk tuk* ride or a 15-minute walk south to the 15th-century **Wat Chedi Luang** on Pokklao Road—built by King Saen Muang Ma and containing a massive *chedi,* damaged by an earthquake, which shook the city more than 400 years ago. In the grounds of the temple, you will see a gigantic gum tree shrouded in silk which, legend has it, will grow so long as the city continues to thrive. Beneath the tree the locals leave offerings of wooden elephants and phallics to the guardian spirit of the city.

Continue west to the intersection of Ratchadamnoen and Singharat Road, to reach the third of Chiang Mai's great temples. **Wat Phra Singh** was built in 1345 by King Pha Yu, and contains a much revered image which was being brought from Kamphaeng Phet to the king of Chiang Mai when the chariot carrying the Buddha broke down. Believing that this was a signal that the image wished to go no further, it was installed in the temple. Besides the small chapel containing the precious Buddha, there is a beautiful 14th-century library decorated with fine carvings.

From Wat Phra Singh, catch a *tuk tuk*—or be prepared for a long walk—to **Wat Bupparam** on Tapae Road, home to a 15th-century temple, since renovated, and to some ferocious five-headed *naga* snakes. Continue east down Tapae Road and within a few hundred metres, you can also drop by **Wat Saen Fang** containing part of a second ring of city walls.

Outside the city walls lie a further 270 temples, although these would take a week to see. For those more frugal

---

A Rush of Progress

Arriving in Chiang Mai on 11 January 1882, after a four-hour elephant ride from Lamphun, Carl Bock was much impressed by the second Siamese commissioner, Pra Udon, who had acquired several European style carriages, which he kept in a couple of bamboo sheds known as the coach house.

The good Pra, who prided himself as one of the most progressive gentlemen of his age had already introduced a floating house on the banks of the Ping River, and as part of his effort to introduce western notions, planned to establish a 'cab stand' as a popular form of locomotion. He was, however, to prove several decades before his time. Until the beginning of the 20th century, Chiang Mai had no roads, and as Bock noted with a touch of irony, the people were "not yet educated up to that pitch of civilization"

---

*T*he woodcarvers of Chiang Mai have excelled themselves since the reign of King Mengrai when they began the elegant wooden carvings of the Buddha that are posted around the city's temples.

with their time we recommend three in particular, although you will need transport to get to them.

Wat Chedi Yot, known as Seven Peaks lies to the north-west of the walled city near the National Museum and has an impressive collection of seven *chedis,* said to have been inspired by a great Mahabodi Indian temple during the reign of King Tilokaraja in 1455. One of the great highlights of this temple and indeed one of the outstanding sights in all Chiang Mai, are the stucco decorations which represent 70 celestial deities, and are examples of some of the finest surviving Lanna art.

South, off Cherng Doy Road, you will find **Wat Suan Dork** (the Flower Garden Temple) which houses the ashes of the kings of Lanna. The main *chedi* was built in 1383 and contains an important relic of the Buddha brought

here on the back of an elephant. Enter the *bot,* to the left, to see a massive 500-year-old Buddha image and to purchase postcards and lucky charms.

If you continue another 1 km (0.6 miles) down Doi Suthep Road, and turn down a long winding lane, you will reach the last great temple: the secluded **Wat Umong**, where a much venerated mad monk, Phra Matta Kaseba, ended his days. The *wat* is quieter and cooler, a forest retreat where people come for seclusion. There are underground cells for meditation, a lake and a small park with exotic birds; a perfect place to round off the day.

Museums

Within easy reach of the city centre, are a couple of charming museums. The most popular is the **National Museum**, on the Superhighway, open Wednesday–Sunday, 9 a.m.–4 p.m., with ancient kilns and a massive Buddha's head, said to be part of one of the largest bronzes ever cast in Thailand. A better option, if you have only limited time, is the **Banyen Folk Art Museum**, on Wua Lai Road, open daily, 8 a.m.–6 p.m., set in a charming old northern-style house selling woodcarvings and antiques. Its proprietor was originally a hilltribes woman who cycled around town selling her wares. These days, she has turned Banyen into one of the biggest antique emporiums in the country. Even if you are not buying, come here just to absorb the delightful atmosphere.

One other institution may be relevant to those contemplating trekking. The **Tribal Research Centre** at Chiang Mai University has a museum and library, open Monday–Friday, 8.30 a.m.–4.30 p.m., with a vast stash of information on the hilltribe people.

Other Attractions

Besides its cultural attractions, Chiang Mai has an abundance of other sights and activities. For river cruises to nearby temples and orchid farms, contact Ping River Cruises at 1 Chiangmai Gow Road, Tel: 234 161.

Animal lovers should visit the **Chiang Mai Zoo**, which is open every day, 8 a.m.–5 p.m. It is the largest in the Kingdom, and is situated some 5 km (3 miles) north-west of town on the way to Doi Suthep mountain.

Chiang Mai also has several colourful markets where the locals, as against the tourists, come to do their shopping. Visit **Somphet Market** on Moonmuang Road or the **Warorot Market** on Wichyanon Road. At either of these, don't miss the opportunity to taste the delicious local delicacies like *khao soi* and spicy *naem* sausages.

Finally for a real breath of fresh air just wander down the old curving roads outside the old city walls where life has changed little. Chiang Mai may well be firmly rooted on the tourist map, but like Bangkok, it is a town that rewards the adventurous.

Shopping

Handicrafts are a Chiang Mai speciality, ranging from woven baskets, and lacquerware to fine woodcarvings, colourful hilltribe products and designer fashion clothes.

To see them visit Sankhamhaeng Road or wander along Tapei or Changklan Road, especially around the Mae Ping and Dusit Hotels.

In some shops you can actually watch tribal crafts being made. At PWO Karen, on the top floor of the night bazaar, traditional footlooms are used to make the the colourful cloth for which the tribe is renowned. Another good place to buy textiles is at the Loom on 27/3 Rajmanica Road or at Bilan at 96/1, Rajchiangsan Road.

For woodcarving and silver, head to Wualai Road and especially around the Banyen Folk Art Museum, whilst at 2 Rajwithi Road is the famous Saraphee Silk Laces renowned for its hand-woven textiles.

 In the evening, and until 11 p.m., there is only one real place to go shopping, and that's the **Chiang Mai Bazaar** on Changklan Road, which contains the most dazzling display of boutiques, galleries, teak shops, craft shops and clothes shops in the Kingdom. You may find places cheaper in Thailand, but you would be hard-pushed to come across such variety.

Wining and Dining

Like *namtoc* in the North-east and *kaeng tai pla* in the South, the Northern Region has its own culinary specialities and Chiang Mai some of the most delightful places to eat them.

Gaeng hang le (a thick pork curry spiced with garlic and ginger) is one of the most common local delicacies and is generally served with *khao niaw* (sticky rice).

No less popular is *khao soi* (a Burmese-influenced dish consisting of noodles made with fermented rice flour and accompanied with sauces and curry). Sometimes the noodles are eaten with *nam ya* (medicine solution), a sauce made from seasoned snake water and served with boiled bitter melon. For the most part, they are served with *nam prik num* (a dip made from ferociously hot green chillis).

But the meal for which Chiang Mai is most renowned is the *kantoke* dinner, a speciality that dates back to the times of the Lanna Kingdom. The name *khan* means bowl, and *toke* a small, low round table, usually made of rattan or lacquerware, around which diners sit on the floor and share numerous dishes. The dinner consists of *gaeng hang le,* (pork curry), *namprik ong* (minced pork cooked with tomatoes, cucumbers, onions and chillis), *cap moo* (fried pork skin), *kaeng kai* (chicken and vegetable curry) and *larb* (minced meat mixed with chillis and mint, eaten with raw cabbage). The dinner is generally accompanied by northern classical dances, exotic hill-tribe shows and of course by coachloads of tourists.

At Night

When it comes to nightlife, Chiang Mai cannot compare with Bangkok. Still, it does have a few appealing options. Just north of Thapae Bridge you will find the Riverside Bar and Restaurant with live bands after 8 p.m. and a terrace, perfect for a sundown drink. Alternatively, try the other famous institution, the Pub, set in lovingly tended grounds on Huay Kaew Road, near the Chiang Mai Orchid Hotel. For those missing Bangkok there is now even a collection of rather basic "girlie" bars along Moon Muang and Kotchasarn Road, as well as discos mainly centred around the big hotels.

Excursions Around Chiang Mai

To see the countless sights around Chiang Mai, either hire a car or motorbike—almost everyone seems to rent them—take one of a variety of tours, or simply catch a bus. Be warned though. The town has two bus stations: the Arcade terminal off Kaew Nawarat Road has services to Bangkok, Chiang Rai, Mae Hong Son, Phitsanulok and Korat and the White Elephant terminal (*chang puak*) on Chotana Road, has services to Sankamhaeng, Lamphun, Fang and Tha Ton.

Most of the sights can be visited in a day, allowing you to return before nightfall. Alternatively, they can be used as a stepping-stone on the route North or South.

Doi Suthep

Chiang Mai's most famous temple lies high up in the hills at the end of a spectacular road that snakes its way for 13 km (8 miles) from town. Doi Suthep's history is as colourful as its temple. It was originally built in 1383 according to legend, to commemorate a turning point in the city's history. Chiang Mai at the time was suffering from severe drought and, as was usual in those days, the king, a man named Gue-Na, went to confide with the most sacred animal in the land, the White Elephant. The White Elephant went to the summit of Doi Suthep, circled it three times, knelt down and died. In memory of this, the king ordered the temple to be built, and since then Chiang Mai has never had a shortage of rain.

There is little left of the original structure though. The present temple dates from the 16th century, but still comprises two magnificent sanctuaries and cloisters filled with gilded *stupas,* said to house a relic of the great man,. On the walls are murals telling the story of the Buddha's life, whilst outside on clear days you can catch spectacular views of Chiang Mai and the surrounding countryside.

To reach the temple, you must either climb a flight of 290 steps or take a gentle ride on a funicular. The car park situated at the bottom contains countless drink stores, rewards for the returning walkers.

Most visitors simply visit the temple by *songthaew* and return to Chiang Mai. A better alternative is to continue 4 km (2.5 miles) further up the road to the Royal Family's northern residence known as **Phuping Palace**. It is set in beautiful gardens and is open to the public Friday–Sunday, when the Royal Family is not in residence.

From the Palace, drive the remaining 3 km (2 miles) along a bumpy road to the Meo tribe village of **Doi Pui**, home to one of Thailand's most colourful hilltribes. Daily invasions of camera-wielding tourists may have brought a wholly new life to these mountain people, but for those who will not have the chance to visit the tribes elsewhere, you still get a sense of their way of life, as well as an opportunity to visit an opium museum and beautiful gardens, and to purchase colourful Meo handicrafts.

Regular *songthaews* for Doi Suthep leave from the White Elephant Gate in Chiang Mai and continue less regularly to Phuping Palace and Doi Pui.

Bor Sang and Sankamphaeng

Almost synonymous with the name of Chiang Mai is the village of Bor Sang, situated 12 km (7 miles) to the east, famous the world over for its colourful umbrellas.

The umbrellas are made from dried mulberry paper stretched over a hub of bamboo spokes and painted with colourful scenes of birds, flowers or butterflies. Some measure as much as 12 m (40 ft) in diameter and can be designed to order. Others are petite ladies' parasols costing as little as Bt50.

In many of the shops you can observe the people at work, painting,

The magnificent temple of Doi Suthep owes its existence to a drought and an elephant. It is said to contain a relic of the Buddha.

cutting or arranging—and often they will run up something for you personally there and then. The umbrellas can be packed easily and make perfect presents and most shops now even offer shipping services.

Umbrellas are not the only wares on offer down the San Kamphaeng. Indeed the road running east out of

165

Chiang Mai, is a veritable high street of factories generating a plethora of beautiful handicrafts of every shape, size and kind. Ceramics, lacquerware, silver, silk, textiles, leather and elaborately carved wooden furniture are all waiting to be haggled over and purchased for bargain prices.

This is the place to see how the traditional lacquerware process works, with small bamboo shaped dishes layered with spray and then handpainted. At silk shops, beautifully dressed sales-girls will invite you to inspect the factory, behind which silkworm cocoons are boiled in vats enabling threads to be unravelled for spinning into weaving silk yarn.

One of the largest silk factories is **Shinawatra** which for 60 years has been producing fine designs and ready-made clothing. For lacquerware the most exclusive collection is to be found at **Chiang Mai Laitong** at 80/1 Mu 3, Sankamhaeng Road. Elsewhere you can see silversmiths and woodcarvers at work, and numerous other traditional crafts.

To get to Sankamhaeng Road you will need transport. If you do not have your own, the best way is to negotiate a tuk tuk driver to stay with you for the whole morning or afternoon and to shepherd you from shop to shop. This should cost a nominal Bt10 or Bt20, or even nothing at all as he receives commission from the shops on anything that you buy. Be sure, however, that he doesn't take you only to the shops where he has a special arrangement.

*T*he people of Bor Sang are modest about their umbrella skills. All it takes is a little dried mulberry paper, some bamboo spokes and an abundance of artistic inspiration.

Lamphun

One of the prettiest day trips from Chiang Mai is to the old town of Lamphun, reached by a road lined with old teak trees. The town was originally centre of the great Haripunchai empire, a Mon kingdom founded in 660 by Queen Chama Devi and defeated by King Mengrai in 1281.

In the centre of town is the famous **Wat Phra That Haripunchai**. It was built more than 900 years ago by King Athitayarat, 32nd ruler of Haripunchai on the site of a former royal palace, and contains a giant nine-tiered umbrella made of gold and weighing

6,498 g (228 oz). Turn to the right and you will see the ancient **Suwanna chedi** and almost directly opposite, the **National Museum**, open daily except Monday and Tuesday, with a collection of sculptures from the 10th century and an unusual Chinese cannon from the Ming dynasty.

Lamphun's other major sight is **Wat Chamadevi**—also known as Wat Ku Kut—situated on the western side of town on the road to San Pa Tong and founded by the second ruler of

Haripunchai in 715 after the death of his mother Queen Chamadevi. Much of the temple has been restored, but enclosed within the modern buildings are the two old *chedis* of Suwan Chang Kot and Ratana, as well as a few remaining standing Buddha images—the rest were stolen by thieves.

From Lamphun, a pleasant little side trip can be taken to the village of **Pa Sang**, lying 12 km (7 miles) to the south-west and famous for its local handicrafts and for its *longans,* a small, sweet-tasting fruit, which resembles a lichee and is most abundant between July and October. Regular buses connecting Lamphun with Chiang Mai take 40 minutes.

M an and beast. An elephant on an afternoon stroll at the training camp of Mae Taem near Chiang Mai.

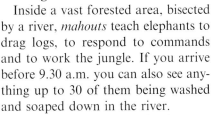

Elephant Camps

A one hour's drive north of town will bring you to the town of Mae Taem, beyond which lies one of Chiang Mai's most famous attractions: the **Elephant Training Centre.**

Inside a vast forested area, bisected by a river, *mahouts* teach elephants to drag logs, to respond to commands and to work the jungle. If you arrive before 9.30 a.m. you can also see anything up to 30 of them being washed and soaped down in the river.

Until a nationwide logging ban was introduced in 1989, many of these same elephants were used to drag timber down to the river, whence the logs would be floated down to saw mills further down stream. These days, the centre caters specifically to tourists, but still remains one of the great highlights of any trip to Chiang Mai.

At the end of the show, you can take bamboo rafts down the river, returning by elephant through lush forest and woodlands. Be sure to bring a camera and arrive early. Coachloads of tourists generally arrive for the second show; by 11 a.m. the place generally resembles an Egyptian camel market.

Trips can be booked by any tour agent. Alternatively catch a regular bus leaving in the direction of Fang. The centre is open from 9 a.m. to 12.30 p.m. daily.

Mae Sa Valley

To reach the charming Mae Sa Valley, take Highway 107 and turn left after 15 km (9 miles) at the town of Mae Rim. The road was originally planned as a detour for trucks, but has since developed into a northern showpiece with elephant training centres, souvenir shops and cultural centres as well as snake farms and waterfalls.

For orchids and butterflies, visit **Sainamphun Farm** signposted to the left and containing more than 50 different types of orchid. Some, like the Miss Udorn Sunshine took ten years to create by crossing two different species. Others were the result of painstaking research undertaken at the Kasetsart University where students pursue courses in Orchidology.

Four km (2.5 miles) further along the main road a turn leads to the **Mae Sa Waterfall** and to a variety of garden resorts and other attractions. Continue to the end of Highway 1096 and bear left onto Highway 1269 to emerge near the town of **Hang Dong**—the road then leads back to Chiang Mai. For those without transport, you would be well advised to take a tour. Ask your hotel reception desk or any of the local travel agents for details.

Doi Inthanon

Magnificently situated in rolling hills, 80 km (50 miles) to the south-west of Chiang Mai off Highway 108 is the National Park of Doi Inthanon, occupying almost 1,000 sq km (385 sq miles) and containing the tallest mountain in Thailand rising to an elevation of 2,565 m (8416 ft).

You can't climb it, since there's a giant military scanning station on top, but you can take walks through dense and moist evergreen forest and along the steep slopes that border the canyoned headwaters of the Mae Pan River. The park contains several waterfalls as well as the impressive **Brichinda Llimestone Cave**, signposted off the main road.

If you are lucky, you may also come across some of the varied and numerous bird life in the Kingdom. Not only does the park play host to the rare Ashy Throated Warbler, but even the much prized Chestnut Bellied rockthrush and the Yellow Bellied Flowerpecker. Bird lists are available at the Visitors Centre and at Park Headquarters, both of which are signposted off the main road.

To see all the sights, the national park authorities recommend private transport. And since the roads to the hilltribe villages are rough and narrow, you would be well advised to use a four-wheel-drive vehicle or a trail bike.

Currently the walking trails are unmarked, but the Visitors Centre does provide details of walking tours and maps and will occasionally even arrange a guide for free. Accommodation is available adjacent to the Hmong village of Ban Khun Klang behind Park Headquarters.

Hilltribes

One of the greatest joys of visiting the North for most tourists is the chance to visit the hilltribes, known as the *chao doi.* These nomadic people, found throughout the region, originated in Southern China and Tibet from where they migrated along various routes into Burma, Laos and Thailand.

In total there are some 500,000 of them, divided into six tribes: namely the Karen, Meo, Akha, Yao, Lisu and Lahu. Each tribe is distinct in language, dress and culture, but they all share certain basic characteristics.

Generally they are highland dwellers, preferring to live above 1,000 m.(3280 ft) Their livelihood is based on slash and burn agriculture, foraging, domestic livestock like black pigs and chickens, and all inter-tribe trade is done by barter. Traditionally the *chao doi* have also shared a common mythology. They believe that they live on top of a dragon and that they have to keep the peace to ensure that it does not move.

Yet within each tribe, and often within subtribes, there are clear distinctions. Akhas are often encouraged to sleep with one another before marriage, whilst young unmarried Karens can only meet with the opposite sex in public. A Meo (Hmong) girl traditionally chooses her partner during the New Year festivities when the young men and women form long lines similar to a Scottish reel. The girl will throw a ball to the boy she fancies. If the boy returns the ball this denotes acceptance, and following several months of courting may lead to ritual bartering for the bride and marriage.

*A*khas traditionally *worship the sun and moon, but when it comes to offerings it's the termite hills that get the chickens.*

As a polygamous tribe, you can often see one boy juggling balls between two girls simultaneously.

Even in sickness, practices differ. Whilst the Mien (Yao) may symbolically burn paper money to appease the spirits, the Karen divine the cause of sickness by examining chicken bones, feathers or grains of rice and then entice the offending spirit into a basket with offerings of specially cooked chicken. By rapidly shutting the top of the basket, they are able to trap the evil spirit and take it into the jungle and bury it.

But the old way of life is changing. Only 15 years ago in most of the Meo tribes, only the headman was allowed

169

to hold money for the whole village, and few hilltribes people met outsiders. These days, the first words many children will learn is "give me one baht". Some hilltribe people now have watches, others have bicycles and transistor radios.

Tourism has provided a whole new way of life. It has made it easier for the hilltribes to sell their products and has provided greater contact with the outside world. But it has also made them prey to greedy tourist agents who ship parties of foreigners into their villages with little concern for the long-term impact on the tribal way of life.

At the same time government rehabilitation programmes aimed at reducing opium cultivation, and new laws preventing further slash and burn have driven many of *khon doi* out of their homes and into the low lands or big cities where prospects are little better. Only in the more isolated villages does the old way of life continue, with offerings to crop grandmother, and the traditional ceremonies that they inherited from their fathers and forefathers.

Below, we include a brief list of the basic characteristics of the six main hilltribes, many of whom you are likely to see on one of the treks.

The Karen
Of all the hilltribes, the most numerous are the Karen or Yang Karing with a population of about 265,000. Largely concentrated in the mountainous area along the western border with Burma, they are probably the oldest tribe, having migrated into Thailand more than 250 years ago. Their economy is based primarily on rice

cultivation, as well as domestic animals, pigs and chickens—many of which are used for ceremonial offerings to appease the spirits of the winds and the rains.

The Meo
The second largest group are the Meo (Hmong), mainly concentrated around Chiang Mai, Chiang Rai and Mae Hong Son, and divided into several subgroups such as the Blue Meo or Striped Meo. The Meo prefer to live at very high altitudes. They grow rice and corn for food, and opium as a cash

A khas not only believe in sex before marriage, but fill their villages with phallic carvings designed to enhance fertility. They now have a population of 33,000!

170

crop. They are the most independent of the tribal people and one of the proudest, worshipping the Spirit of the Sky who they believe created both the world and their own way of life.

The Akha

The Akha originated from Yunnan in Southern China, where they belonged to the tribal group known as the Lolo. There are thought to be around 33,000 of them living mainly in extended family units, the hallmark of traditional Akha life. Akhas are strict animists believing that the spirit and human worlds at one time lived together in harmony, but that discord led to their separation. Akhas worship the sun and the moon, and they fear the spirits in the swamps and termite mounds who are appeased by offerings of chickens.

The Yao

The Yao, or Mien, originated in Southern China over 200 years ago from where they migrated across the waters to Hainan, Thailand, Vietnam and Laos. In total there are some 25,000 of them spread mainly around Chiang Rai, Phayao and Nan.

Yao Anecdote
The first Yao, according to the traditional wisdom of the mountain tribes, was neither an Adam nor an Eve, but the offspring of a dog named Pan Kou who defeated a cruel tyrant, and as a reward was given a Chinese princess to marry. Their son was the first member of the Yao tribe, who have since grown to the extent that there are now some 30,000 settled in northern Thailand around the provinces of Chiang Rai, Phayao and Nan.

To spot them, look out for their teeth capped with gold—a popular sign of wealth—their ankle-length tunics and thick purple sashes around their neck. The Yao believe in extended families and polygamous marriages, and have traditionally cultivated opium. They also worship their ancestors by sacrifices of pigs and chickens.

The Lisu

The Lisu are the most widely dispersed of all the hilltribes, spread over nine provinces of the north. In total there are some 24,000 of them, divided into the Hua Lisu and the black Lisu groups. Originally, they came from Southern China and only began to migrate to Thailand 60 years ago. These days they derive most of their income from the selling of domestic animals like pig and cattle, and by growing rice, corn and opium.

The Lahu

The Lahu are of Tibetan origin and number around 55,000, divided into different subtribes and concentrated mainly around the district of Fang and north of Chiang Rai. Poorer than the other tribes, they practise primitive slash and burn cultivation of crops, including opium.

You can often distinguish the men by their silver buckles and black turbans, and the women by calf-length tunics with yellow or white embroidery. The Lahu believe in a village spirit named Ghomuntawe, and a house spirit named Bobar. If the people are possessed, a spirit doctor exorcises the evil phi using a special pronged spirit fork.

Trekking

The best way to see the traditional ways of the hilltribes is by taking organized treks, which can be arranged in any of the major centres. Chiang Mai itself boasts some 50 trekking agencies, with the other major centres being Chiang Rai, Mae Hong Son, Pai and even Mae Salong.

Typically a trek might start with a jeep ride to a point some distance outside town, followed by a two- or three-hour walk to an appointed village at which to spend the first night, eating and sleeping in the headman's house. Following days could include further walking—for up to five or six hours

Rafting along the northern rivers as part of a trek can be both idyllic and inspiring when you have a man with a pole doing the work.

along narrow mountainous paths—elephant riding, river rafting on bamboo floats, or a combination of all these.

A more leisurely alternative is an air-conditioned bus tour offered by some hotels and tour operators, where the most you'll need to do is step out, take pictures and perhaps bargain for one of the beautifully embroidered bags or garments made by the tribal women.

Whatever trek you opt for, it is well worth checking around to find both a reliable guide and a well-known agent. A good guide makes for a wealth of understanding and provides the communication channel between the tribespeople and yourself. With a poor guide, you will be limited to seeing, whilst missing out on any real insight into their way of life. Avoid groups with more than ten people, and never go alone.

The ideal time for trekking is between October and February. At night it can be cold, so bring a sweater and a torch, and if you like western comforts, a couple of loo rolls and bars of soap. Akha villages may have charm, but they are short of luxuries; and if grunting pigs and smoky rooms are not to your liking, you would do better to opt for a day trip or stay in your hotel in Chiang Mai.

Treks can also be made during the rainy season, although muddy tracks and leeches can stifle the enthusiasm of even the most avid tribal spotter.

Many hilltribes now expect money for photos. Don't give it to them. Instead you should bring tobacco or postcards for the adults and little gifts for the children.

If while approaching any type of hilltribe village you see waist-high bamboo stalks bound together in a tripod and adorned with white pieces of material, whatever the guide may say to you, do not enter this village. Most hilltribes are animists and this particular sign means that they are exorcising evil spirits which they believe have entered the village—and under no circumstances are visitors welcome at this time.

Finally when trekking do not expect to discover untouched tribes. If you are lucky you may come across people still living in their traditional way. And if you are unlucky, you will be greeted by tribespeople dressed in T-shirts, selling Coca Cola and smoking Marlboro cigarettes. But whatever your guide or agency tell you, tribal tourism is endemic, and there will always be other people who have got there before you.

The TAT office in Chiang Mai, Tel: 248 604, provides lists of official trekking agencies and it is often worth checking with them before you sign on. Pirate organizations are not unknown.

The Mae Hong Son Circuit

To get away from the crowds, you must leave Chiang Mai and head west into the vast region that borders Burma and which contains spectacular hills and vast underground caves, wooded valleys and some of the wildest and most rugged terrain in the region.

Years ago it was inaccessible but for paths and rivers forded by elephants and buffalo. These days it can be reached by a 30-minute flight from Chiang Mai. But like many of the trips in northern Thailand the joy is the ride rather than the arrival—and the circuit to Mae Hong Son through Pai and Mae Sariang offers some of the finest scenery that the north has to offer.

To visit these places you can either take public transport or hire a car from Mae Hong Son or Chiang Mai.

173

But if you are driving, be warned: the road between Chiang Mai and Mae Sariang has more than 1,000 hairpin bends and is exceptionally demanding even when conditions are good. And whilst traffic is rare, buses hurtle along taking up most of the road—and accidents are not uncommon.

Pai

This charming town is situated on the banks of the Pai river nestling on the mountainside 135 km (84 miles) from Chiang Mai.

To get there, drive north from Chiang Mai on Highway 107 and at the town of Mae Taem take a left turn onto Highway 1095. From here the road curves its way through the hills, through teak and bamboo and past a couple of well-signposted waterfalls before descending into the Pai valley. The town itself marks a halfway point between Chiang Mai and Mae Hong Son and is perfectly placed for spending some time recuperating from the journey.

Pai is set in stunning scenery, ringed by mountains and, during the months of February and March, brilliantly covered in a blanket of bright coloured flowers. Around the valleys are scattered Lisu, Lahu, Karen and Shan hilltribes and treks and rafting can often be organized by the guesthouses along the river.

Pai is a good place to walk around, a breath of fresh air after the crowds of Chiang Mai. Many of the houses still have their roofs made from leaves in the traditional fashion that was once prevalent throughout the north. For sheer relaxation, you can even have a traditional massage and herbal sauna.

Soppong

From Pai, continue to the small town of Soppong, situated 46 km (29 miles) further west at the end of another beautiful stretch of road. It's a pleasant enough town, and a gathering point for hilltribes, especially the colourful Lisu, dressed in their blue and yellow tunics.

The main reason to come to Soppong though is to see the limestone cave of **Tham Lod**, which lies 9 km (5.5 miles) further, signposted down a bumpy dirt track.

The cave is made up of a gigantic limestone cavern through which flows the Nam Lang River exiting a couple of km beyond the entrance. Along the underground river, the cave leads through galleries of weird and wonderful stalactites and through a maze of ancient burial grounds and chambers said to be inhabited by the *phi* or spirits.

At dusk, millions of swallows exchange places with bats in a staggering display of aerial agility, astonishingly managing to avoid the seemingly inevitable collisions.

Guides and lanterns can be hired from outside the cave entrance. Be warned, however: during the rainy season, you may have to ford the river in numerous different places.

If it is late and you do not want to continue on to Mae Hong Son, there is simple but pleasant accommodation at Cave Lodge just 1 km (0.5 miles) further down the track. The huts are run by an Australian caving enthusiast who will occasionally organize trips to other more remote caves in the district, as well as to tribal villages along the Burmese border.

Mae Hong Son

Squeezed between mountains at the end of one of the most spectacular roads in Northern Thailand is the town of Mae Hong Son (the City of a Million Mists).

Long isolated from the rest of Thailand by its geographical situation, it was not until 1832 that the Prince of Chiang Mai first sent an expedition into the area in search of the highly valued white elephant. So successful was the expedition that a small settlement was founded and, half a century later, Mae Hong Son became a provincial capital.

It took another 50 years, however, before the elephant could be entirely relegated and the motorcar used in its place. Today the town not only has cars, motorbikes and a small airport, but in 1989 acquired its first set of traffic lights. Since then development has been rapid, with paddy fields giving

The road to Mae Hong Son winds its way along the north-west border with Burma. The most spectacular stretch lies between Pai and Soppong.

way to new building projects and, most recently, the arrival of two luxury hotels. But if Mae Hong Son has suddenly become fashionable, it continues to retain much of its charm. The town still consists of two main streets, with a few Burmese-style temples and imposing views of the mountains. More than half the population are Shan, with many others from the various hilltribes and only 2 per cent of the population Thai.

For much of the year, and especially during the winter months from November of February, temperatures in Mae Hong Son can fall as low as 5°C (40°F) with early morning mist and dew. During December, wild sunflowers known as *buatong* dot the valleys and the higher slopes. Even then, you would be well advised to bring a sweater.

Around Town

For a brief walking tour of the town, start at the market on Singhanaat Bamrung Road, preferably before dawn, where you may occasionally see Meo and Karen hilltribe villagers in their traditional costumes buying vegetables.

*E*lephants were the reasons why it started. Temples are the reason it has thrived. Mae Hong Son still has its fair share of both. Here is the magnificent Wat Hua Wiang.

After breakfasting on *joke mu* (hot rice gruel soup with pork and soybean) or roasted frog, the town's other major speciality, visit the wooden decayed-looking structure of **Wat Hua Wiang**, lying less than 100 m (328 ft) away on Panetwattana Road.

Continue 300 m (984 ft) to the south down Khunlum Phra Athit Road and turn left to reach **Jongkhum Lake**, used some 150 years ago as an elephant bath, now scene of early morning runners and fitness fanatics.

The lake is also home to two of the town's most delightful temples, overshadowed by the hills and especially beautiful in the early morning mist. Inside **Wat Chong Klang** is a collection

A Cause for Celebration

The people of Mae Hong Son relish a good celebration, and what could be better than an occasion marking the initiation of novices into the monastic life. On that great day, held in the first week of April, the young boys dress in Thai Yai-style clothes decorated with flowers, bathe in perfumes made from herbs and are carried through the city to the sound of long drums and cymbals. On the final day, in front of their families and crowds of colourful onlookers, the young men are taken to the temple where they receive a set of robes, and are accepted into the highest order in the Kingdom, to become a Buddhist monk or novice. Still, the people of Mae Hong Son have other reasons to party. In December they hold a Miss Hilltribes Contest. The event is accompanied by a big fair and attracts vast numbers of nubile young tribeswomen from the surrounding valley—who hardly surprisingly attract even larger numbers of acquisitive young men from the nearby towns.

of carved wooden figures brought from Burma and representing some of the former lives of the Buddha. Outside, another Burmese style *chedi* of **Wat Chong Kam**, built by the Shan people nearly 200 years ago.

The last of Mae Hong Son's temples lies high above town. **Wat Phra That Doi Kong Mu** was built 150 years ago under the reign of the first governor to contain relics of the Buddha. The chief reason to come here, though, is for the awesome views of the surrounding hills, of the tiny town below and of the incongruous airport landing strip in the corner. The temple can be reached by a road that passes Wat Phra Non or by a 20-minute walk.

In the evening, dine at the Fern Restaurant on Khunlumprapas Road for the best Thai food in town or try one of the many backpacker restaurants serving milk shakes and muesli. Be warned though. Restaurants close early, and besides the odd nightclub, entertainment is mainly centred at the Holiday Inn Hotel and at the nearby Tara Mae Hong Son which hold tribal dancing and other northern cultural shows—as well as discos.

Around Mae Hong Son

You won't need transport to see most of the sights around Mae Hong Son. The town has probably more tour agencies per capita than any other city in Thailand. Popular excursions are run not only to the long-necked village (Padang) and Tham Pla Cave, but also to nearby tribal villages, waterfalls and caves. Rafting and elephant riding can also be arranged along the Pai River, 4 km (2.5 miles) south of town. Still for those who want to explore further afield, jeeps and motorbikes can be rented.

Side Trip to Mae Aw

This picturesque tribal village lies 45 km (28 miles) to the north-west of Mae Hong Son, high up in the hills, and is reached by a steep and treacherous road. The turning lies 17 km (10 miles) north of town off Highway 1095 from where a left turn leads past the small farming community of Huai Khan to the **Pha Sua** waterfall, a beautiful cascade with deep pools where you can stop for a refreshing bathe—in the dry season only.

Beyond Pha Sua the road steepens, twisting around the hills through thick dust—or in the rainy season mud—and emerging after 24 km (15 miles) at the Meo (Hmong) town of Napapak. There is a guesthouse here and a thriving tribal community. The people still dress in their distinctive costumes with the long black trousers, their beautiful silver bracelets and intricately embroidered jackets. But civilization has arrived in less subtle forms and occasionally at weekends you may even find them watching their favourite sport—football— played on a proper pitch outside their huts.

From Napapak, the road levels out, leading a further 4 km (2.5 miles) to the village of Mae Aw, situated in magnificent scenery close to the Burmese border. The village is inhabited by former members of the KMT (Kuomintang), a group that migrated from China and who traditionally survived by trading opium, though these days other crops are more in evidence.

Several agencies now organize the trip, but there is is no official accommodation, so you must either return to Napapak or backtrack all the way back to Mae Hong Son. Make sure you leave early.

The Padang Tribe

One of the strangest, least known tribes in South-east Asia inhabit the region around Mae Hong Son. They are known as the Padang (Giraffe People), and their women are distinguished by elongated necks, some of which stretch to 30 cm (12 ins).

The necks are formed by placing gold rings on during adolescence and have become an integral part of a culture which once stretched throughout much of the Asian and African continent. For the Padang equate beauty with the length of the neck, and marriage and family honour have depended on it. Traditionally, the ceremonial rights of the Padang women begin at the age of five, when the first rings are put around the necks of the young girls. Two years later, under the light of a full moon, further spirals and golden rings are added, gradually stretching the neck until the girl reaches maturity.

These days though, it is a dying tradition with only around 2,000 of the total Padang population of 40,000 people wearing neck rings. Many of the young girls now remove the rings at an early age before the necks have become deformed.

Even these people are not originally from Thailand, but from Burma. At the behest of the Thai authorities and in exchange for permanent residence and money, several of them have moved over to two districts of Mae Hong Son where they pose for tourists—entry costs Bt300—and weave shirts and sarongs for sale in the local market.

Some visitors now find the whole idea of a tribal village for tourists distasteful. Those that do would be well advised to give the village a miss. Still, the lives of the Padang people in Thailand are preferable to their lives in Burma, and the Padang are there of their own free will.

On the way back from the village, if caves and fish are an attraction, you can visit the popular tourist gathering point at **Tham Pla**, signposted 17 km (11 miles) from Mae Hong Son on the main road. Beyond the car park is a big temple and an underground lake, in which giant blue sacred carp swim around contentedly. Food consisting of bread and peanuts is for sale at the entrance—and people come from all around to make merit by feeding the fat and illustrious creatures.

Trips to the Padang Village and Fish Cave are organized by most travel agents. Because of the relative inaccessibility of the long-necked tribal village, using your own transport is not recommended.

From Mae Hong Son to Chiang Mai (South)

There is no need to backtrack to Chiang Mai on Highway 1095. A perfectly adequate, although extremely winding road, leads through staggeringly beautiful countryside via the towns of Mae Sariang and Hot. It is only 360 km (225 miles), but you would be foolhardy to do the journey in a day—and as with the route to Pai, accidents are by no means uncommon.

Mae Sariang

The town of Mae Sariang (160 km, 100 miles) has two boasts. It was an old smuggling town, and still acts as a major conduit for timber and livestock from Burma, and it enjoys a quiet river setting.

There's not a lot to see though, save for a small market, selling local delicacies like chicken's feet and the small Burmese-style temples of Wat Utthayarom and Wat Sri Boonruang. Several hotels do, however, make pleasant stops for those continuing to Chiang Mai and occasional trekking trips can borganized to the surrounding region.

Side Trip to Ban Mae Sam Lap

To get to Ban Mae Sam Lap, the border trading town 52 km (32 miles) to the west of Mae Sariang is an adventure in itself. You must ford a river in at least 15 places, follow a dirt track, Highway 1194, and finally arrive in a place where nobody speaks a word of English.

The few visitors who make the trip generally prefer one of the irregular *songthaews* that leave from Mae Sariang, but even these have a record of getting stuck in the dirt—women pay extra since they have less pushing power.

The best time to arrive in Mae Sam Lap is early in the morning when the markets are most crowded and the smuggled goods are being brought across the river from the opposite bank.

Northern Dialects

Saying *sawadee kap* to a northerner could be like saying *bon jour* to an aboriginal. For whilst some 80 per cent of them speak loosely-related languages pertaining to Thai, the majority converse in local dialect. In some cases this may be *kham meuang* or northern Thai, in others *shan* or *tai lue* or the tribal languages of the Meo *(Hmong)*, Mien *(Yao)*, Lahu, Lisu, Karen and Akkha. Many of these tribal languages derive from Austro-Thai or the Sino-Tibetan group of languages. Some do not use words for greeting, others have no word for food or for numerals. Thus in one dialect rather than saying 'four pigs', the people say 'pig, pig, pig, pig' The northeasterners, however, go a step further. In some parts of Isaan, they even have a dialect with seven different tones, so that the same word can mean seven different things.

*W*aterfalls in the
*north are abundant, but to see
the best you must visit the area
near the Ob Luang Canyon and
Doi Inthanon Park.*

From the riverside, boats cross to
Burma, just a few hundred metres or
yards away, an area controlled by the
Karen Liberation and stretching for
hundreds of miles—though you'd be ill
advised to cross.

Before leaving Mae Sariang, check
on road conditions and the situation
on the border. Currently a new road is
being put through, but completion is
likely to take several years.

There is no accommodation at Mae
San Lap, so you must backtrack to
Mae Sariang, from where the road
branches. To the south, Highway 1085
leads along the border to Mae Sot.
And to the east, Highway 108 contin-
ues via the spectacular Ob Luang
Canyon to Hot.

Hot

With a name like Hot, it is hardly surprising that this town's major commodity is boiling springs, although you will have to visit one of the private resorts further up the road to the north to find them. For those with no such needs, there are several other sights in the vicinity including a pine reafforestation scheme, the spectacular **Ob Luang Canyon**, to the north, and **Doi Inthanon National Park**.

From Hot, Highway 108 loops back to Chiang Mai (90 km, 55 miles) via the **Mae Ya Waterfall**.

From Chiang Mai to Chiang Rai

North of Chiang Mai, rice fields give way to teak forest and outcrops of granite, with the foothills of the Shan mountains, bisected by the Kok River flowing down from Laos.

The region is inhabited by a large number of hilltribes, although these have been heavily touristed, and sprinkled with an abundance of caves. Only as you approach Chiang Rai does the land flatten, descending into the vast fertile plain wherein lies Thailand's northernmost provincial capital.

Overland

There are three ways of getting from Chiang Mai to Chiang Rai. Either you can take the 30-minute flight with Thai Airways from Chiang Mai, or a long-tailed boat from Tha Thon down the Kok River. Or you can go overland.

If you opt for the overland trip, there are two routes. The first is on Highway 107, which passes via the Elephant Training Camp of Mae Taeng and the signposted turning to the beautiful **Chiang Dao Caves**. Fifteen km (9 miles) before the town of Fang, you turn right down Highway 109, a difficult and narrow road to Mae Suai from where it is a further 50 km (31 miles) to Chiang Rai.

The alternative route on Highway 1019 via Wiang Pha Pao is considerably faster with a good road, curving through hills and valleys, past the famous **Nang Kaeo** spirit house where villagers customarily donate wooden phalluses, and joining Highway 1 just 40 km (25 miles) from Chiang Rai.

Bock's Legacy

When Carl Alfred Bock, author of *The Head Hunters of Borneo* came to Siam in 1881, he was struck above all by the delightful simplicity of the people and their awe for elephants. A Norwegian natural scientist, born in Copenhagen in 1849, Bock had earlier visited Indonesia to study zoology and ecology. After arriving in Bangkok, he travelled to Chiang Mai and Muang Fang with the assistance of His Majesty King Chulalongkorn, who placed at his disposal steamers, boats, elephants and coolies. Although Bock was captivated by the charm of the Siamese and especially the goodness of the Enlightened Ruler, the 14-month journey was to be his last and, in 1896, he joined the diplomatic services as Swedish-Norwegian Vice Consul in Shanghai. His legacy is a book on Temples and Elephants and several ethnographic exhibits including bronzes, now kept in the Ethnographic Museum in Oslo. Bock died in 1932 after having been awarded the Order of the Rose by the Emperor of Brazil, and a gold Medal by the Geographical Society of Lisbon.

Journey Down the Kok River

For those without transport, undoubtedly the most spectacular, but the least comfortable, way to arrive in Chiang Rai is by boat from Tha Thon on the Kok River, situated 190 km (120 miles) north of Chiang Mai. This is the place where the 19th-century Scandinavian explorer Carl Bock encountered wild buffalo and tigers, cutting his way through thick jungle before taking the route to Chiang Rai.

Tha Thon is a charming little town, easily reached by bus and dominated by a giant white Buddha situated on a slight knoll on the hill. There are now several guesthouses and restaurants on the river, the best and most expensive being the Mae Kok River Lodge, Tel: 053 215 366, built out of teak and set amongst coconut palm plantations with fine views of the river. The Lodge has a travel and trekking agency called Track of the Tiger which organizes trips along the Mae Kok (Kok River) and into the surrounding hills to visit the local tribes.

From the small pier situated close to the bridge, long-tailed boats, powered by ten-foot propeller shafts, leave every day at 12.30 p.m. for the four-hour trip to Chiang Rai, although during the dry season the journey can take considerably longer, depending on how many times you get stuck. There are no cushions, no toilets and little room to stretch your legs. But the scenery is spectacular, passing through mountains and deep gorges, and past hill-tribe villages, although the boat rarely stops.

For those with the time, a better alternative is to hire rafts from Tha Thon, which take three days to get to Chiang Rai. You can hire guides, stay overnight in the villages and even arrange to go elephant trekking along the way. The rafts are, however, basic; with only a roof to shade you from the sun, and a bamboo floor to separate you from the water. Generally they need to be booked a week in advance. For details enquire at the pier.

Until a few years ago much of the area along the Kok River was considered bandit country. Today, there's little trouble along the route, although as a precaution boats often carry a soldier, generally identified by a smiling face, a big gun and a predisposition to sleep.

Regular buses leave from the Chang Phuak Bus Station in Chiang Mai for Fang from where *songthaews* proceed to Tha Thon.

Chiang Rai

If you're arriving in Chiang Rai expecting drug barons and opium lords, be prepared for a disappointment. Thailand's northernmost provincial capital has neither one nor the other, but is a sleepy unprepossessing city with few sights and even fewer charms.

According to legend, it was built, as was often the case, when an elephant strayed along the Kok River and stopped on this exact spot. Its founder was King Mengrai, the man who went on to establish Chiang Mai. His celebrated statue is still to be seen to the east of town, covered in flowers and surrounded by little wooden elephants

The riverine village he once looked over is now a modern town undergoing something of a boom, largely as a result of tourism. Apart from the statue, Chiang Rai's main attractions are its temples. Pleasant walks can be taken to a number of these, notably around **Wat Phra Kaeo**, once home to the famous Emerald Buddha, now containing a replica made from Canadian jade stone, carved in China.

By turning off Trairat Road and following Saengkaeo Road, a short walk will take you to the 14th-century **Wat Ngam Muang**, less well known, but more distinguished looking with its naga stairway and ancient brick *chedi,* said to enshrine the remains of King Mengrai.

From here, by veering to the north, it is a 5-minute stroll to the Burmese-style **Wat Doi Tong,** which offers fine views of the river below, and a glimpse of the old part of town.

To the east of Wat Phra Kaeo near the boat pier (*Tha Rua*) is the last of Chiang Rai's major temples. **Wat Pra Singh** was built during the reign of King Maha Proma in the late 14th century and has a northern-style bell tower, a Bhodi tree from India and even a stone Buddha footprint with ancient Khmer script.

From the pier on the river, short boat trips can be organized to the Karen village of **Ban Ruammit** for elephant rides, or to go further afield to other hilltribe villages. Boats generally leave at 10 a.m. and continue to Tha Thon. But be warned. These places are frequently overrun by tourists and are unlikely to provide anything more than a passing glimpse into the hilltribe's way of life.

Chiang Rai does, however, have some of the finest hotels in the region as well as cheap and cheerful guest-houses on the river. In the evening, there are several good places to dine.

The biggest lure of Chiang Rai province is to be found not in the city, but to the north, along the Mekong, in the towns of Chiang Saen and Mae Sai, and the wild areas along the border known as the Golden Triangle. Treks ranging from one-day luxury tours to a full week of walking can be organized in almost any travel agent or hotel along with day trips to every imaginable site in the vicinity.

Opium and the Golden Triangle

The most infamous region in Southeast Asia lies north of Chiang Rai, beyond the banks of the Mekong River: a vast tangled mass of jungle extending deep into Burma, the Shan States and into neighbouring Laos.

The Golden Triangle is the second largest supplier of opium in the world—The Golden Crescent in Afghanistan takes first prize—producing some 2,500 metric tons annually and accounting for some 40 per cent of the entire world production. It is also home to the undisputed opium king—Khun Sa—and to mountain tribes and private armies.

For centuries, the opium trade was largely in the hands of the Chinese, although the Sumerians in 5,000 BC had been avid opium users. It was during the 1960s, however, that opium production exploded with the advent of the Vietnam War, when the American CIA, the Shans and the Chinese Kuomintang Army (KMT), all became involved in a massive network of profit, deceit and self interest in order to fund their armed struggles.

183

Prince of Poppies

Chang Chi-fu, Opium King, Prince of Poppies, and the man known throughout the world as Khun Sa, was born in 1932 in the Shan States of Burma. A former member of the Chinese Kuomintang Army (KMT), Khun Sa went on to become leader of the Shan United Army (SUA) in the late 1960s, a group fighting for independence from the Burmese government—and financing its struggle through the sale of opium.

In 1967, Khun Sa was arrested in neighbouring Laos, but escaped after bribing officials. During the 1970s he bought up vast quantities of opium, refining it into heroin along the Thai-Burma border and in so-doing becoming the most powerful opium lord in the Golden Triangle.

In 1990, the US put out an indictment for Khun Sa's arrest. But the bumptious man continues to avoid the world's wrath and—surrounded by thousands of armed troops living in fortified tunnels and with a cache of weapons including heat-seeking missiles—remains the most formidable single force in the opium wars.

Following the end of the Vietnam war, the DEA, the US Drug Enforcement Agency launched an unprecedented war against international traffickers, but has been hindered by international boundaries and the huge cache of arms.

Today the war against opium continues. But whereas once it was centred in and around Chiang Rai, now it has shifted over the borders into Shan-controlled areas of Burma, reached only by horse over hundreds of miles of mud paths known as opium tracks.

With the help of vast Western and international resources, the Thai government has succeeded in slashing opium output to about 30 tons a year, and has persuaded many of the hill-tribe people to substitute cash crops such as strawberries or cabbages for opium. Much of the Golden Triangle area in Thailand now has a bucolic calm about it, and you are more likely to run into five-star hotels and groups of trekkers than drug smugglers or armed bandits.

Only occasionally will you come across poppies. They are planted around September at the end of the monsoons, and take three months to produce the white, mauve and red petals that dot the higher slopes of the mountains. When the petals fall, they reveal a green seed pod inside which is a creamy resin, extracted by hand then left for two days to congeal before being wrapped in dried poppy petals. This can then be refined into heroin and shipped out to markets around the globe.

Chiang Saen

To see the Golden Triangle you must head north of Chiang Rai, to the sleepy town of Chiang Saen on the banks of the mighty Mekong River. The town has both a remarkable history and setting to recommend it. Between the 10th and the 13th centuries, Chiang Saen was the seat of power for one of the earliest northern principalities. It was from here that Mengrai first unified the warring factions and started on his long march culminating in the foundation of Lan Na.

A short tour can be made—best to use a bicycle—starting near the old gateway to the west at **Wat Pa Sak** (Teak Forest Temple). It's the oldest of

Chiang Saen's ruins and was built in 1295 by King Saen Phu on the spot where he planted 1,000 teak trees. Continue 2 km (1 mile) further north and you will find the base of **Wat Phra That Chom Kitti**, reputed to house a part of the Lord Buddha's forehead, and offering spectacular views of the Mekong River below. Return to the city gates and visit the diminutive **Wat Phra Rod** and almost directly opposite the imposing **Wat Chedi Luang**, built in 1331 and measuring 58 m (190 ft) tall.

Countless tribal villages dot the hills of the Golden Triangle, offering an invitation to trekkers. Luxury? So long as you don't mind a pig under your bed!

The people of the North are still more than happy to indulge in a little sideline— like growing opium. In a good year the region still produces as much as 30 tons.

Once found everywhere in the north, monkeys are more often than not kept in captivity. Still some of them at least enjoy posing for tourists.

Afterwards, you can stop off at the **National Museum**, open Wednesday–Sunday 8.30 a.m.–4.30 p.m., which lies next door to Wat Chadi Luang and houses a fine collection of *Chiang Saen* artefacts, dating as far back as Neolithic times, as well as an impressive display of hilltribe handicrafts and Burmese lacquerware.

For those with the time, a delightful side trip can be taken east to the village of **Chiang Khong**, site of a small town on the Mekong River. Occasionally you may be able to find a boat to take you there, a trip taking anything from three to five hours. The alternative is a an abysmal dusty potholed road, which is currently under reconstruction.

Ban Sop Ruak

From Chiang Saen, continue 11 km (7 miles) west to Ban Sop Ruak, the official point of the Golden Triangle. The spot is marked by the confluence of the Ruak and Mekong Rivers forming three national boundaries. To the south lies Thailand, to the east Laos and to the north-west on the narrow promontory, Burma, now known as Myanamar.

You would not know that this was the most famous sight in Thailand, if there wasn't a big sign announcing it, and crowds of other visitors looking for it. Many people find this one of the biggest disappointments of the north. Still, if you fight through the souvenir stalls selling Golden Triangle T-shirts, you can take an expensive boat tour around the official sandbank, although during the rainy season it is often submerged.

Mae Sai

When you reach the lively border town of Mae Sai, you have got to the end of the road. Beyond lies Burma and the

Gambling on the Golden Triangle

One of the latest intrigues to befall the legendary Golden Triangle concerns not the drug king pins or money laundering, but plans to build an international casino. The plush resort will incorporate a 300-room hotel, an 18-hole golf course, a helipad and a hovercraft port. But insiders claim the real lure will be the spinning roulette wheels and blackjack tables. Neither the Thais nor the Burmese will officially admit it is there. Still you can see the foundations going up on an island in the Mekong, and there is no shortage of people prepared to place bets on the outcome.

town of Tha Khi Lek, reached by a footbridge that crosses the Sai River.

Most visitors wing their way through the town on their way to and from Chiang Rai. Better to use this delightful town as a base to explore the surrounding region.

Aim to get to the bridge at dawn when the border is opened, and hundreds of tribespeople, Burmese and

Burmese puppets hang forlornly as their manufacturers cross the bridge at Mai Sae to buy Thai tomatoes.

Thais stream across in both directions bringing over fruits and handicrafts and, illegally, jade and drugs. Although foreigners are not allowed over into Burma, the area up to the entry post is a photographers' delight and the perfect spot from where to watch the hilltribe children pose for tourists, or the street vendors haggling over tomatoes and less identifiable Burmese vegetables.

Beyond the bridge, stalls line the main street, **Paholyothin Road**, selling fine Burmese-puppets and lacquerware as well as jade, hilltribe silver and Burmese style tapestries. The tapestries known as *kalaga* are especially beautiful, made with intricate designs, sewn with gold, silver and velvet. Such is the quality that many dealers now travel all the way from Bangkok and Chiang Mai to buy them here.

To get a reasonable price, you must bargain hard, as easy money in the past has inflated expectations and often the locals will start by asking the most outrageous sums. Also beware fake gems. Mae Sai may offer good opportunities for the specialist gemologist, but for many a visitor, it can easily end in disaster.

After exploring the shops and markets, a pleasant walk can be taken to the temple of **Wat Doi Wao**, situated on a hill to the west of the main street. The temple is reached by a flight of 207 steps and is said to hold one of the Lord Buddha's hairs. It also offers some of the finest views of the surrounding area.

Mae Sai has two other easily accessible attractions: **Tham Luang** (Great Cave) is 6 km (4 miles) to the south of town signposted on the right; and **Tham Pla** is a further 7 km (4.5 miles) off the main road at Ban Tham. Hotels and guesthouses will be able to supply details.

In the evening Mae Sai tends to a fairly basic form of entertainment. But the town does have a pub. The Frontier Saloon, is situated opposite the cinema on Paholyothin Road, serves draught beer and Jack Daniels whisky, and has a live band playing some of the best rock music on this side of Bangkok.

Side Trip to Doi Tung

West of Mae Sai off the road to Chiang Rai is one of the most popular sights in the vicinity. The famous hillside temple of Doi Tung is perched some 2,000 m (2188 yds) up the mountain and is worthy of a trip for the scenery alone.

The access road is Highway 1149, a turn off from the Chiang Rai-Mae Sai Road—and there are no shortage of *songthaews* doing the trip.

The road climbs steeply, passing the Queen Mother's summer residence and numerous neatly planted fields, courtesy of a massive Royal-sponsored agricultural project designed to help the tribes re-integrate into normal life. The people here, Akhas, Shans and Lahus, are encouraged to grow cabbages, cucumbers and strawberries and to make up for their loss of income—opium was formerly a more remunerative source of funds—the government has built them new model settlements and schools.

Along the wayside stop to look at the various tribal handicrafts now churned out with untold enthusiasm, and keep your camera handy for the magnificent views along the way.

At the end of the road is **Wat Phra That Doi Tung**, regarded as the holiest sanctuary by the residents of Chiang

Rai and by the Shans in Burma. The temple was built by King Achutaraat of the Yonog Kingdom in AD 911 and is believed to enshrine part of the left collarbone of Buddha.

Beyond the *wat,* a rough, almost impassable dirt track leads along the Burmese border back to Mae Sai. A better alternative though is to retrace your steps back to the main road.

Mae Salong

High in the hills at the end of a stunning drive through mountains and small rice-growing settlements is the town of Mae Salong, renamed **Santikiri**, signposted 67 km (42 miles) north-west of Chiang Rai on the newly paved Highway 1130. This delightful

First it was opium but now Mae Salong's intrepid merchants have an alternative—herbal tea—the most famous in the Kingdom. The locals, however, prefer illicit and extremely potent liquor.

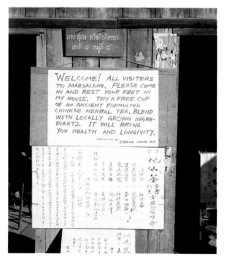

village is as remote as you can find—but still has the pleasures of good accommodation and bracing mountain air.

Many of the wooden houses are built up the mountainside, others in traditional Chinese-style with each door guarded by protective spirits. Even the people look different and often you can hear the people conversing with one another in Mandarin. Mae Salong's architecture and the towns inhabitants reflect a historic quirk. For the town is largely inhabited by former members of the Nationalist Kuomintang Army, KMT, the remainders of Chiang Khai Shek's Nationalist army who fled from China after the 1949 revolution.

For years the KMT maintained a monopoly on opium trade inside both Burma and Thailand, taxing Shan opium caravans entering Thailand and collecting tribal opium in order to finance their dream of reconquering China. These days, however, the communist threat has gone and the people have substituted poppy cultivation with tea, vegetables, herbs and tourism. Today throughout Thailand, Doi Mae Salong tea is considered the best in the kingdom and theoretically you could find no better place to have a "cuppa"—although sometimes they only offer Liptons.

To explore the town, start off the morning—6.30 a.m.—by visiting the fruit and vegetable market opposite the Mae Salong Guest House where every morning, Akha, Meo and Yao hilltribes dressed in all their finery trudge into town to sell sweetcorn.

Continue along the main road, which follows the valley, to reach the

189

main market where stalls sell the famous *khanom jiin nam ngiaw,* a Yunnanese noodle concoction, as well as herbal remedies for impotence and flatulence, floral teas and extremely potent illicit liquors.

Trekking can sometimes be arranged into the surrounding region from guesthouses with more unusual forms of transport, involving rides on mule back along the ridge overlooking the Burmese border. Enquire on arrival.

Side Trip to Ban Hin Taek

If you backtrack some 13 km (8 miles) along the main road, a small turning next to a row of stalls selling hilltribe crafts leads to the village of Ban Hin Taek, scene of some of the most frenzied drug wars in Thai history.

There are several tribal villages in the vicinity and a Christian Akha village, converted by local missionaries. But the road to Ban Thoed Thai

---

A Satisfactory Outcome

One of the great turning points in the war on drugs took place on 21 January 1982 when the Thai border police and Shan United Army under Khun Sa fought a mass battle for control of Ban Hin Taek. The military used helicopters and light aircraft, and the Shans, machine guns and mortars, previously supplied by the Thais. The Thais claimed victory when the Shans were forced to withdraw over the border. The Shans maintained it was a draw—and departed with 200 mules loaded with heroin, still intact. Times have changed, however, and so too the names of the places. Mae Salong has been re-christened Santikiri (Hill of Peace) and nearby Ban Hin Taek, Ban Thoed Thai (Independence Upholding Village)

---

remains difficult and often impassable —and is best done either by *songthaew* or as part of a trekking group, which can be organized in Mae Salong.

From Mae Salong, most people return down the mountain to Mae Chan where the road rejoins the highway connecting Mae Sai to Chiang Rai. Alternatively you can continue west of Mae Salong on a spectacular road to Tha Thon 50 km (31 miles) beyond. Although much of the road is surfaced, certain stretches may still be dirt. Enquire locally for up to date information.

Phayao

Magnificently situated on the banks of a fairy-tale lake, hemmed in by distant hills, is the sleepy town of Phayao; a perfect stop-off point on the way north or south.

The town was established as capital of a small principality more than 900 years ago, although it was abandoned during the 18th century. Its charms today are of a natural rather than a historical nature, and few pleasures are greater than a short boat trip in one of the town's elderly paddle boats.

For lunch try one of the countless open air restaurants serving freshwater fish, and especially the famous *pla bu* (the bamboo fish), a local delicacy, which is often exported to Hong Kong and Singapore. The best way to eat it is steamed or poached *pla bu pae sa* in a ginger and sweet chilli sauce, with plain rice.

Further around the lake to the north—reached by a left turn off the main road—is **Wat Srithomkomkam**, said to have been founded on the spot where a bird dropped a seed which

immediately sprang into a leafy tree. Inside the temple you can see the famous **Phra Chao Ton Luang Buddha** image dating from the 15th century and built of brick and stucco, covered in gold leaf. Outside, join monks in saffron robes making merit by feeding several large, overweight goldfish.

*M*ost of the trees were cut down in Nan province during the mid 1970s. But the military left just enough to keep the locals happy and for the communists to hide in.

*P*hayao's attractions are as clear as its waters, and who can blame the local fishermen for being not a little dazzled by them.

Nan

Fifty km (31 miles) south of Phayao, the road forks. To the right, the main Highway 1 continues to Lampang. And to the left Highway 103 cuts across towards Nan, one of the quietest and most rugged areas of the north. Nan, long isolated by geographical and political borders, has a surprisingly grand history. It was the

original seat of an ancient kingdom and during the 13th century, Khun Fang, brother of the founder of Vientiane, set up court in War Nakhon 70 km (43 miles) north of the provincial capital. Burmese and Laotian influences are to be found throughout the older part of town—especially in some of its magnificent temples.

To get an idea of the past, drop in at the **National Museum**, open Wednesday–Sunday, housed in a former palace built in 1903 by the ruler Phra Chao Suriyapong Phalitdej. Besides a collection of woodcarvings, *lanna*-style Buddha images, ceramics and betel nut sets there are also write-ups on the tribes of the region and a famous black elephant tusk, regarded as the province's most valuable treasure.

Three other sights are worth visiting. Opposite the museum is **Wat Chang Kham Wora Vihara**, a royal monastery built in 1547 and containing a Buddha image of solid gold discovered only in 1955 when the plaster covering broke, revealing the image beneath.

About 100 m (110 yds) further on the opposite side of the road is the 16th-century **Wat Bhumin**, Nan's most famous temple with beautifully carved wooden doors, placed around the four sides of the main shrine. Inside are fine murals, some of which have been restored, depicting Nan's past and episodes from the life of the Buddha.

Two km (1.5 miles) to the southwest of town on the far bank of the Nan River is the last major temple. **Wat Phra That Chae Haeng** is dominated by a vast *naga* snake and contains a 55 m (180 ft) high golden *chedi* and dazzling gilded umbrellas.

> **Touch of Turbulence**
> Nan's heyday during the 13th century gave way to more turbulent times during the 1970s when the communists decided that the forested hills around provided perfect hiding ground for their headquarters and an ideal spring-board for their onslaught on the entire country. But the Thai military had other plans. They bombed the area, cut down the trees and flushed out the communists— hence the vast cleared areas. Still, a handful of communists are said to inhabit the border area, and roadblocks and army trucks do occasionally break the calm. That has not stopped growing numbers of tourists from visiting the town. The TAT now claims it as one of the last beautiful frontiers in Thailand.

Whilst wandering the streets look for the town's most famous commodity—a blue cotton cloth called *mohom*, much favoured by the Thai farming fraternity. If you buy some make sure you wash it at least once before wearing it as it has a habit of shedding its rich blue dye onto unsuspecting skin.

Visitors keen to support hilltribes should seek out the **Ockenden Venture Handicrafts Centre** near the centre of town, which sells beautiful handicrafts and woven baskets, and uses the proceeds to support the tribes themselves.

Nan has little of the bustle of surrounding towns. There are few bars and most restaurants close at 9.30 p.m., except for an excellent pasta restaurant run by a jovial Swiss-Italian. Only for two days in October is the sleepy town transformed into a boisterous melee of people. For this is the time of the annual boat race marking the end of the rice harvesting festival. Villagers come from all over the region to sell their wares, fruits, flowers and locally made wickerware or just to watch. Boats are brightly painted and adorned with flowers, punted by up to 30 people in a boat. The timing of the festival varies each year according to the moon so check with the TAT.

Excursions from Nan

Beyond Nan town and the sparsely covered valleys supporting corn, rice and citrus fruits lies some of the most magnificent scenery in the north, although you will need either your own transport—or should arrange a tour through Fhu Travel on Sumondeavarag Road—to explore it.

Doi Phuka National Park

For a full days' circuit, head north on Highway 1080 and at the town of Tha Wang Pha (40 km, 25 miles) take a right turn on to Highway 1170 to the town of Pua. Just before the town centre, take another signposted right turn towards the Doi Phuka National Park. From here a tarmacked road climbs steeply into the hills, with spectacular views across the valley to Laos. Several tribes live in the vicinity, although trekking is not easily arranged. By following Highway 1256 and Highway 1031 you can make a circuit, returning to Nan via the towns of Ban Puk Heuk and Ban Lak Lai. Alternatively, extremely basic accommodation is available in the town of Pua in the form of a drive in brothel. Transport is imperative, but only to the Park!

Na Noi

This tiny village 65 km (40 miles) south of Nan has become something of a celebrity as near here film makers shoot much of the wild scenic drama movies shown in cinemas around the country. To get there drive, or catch a *songthaew*, along Highway 101 to Wiang Sa, before turning onto Highway 1026 to Na Noi. Continue 5 km (3 miles) past Na Noi to **Sao Din** with its picturesque valley and cliffs.

Afterwards, if you have the time, return to Nan on a circular route on dirt tracks via Mae Charim or continue to Phrae and Uttaradit. Make sure you do the trip in daylight. And enquire about conditions before leaving.

The Eastern Border

From Nan, a dense network of roads leads further north to Chiang Rai and to Chiang Khong through a countryside of rolling hills and further afield paddy fields and the Mekong River. There are few places to stay along the way though—and few people speak English. Still, by leaving early in the morning, it is possible to travel via Pua and Chiang Kham to Chiang Khong, from where you can continue to Chiang Saen on Highway 1129 or alternatively cut across to Chiang Rai. Enquire about conditions prior to departure. From Nan it's also possible to head south, via the towns of Na Noi and Fak Tha (140 km, 87 miles) along the eastern side of the Sirikit reservoir to the spectacular **Sak Yai National Park**, home to the thickest teak tree in the world, and from here to Uttaradit or even Chiang Khan.

But the roads are small and treacherous, there are army checkpoints and you would be well advised to backtrack on Highway 101 to Phrae and beyond to Uttaradit and Phitsanulok and into the North-eastern region.

Where the Arid Lands Mix with Elemental Charms and Ancient History

The people of Isaan are said to have got the short straw. They inherited an infertile, vast and arid land, jutting out towards Laos and Cambodia. But to complement that, they were given charm and goodheartedness, strength and endurance—and they are spoilt with some of the greatest ancient ruins on earth.

To the north-east of Bangkok, the land opens out into endless plains, high rocky plateaus and barren scrublands stretching to the Cambodian border and up to Laos along the banks of the Mekong. This vast tract of land is known as Isaan, Kingdom of Shiva, a land dessicated by drought, beautiful and forgotten. Until recently, it was almost inaccessible. Today, it remains the least visited part of the Kingdom, yet one which perhaps more than any other rewards the traveller.

Geographically, the area is largely made up of a giant plateau, which is 150 m (492 ft) above sea level, and is intersected by ridges and mountains. The soil is sandy, layered upon salt, making much of the land inhospitable to cultivation. During the rainy season much of Isaan is flooded, and during the dry season the earth is parched.

On the plateau live a third of the population—farmers and traders. They make their living predominantly from rice, but in the poorer areas from sweetcorn and tapioca. Although recent dam projects have alleviated at least some of the problems caused by shortage of water, Isaan remains poor. It has more than 40 per cent of the

Surin's most famous inhabitants are elephants, as demonstrated by this illustrious creature.

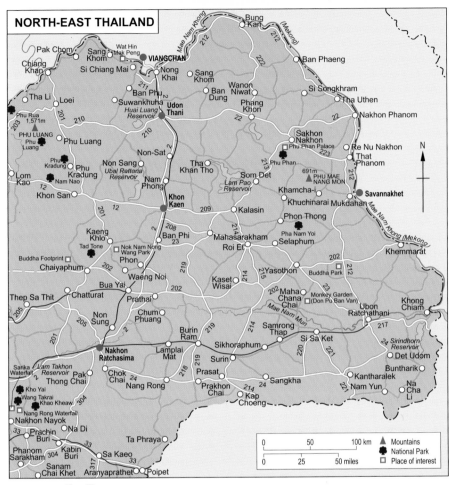

NORTH-EAST THAILAND

M ap of the North-east.

Kingdom's rice-growing area, yet it produces less than a third of the annual national crop.

The people are mainly Lao and Khmer with a sprinkling of Thais. They live mainly in small rural communities, tiny dots on the endless plains. Although big cities like Ubon and Khon Kaen have sprung up, the real Isaan lies outside the modern trading centres, among the rice fields.

For almost 400 years, the land known as Isaan formed part of the great Khmer empire, which stretched from Angkor in Cambodia west to the Central Plains and as far as Phetchburi in the South of Thailand. Today many beautiful ruins can still be seen at Phimai and around Buriram and Surin. Archaeological finds in Ban Chiang and the surrounding area also suggest that the land may have been inhabited more than 5,000 years ago by a people who were the forerunners of one of the earliest Bronze Age civilizations.

Isaan is not an easy place in which to travel. With the exception of Khon Kaen, there are no luxury hotels. Few people speak English and, despite a network of good tarmacked roads, the distances between the major sights are substantial. But there is something special about the region that can be found nowhere else in Thailand; the lure of vast open spaces, the hospitality of the Isaan people and the bare harsh landscape of dusty tracks running to a distant border.

The best way to see the North-east is to hire a car or motorbike, either from Bangkok or any of the main towns. Although there are buses, trains and even aeroplanes, the quintessential flavour of the far provinces is to be found away from the main roads in the villages, in the people harvesting the rice, in the markets and stalls.

A good route would take you from Bangkok to Korat, Buriram and Surin, along the Mekong River and up to Nong Khai, from where you can either cross to the Northern Region via Loei and Phitsanulok, or return to Bangkok by train. Parts of the trip can also be easily covered from any of the major cities in the North-east. But Isaan needs time and it needs effort. And if luxuries are important, it would be better to opt for another region.

*H*igh up on the hill way above the Friendship Highway, a grand white Buddha image welcomes travellers to the world of Isaan, the poor man of Thailand.

The Friendship Highway

The main road running North-east starts from Saraburi, 100 km (62 miles) north of Bangkok, and is known as the *Mitraparp* or Friendship Highway. It was built with American aid in the

1950s and used during the Vietnam war to carry supplies to US airbases in Udon Thani, Khon Kaen and Korat. In 1975, after the fall of Saigon, the Americans evacuated their airbases, but the narrow strip of tarmac remains, carrying trucks filled with rice and tomatoes and tapioca from Thailand's far provinces to the the capital of Bangkok.

A huge white marble Buddha high up on the mountainside some 45 km (30 miles) from Saraburi, marks the entrance into the vast region of Isaan. The Buddha is at **Wat Teppitakpunnaram**, on the last hill before the Korat Plateau, and can be reached by taking a right turn. Two staircases lead up to the Buddha, staring impassively over the north-eastern plains and the narrow thread of mountains stretching into the distance. From here the Friendship Highway extends a further 570 km (354 miles) to the town of Nong Khai on the Mekong River, connecting the northern tip of Isaan to the prosperous region of the Central Plains.

Side Trip to Khao Yai National Park

South of the Friendship Highway, spread across the foothills of the Dongrak mountain range lies Thailand's oldest and best known National Park. Khao Yai (Big Hill) occupies a total area of 2,168 sq km (837 sq miles) and boasts one of the largest concentrations of wildlife in the country.

Twenty five large mammal species alone are said to live in the vast tracts of dense evergreen including Asian wild dog, clouded leopard, black bear, tiger and elephant. With a little bit of luck, and preferably a large pair of binoculars, you may also see some of the Kingdom's most colourful birdlife; orange-breasted and red-headed *trogons,* moustached *barbets,* great slaty woodpeckers and possibly the largest concentration of hornbills in South-east Asia.

Although organized tours are now the recommended way of seeing the park, enthusiastic walkers will find plenty else on offer. Try one of 11 marked trails listed at the Visitors Centre. They are for the most part signposted at irregular intervals, although you should try to get a map from one of the park wardens. One of

One of the simpler joys of travelling through Thailand is a walk through one of its great National Parks. And what better than the oldest of them all— Khao Yai or "Big Mountain".

the most popular will take you from the Visitors Centre along elephant tracks to the **Nong Pak Chi Watchtower** situated some 8 km (5 miles) to the north. Try to get there in the early evening when the animals come out to feed, and ideally bring a guide to avoid spending the night searching for a route back home.

A day can also be easily spent around one of the many waterfalls that scatter the park, especially around the **Haew Suwat Waterfall** that lies some 7 km (4.3 miles) east of the Visitors

198

Centre. Walk a further 1 km (0.6 mile) from here to get to the **Haew Sai Waterfall** and a further 2 km (1.2 miles) to the **Haew Pratun Waterfall**. Those with surplus energy can then cut west along an extremely poorly signposted path back to the Visitors Centre.

The best of all options though is transport, and the ideal time to explore the park at dusk, when elephants cross the road or can often be found at the elephant salt lick north of the Visitors Centre on the road to Pak Chong.

For those who haven't got wheels, several hotels now run night jungle spotting tours where you may see *sambar,* barking deer or elephant, frozen in the beam of a spotlight carried on the back of a jeep. Trips can also be taken to a nearby limestone cave inhabited by vast numbers of wrinkled lipped bats. Tours of the cave and walks through the forest can be organized through Jungle Adventure Tours, Tel : 044 312 877.

Nakhon Ratchasima (Korat)

Visitors expecting to find a heap of Khmer ruins in Nakhon Ratchasima, commonly known as Korat, are likely to be disappointed. Reminders of the Americans—bars and massage parlours— who used the place as an airforce base during the Vietnam war are more in evidence than their ancient predecessors.

Still, with its lure of reasonable hotels and restaurants, this pleasant if uninspiring town has established itself as the main stepping-stone to some of the greatest ruins in Isaan.

> **Mouhot's Hell**
> "A nest of robbers and assassins, the resort of all scum of the Laotian and Siamese races" wrote the 19th-century French naturalist Henri Mouhot of Korat. Mouhot's distaste for the place derived from the abundance of bandits and vagrants who had escaped from slavery and prison, and who pursued the caravans. Even the town's inhabitants he found "impertinent and disagreeable", and much prone to "gambling and opium-smoking".

Before starting on a temple spree, three sights are worth looking at. On the the west side of town in front of the old gate of **Prat Chumpon** you will come across the statue of Thai Surani, wife of the Governor of Korat who, in the year 1826, when the town was under siege invited Prince Anuwong and the Laotion army to a party. As soon as they had drunk sufficient quantities of alcohol, she signalled to the concealed Thai soldiers, who rapidly attacked and overpowered their aggressors.

Further south down Ratchadamnoen Road is another monument to history. The **Mahawirong National Museum**, open from Wednesday–Sunday 9 a.m.–12 noon and 1 p.m.–4 p.m. and situated within the grounds of **Wat Sutchinda** contains a fine collection of Khmer art, a famous Buddha statue and several door lintels from the surrounding region.

One last sight, in the centre of town, is the remains of the old fortifications. These are relics of the 13th to 16th century when this was an important and influential town guarding the frontier with Cambodia.

In the evening, Korat offers two widely differing forms of entertainment. On the one hand there are nightclubs—left over from the days of the US, but still containing some of the same old faces— and on the other, the night bazaar on **Manat Road**, which sells local souvenirs, handicrafts and fried grasshoppers and is open from 6 p.m.–11.30 p.m.

Before leaving town, visit the tourist office (TAT) in Korat at 2102–2104 Mitraparp Road, Tel: 243 427, which can advise you on some of the sights in the vicinity and distributes the latest information on events throughout the North-east.

Pak Thong Chai and Dan Kwian

A 40-minute drive to the south will bring you to the village of Pak Thong Chai, famous for its silk weaving.

The silk is made by extracting thread from cocoons, refining it, setting intricate patterns, dying and finally weaving. In the 1930s it was the favourite fabric for Bangkok high society, who donned a p*anung* for social calls. Now that trousers and polyester have taken precedence, silk manufacturing has since gone into decline, but can still be seen at the **Sri Thai Silk Factory** and a handful of other shops along the main road.

A short distance east as the crow flies, but a considerably longer distance by road, is the town of **Dan Kwian**, best known for its pottery, although there is also an open air wooden cart museum. The clay comes from the banks of the Moon river, is woodfired

at high temperatures, and is unglazed. Watch the process and take your pick of the traditional water jars, ceramic jewellery and murals.

Side Trip to Phimai

The pride of Korat, and indeed of Isaan, lies 68 km (42 miles) to the north-east of town in the small village of Phimai. Nobody quite knows who built this majestic temple, or why, or indeed precisely when. But archaeologists conjecture that it was probably started during the reign of the great King Jayavarman Vi, sometime during the 12th century, and that it formed part of an old city covering an area 1,000 m (3281 ft) by 560 m (1837 ft).

You won't need to know the history to enjoy it though, for Prasat Phimai has an uncanny resemblance to that of the Angkor Wat, the magnificent complex across the border in Cambodia to which it was once connected by road.

Four gates dominate the ruins, the largest preceded by a *naga* bridge at the foot of which stand lion guardians, with the roof supported by *garudas* and *nagas*. The walls are covered with intricate engravings of flowers, lions, elephants and monkeys, and of Rama killing the *Asura* (demon) named Wirat, a former deity who was turned into a devil by Shiva as a punishment for being a ladies' man.

Inside the inner courtyard stand two small stupas (*Prang Phromathat* and *Prang Hin Daeng*) and, in the centre, an ornately carved dome (*Prang Prathan*) with four doors and a lintel finely carved with scenes from Mahayana Buddhism.

Outside in the gardens is an open air museum, open daily 8.30 a.m.–4 p.m.,

with a collection of ancient statues, friezes and lintels of Buddha, gods and monkeys. These exhibits were gathered from Phimai and other Khmer sites throughout the North-east.

A pleasant way to round off the afternoon is with a trip to an extra-ordinarily large Banyan tree called **Sai Ngam** which lies 2 km (1.2 miles).down

An exquisite example of Khmer architecture, Phimai was said to have been modelled on nearby Angkor Wat.

the road and is said to be the biggest in the world. Certainly if it's not, it must have a higher concentration of spirits. To see them, just explore the little shrines and note the yellow silk often tied around the bark to keep the tree spirit warm.

Phanom Wan

This 1,000-year-old temple, like many sights in Isaan, is not easy to get to without your own transport, but is certainly worth the effort. You will find it a short distance off the main road some 15 km (9 miles) north of Korat near the village of **Ban Long Thong**.

Prasat Hin Panomwan means the stone castle of Phanom Wan. It, has fine lintels and inside is adorned with a few remaining Buddha images—the majority of them have been taken to the open museum in Phimai. The Fine Arts Department is renovating it, but it's a tranquil place with a certain wild grandeur and few tourists. Buses run to the crossroads from the main terminal in Korat, although you will have to walk the remaining 5 km (3 miles) or catch a *songthaew*.

Buriram and Monsoon Country

To see the real Isaan, you must journey east of Korat into the vast arid countryside around Buriram, a region known as Monsoon Country after a book by well-known author Pira Sudham. For much of the year, the land is parched under the searing heat, and during the rainy season huge tracts of farmland are flooded.

Centuries ago, this province was part of the Khmer empire, and for almost 400 years extended from Angkor in Cambodia to north-east provinces.

Today its ancient sanctuaries and ruins provide some of the finest examples of Khmer art in the region. If you are driving, take any of the turnings off the main road, Highway 24, and you

will enter the world that Pira Sudham writes of, a world of plodding water buffalo, of sun-hatted women knee-deep in mud and endless rice fields stretching to a distant horizon.

When you have two fine young water buffalo and a cart filled with rice, what more could a man wish for?

Pira Sudham

He was born in a small rice farming community near the Cambodian border and has gone on to become one of the the best-known literary figures in Thailand. Pira Sudham left his village at the age of 14 to become a temple boy in Bangkok. He subsequently attended university abroad, but he never forgot Isaan, and in his books, he provides a window on the rural farmers, on their hopes and poverty and the corruption around them. His most famous works are *Monsoon Country* and *People of Isaan,* stories of the pressures of development and of social alienation. Almost alone amongst Thai authors he writes in English, providing a unique insight into a largely forgotten world. In 1989, Pira Sudham was nominated for the Nobel prize for literature.

Phanom Rung

This splendid mountaintop shrine lies 120 km (74.5 miles) east of Korat and, like Phimai, has become one of the great architectural sites in Isaan.

Phanom Rung rests on top of an extinct volcano and, as evidence of the Khmer belief that the higher the temple, the more important the shrine, reflects some of the finest of all Khmer artistry.

Three laterite staircases, flanked by sandstone columns shaped like lotus buds, ascend through successive levels past Brahman purifying ponds to the grand entrance, lined by sculptured sandstone columns.

At the summit, which offers spectacular views of the flat countryside around, you will come to four galleries enclosing the central *prasat.*

History relates that Phanom Rung was built during the reign of King

Isaan's Phanom Rung monument to the ideals of the Khmer empire was left deserted and fallen down until the Fine Arts Department put it back together.

Suriya Voraman VII of Cambodia to worship Shiva, the Hindu god of the Universe. It nearly fell down during the early 20th century, but thanks to a massive restoration project taking 17 years, you can now see it again in all its glory.

Almost everything here is symmetrical, from the doors to the windows and the intricate *naga* bridges—there are only three of them now left in Thailand. Note too the great five-headed *naga* snakes, the engravings of

The Missing Lintel

One of the great episodes of Isaan folklore took place in the early 1960s when a famous reclining Vishnu lintel went missing from Phanom Rung only to reappear in March 1973 in the Art Institute of Chicago. The Fine Arts Department lobbied for the return of the prized artefact, Carabao, one of Thailand's most famous rock bands featured a song *Give us back our Phra Narai Lintel,* the Thai government held high-level discussions with their US counterparts; finally in November 1988, the precious lintel was returned and placed in its original resting point, where it can be seen in all its glory.

elephant heads and of Kala, God of Time and Death—and feel if only for a moment the invisible power of times gone by.

To get to Phanom Rung head to the village of Prakhon Chai, some 120 km (74.5 miles) east of Korat on Highway 24, and shortly before you get there, follow a signpost to your right. Buses also run to the town of Nang Rong from where you must catch a *songthaew* or motorbike. A better option: take a tour.

Phanom Muang Tham

Some 7 km (4.3 miles) east of Phanom Rung, but accessible by car or motorbike taxi, is Buriram's other great monument—the 10th century temple of Phanom Muang Tham.

King Jayavarman V was responsible for this remarkable edifice made up of five ancient prangs set around four lotus ponds and enclosed by a laterite wall. Time has taken its toll and much of the temple is now in ruins, but like the great Humpty Dumpty, the Fine

Arts Department is busily putting it back together again.

If you are fortunate enough to get there before they do, you will find a crumbling cascade of weathered rocks set around triple gateways at four cardinal points—and in the inner courtyard, several delicate carvings from Brahman mythology.

There is accommodation at Buriram town, some 65 km (40 miles) to the north on Highway 219, but most visitors continue to Surin situated a further 80 km (50 miles) to the east along Highway 24 and Highway 214.

Surin

The name of Surin is synonymous with the great beast of the land, the *chang* or elephant, which for centuries roamed the jungles of South-east Asia, and in more recent times worked the logging areas.

Don't expect traffic jams of elephants though, since for most of the year, Surin is just a quiet town full of Chinese-fronted shop houses, with a slow ebb to it and few tourists. Only during the three day annual round up in November does the town come to life when more than 100 elephants from all over the North are brought here to stage races, tug of war, log pulling contests and to play football. The festival was organized to preserve the skills of the local people, and tourists descend in their thousands.

You can see elephants at other times of the year, but you will have to go the the **Taklang** village, situated 59 km (36.5 miles) to the north off Highway 214. The people here are from the Suay Tribe, a people who migrated from Attapeau Sanpae in Laos, and who, during the reign of King Suriya-marin of Ayutthaya, built a formidable reputation by catching one of the royal white elephants. One Suay chieftain, named Chiengpoom, was even a governor of Surin and had the eminent title of Phraya Surinpakdee Srinarong Janguang.

Today the fearsome reputation of the Suay has waned and the number of elephants with them. Many of the *mahouts* are forced to take their elephants to the big cities to earn a living posing for tourists, only returning to Surin for the round up in November. But there are always a few elephants wandering around in the rice fields and the people are more than happy to display some of the skills which have made the *mahouts* famous nationwide. Tours can be organized from Surin, but impromptu visitors are also welcome.

On the way back from Taklang, a delightful little side trip can be made to the silk weaving village of **Kha-wowsinrin**, signposted to the left 14 km (8.7 miles) from Surin, where the Queen herself presided over the opening of a home industries project. These days silver trinkets and Khmer bracelets are more in evidence than silk, and most of the restaurants have no food. Still, there are a few other small villages that can be explored further down the road.

Surin itself has a lively morning market where people from the surrounding region come to barter their goods. Get there at around 7 a.m. before the heat of the day and feast yourself on real Isaan food. Try fried sour pork sausages (*sakrok pleaw*) or *laab phet* (minced duck meat with spices) or even *tapwan* (sweet pork liver), which is probably the hottest dish that you will ever come across. Also famous is sticky rice or *khao niaw*. It's a chunk of rice containing starch that sticks together and is easy to eat by hand, like bread.

Most Isaan food requires little cooking since the majority of villagers spend their days working the fields. Often, they catch fish in the rice fields, pound them with a mortar into a kind of paste add chilli pepper and onions —and that's their lunch. It is called *palat,* is fearsomely hot and extremely malodorous.

Other equally distinctive and exotic dishes abound such as fried ants and frog curry, although the locals will rarely waste such delicacies on an unappreciative foreigner.

In the evening, a good place to go for less adventurous fare is the **Artiste Pub** on Thanon Jet Pamroong, which sometimes has live bands. Surin also has several nightclubs situated along the Lac Meung Road around the Mars Party House and at the Rome Pub and Palace Disco. Occasionally, if you are lucky, you may even catch the locals dancing the famous *Ruem-unre* (pestle dance) and *Ram Trut* (New Year's dance) or playing something known as Thai rugby with a coconut.

Side Trip to Prasat Bay Kream

South of Surin, lying on the exact border with Cambodia, a narrow track leads through elephant grass to the three ruined Khmer temples known as **Prasat Bay Kream**, **Prasat Ta Muen Toj** and **Prasat Ta Muen Tam**.

The temples were constructed in the reign of Khom's King Chai Woramun the 7th, around 1700–1750 BE according to the Buddhist calendar, and have some fine old sandstone carvings–covered in an abundance of undergrowth.

Until recently, the temples were closed to outsiders, with land mines scattered liberally in the vicinity. Most of the area has now been opened although there are still a couple of army checkpoints. To get there take Highway 214 to Prasat and 10 km (6 miles) further, turn right onto Highway 2021 to Ban Ta Meung. From this tiny village, you must take a left turn down a dusty track for 12 km (7.5 miles) until you reach the temples.

For those without the transport and who cannot speak Thai, a better alternative though is to talk with Pirom at the Pirom Guest House who has a landrover and extensive knowledge of the local area.

A good way to round off the trip is to visit the delightful 11th- or 12th-century temple of **Prasat Ban Phluang** signposted just 1 km (0.6 mile) before the town of Prasat. It is a tiny place that has been extensively restored and has a fine carving of the god Indra riding an elephant over the eastern facing door.

Ancient stone monuments dot the arid plains of Isaan. Here is a relief carving from Prasat Ban Phluang.

Side Trip to Khao Phra Viharn

The last great side trip that can be taken from Surin or Si Sakhet is to the temple of Khao Phra Viharn, one of the most venerated shrines in Southeast Asia. Until 1963, it was one of Thailand's major tourist attractions. Then came the decision of the World Court that the area be awarded to Cambodia. Now, the 11th-century cliffside temple is once again being promoted, although you may only be able to see it from a distance.

To get to Khao Phra Viharn from Surin, follow Highway 214 to Prasat, then branch off to the left on Highway 24. After 130 km (80 miles), turn right down Highway 221. Phra Viharn National Park lies 40 km (25 miles) beyond the town of Kantharalak at the end of a stunning stretch of road into the hills. The spot is marked by a car park, and 100 m (328 ft) further on by a look-out point with awesome views of the countryside and of the distant temple with a Cambodian flag.

Beyond barbed wire fences, a path climbs up the other side of the hill to **Phra Viharn**, stretching for almost 1 km (0.6 mile) across the mountainside and rising through a succession of *gopura* (vestibules) to the top .m.ost sanctuary, that honours the god Shiva. Inside are crumbling lintels, pillars covered in moss and hallways that once served as ammunition depots for troops during the Cambodian conflict.

Currently visitors wishing to go beyond the look-out point must get a special pass. There are, however, plans to re-open Phra Viharn as a major tourist attraction and even to restore it. For further details, enquire at the official tourist office (TAT) in Bangkok or with the authorities in Surin, Kantharalak or Ubon Ratchathani.

Basic accommodation can be found 50 km (31 miles) from Phra Viharn at the town of Kantharalak. To get there catch a bus from Surin or Ubon.

The Emerald Triangle

South-east of Surin the land opens out into one of the most beautiful and exhilarating areas in Isaan. Wide open spaces give way to forested mountains and distant views of Cambodia and, further north, of Laos.

The locals call it the Emerald Triangle, the region where the three borders meet, an area largely untouched by tourists, where goods move silently across borders.

The people here are largely Khmer and Lao and their friendliness is tempered only by their lack of English. Their charm does much to makes up for the lack of hotels and luxuries, for this remains very much the territory of the adventurous, where for a few days you can experience a different side of Thailand.

From Surin to Ubon

From Surin drive to Kantharalak and 23 km (14 miles) further on take a left turn down Highway 2248 towards the village of **Nam Yun**. After a few km the road turns to dirt, cutting through vast arid areas, cultivated with sweetcorn and tapioca.

Nam Yun is little more than a speck on the map with a few shops, a petrol station and an incongruous Catholic school, but makes a pleasant spot to stretch your legs. Afterwards continue the 28 km (17 miles) to **Na Cha Luai** a friendly little market town with charming little wooden-fronted houses, but with no hotels. If it is late and you need somewhere to stay, try the *wat* on the outskirts of town, beyond the market. There's a hall with wooden floors where laymen can sleep. You should, however, ask permission from the abbot and leave a donation in the morning. Traditionally women have not been able to stay in *wats,* but the situation is changing and especially in Na Cha Luai presents no problem.

Na Cha Luai is the perfect spot from which to explore some of the little dirt tracks that run off the main road, but ideally you should have a guide or someone who speaks English. At dawn it makes a pretty sight. The hills are covered in mist, the workers

Let There Be Rain

In olden times, one of the most important methods of producing rain was known as *Bamrun Na* (Clashing of Tusks). H.G. Quaritch Wales describes it thus: "Two elephants were tied to posts with strong ropes of sufficient length to allow their tusks to meet, but not long enough to allow them to inflict a wound. These animals, much excited would rush at each other in an attempt to fight and their tusks would clash, giving forth a loud sound. It appears that the clashing of tusks was a magical imitation of thunder intended to inspire the rain gods with fear". These days in parts of the arid north-east, locals use an alternative measure. During a really severe drought a Siamese cat is placed in a cage and carried around the village whilst people pour water over its head and call for rains. The ancient right is, however, considered only partially effective.

are leaving for the fields, and the land is a sea of haze and water buffalos.

Along the streets you often catch sight of local farmers, their skins blackened by the sun, carrying archaic looking double barrelled shotguns. These peasants have often just returned from their cross-border forays, killing birds, pigs and buffalo in Laos and Cambodia, where the jungles still provide a natural habitat and where deforestation has yet to take hold.

To see the beautiful National Park of **Phuchong Nayoi**, backtrack 9 km (5.5 miles) to the village of Keng Luang and follow a small dirt track, which leads past the park gates to a small car park. If you walk down a steep path, you arrive at a hidden waterfall which bubbles over the mountainside. It's a good spot for a picnic,

but swimming is not recommended. The current is deceptively strong and every year carries away several victims.

Back on the main road, continue a further 90 km (56 miles) past the town of Buntharig and the Sunthon Reservoir, passing some of the most arid landscape in the north-east, to the town of Phibun Mangsahan where the route forks. To the left Highway 217 leads to Ubon Ratchathani, the major city in the region and to the right Highway 222 leads to Kong Chiam.

Kong Chiam

This delightful little town lies at the confluence of the Moon and Mekong rivers, just a short distance from the Laotian border. With its spattering of small guesthouses, it makes a perfect base from which to explore the surrounding region.

From the waterfront next to the town *wat,* hire a tiny motorboat to take you out on the two coloured river, the spot where the dark lurid green of the Moon mixes with the brown of the Mekong. On one side is Thailand and on the other, Laos, and in the far distance, the hazy mountains of Cambodia.

After exploring the town with its wooden houses and riverine bars, a pleasant side trip can be taken to the picturesque Kaeng Tana rapids situated within the **Kaeng Tana National Park**. The best way to get there is by the ferry which crosses regularly over the Moon River up till 6 p.m., from where the Park is a further 10 km (0.6 mile) on dirt track. Accommodation is available although this should be booked in advance through the National Parks Division, Tel: 579 4842.

Walks to several signposted waterfalls and caves are an additional attraction.

Pha Taem and Chong Meck

Some of the oldest cave paintings in Thailand are found at the historic **Pha Taem Cave**, 19 km (11.8 miles) north-west of Kong Chiam, off Highway 2134 near the village of Nong Pheu. The paintings—pictures of human figures, hands, elephants, fish and animal traps—are set on a high and precipitous sandstone cliff that extends some 400 m (438 yds). Along with finds at Ban Chiang, they are evidence of settlement of the North-east by an early civilization. According to archaeologists they date back 2,000–4,000 years, and are painted with pigment made from animal blood, vegetable gum and local soil. Within walking distance of the paintings are caves and several waterfalls with spectacular views of the river below.

One final attraction within easy reach of Kong Chiam, is the town of Chong Meck on the Lao border reached by driving south of town on Highway 217. From near the car park, you can walk across into Laos, although you will have to leave cameras or any other bags at the Thai Immigration Office.

There is a prosperous little market between the two official borders selling Heineken beer, 1983 vintage Bulgarian wine from Sophia and Vietnamese whisky as well as beautiful pots and wooden carvings.

From Chong Meck, drive a distance of 50 km (31 miles) back to the crossroads at Phiboon Mangsahan from where Highway 217 continues to Ubon Ratchatani.

*P*oor in wealth, but rich in humour, Isaan people still find plenty to be happy about.

Ubon Ratchathani

Ubon Ratchathani, City of the Royal Lotus Flower and sprawling provincial capital has two boasts. It was once a US airbase, and it hosts one of the most beautiful celebrations in Thailand.

The event takes place at the end of July when the people make candles shaped like temples and mythological creatures. Some of them are up to 3 m (10 ft) tall and are paraded three times around the local *wat* in a rite of purification. Traditionally the candles were used by the monks during the dark lenten days when, under rules which were laid down by the Buddha, they were not allowed to leave the *wat* for three months during the rainy season.

At other times of year, visit the delightful **Hat Wat Tai Island**, set in the middle of the river with an abundance of restaurants on jetties. You can even get a good and traditional massage in Ubon at the New Powate massage centre on Pichit Rungsun Road. In the evening, Ubon offers several good places to eat. Try Memoon Floating Restaurant or the wonderously named Talat Sod besides the Mun River. Many of the stalls sell grasshoppers and other strange-looking concoctions. If you do not know what to order just point at a dish and ask for *"nam yen"* (cold water) or *"nam cha"* (tea) if it turns out to be ferociously hot.

For tours around Ubon and local information visit the TAT Office, 264/1 Khuan Thani Road, Tel: 377 008.

Forest Temples

Two forest temples lie within easy reach of Ubon. The first is **Wat Nong Pa Phong**, 10 km (6 miles) to the south of town which was set up by the renowned monk Acaan Chaa. For the last ten years he has been in a coma, but still alive—testimony to the strength of mind over body.

Around the temple are thickly wooded groves containing the monks' simple quarters, with signs of Buddhist theology attached to the trees, declaring in English the true meaning of life.

Afterwards you can continue to **Wat Pa Nanachat Beung Wai** (International Forest Temple), situated 8 km (5 miles) away, off Highway 226, and home to several American, English and German novices. Unlike the monks who reside in *wats* throughout the Kingdom, the forest dwellers live a life of contemplation and solitude. They do not study the languages of Pali and Sanskrit, but live a more stringent and practical life. Often they spend long periods of time in strict seclusion, meditating to achieve greater awareness and consciousness of the frailty of the human self and the temporal nature of all things.

The forest tradition, however, is no longer confined to Thailand. Recently monasteries were opened in the West at Chithurst in England, as well as in France, Italy and Switzerland.

The Mekong Route

From high up in the icy Himalayas, the great Mekong River flows down through southwestern China forming the border between Thailand and Laos before flooding into the South China Sea. Along the way it passes through Northern Thailand between the towns of Chiang Khong and Chiang Saen. But it is in the North-east that the river is seen at its most beautiful, flowing through the undeveloped countryside on its long course to Vietnam's Mekong Delta.

Between Ubon Ratchathani and Nong Khai lies one of the most scenic stretches of the river. The route offers glimpses of the Mekong, deep gullies through the hills, miles and miles of rice fields broken by small villages and the distant outline of the mountains of Laos. It is an area with good roads,

211

*T*he Mekong River
runs down from China through
Laos and into Vietnam. On its
way it passes through north-east
Thailand before emptying into
the South China Sea.

but largely unspoilt, with the attraction
of being far away from western civilization.

There are few good hotels along the
route and like the journey through the
Emerald Triangle, private transport is
an advantage if not a prerequisite.
Buses do go along Highway 212, but
the joy of the journey is the moving
and the opportunity to stop along the
way rather than the arrival.

From Ubon to Mukdahan

Start at Ubon and drive north-east on
Highway 202 to the small town of
Khemmarat, a picturesque market
town strung along the west bank of the
Mekong.

After exploring the narrow streets
with their charming wooden houses
continue along Highway 2034 for 50
km (31 miles) until you see the strange
mushroom-shaped rocks on your left.

These spectacular rock formations
are part of **Phophatep National Park**
signposted down a tarmacked road.
The Park can provide a good break, or
a pleasant longer stay, and is a good
stop-off point before continuing to the
sprawling town of Mukdahan, which
is squeezed between mountains on the
banks of the Mekong River. Mukdahan was one of the first border towns

to open a checkpoint between Laos and Thailand It remains a major centre for border trade; trucks filled with consumer goods and soap powder cross over the Mekong by ferry to the town of Savannakhet situated directly opposite on the far bank of the river. Often you may hear the inhabitants speaking French.as the majority of the inhabitants here are from Lao—a former French colony— with the Thais being a minority. It is possibly no coincidence that the only real French bakery on this side of the Mekong is situated in Mukdahan, and is run by an old Thai couple. Baguettes come out of the oven at 6 a.m.

That Phanom

The road beyond Mukdahan follows inland for a little over 45 km (28 miles) to That Phanom, a small town set on the banks of the Mekong. A few km before you reach the town, a right turn leads down a dirt track, which runs parallel to the main road past the small rural communities that live along the river bank.

That Phanom is best known for its Laotian-style *chedi,* the most revered in Isaan. According to some archaeologists it was built more than 1500 years ago, but collapsed in 1975 after four days of torrential rain. The calamity was considered highly inauspicious— ceremonies were held and offerings made to appease the capricious spirits. But the King went there and funded the rebuilding of the *chedi* and in 1978 it was restored to its former glory. The *chedi* is 57 m (187 ft) high and decorated with 10 kg (22 lbs) of gold, surrounded by cloisters filled with Buddha images. Inside the courtyard is a small museum with a display of pictures and short write-ups on the history of the temple, its destruction and its rebuilding.

Boats can be organized from the river bank for short trips down the Mekong.

Renu Nakhon

For a delightful little side trip, drive 11 km (7 miles) north-west to the town of Renu Nakhon, a village famed for its weaving. At the big market next to **Wat Phra That Renu Nakhon** you will find a vast display of children's cuddly toys and *mutmee,* a form of silk made from dyed threads as well as the triangular pillows for which the Northeast is renowned. Afterwards, wander down the main street to the shops and small restaurants where you can feast on *som tam* and freshly caught fish from the Mekong.

Nakhon Phanom

The attraction of Nakhon Phanom, the sprawling riverine town that lies 50 km (31 miles) north of Renu Nakhon is its setting. The city hugs the river offering magnificent views over the Mekong to the mountains of Laos and the Laotian town of Thakhek. There is little else that is particularly memorable about the town though, except the signs telling you that guns are banned. Still you can visit the busy market and relax at the little restaurants overlooking the river.

From Nakhon Phanom you have the option of two routes. The first cuts across to **Udon Thani** via the town of Sakhon Nakhon, which is known more popularly as Nakhon Nowhere, and the historic village of Ban Chiang.

*N*eatly dressed children pedal back to their villages. Some live as far as 15 km (6 miles) from the nearest school.

The second, Highway 212, follows the arch of the Mekong River for another 300 km (186 miles) to Nong Khai. By leaving early, you can complete the trip in a day, driving through eucalyptus, tobacco and tomato plantations; there are occasional glimpses of the river and views of the distant mountains of Laos to the east.

Pleasant breaks can be made at the towns of Ban Pheng after 80 km (50 miles) and Ban Kan after 160 km (100 miles). It is better though to continue on to Nong Khai in time for a refreshing sunset drink beside the river.

Nong Khai

When you reach Nong Khai you have got to the northernmost point in Isaan. Beyond lies Laos and the capital of Vientiane situated 30 km (19 miles) upstream of the Mekong River.

A major trading town and a charming French influenced provincial capital, Nong Khai is a popular gathering point for tourists in the north-east. And whilst the majority of visitors who come to Nong Khai by rail from Bangkok do so primarily to catch the ferry to Laos, the place merits at least a full day's stay.

The most pleasant part of town lies in the area around Meechai and Rimkong Road with tree shaded avenues. There are fine old wooden houses—amongst a spattering of new ones—and an unlikely market selling politburo style hats and Czezoslovakian binoculars brought over from Laos at fantastically low prices.

For a further unexpected site, head 4 km (2.5 miles) to the east of the town to the eclectic **Wat Gugaew**, filled with statues of Hindu divinities, Buddhas and dogs smoking cigarettes. The gentleman responsible for this creation was none other than the famous monk Luang Pu (Venerable Grandfather) who set it up in 1978 as a demonstration of how all religions should work in unison.

In the evening, a delightful way to see the river is to take the boat that leaves at 5 p.m. or 6 p.m.—depending on the time of year—from the ferry pier on Hai Sok Road for a sunset cruise on the Mekong. On your return, try one of the restaurants strung along the river, serving steamed fish and other local delicacies.

Occasionally you may get *pla buk,* the giant fish of the Mekong. The season starts in April and lasts until June. During that time the waters around Nong Khai, Chiang Khong and Chiang Sen are a hive of activity. The fish can weigh up to 300 kg (661 lbs). Any catch will be accompanied by great local celebrations and failure by the offerings of wooden phalluses to the river to fertilize the waters.

At other times of the year when the river is low, you can almost walk to Laos, but this is not recommended, because the currents are strong, and each year the river claims victims. Traditionally the people believed that if the river did not take its sacrifice then the rains would not come and their crops, predominantly tomatoes, would be spoilt.

The Mekong (West of Nong Khai)

The most idyllic stretch of the Mekong River extends west of Nong Khai and a good excursion can be easily made to the towns of Si Chiang Mai, Sangkhom and Chiang Khan. Cheap but reasonable accommodation is abundant and there is no shortage of waterfalls and caves to break up the journey.

Many people travel the route by bus. Some of the more athletic use bicycles, which can be rented in Nong Khai. Unlike the eastern route, the road also follows the river more closely, and you can sometimes see villagers panning for gold and small boats scurrying across the river.

Si Chiang Mai and Sangkhom

Spring-roll wrappers—produced by Vietnamese—and Saturday cockfights are the chief claims to fame of the village of Si Chiang Mai, on the banks of the Mekong, 40 km (25 miles) west of Nong Khai on Highway 2186. It's a pleasant if uninspiring town, laid out on a grid system and can provide a useful resting place for the night or a good lunchtime break on the route further west.

From Si Chiang Mai, Highway 2186 continues through grand countryside past little villages, winding through the hills to **Wat Hin Maek**, situated on the right hand side at 83 km (52 miles). This beautiful forest temple inhabited by a strict monastic Buddhist sect known as *thuthon*, contains a preserved corpse of its founder and various monastic retreats built on the edge of the river.

*Q*uintessence of the *Mekong's romance. Sunset looms over to Laos from the river bank near Chiang Khan.*

After passing the signposted **Than Thong Waterfalls** —good for a quick swim—the road continues through the hills before descending into the town of Sangkhom, the perfect place to spend the night in one of a handful of charming guesthouses on the river.

Those with the energy can rise at dawn the next day to visit the **Buddha Cave** of Phatak Sova, 2 km (1.2 miles) east of town and reached by a steep 45-minute hike up the mountain, from where you get superb views of the Mekong River and Laos and, occasionally, of gold panners, mainly old women digging in the sand. Afterwards, for pure relaxation try the old herbal-style saunas at the River Huts or DD Guest Houses with their perfect views of the river.

216

Chiang Khan

Situated at the end of an even more spectacular piece of road that snakes its way through the hills with stupendous views of the river is the sleepy town of Chiang Khan. Largely made up of wooden houses and set along the banks of the River it has striking views of the mountains beyond.

Shortly before you get there, you will pass a right turn to the **Kaeng Khut Khu Rapids**, which are best during October and November, but a good picnic spot at any time of year.

Besides the rapids and the delightful **Wat Pa Klang**, located in the centre of town, the pleasures of Chiang Khan are purely visual. All you need is time—and a camera. Wander down to the river and hire a boat to take you upriver, or explore the little streets and side stalls where the locals sit drinking Mekong whisky.

It was to the west of Chiang Khan that long-simmering border tensions between the Laotians and the Thais exploded in 1987. Today, however, the place has an air of calm about it and you can rent boats to see the small hill where the action took place. This is the last time you see the Mekong River until it reappears again in Chiang Kong in the Northern Region.

From Chiang Khan, most visitors head south to Loie town, but it is possible to continue by road as far as Tha

Li. This is a small town within easy reach of the Heuang River, just 8 km (5 miles) from the border with Laos.

Loei

The province of Loei is known as the "Siberia of Thailand" and is rich in mountains, caves and waterfalls, but there are freezing temperatures during the months of November and December, and the infrastructure is among the most basic in the country. Indeed until roads were built, the place was almost wholly inaccessible.

Today it has transport—buses and a three times weekly plane from Phitsanulok—but preserves something of the wild border feel, with its refugee camps and its singular local dialect.

Buses from Nong Khai arrive in Loei town, the rugged provincial capital situated 45 km (28 miles) south of Chiang Khan. It is better to continue on to Phu Kradung, the spectacular National Park lying 82 km (51 miles) to the south off Highway 201.

Phu Kradung

Even before you arrive, you can see the 60 sq km (23 sq miles) plateau, covered in mists in the early morning and surrounded by forest. Legend tells that the Park was named Phu Kradung (Bell Mountain) when a mysterious chiming sound echoed down to the surrounding villages at certain times of the year.

If you plan to climb the hill you should start early—the Visitors Centre closes at 3 p.m.—and prepare for a major hike. Porters can be hired next to the Information Centre to carry bags or, for an extra payment, they will even carry you. From the foot of the trail a signposted path climbs steeply through oak, pine and beach trees for some 5 km (3 miles) before emerging onto a vast plateau carpeted with grass and pine trees and, during March and April, with rhododendrons and daisies.

Enthusiasts generally rise at dawn and head to **Pha Nok Aen**, on the eastern edge of the plateau to witness the sunrise, and to Lomsak Cliff in the evening, some 12 km (7.5 miles) to the west for sunset. That still leaves lots of time to explore the 50 km (31 miles) of trails in the Park where if you are lucky you may run into an elephant—the Park is said to have 20—or, more often, into a ferocious mole, known as the eastern mole, which is found in abundance on the plateau and lives on a diet of lizards, mice and small birds.

To explore Phu Kradung away from the crowds, go on a weekday, and take walking shoes and a sweater. At night, temperatures can drop to freezing and even the locals appear to survive only on copious amounts of local whisky.

Phu Luang

For those with time, another magnificent Park lies in the vicinity, although it is harder to get to and more difficult to arrange. **Phu Luang Wildlife Reserve** lies near the town of Wang Saphung, some 50 km (31 miles) south of Loei off Highway 201 and is renowned for its high concentration of wildlife, including elephants and deer.

The best way to organize a visit is through the Tourist Information Centre in Loei, Tel: 811 776, or the Loei Administration Service, Tel: 800 776.

776.

If you turn up on spec, nobody at the Park Headquarters speaks a word of English, and even if they did, they would probably refer you back to the authorities in Loie. Groups are preferred, and you should make arrangements well in advance.

Khon Kaen

Nightclubs and supermarkets are the only real attraction of Khon Kaen, the administrative centre of Isaan and the one city in the north-east that can claim to have a university, to which people go to study agriculture and the production of carrots.

Like Korat and Udon, it was a US airbase and, like these cities, is more of an arrival and departure point than a destination in itself. There is, however, a **National Museum** on Kasikorn Tungsang Road with a collection of bronze and pottery from Ban Chiang, open Wednesday–Sunday 9 a.m.–noon and 1 p.m.–4 p.m. Eleven km (7 miles) south of town you can also visit the famous village of **Ban Chonnabot** known throughout the north-east for its production of silk. Buses leave from the terminal on Si Chan road near the nightmarket.

Whilst wandering around Khon Kaen, look out for *kunchien* (air dried pork sausage). The Chinese all over the country consume it in large quantities for breakfast. It is made from pork, and smoked and dried over a long period of time and tastes like a cross between black pudding and fermented pigs' trotters.

*S*ilk has rapidly become *Khon Kaen's greatest gift to the North-east.*

 ## Ban Chiang

Every archaeologist or historian will at some stage end up in the small village of Ban Chiang, a typical north-eastern settlement, but for the astounding discoveries that date back more than 5,000 years.

The first pots were discovered in 1966 by a young American student named Stephen Young. Later finds were sent for thermo-luminescence tests and were dated between 3,600 BC and 3,000 BC. Over the next two decades more than 18 tonnes of bronze, of iron tools, utensils, pots and skeletons were uncovered.

In 1974, the Fine Arts Department of Thailand and the University of Pennsylvania launched a joint venture

The joys of Isaan are found not in its cities, but away from the hustle and bustle in the rice fields that stretch to an endless horizon.

Chiang Khwang in Laos and settled here.

In the centre of town, a museum, open Wednesday–Sunday 9 a.m.–noon and 1 p.m.–4 p.m. displays black and white photographs and original red painted pots, clay crucibles and bronze tools. Many of the pots were made from clay mixed with rice husks to create a more durable body. Some were used as burial urns, others to carry water or store food.

A few hundred metres away from the museum there is an open excavation pit containing human skulls and pot rims. Outside the excavation pits cheap imitation pots are for sale and a few of the originals too, although the sale of this is strictly outlawed by the Fine Arts Department.

Ban Chiang can be reached only by taxi or by buses, which leave every hour from the Thai Isaan market in Udon Thani or, alternatively, by Highway 22.

There is nowhere to stay in Ban Chiang, so you have to head back to Udon Thani, the main provincial town and transportation hub in the area, which lies 50 km (31 miles) to the west. If you have never visited a Thai-style nightclub before, this is the place to try it. To find one, just wander down the street and look out for the flashing lights. You won't have to go far.

on Ban Chiang and adjacent sites to verify the early discoveries. The results prove beyond doubt that the region had an advanced cultural and technological development which may have predated civilizations in China.

Sometime around 200 AD, the people of Ban Chiang moved away, leaving the place deserted until 200 years ago when four families migrated from

Abundant Fruits Ripening on Eastern Shores

On the sun-blessed stretch of land that cuts its way east along the Gulf of Thailand lies the region famed for its fruit orchards and green valleys. But to papayas, mangos and durians have been added beaches and islands, gemstones and fishing villages. In fact so many attractions that the people of Bangkok are trying to turn this into a weekend riviera.

Where the rolling hills of the north-east meet the Gulf of Thailand is lush countryside, a vast orchard stretching along a narrow strip of coast to the Cambodian border. Here the rainfall is high, the countryside fertile and, off-shore, there is an abundance of fish and islands.

Economically too this is the region of wealth: of gas pumped offshore from the vast industrial complexes of Mata Phut; and of gems extracted from the mining town of Chantaburi,

*F*ruits *in the Gulf are as abundant as fish. Here a local picks papaya.*

home to the biggest sapphire-producing region in Thailand. But above all, the Gulf of Thailand is renowned for Pattaya, the small fishing village which in ten years has been transformed into a vast entertainment metropolis on the beach, surrounded by condominiums and golf courses, elephant *kraals,* water parks, and crocodile farms. Only beyond Pattaya does the region return to normal, with the sleepy towns of Ban Phe, the idyllic island of Ko Samui and the smaller fishing towns, destinations for those with a little more time and sense of adventure.

The Gulf of Thailand is the easiest region to explore. A constant flow of buses runs from the bus terminal on Sukhumvit Road, opposite Soi 42, to Chonburi, Pattaya, Rayong, Ban Phe

223

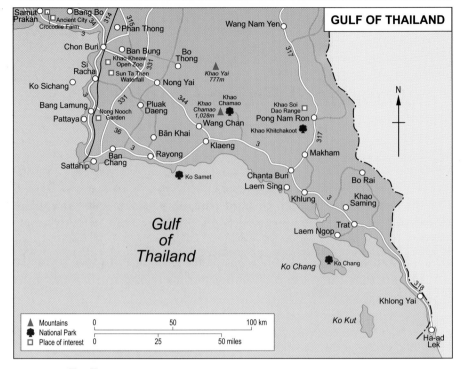

Samut Prakan — Bang Bo — Ancient City — Crocodile Farm — 314 — 315 — Phan Thong — Wang Nam Yen — **GULF OF THAILAND**

Chon Buri — Ban Bung — Bo Thong — Khao Kheaw Open Zoo — 331 — 317 — Si Racha — Sun Ta Then Waterfall — Nong Yai — Khao Yai 777m — Ko Sichang — N

Bang Lamung — Pluak Daeng — 344 — Khao Chamao — Khao Soi Dao Range — Nong Nooch Garden — Khao Chamao 1,028m — Pong Nam Ron — Pattaya — Wang Chan — Khao Khitchakoot — Ban Khai — 36 — 3 — Klaeng — 317

Ban Chang — Rayong — Makham — Sattahip — 3

Ko Samet — Chanta Buri — Laem Sing — Bo Rai — Khao Saming — Khlung — 3

Gulf of Thailand — Laem Ngop — Trat — Ko Chang — Ko Chang

Khlong Yai — 318

▲ Mountains — 🌳 National Park — ☐ Place of interest — 0 — 50 — 100 km — 0 — 25 — 50 miles — Ko Kut — Ha-ad Lek

M *ap of the Gulf of Thailand.*

and Chantaburi. Only at the far tip, beyond the town of Trat and around Ko Chang, is transport less frequent. But even here, development plans are being drawn up; plans that in time will turn this into yet another major international string of beach resorts.

From Bangkok to Bang Saen

Only 15 years ago, there was an old bumpy road leading from Bangkok down the Eastern Seaboard, through salt farms and mangrove forest to the provincial town of Chonburi. Now the four-lane Bang Na Trat Highway cuts

the travel time from Bangkok by half, but misses most of the local colour with fishing villages replaced by gas stations and factories.

Still, by taking the old Sukhumvit Highway to Samut Prakarn, a pleasant trip can be made, stopping at the Crocodile Farm and at the Ancient City before continuing to Chonburi and Pattaya. The trip can easily be done in a day, with the option of a longer stay.

Chonburi

The first major town on the drive south-east is an unspectacular provincial hub best known for its annual Buffalo Festival, held around the first full moon of the eleventh lunar month—which is generally at the end of October.

Chonburi's only other claim to fame lies in its associations with a great king in Thai history. Taksin, a former general, was credited with expelling the Burmese from Ayutthaya in 1767. He later went insane and was bludgeoned to death with a scented sandalwood club, but remains a regional hero.

A statue of Taksin stands outside **Wat Yai Intharam** near the old market in the centre of town where he is supposed to have spent a night. Inside there are murals depicting the Buddha's struggle with Mara, the spirit of evil, and roof finials, moulded with stucco angels kneeling in prayer.

Ang Sila

The sound of workers chipping away at granite pestles is the first noise you are likely to hear at Ang Sila, the small fishing port lying 5 km (3 miles) beyond Chonburi. Besides prolific production of these instruments, used to pound chillis, the town is famous for pickled fish, and woven cotton fabric, which can be purchased at the nearby stalls. After looking at the shops, visit the sleepy pier to the south, to which are tied dozens of brightly painted fishing boats, and where odours of the famous *nam pla* sauce fill the air.

A couple of km further east overlooking the bay is Khao Sam Muk hill with a striking chinese temple called **Sala Jao Mae Saam Muk**, dedicated to a young lady named Muk who, after a forlorn love affair, leapt off the cliff.

From Khao Sam Muk, the road curves around the bay before descending into Bang Saen.

*T*he Gulf of Thailand *is loved by poets for its inspiration, by fishermen for its catch, and by holidaymakers for its beaches.*

Bang Saen

Most visitors miss out Bang Saen, the small town 10 km (6 miles) from Chonburi, in their haste to get to Pattaya. However, locals savour the area and have turned it into a very popular weekend beach resort.

Bang Saen has two attractions that are especially worth visiting. Along the beach road is a giant water park called **Ocean World**, with water slides, swimming pools and children's paddling areas; and on the campus of Sinakarinwirot University at the **Scientific Marine Centre**, open Tuesday–Sunday 8.30 a.m.–4 p.m., the largest aquarium in South-east Asia has displays of sea horses, corals and rabbit fish shown in tanks weighing up to 200 tons.

The beach itself stretches for around 1.5 km (1 mile), fringed by palm trees, only the sand a little dirty and the water a little murky. But it is possible to swim, and there are few foreigners; there is a charming air of faded old-worldly grandeur.

In the nearby restaurants try the local delicacies like *pla muuk* (squid) and *khai maeng da talay* (crab's eggs).

From Bang Saen, a pleasant side trip can be taken to the **Khao Khiao Zoo**, 14 km (9 miles) to the south-east, which occupies some 480 hectares (1,200 acres), contains more than 50 species of wildlife, and has one of the largest bird aviaries in the country. Accommodation is available, but it should be booked ahead at the Dusit Zoo in Bangkok.

Pattaya

Thailand's most notorious beach resort lies just 45 km (28 miles) south-east of Bang Saen, signposted down a narrow lane that crosses over a bridge parallel with a shallow bay filled with fishing boats.

Pattaya's reputation has not been made without good reason. Its ingredients of available young girls, or boys, its endless beer bars and nightclubs and whole-hearted dedication to the pleasures of *sanuk* once made it the most popular gathering point in Thailand.

These days it has also become a byword for dirty beaches, polluted waters and overcrowding, and an example of the sort of tourism which Thailand is now trying to avoid.

King Taksin started the ball rolling when he camped his army here some 200 years ago. But it was not until the Americans, who were stationed at the giant air base at U-Tapao during the

---

Almond Eyed Beauties

As far back as the 17th century, reports of the beauty and joyousness of the Siamese inhabitants were emerging from explorers who sailed up the Chao Phya River. One Englishman of the name Samuel Purchas reported "His power is great, usually warring with 1,000 elephant and 2,000 men. The zone is hot,the women beautiful and the inhabitants much given to pleasure and ryot". 19th-century naturalist Carl Bock did not entirely agree. He found the men and the women almost indistinguishable because of their short haircuts, and complained that they painted their faces white.

*M**ap of Pattaya*

226

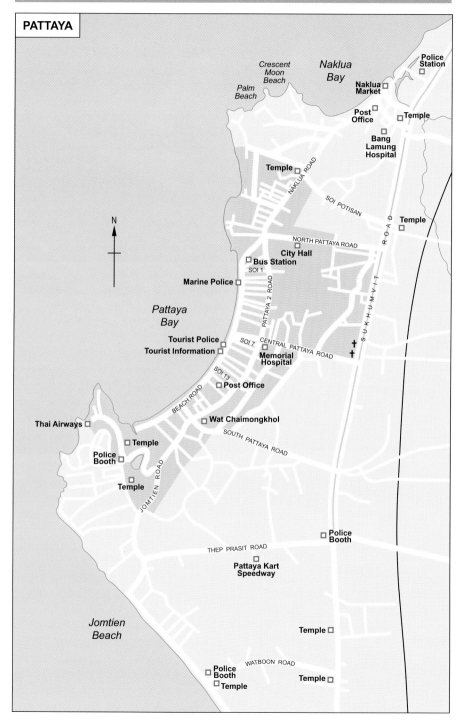

PATTAYA

Crescent Moon Beach

Naklua Bay

Palm Beach

Police Station

Naklua Market

Post Office

Temple

Bang Lamung Hospital

Temple

NAKLUA ROAD

SOI POTISAN

SUKHUMVIT ROAD

Temple

N

NORTH PATTAYA ROAD

City Hall

Bus Station

SOI 1

Marine Police

PATTAYA 2 ROAD

Pattaya Bay

Tourist Police

Tourist Information

SOI 7

CENTRAL PATTAYA ROAD

Memorial Hospital

SOI 13

BEACH ROAD

Post Office

Thai Airways

Wat Chaimongkhol

Temple

SOUTH PATTAYA ROAD

Police Booth

Temple

JOMTIEN ROAD

Police Booth

THEP PRASIT ROAD

Pattaya Kart Speedway

Jomtien Beach

Temple

WATBOON ROAD

Police Booth

Temple

Temple

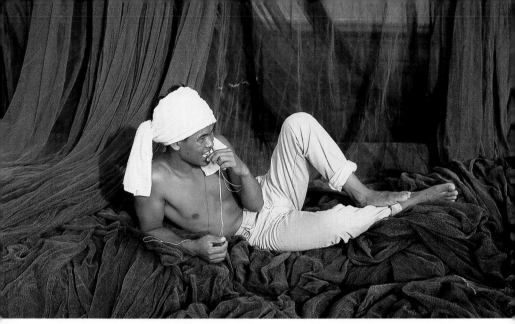

Vietnam War, were sent on rest and recreation that the place boomed.

Over the next decade, rooms sprang up everywhere and fortunes were made. Then came the poor planning and overcrowding which have transformed the sleepy fishing village into a sprawling heap of bars and nightclubs.

That's not to say everyone is disappointed. Nearly a million visitors still descend on the town every year to party, to stay in its smart hotels, to play golf and to dine on delicious seafood. And whilst some may be unhappy, most leave with memories if not of joy, then of the most extreme place they have ever visited in their lives.

Orientation

Pattaya has a 4 km (2.5 mile) road that runs alongside the beach and further inland another parallel road with short lanes or *sois* interconnecting them.

The two main streets known as Beach Road and Beach Road 2 are

A fisherman on the Gulf takes a break from the ardours of a life on the sea.

one-way streets, and minibuses taking passengers cost a flat Bt5.

For quieter places to stay you must head to the northern part of town. It's less crowded, more exclusive, given over to smarter massage parlours and to fine restaurants. Southern Pattaya is where the cheaper places are to be found, nestling between bars and rows of stores selling fake Gucci bags and Rolex watches.

Continue beyond South Pattaya and you will come to another headland known as Hat Cliff, where the exclusive Royal Cliff Beach Hotel is situated in its own little world and, further around, the long crescent-shaped bay known as Jomthien.

The seven km (4 mile) beach with its wide strip of sand and palm trees was until recently overlooked by developers, but has now become a booming concrete jungle. Five-star hotels, condominiums and ugly shopping arcades, cater largely for Thais and for the sprinkling of foreigners who seek an alternative to touts and beer bars.

Around Town

Before going anywhere, drop in at the Tourist Office at 382/1 Pattaya Beach Road, Tel: 428 750, which provides updates and useful information on festivities and attractions in the region and is open seven days a week.

Afterwards you can shop for gems, jewellery, silk, handicrafts, or Thai fishermen's trousers in the shopping centres, stalls and fashionable boutiques that line Beach Road and are adjacent to the major beachside hotels.

Pattaya also has a water park, conveniently situated just a few km from the centre of town at 345 Jomthien Beach Road and easily reached by minibus.

Finally for good views of town, climb the hill off South Pattaya Road where there is a big Buddha image, staring serenely towards the nightclubs below.

Day Excursions

To discover the area around Pattaya hire a car or jeep in town or take one of the organized excursions arranged by hotels and travel agents. First stop for many visitors is the village of **Nong Nooch**, 15 km (9 miles) to the east and set in 550 acres of exotic palms, orchids and cacti. Daily shows at 10 a.m. and 3 p.m. feature folk dances, martial arts and cock fighting. Accommodation is available in bungalows, which should be booked in advance at their Pattaya office, Tel: 429 321.

Closer to town, is the **Mini Siam**, the third miniature town of its kind in the world featuring more than 100 historic towns on a 1/25th scale. Those with an interest in elephants should head to the **Elephant Kraal**, located behind the Pattaya Orphanage on the Sukhumvit Highway, where performances take place daily at 10 a.m. and 2.30 p.m.

Whilst for those with equestrian aspirations, visit the **Reo Park Ranch**, 30 minutes from the city on Highway 3 near the Siam Country Club.

Pattaya even has its own car racing track at the Bira International Circuit, some 14 km (9 miles) to the east on the road to Rayong, Highway 36, where at weekends events range from pick-ups to motorcycles to Formula 3 racing cars.

Golfers can take their pick of three courses in the vicinity. At the Siam Country Club, Tel: 428 002, signposted at km 145 on the Sukhumvit Highway you will find an 18-hole course, whilst a 40-minute drive towards the town of Sattahip will bring you to the Royal Thai Navy Golf Course, Tel: 428 422. Also highly acclaimed is the Bang Phra Course near Chonburi with a motel, a swimming pool and reasonable green fees. Reserve beforehand.

Beaches and Islands

The islands around Pattaya were once as colourful as their names. These days **Ko Larn**, **Ko Sak** and **Ko Pa** are no longer unspoilt, but they still make pleasant side trips and good, if expensive, places to eat the local seafood. Regular speedboats run to Ko Larn (Bald Island) taking 20 minutes. Cruises by converted fishing boats take one hour. Ticket booths are opposite

Beaches and hotels are abundant, but to find the real Pattaya you must go out at night.

the TAT office on Beach Road. Tours can arranged leaving at 8.30 a.m. and returning at 5 p.m.

Beyond Ko Larn, you can visit the smaller islands of Ko Sak as well as **Ko Lin** and Ko Pa. Boats can be arranged along the waterfront.

For the best mainland beaches within easy distance of Pattaya, catch a minibus to **Jomthien**, 7 km (4 miles) to the south. Waterskiers, windsurfers and sailors should head to the northern end of the beach close to Surf House, where more than 20 different schools rent equipment and provide lessons.

Scuba diving courses can be booked ranging from one day in a swimming pool to three-day offshore island excursions. Enquire at Seafari dive shop, Pattaya Beach Road, Tel: 428 126.

Some hotels now organize deep sea fishing trips ranging from one day to a week, on fully equipped boats. Barracudas, sharks and marlin are frequently caught. Charges are generally reasonable and the catch is good, especially during the winter months. Enquire at your hotel.

Nightlife

You won't need a guide to show you Pattaya's nightlife. Bars and nightclubs are endemic—the only constraints are your own morals and the size of your wallet.

As a rule, if it's beer bars you are after, head for the area around **Soi Diamond**, which is a magnet for every form of bar, strip joint or show. Bars do not generally charge entry fees, but as in Bangkok, always check before ordering a drink.

Dotted along Beach Road you will also find boxing rings, discos like the Marina—best after 2 a.m—and countless other drinking establishments.

Transvestite bars are another Pattaya speciality. For internationally renowned cabarets, visit Tiffany on Pattaya 2 Road, Tel: 429 642. Shows begin at 7 p.m., 8.30 p.m. and 10 p.m., but such is the demand, you should arrive early or book seats in advance. At 78/14 Pattaya 2 Road, is the famous Alcazar transvestite cabaret, Tel: 418 746, with shows at 7 p.m., 9 p.m. and 10 p.m. and a photocall of the "girls"

230

in the car park after the performance.

Finally, for those wanting good food, Pattaya has plenty of restaurants. For cheaper food, try the markets in the area near Soi Diamond. Elsewhere its chips, *nachos,* pancakes, hamburgers and yet more bars.

From Pattaya to Ban Phe

From Pattaya follow Highway 3 past the fishing village of Ban Saray and the old US airbase at U-Tapao to the town of Rayong, famed for its malodorous *nam pla,* a sauce made from fermented fish, salt and garlic. After visiting the **King Taksin Shrine** situated at Wat Lum Mahachai Chumpon and the old fishing port, continue to the village of Ban Phe.

Ko Samet

Eighty five km (53 miles) east of Pattaya and a world away is the beautiful palm-fringed island of Ko Samet former home of Sunthorn Phu, one of Thailand's greatest poets.

The island nestles just 40 minutes offshore from Ban Phe and is easily reached by fishing boats which leave regularly for Na Daan Pier.

Unlike Ko Samui it is relatively small and as yet uncluttered by large hotels. What's more, along the eastern side it has good beaches running almost the entire length of the island.

At the northern end is **Hat Sai Kaeo**, a 15-minute walk from the landing stage. With it's fine sand and turquoise seas it has, not suprisingly, become a popular gathering point with countless bungalows and restaurants.

Sunthorn's Legacy

Besides being a poet of considerable standing, Sunthorn Phu was also a man of admirable will, although his true character and origins remain under fierce debate. One of several works contends that he was the son of a coal transporter who first demonstrated his poetic gifts by writing on the walls of the local temple. Another, by the late poet Prince Prem Purachatra, suggests that he was the son of a wet-nurse who became a government clerk, only to be jailed as the result of prolific drinking and a heated affair with a lady of the palace. Phu is subsequently said to have emerged to become a retainer and poet in the court of King Rama IV. One last account by one Montri Umavijana, concludes that Sunthorn Phu, a romantic and a man of talent, died poor and disillusioned. Few doubts exist, however, on the quality of his work. In 1987, the United Nations Educational Scientific and Cultural Organization (UNESCO) belatedly recognized him as one of the world's most eminent poets.

To the south is **Ao Phai** (Paradise Beach) a delightful stretch of palm-fringed sand leading to **Ao Thap Thim** and **Dantawan** (Sunflower Beach) and beyond to the long crescent shaped **Ao Wong Duan** (Seahorse Beach), the most developed beach.

Continuing south of Ao WongDuan you will come to **Ao Thian** (Candlelight Beach) made up of rocky coves and further around the island, a sprinkling of less developed beaches where people come to camp out on the sand.

In 1981, the eastern part of Ko Samet was declared a nature reserve, and overnight stays were banned. But today you will find accommodation, most of it basic and expensive, all around the island. At weekends or bank holidays, especially, it can be almost impossible to get a place to stay. But during the week it remains quiet and beautiful with just the odd mound of rubbish as a reminder that anyone was ever there.

Daytime activities on Ko Samet consist almost exclusively of swimming in

Sunthorn Phu may not have known it, but when he came to Ko Samet in search of his muse he set a trend. Now fleets of boats dutifully await the next batch of inspired "poets".

Map of Ko Samet.

the clear turquoise waters, short boat trips and walks around the island. Don't expect much in the way of night entertainment though. Besides malarial mosquitoes—you should take prophylactics—and Bill's Garage Disco on the main road near Hat Sai Kaew, most people sit on the beach drinking Mekong or retire early to bed.

For those in search of greater luxury than can be found on Ko Samet, the mainland strip from Ban Phe to Klaeng along Highway 3145 offers a number of hotels and resorts with long

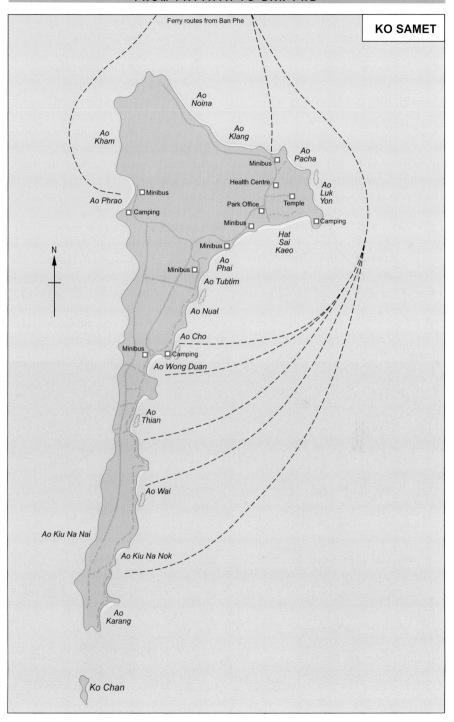

KO SAMET

Ferry routes from Ban Phe

Ao Noina

Ao Kham

Ao Klang

Minibus

Ao Pacha

Health Centre

Ao Luk Yon

Minibus

Ao Phrao

Park Office

Temple

Camping

Minibus

Camping

Hat Sai Kaeo

N

Minibus

Ao Phai

Minibus

Ao Tubtim

Ao Nual

Ao Cho

Minibus

Camping

Ao Wong Duan

Ao Thian

Ao Wai

Ao Kiu Na Nai

Ao Kiu Na Nok

Ao Karang

Ko Chan

stretches of white sand and relatively clean water whence day trips can be arranged to Ko Samet.

From Ban Phe to Chantaburi

Somewhere beyond Ban Phe, you cross an invisible line marking the furthest point for weekenders from the capital. The main road, Highway 3, is still crowded with trucks carrying fresh

*K*ing Taksin came to Chantaburi to rally his forces, and the Catholics, to avoid persecution. Now people come to admire its old-world architecture.

produce to the capital, but there is a slower feel to the place, the people are friendlier, the hills higher and more tropical and the Thais increasingly replaced by people of Khmer origin.

This is the area known as the orchard of Thailand, producing much of the nation's fruit from its plantations of mangoes, durians and papaya. For much of the year stalls line the road, where you can stop to try some of finest fruits the Kingdom has to offer.

Chantaburi

Magnificently situated in lush hills is the town of Chantaburi (City of the Moon), the gem capital of Thailand.

Taksin came here in 1767 to rally his forces before re-taking Ayutthaya. But the architecture of the town also reflects earlier occupations by the

Sunsets on Ko Chang are as abundant as pineapples, but are always in season!

Bt25,000 a carat. Potential purchasers should beware: fakes are abundant.

To see where the gems come from you head north of town on Highway 3249 to the area that is known as **Khao Ploi Waan** (Sapphire-Ring Mountain).

In the past, all you needed to do was to wander down any dirt track to come across groups of miners digging holes with spades and buckets. The earth would then be sifted by members of the family, and any gems sold in the local market. These days a lot of the mines have tractors and the earth is pumped up through jet pipes of water. Vast tracts of forest have been cleared leaving gaping scars and countless holes for the unwary to fall into.Some miners strike it lucky, and in the nearby towns you may see flimsy corrugated mining shacks with television aerials and brand new jeeps parked outside. The majority make little more than Bt100–Bt200 a day.

In nearby Pailin, across the border with Cambodia, the world's biggest ruby was uncovered at the turn of the century. Generally however the gems mined around Chantaburi are smaller and less pure, and these days because of shrinking supply, traders often import or smuggle stones from Sri Lanka, Australia and Laos.

On the way back to town, look for stalls selling delicate reed mats, known as the *sua Chantaburi*. These are made

French, and, centuries before them, by the Khoms, a powerful Indian-influenced kingdom in Cambodia.

To explore the old part of town, wander down to the banks of the Chantaburi River, which meanders past old wooden houses. Many are still inhabited by Vietnamese Catholics who fled to Thailand in the late 19th century after persecution from the Vietnamese Emperor Gia Long.

The Vietnamese Catholics are also responsible for the unlikely looking **Church of the Immaculate Conception**, the largest Christian church in Thailand, situated over the bridge on Tha Luang Road.

Continue to the **Gem Market** off Trok Kachang Road, to the south-east of town, where purchasers from all over the world gather to examine piles of gems, red rubies and star sapphires. Many of the gems are sold in lots of up to 100 stones, priced at as low as Bt50 a carat. Top-graded sapphires may command prices more than from tanned reeds and spun into mats in the small village of San Hin on the outskirts of town

Phliu Waterfall National Park

A 30-minute drive south-east of Chantaburi on Highway 3 will bring you to the beautiful Phliu Waterfall signposted off the main road to the left. The Waterfall was much favoured by King Chulalongkorn, Rama V, who built a mausoleum there in 1876 in memory of his Royal Consort Queen Sunanda who died when she capsized on the river near Bang Pa-In in 1876. To escape the crowds, try to get there during the week. Around the waterfall you can follow trails up the hillside and afterwards treat yourself to *khai yang* (barbecued chicken), Mekong whisky and other fortifying substances. Buses leave for the park from in front of the Chantaburi municipal market.

Trat and Ko Chang

The last provincial town before you reach the Cambodian border is little more than a throughway for most travellers. For 19 km (12 miles) beyond Trat, along Highway 3148 lies one of the last undiscovered gems in the Gulf of Thailand: the 52-island National Park of Ko Chang.

To get there you must drive or catch a *songthaew* to the small town of Laem Ngop from where boats leave twice daily to Ko Chang, taking an hour and a half.

Although Ko Chang and the surrounding islands have only recently been primed for tourism, they are no stranger to royalty. King Rama VI visited Ko Kood in 1911. And before that King Chulalongkorn, Rama V, visited Ko Chang in 1889. Near Nonsee Waterfall in Ko Chang, there is still a stone bearing Rama V's initials.

The chief attractions of Ko Chang, though, are beautiful beaches, and inland, the largely forested interior, which still provides a natural habitat for wildboar, deer, langurs, gibbons, and wildfowl. Several waterfalls and caves can be reached on foot or by motorbike. Boats generally stop first at Klong Sond, situated on the north-west side of the island before continuing to the more beautiful **White Sands** *(Sai Khao)*, **Klong Prao** and **Bang Boa**. Accommodation ranges from basic wooden huts to more comfortable bungalows, but these days plans are afoot to extensively develop the island.

Instead of taking the boat to Ko Chang, you can also visit the smaller islands of **Ko Kradat** (Paper Island), **Koh Maak** (Areca Nut Island) and **Ko Kood** which lie further to the south. These can only be reached directly from Laem Ngop and contain a spattering of resorts. For details, enquire on arrival at the pier.

One word of warning. Ko Chang is a high danger zone for malaria and the authorities in Bangkok strongly advise anti-mosquito repellent and, better still, a mosquito net. Prophylatics such as Maloprim and Nivoquin have proved ineffective as the mosquitoes are in many cases immune to them. For further information, contact the Malaria Division in Bangkok, Tel: 281 6650.

Art and Culture

The first works of art in Thailand were pots made from clay, decorated with bright colours and dating back thousands of years. Then came cave paintings, beautifully carved stone Buddha images, great epic poems and dances.

Many of the early works were influenced by the great ancient civilizations of India and China, by the Khmers and even the Greeks. But to the originals, the Thais added their own interpretations and colours, to their temples, golden spires, and to their dances, a greater sensitivity. The results reflect not only the calm and unity of the Buddhist Kingdom, but above all the character of the Thais with their love of beauty, of colour and joie de vivre.

Exquisite movement underlies the highest form of drama: the Thai dance traditionally only performed before kings.

Dance and Drama

There can be few things in life that inspire the Thais to such a pitch of fervour and delight as a dramatic presentation of the Ramakien. This great epic colours their dances, and their woodcarvings and even their temples.

The legend is taken from the great Indian epic, the *Ramayana.* The story tells of Rama and his beautiful wife Sita, who are banished to the forests by the King of Ayutthaya, and of Sita's abduction by Ravana, the ten-headed demon King. But after numerous battles with birds and monkey armies, Rama wins her back and triumphantly takes her back to the court where he reclaims the throne.

Readings of the *Ramakien* can last for days. Normally, however, only a few of the 136 episodes will be presented, thereby providing a digestible amount, whilst allowing the audience to participate in a myth to which they are completely accustomed.

The Ramayana is also the subject of shadow puppetry, and of Thai classical dances known as the *Khon* dances and the *Lakhon* dances. These largely developed out of the royal courts of ancient Siam where they were acted before the king in lavish costumes. *Khon* dances were traditionally performed by men concealed behind brightly coloured ornate masks and the *Lakhon* dances, by women.

The characters do not speak, but each movement of the hands reflects a subtle change of mood or feeling. To the Thais the movements are a story without words and the figures, symbols behind masks. But to visitors it can seem like a drama with no action, a play with no scenes.

Literature

At the heart of Thai literature are the two great themes of the Ramayana and Buddhism. These influenced not only the very earliest tales passed on by word of mouth, but have provided a strong framework even for contemporary literature.

The core of the Buddhist philosophy is to be found in the *Jataka Tales,* which relate stories of the 500 earlier lives of the Buddha. These tales, found throughout the Buddhist world, expound a particular virtue on the long journey to Enlightenment, and were to provide a model for the tragic hero in Thai literature.

During the early 19th century, a new romantic genre found expression through monk and poet Sunthorn Phu (1786–1855). Strong-willed, controversial, a man of the people, Phu took legends of old and recreated them in simple verse; a sort of Thai Homer, who touched the common people with his universal themes of love and loss.

The Thai love for poetry extended to other works too. Much of Shakespeare was translated into magnificent Thai by King Vajiravudh; so successfully, in fact, that the *Merchant of Venice* was once thought of as a Thai play.

In contrast to earlier works, modern Thai literature has tended to focus on more secular matters. Letters from Thailand by Botan, Thailand in Crisis by S. Sivaraksa, A Child of the Northeast by Kampoon Boontawee and People of Esarn by Pira Sudham are just some of the best-known works of the century which have been translated into English. The books have tended towards a fierce realism. Yet what has emerged is also essentially Thai in spirit, mixing Buddhism with contemporary life and the new challenges and uncertainties of a changing world.

Image from the Ramayana—*Thailand's best known epic.*

Music

The classical orchestra in Thailand is called the phipat and was traditionally used to accompany the Khon and Lakhon dances.

The orchestra is made up of five woodwind instruments and one percussion instrument. These give rise to strange twanging melodies especially composed to convey dramatic moods like anger, sorrow, conquest or fear.

The most common instruments in the classical Thai *piphat* are the *peenai,* an oboe-like instrument with a bulging wooden body, *ching* or finger cymbals, and *king wong yai,* a semicircular set of graded gongs. The most-prized instrument is the *ranart,* a curved wooden xylophone, which emits a tinkling sound often compared to summer rain. There is also a *taphon,* a barreldrum made with wood from a jackfruit tree and often a *saw duang,* which is a two-stringed instrument resembling a croquet mallet.

Thailand has even developed its own brand of popular music. It sounds like a cross between Arab music and accelerated second-rate pop, and is so popular that the ancient classical sounds are now becoming almost obsolete.

Religious Art

The greatest and most visible expression of Thai art is to be found in its religious figures, in the statues of Buddha, glittering temples and dazzling spires pointing to the skies. Many of the temples are adorned with intricate mosaics of coloured glass and porcelain, others with woodcarvings and elaborate designs fashioned from inlaid pieces of mother of pearl, or powerful mural paintings.

The images often depict the future Enlightened One as a man or an animal, or the Buddha's victory over the tempter Mara. Sometimes they show the serpent or *naga,* who protected the Buddha with its hood from the rain and sunshine, and coiled its body up into a seat for the Buddha to sit on.

The Buddha figure itself by tradition has 32 major features and 80 secondary features, although only a few are actually represented in art. The body is to be of harmonious proportions with broad shoulders and narrow hips. The eyes are downcast, shaped like lotus buds, the mouth smiling gently to enhance the aura of inner peace. The lobes of the ears are long, denoting wisdom, and the fingers are curved.

The stance of the figure and position of the hands also has symbolic importance. A Buddha standing with his right hand placed over his left and his eyes open is in a position of "mindfulness". The posture recalls the Buddha after enlightenment, when he stood still under the *bodhi* tree for seven days considering the suffering of all living things. The Buddha with both hands held to his chest, the right palm over the left, is in a position of "contemplation" and with the right hand raised is "dispelling fear". The most popular pose is that of *bhumisparsha mudra* (earth touching), with the right hand on the knee pointing down to the earth. This represents the Buddha at the moment of enlightenment, when an earthquake occurred and a profusion of lotus blooms appeared.

Early Buddhas, especially those from the pre-Khmer Period, tend towards rigid symmetry with squarer proportions and with curved eyebrows. During the Khmer and Lopburi periods they became more finely delineated, with a greater use of expression, often dressed like Kings or seated on the great *naga.*

As the centuries went by the Buddhas became more perfect, more majestic and more serene, the solidity of the early works being replaced by a fluid sensitivity. During the Sukhothai period, the highpoint of Thai art, they acquired the serene oval faces, the delicately shaped brows and the timeless feel of calm and enlightenment. In the later Ayutthaya period, the Buddha figures became more elongated with more stylized features, rich ornamentation and heads topped by a lotus bud. In the Bangkok period, few innovations have been made, with the figures copied from earlier styles.

But sculptors of the later periods continued to depict the Buddha in the traditional poses—walking, standing, sittin and reclining, the final position of the Buddha on his deathbed at the moment of attaining nirvana.

Characteristics of the Major Periods

Pre-Khmer (5th–10th Century AD)
The sculpture of this period is very similar to that of the Gupta dynasty in India during the 4th–8th century.The main features are curved eyebrows joined at the bridge of the nose, rigid symmetry, body and limbs modelled as if sexless and large spiral curls of hair.

Khmer and Lopburi (7–10th Century)
The faces in this period are more finely delineated and individual, with greater use of expression. Often the Buddha is depicted as universal emperor wearing long ear pendants and jewelled collars, with the *ushnisha* ornamented with lotus petals. The images reflect the Khmer belief in the divinity of the King and Buddha.The main features are the predominance of stone carving, hair that looks more like scales and long ear lobes, and the Buddha image is often depicted seated upon the coils of the great *naga* serpent.

Lan Na (13th–16th Century)
The sculptures produced in the Lan Na Kingdom reflect influences from Haripunjaya, Angkor, Sukhothai, Sri Lanka, India and Burma. The early images were stronger, more virile, clothed in an open robe. Later they became more elongated without the richness and grandeur.The main features are a plump oval face, pronounced nose, small mouth, heavy solidity of the body with large shoulders and narrow hips

Sukhothai (13th–15th Century)
The Sukhothai period is regarded as the highpoint of Thai art. The Buddha is depicted in a state of full enlightenment, with relaxed muscles, an enduring serenity and soft, slightly feminine features.The main features are a long and oval face , a nose shaped—according to the sculptures—like a parrot's beak, arms that are long and sinous like the trunk of an elephant, a curved sweep of the arched eyebrows, and hair that forms a delicate v shape at the top of the brow. The legs of seated figures are raised one above the other.

Ayutthaya (15th–19th Century)
The sculpture at Ayutthaya was influenced by Sukhothai and Khmer styles. The images and gestures are more varied than in other periods, with greater emphasis on ornamentation and on §a new form of Buddha—Buddha Crowned in Monastic Robe. In the late 17th century, this movement reached its peak with images made from bronze, stucco, wood, silver and lacquer The main features are highly stylized features and an elongated body. The head is topped by a cone of flat rings decorated with the lotus bud, jewels are added around the neck, on the arms and across the chest, and decorated wing-like ornaments extend beyond the

ears. There is a predominance of images showing the Buddha seated in the position of victory over Mara.

Bangkok (18th Century)
No new style. Figures copied from the Sukhothai and Ayutthaya periods and encrusted with gold and gems.

For a people who can run up beautiful flower bracelets and fine celadon pots the highest form of artistry is still reserved for the Buddha itself. Here from the Khmer and Lopburi period.

241

Island Beach Paradise Amidst Turquoise Seas

When the gods made Thailand, they sprinkled it with an abundance of sparkling white beaches and islands. They added turquoise seas, crystal sands, rich marine life, and to complete the idyllic picture—some of the best seafood in the region. Those gifts may no longer be a secret, but to most visitors, they remain an unending lure.

South of Bangkok and along the narrow strip of land that snakes its way down the Malay Peninsula for over 1,100 km (700 miles) lie the beaches for which Thailand is renowned; miles of white sand, of palm trees and, offshore, there are dazzling islands and spectacular rock formations.

This is the location of legendary Phuket and Ko Samui, of Krabi and of the lesser known island National Parks of Ko Tarutoa, Ko Surin and

Commuting in the South has its advantages. Even the fishermen find no traffic jams.

Ko Similan. It is also the place from which the best seafood comes, where the ferociously hot fish-kidney curry (*keng tai pla*) and the sumptuous prawns with coconuts (*tom ka kung*) is made.

Many of the island resorts now have five-star hotels and luxury swimming pools, fine restaurants and watersports. Others, simple bungalows with fishing boats and colourful villages. Away from the main tourist destinations, there are still uninhabited islands reached only by chartered boats or sailing cruisers where there is nothing to disturb the sound of the sea and of birds overhead.

Besides its beaches, the South also has other attractions, although many of them are rarely visited. Some of the

243

most impressive scenery is found along the west coast—staggering limestone cliff formations and rain forest, caves and waterfalls. Even down the east coast, with its flatter landscape and endless coconut plantations, there are lakes, bird parks and tropical paradise islands.

Between the 8th and 13th centuries, the South was an independent kingdom and part of the Srivijaya empire, which ruled a string of principalities in Indonesia, Thailand and Malaysia. Even today the region is still dotted with old cities, and historical monuments in the towns of Nakhon Si Thammarat and Songkhla.

History has also shaped the character of the southern inhabitants known as the Thai Pak. Southerners are proud. They are also different to the people of the Central Plains, with a distinct dialect and a distinctive architecture. In the extreme south, and especially beyond Hat Yai, *wats* give way to mosques, and Buddhists to Malay Muslims, with veils and the feel of Malaysia. These people have long seen themselves as independent, and for decades have been fighting for secession. But these days trouble is rare, and the few visitors who make it here are more likely to find smiles and charming scenery than radical independence seekers and fundamentalists.

Because of the vast distances involved, most visitors travelling south from Bangkok prefer to head directly for the beaches by train or by bus. But driving offers a wonderful opportunity to explore the region. There are good roads and plenty of accommodation along the way. Indeed for those with the time, a circuit can be made driving down the western coast, crossing over to Hat Yai and down as far as Narathiwat on the Malaysian border, then returning up the eastern coast via Surat Thani.

For those who cannot face the long distances involved and who prefer the immediate luxuries of some of the finest hotels in Thailand among some of the most beautiful surroundings, there are also direct flights from Bangkok to Ko Samui, Phuket and Hua Hin.

Phetchburi

Temples and caves are the chief attractions of Phetchburi, which was formerly known as Muang Phribphli, the historic town 150 km (90 miles) south of Bangkok. The city was originally an old Mon settlement and, until the late 13th century, part of the mighty Khmer empire. During the Ayutthaya period (1350–1767), it even became a centre for trade, religion and art. Today, its 30 temples spanning more than five centuries provide a rich architectural setting against a backdrop of hills stretching west to the border with Burma.

For an easy tour lasting a couple of hours, start west of Chomrut bridge, at the impressive **Wat Yai Suwannaram**. Built during the reign of King Chulalongkorn, Rama V, it is famed for its murals of the Ayutthaya period and intricately carved doorway. Leave Wat Suwannaram and passing the temples of Wat Borom and Wat Trai Lok, turn first right to get to **Wat Kampaeng Laeng**, the oldest site within the city, dating back to the 13th century,

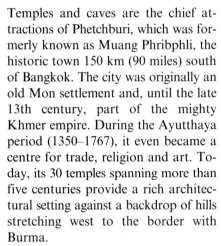

with five Khmer *prangs*, one of which contains a Buddha footprint.

To see the next temple, turn first right to Wat Uthai and cross over the river to **Wat Mahathat**, a late Ayutthaya-style temple, which is home to 198 Buddha statues.

Catch a *songthaew* or tricycle to see the last and, in many ways, most beloved of Phetchburi's temples. **Wat Bandai** lies west of town, reached by a narrow footpath that leads up the mountainside past a cave full of stalactites. Legend has it that the temple was built by a rich businessman with the help of his mistress and wife. The wife built the *bot*, the mistress, the *viharn* and the businessmen, the pagoda, which leans symbolically towards the *viharn*.

One other sight not to miss is the palace complex of **Phra Nakhon Kiri** situated on Khao Wang Hill further to the east. It was built by King Mongkut in 1860 and used as a holiday retreat away from Bangkok, and as an observatory, from which the king, a noted astronomer, studied the movements of the stars. Besides having numerous temples, including a large white one that resembles an iced cake, it is a perfect spot to be at sunset, with fine views of the city and the far-off Kaeng Krachan National Park's forested hills stretching towards the border with Burma.

A ten-minute *songthaew* ride to the south along Ratchadamnoen Road

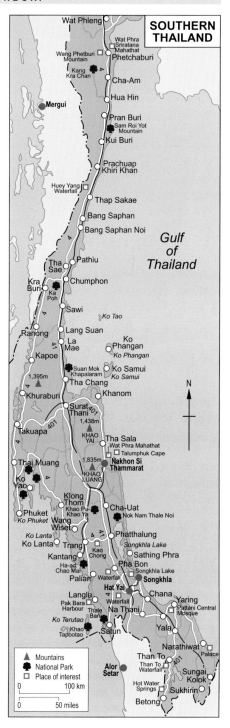

Map of the *Southern region.*

245

*A*ncient Buddhas line the walls of the Khao Luang Cave in Phetchburi, watching over the wellbeing of its inhabitants. They didn't help King Mongkut though—he died of malaria in the nearby swamps in October 1886.

The godfathers, through a network of underground contacts, have helped support leading political and military figures throughout Thailand and, in exchange for funds, have been able to pursue their interests more or less unhindered. Visitors have little to fear, and for the most part the inhabitants, though unused to tourists and lacking mastery of the English language, are both friendly and helpful.

The town can be easily reached by trains which leave Bangkok's Hualamphong Station five times a day or by regular buses from the Southern Bus Terminal on Charoen Sanitwong Road in Thonburi.

will bring you to the magnificent **Khao Luang Caves**. Descend a flight of steep steps and enter a vast cavern illuminated by shafts of light, where the locals have installed Buddha images and are busily attaching gold leaf to them in the hope of making merit. By hiring a guide from the entrance—normally a child who speaks no English— you can wander beyond the main cave into smaller chambers, where niches in the rock contain other Buddha images, more beautiful and less visited.

Phetchburi has a darker side as well and is renowned as the biggest centre of *go sao* (godfathers) in the Kingdom.

Side Trip to Kaeng Krachan National Park

Set in one of the last great forested areas of Thailand near the Burmese border is Kaeng Krachan National Park. Not only is this the largest park in the Kingdom, covering an area of 2,915 sq km (1125 sq miles), but it offers some of the best trekking opportunities within easy reach of Bangkok.

You won't need transport to get there either. Regular buses leave from Phetchburi to Tha Yang, a small town 18 km (11 miles) to the south from where *songthaews* leave for the Park. For those with a car, it's a distance of

50 km (30 miles), reached by a right turn down Highway 3175, shortly after Tha Yang, from where the park is signposted.

First stop should be the Visitors Centre, situated 5 km (3 miles) inside the gates—in a disappointingly arid and bald area, in the dry season—close to the Kaeng Krachan Dam and the landscaped reservoir.

But beyond lies a vast tract of virgin forest, which covers most of the park and is made up of deciduous and rain forest with *takien, yang, tabaek, teng* and *krisna* trees.

To explore the park, it's best to take one of the treks organized by the National Park staff. Treks normally last for around six days and nights, and include a stop near the spectacular nine-level **Thortip Waterfall** and plenty of trails through jungle and scrub. On your return journey, you may even have to build a raft. Be warned though. Your itinerary will have to fit in with other groups, and there is no way of knowing beforehand exactly when a trek will leave.

For most of the year butterflies, gibbons and hornbills can be seen in abundance and, if you are lucky, elephants, black bears, serow, barking deer and wild boar. There are even said to be tigers and the illusive tapir living close to the Burmese border, although these days, sightings are rare.

If you are contemplating a trek, bring a thick sweater as it can get cold at night, torches, mosquito repellent and footwear for walking through rivers—as well as biscuits and chocolate if you don't like the idea of a staple diet of chillied noodles, cabbage and eggs.

Hua Hin

Weekenders from Bangkok rush to the town of Hua Hin, which lies 65 km (40 miles) south of Phetchburi, for its beaches, its condominiums and its air of old- worldly grandeur.

Those with more time wander along the seafront, explore the adjacent bays to Chopstick Hill and take excursions into the surrounding countryside.

Don't expect palm trees and white sands though. Hua Hin is more like Brighton than it is like Phuket and whilst it does have reasonable beaches, most people sit in deck chairs rather than swim in the slightly murky water.

It was Prince Chakrabongsae who first came across the spot in 1910 during a hunting trip. So captivated was he that he built himself a holiday villa, and other members of royalty quickly followed suit.

Memories of those days can still be found at the old Railway Hotel, recently renamed the Sofitel Central Hua Hin. It was built in 1921 by Prince Purachatra, the Director General of

---

A Worrisome Business

It was on 24 June 1932, whilst King Prajadhipok, Rama VII, was in residence at Hua Hin's Klai Kangwon Palace (Far from Worries) that the news came through that a junta of 27 army officers had seized power and ended the absolute monarchy that had governed the country for centuries. The King immediately responded by unconditionally accepting the new constitutional terms. Indeed so promptly did he reply that the coup leaders, feeling that they had offended His Majesty, sent a telex to apologize.

the state railway, and for many years housed the fashionable gentry who fled the heat of the capital to play golf, to drink champagne and listen to serenading orchestras.

During the early 1980s the Railway Hotel again had its moment when it played the part of Phnom Penh's leading hotel in the film *The Killing Fields.*

Today, it is newly painted and restored. It still provides the finest accommodation in town, with teak floors and *fin de siecle* ceiling fans. In addition its hedges have been clipped to look like giraffes and elephants.

Even if you are not staying there, the hotel is still a good place to go for afternoon tea and cakes on the veranda, or in the evening for jazz in the basement.

For another glimpse of old Hua Hin, visit the delightful old railway station to the west of town with its royal waiting room.

These days, although Hua Hin has grown rapidly with condominiums and an occasional beer bar, there's plenty of things to make up for it. Golfers should head straight to the famous Royal Hua Hin Golf Course, Tel: 511 099, built by a Scotsman in the 1920s and still going strong.

Others may take advantage of pony rides and windsurfing and deckchairs along the beach.

One of the highpoints, though, is the lovely old rickety pier, especially colourful in the early morning and late evening when fishermen are loading and unloading their catches.

In the evening, wander down towards the pier where you will find many of the seafood delicacies for which the South is renowned.

Pala-U Waterfall

For a magnificent drive—and the reward of a cool swim in a waterfall at the end—head 75 km (45 miles) north on Highway 3218 to the Pala-U Waterfall, signposted up an extremely steep slope beyond the park gates.

From the base of the waterfall, follow the path that criss-crosses the river, over giant boulders and past beautiful pools of water, which are ideal for swimming.

Each of the eleven levels gets increasingly more spectacular, although you'd need a guide and two days of walking to get to the top.

Best just to find a spot—come during the week when its quiet—bring a picnic and some binoculars and, if you are are lucky, you may even see some of the park's famous birdlife.

There's nowhere to stay so you must return to Hua Hin or take the difficult and unsignposted dirt track to Phetchburi. Day Tours can be organized by a number of travel agents in town.

Cha-am

This pleasant seaside resort lies 30 km (19 miles) north of Hua Hin and can make a good day's excursion—and if you like it, a longer stay. It's a popular and unpretentious Thai resort with a long stretch of sand—generally overrun with motorboats, a charming port, where you can watch fishing boats heading out to sea and, inland, old wooden houses and rice paddies. Further up the coast from Cha-am are several vast sprawling hotel complexes, notably the Regent Cha-am.

Buses run regularly between Cha-am and Hua Hin taking 45 minutes.

Side Trip to Khao Sam Roi Yot

Highway 4 south of Hua Hin, parallels the sea for 15 km (9 miles) at first, passing near the small village of Khao Tao before turning inland through pineapple plantations and strangely shaped hills. The hills are called Khao

T he people of the South pride themselves on their beaches and their islands, but also like to indulge in a little worship.

Sam Roi Yot or Mountain of 300 Peaks, and can be reached by a sign-posted left turn near the intersection with Pranburi at km 286. Here, on 18 August 1886, King Mongkut conducted his fateful expedition to witness the eclipse of the sun. Accompanied by European observers and dignitaries, including the governor of Singapore, he journeyed into the marshy uplands from his palace in Phetchburi.

The eclipse took place just four minutes earlier than Mongkut had predicted, and the reputation of the Thai monarchy reached new peaks. But the King's triumph was short-lived and, two months later, he died of malaria.

The area has since been turned into a National Park and is liberally sprinkled with caves and limestone outcrops— best reached by boat from the Park Headquarters.

Keen walkers have the choice of several trails where occasionally you may spot monkeys—crab-eating macaques and dusty langurs—or the serow, which resembles a strange-looking antelope, as well as large numbers of marsh birds and waders, which have made the park a popular gazing spot for ornithologists.

Trips to the park can be arranged for you by most hotels and travel agents in Hua Hin. Alternatively you can catch one of the fairly infrequent market delivery trucks from the crossroads at Pranburi.

Prachuap Khiri Khan

This sleepy fishing town, known as the Village among Mountain Chains, lies a further 90 km (56 miles) south of Hua Hin situated on a long sweeping bay surrounded by hills.

It is a small, undeveloped Thai resort, with neither the luxuries nor the royal notability of its nearby neighbour. People come here to get away from it all, to watch old women collecting shells in buckets and shaking the tamarind trees with bamboo poles, and to indulge in the favourite pastime of eating seafood at the numerous small restaurants along the beach or at the night market near the pier.

One sight not to miss though is **Mirror Mountain** (*Khao Chong Kra Chok*), south of town. Climb 425 steps and you will come to the small pagoda of **Wat Thammikaram** containing relics of the Buddha and thronged with monkeys.

Continue around the left side and down a precarious metal ladder to see the hole which is supposed to mirror the sky—though quite why is anyone's guess. If you haven't got a head for heights, better just to admire the spectacular views from the top as you look down on the long curving beach of Ao Prachuap backed by an inlet of mangroves.

To the south of Ao Prachuap is the smaller, more secluded **Ao Noi**; and beyond the picturesque **Ao Khan Kradai**, where a narrow path leads up the side of the headland to **Tham Khan Kradai**. This small cave *wat* houses a 30 m (98 ft) reclining Buddha, and rows of smaller Buddhas stretching back into the darkness. At the entrance, a monk sells candles. But to be safe, bring a torch.

Outside the cave is a curious temple with mother of pearl steps and dragon banisters, a ferocious green guardian, and a grotesque brown-painted plaster statue depicting two men fighting and a woman having her bottom bitten by a goose—the inevitable consequences of adultery.

From Prachuap Khiri Khan to Chumphon

South of Prachuap Khiri Khan, the road passes inland from beautiful Ao Manao Bay—currently off limits—and 45 km (28 miles) further near the town of Thap Sake, famous for its Wanakon Beach. Continue 115 km (70 miles) further south and you will pass a turning for the town of Pathiu and Ban Tah Samed with its palm-fringed bay and sprinkling of offshore islands reached from Pak Nam Chumphon.

At the provincial town of Chumphon, the main road branches. Down the east coast Highway 41 continues inland towards Surat Thani and the jump-off point for Ko Samui. And to the west, Highway 4 cuts across to meet the coast at Ranong and continues down to Phuket.

Ranong and the West Coast

The wettest, lushest and one of the least populated provinces in Thailand lies south-west of Chumphon past the town of Kraburi, the spot that marks the narrowest stretch of the peninsula.

Ranong is a cluttered mishmash of charming old buildings built by the immigrant Hokkien Chinese, thriving markets and ugly modern shop fronts.

One house worth visiting is the former residence of the provincial governor Koh Su Chang, situated to the north of town off Ruang Rat Road.

Afterwards you can drop by the town's best-known attraction: its hot springs, situated 2 km (1 mile) to the east at **Wat Tapotharam**, within the grounds of Raksawaring Park. These comprise three wells—father, mother and child—filled with bubbling sulphurous water at a temperature of 65°C (149°F). Get there at dawn to see the monks from the *wat* line up with their buckets and kettles to draw water from the father well. For those whose thoughts turn to breakfast, the nearby stall owners thoughtfully provide eggs, which you can boil in it. Visitors with larger budgets will not have to come this far. At the **Jansom Thara Hotel**, situated close to the turn-off, the water is piped from the hot springs to the bath, the swimming pool, the jacuzzi and the drinking water taps.

Continue past the springs for 6 km (4 miles) along a scenic stretch of road to get to the old tin mining village of **Hat Sompan**. There's little tin mined these days, but outside the village *wat,* the river forms a large pool where you can make merit by feeding the gigantic carp on watermelon and peanuts.

A Question of Hospitality

Eminent Siamese households of the early 20th century held back nothing when it came to ingratiating themselves with honoured guests. Every comfort would be provided, from the best food to the finest company. So much so that it was considered wholly inconsiderate for a guest to be left to sleep alone. Thus a new arrival would commonly find himself in the company of a sister, a number two wife, an aunt, even a daughter, but never a number one wife.

Don't try to catch them though. Legend has it that they are possessed by potent spirits and that anyone who touches one will contract leprosy.

Victoria Point and Hat Charndamri

Two attractions lie within easy reach of Ranong town. The first is the provincial fishing port 8 km (5 miles) to the south-west, home to colourful fishing trawlers and long-tailed boats that ply to and from Victoria Point in Burma.

Foreigners are not allowed to cross. That reward is reserved for Thais and Burmese. But you can watch the hive

*R*anong *is more than just a gateway for traditional sea traffic. Hundreds depart illicitly to Victoria Point in Burma to indulge in a little local pastime known as smuggling.*

of activity and take pictures of the Burmese flocking over to shop for jewellery and more basic commodities like powdered milk.

In the evening, drive to Hat Charndamri, signposted 10 km (6 miles) to the north of town and take a pew on the verandah at the Jansom Thara Beach Resort. Order a drink—and sit back to watch the sunset over Victoria Point and across the La-Un estuary—one of the most scenic settings in the region.

From Ranong to Phuket

For a rewarding excursion, drive south from Ranong to Phuket stopping at the National Parks of Laem Son and Khao Lak-Lamru—and if you have the time—the beautiful Surin Islands. You won't find luxury, but you will see some of the most unspoilt surroundings in the region. Buses leave from Ranong Terminal and you can ask to be dropped off at the turnings. Alternatively enquire about day trips from Phuket.

Laem Son National Park
First of the National Parks, off Highway 4, is Laem Son (Pine Cape). It is 58 km (36 miles) south of Ranong, signposted to the right along a dirt track leading through mangroves and over three precarious wooden bridges to the Park Headquarters.

Cottages can be rented in the Park or at Komain Villa shortly before you get to the visitors' area. Alternatively, camp on Bang Ben Beach, a long and deserted stretch of sand, backed by a large picnic area under casuarina trees.

Dream up an island and they will show you a world. Local fishing boats ship modern Robinson Crusoe hunters to the South's Island National Parks.

It is very quiet with just the sound of birds and the waves and, offshore, the islands, nine in all, which can be visited by boats rented out from the park staff. To camp on the islands, bring your own food and organize a boat for the return journey.

Turtles come ashore to lay their eggs in this peaceful area and for much of the year the coast is home to herons and egrets, white-breasted kingfishers and white-bellied sea eagles.

Surin Islands
To get to the jump-off point for the magnificent Surin Islands, continue 50 km (30 miles) south of Laem Son on Highway 4, and turn off to Ban Hin Lat fishing pier, from where boats can be hired for the four-hour trip.

The chief attractions of these islands—there are five in all—are fine corals, turtles and crystal clear waters. The islands are also home to the last of the Moken sea gypsies. Between April and November, however, the seas can be rough and boats hard to come by.

Khao Lak-Lumru National Park

Follow Highway 4 south passing the junction, Highway 401, for Khao Sok National Park; after 35 km (22 miles) you will reach a signposted turn-off to Khao Lak-Lumru National Park, a long sandy strip of beaches and rocky coves and, inland, of tamarind and hopea trees. The park is a good place to stop and wander for a couple of hours—and for those who prefer a longer stay, to rent bungalows.

Phuket

The pearl of Thailand's tourist industry, the largest and the most popular island in the Kingdom, lies just a stone's throw off the mainland, surrounded by the waters of the Andaman Sea.

Phuket (pronounced poo-ket) has some of the most beautiful beaches and some of the finest accommodation in the land, with miles of white sand and offshore, numerous islands and coral reefs.

A British Love

"I know of no place with so much value" wrote Captain Francis Light of the British East India Company on arriving on the sun-blessed island of Phuket in the early 1770s. What Light was referring to was not sand, but tin—vast amounts of it—which have since made the province one of the richest in the country. Notwithstanding his find, Light still had enough time to enjoy himself. Whilst on the island he fell in love with a local girl of Thai-Portuguese descent, and as a result ended up postponing his departure for several years.

It has an area of 810 sq km (315 sq miles) bisected by a ridge of mountains, which runs down the west coast, cutting the shore into a series of bays, inland National Parks and waterfalls.

The first known inhabitants of the island were a nomadic people, forebearers of the Chaoloy sea gypsies. During the 17th century, Phuket attracted Europeans, mainly British and Portuguese lured to the island by its vast reserves of tin. These days, Phuket plays host to nearly one million tourists—almost six times the total population of the island. And every year, more new concrete developments, more discos and malls line the seafront.

But whilst Phuket is no longer the undiscovered island of yesteryear, it has managed to preserve much of its character. Indeed Phuket offers something for everyone, whether its waterskiing, sailing or simply sunbathing and dining.

In the early morning, there are fishing boats to watch, nearby islands or markets to visit and, in the early evening, walks on the beach and the sight of the sun setting over the Andaman, best viewed from Promthep Cape or from the comfort of the Boat House on Kata Beach.

Although Phuket is a year-round tourist destination, the ideal time to visit is between November and February when the weather is fine and the surrounding islands of Ko Similan, Ko Surin and Ko Phi Phi are at their most beautiful.

*M*ap of Phuket.

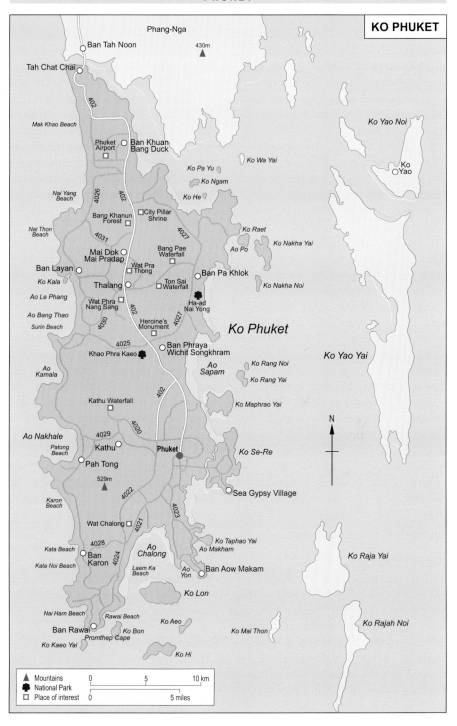

KO PHUKET

Phang-Nga

Ban Tah Noon

430m

Tah Chat Chai

402

Mak Khao Beach

Ko Yao Noi

Phuket Airport
Ban Khuan
Bang Duck

Ko Wa Yai

Ko
Yao

Ko Pa Yu

Nai Yang Beach

4026

402

Ko Ngam

Ko He

Bang Khanun Forest
City Pillar Shrine

Nai Thon Beach

4031

4027

Ko Raet

Ao Po
Ko Nakha Yai

Mai Dok
Mai Pradap
Bang Pae Waterfall

Ban Layan
Wat Pra Thong

Ko Kala
Thalang
Ton Sai Waterfall
Ban Pa Khlok

Ao Le Phang
Ko Nakha Noi

Wat Phra Nang Sang
402

Ha-ad Nai Yong

Ao Bang Thao
Surin Beach
Heroine's Monument

4030
4027

Ko Phuket

4025
Ban Phraya Wichit Songkhram

Khao Phra Kaeo
Ko Yao Yai

Ao Sapam
Ko Rang Noi

Ao Kamala
Ko Rang Yai

Kathu Waterfall
Ko Maphrao Yai

N

Ao Nakhale
4029
4020

Patong Beach
Kathu
Phuket
Ko Se-Re

Pah Tong

529m

Karon Beach
4022

Wat Chalong
4021

4023

Kata Beach
4028

Ko Taphao Yai
Ao Makham

Ban Karon
Ao Chalong
4024

Ko Raja Yai

Kata Noi Beach
Laem Ka Beach
Ao Yon
Ban Aow Makam

Ko Lon

Nai Harn Beach
Rawai Beach

Ko Aeo

Ko Rajah Noi

Ban Rawai
Ko Bon
Ko Mai Thon

Promthep Cape

Ko Kaeo Yai
Ko Hi

▲ Mountains
🌳 National Park
☐ Place of interest

0   5   10 km

0   5 miles

255

Most visitors arrive in Phuket town. From here *songthaews* serve all main beaches. Cars, jeeps and motorbikes can be rented by the day or week. Be warned though. As yet there is no ring road and transferring from A to B can take considerably longer than the map might suggest.

The Beaches

Phuket has more than a dozen white beaches to choose from, broken up by coves and hills, each with their own charm and their own characteristics. We list five of the major beach areas. They are all situated along the west coast since the east coast is unsuitable for resort development.

Since few people stray far afield, your choice of location is likely to determine the outcome of your holiday.

Patong

The most developed, the brashest and, perhaps, the most beautiful of Phuket's beaches, dominated by a 25-storey hotel and with shopping arcades, supermarkets, restaurants and bars that rarely close.

This is the place to come to for nightlife and watersports and raucous times. People wanting peace and quiet should stay away.

Kata and Karon

Further to the south are Kata and Karon, quieter family beaches with long white curving stretches of beach, with high-standard hotels and a less boisterous nightlife, although never a shortage of things to do. The beach is divided in two, separated by a headland with the pretty Kata Noi tucked away in the southern corner.

Surin/Pansea

To the north of Patong is Pansea, the most exclusive beach, home to the Amanpuri and Pansea Hotels. This is the place to relax in some of the quietest, most idyllic surroundings.

Don't expect much nightlife though. Pansea is isolated and self-contained and for those not wanting to move. Also be warned: the weather during the monsoon season creates vicious undercurrents and can make swimming unsafe.

Nai Harn

Close to the southern tip, squeezed between two rocky headlands, is Nai Harn, with some of the last remaining beach bungalows on the island and the large and ugly Yacht Club.

Currently a major project is under way to build yet more hotels, but it's still pleasant and still some way off the beaten track—although during the monsoon months, waves are big—and swimmers should beware.

Rawai

Beyond Nai Harn, at the southern tip is the small fishing community of Rawai, home to the Chaoloy sea gypsies and to a line of simple bungalows. The beach is not so clean and not good for swimming, but the offshore islands of Ko Lone and Ko He are easily reached and there's still the feel of somewhere largely untouched by tourism.

Phuket Town

The main town of Phuket is, for most visitors, little more than an arrival and departure point. If you spend a couple of hours wandering the streets, you can

still get an impression of the old town where the old tin and rubber barons once upon a time resided in all their glory.

Sights not to miss are the beautiful old houses, set between newer hideous ones, along Yaowarat, Phang Nga and Dibuk Roads and especially the former

Dropped from the heavens, a Phuket parachutist takes the plunge into paradise.

mansion of **Phra Oraam Saakhor-nakhet**, now the Phuket office of Thai Airways International on Ranong

257

Road. Turn left and you will get to the famous **Saan Jao Pud Jo** temple, on Ranong Road, scene of the famous annual Vegetarian Festival.

Afterwards, visit the busy vegetable market—from where local buses depart at irregular intervals for all the beaches.

Also visit the nearby shops and department stores, where you can buy the pearls for which Phuket is now famous, painted wooden birds, pewterware hipflasks and tankards, intricately woven lipao vine handbags, Thai silk and Phuket batik.

For some of the best views of town, climb the summit of **Khao Rang**, at the end of Kaew Simbi Road. Neighbouring Khao Toh would be even better, but is the site of a Channel 7 TV station.

A haven of calm in a turbulent world, Phuket's beaches provide a little something for everyone.

Island Activities

When you are bored with beaches, Phuket offers a wide range of activities tuned to every need and price.

Golfers generally head for Hat Surin Golf Course on Surin Beach, Tel: 830 00, with nine holes, or Phuket Country Club, Tel: 211 523, Bantungtong, Kathu with an 18-hole course, said to be one of the finest in the country.

Tennis is available at many big hotels, although generally for guests only.

For exotic sealife, visit the **Marine Biological Research Centre**, open daily 10 a.m.–4 p.m., on the southernmost point of Laem Panwa, set up seven years ago with displays of more than 100 species of fish and unusual crustaceans.

Phuket also has an orchid garden as well as a cultural village off Thepsatri Road, built on the sight of an old tin mine and containing an extensive range of handicrafts from all over the country.

For crocodile wrestling and southern Thailand's largest collection of fresh water and estuarine alligators, visit the **Crocodile Farm**, which is open daily, on Chana Charoen Road.

W hen dusk falls over the grand landscape of Phuket even the palm trees are transfixed.

In the early evening, the most popular spot is **Promthep Point** on the southern tip of the island where vast crowds gather to watch the sun setting over the Andaman Sea.

Finally for those who want to get away from it all, head to **Khao Phra Taew National Park** in the north of the island with its famous **Tone Sai Waterfall** or to the beautiful **Mak Khao** and **Nai Yang Beach** on the north-west of the island, where for an afternoon you can escape into a still largely forgotten world.

Stop by the TAT at 73–75 Phuket Road, Tel: 212 213, for details of excursions. Alternatively ask at any local travel agent or see the latest issue of *Phuket Magazine,* which can be bought in most newsagents or bookshops.

Island Circuit

To explore the island, hire a motorbike or jeep for the day from any of the travel shops. But check the vehicle before leaving—and be warned—there is no satisfactory ring road around the island and some of the roads are extremely difficult. If you find roads too steep or forbidding, backtrack to the main road and follow signs for the next turning.

Begin at **Mai Khao** in the far north of the island, off Highway 402. It is a 9 km (5.5 mile) stretch of white sand and casuarina trees, and from November to February giant turtles come ashore to lay their eggs.

Continue to **Nai Yang**, the National Park Beach with its National Park bungalows and a picnic area.

Some 5 km (3 miles) south of Nai Yang, the adventurous can take a right turning to secluded **Nai Thon** and **Bang Thao Beach**. Those who do not relish the prospect of a dirt track, steep inclines and an astoundingly difficult road can continue along Highway 4031 and Highway 402 to the old capital of Thalang, before turning right at the Heroine's Monument and heading to beautiful and secluded Surin and Pansea Beach.

Beyond Pansea, a road leads around the coast to Kamala, branching left up another difficult dirt track that twists through the hills, past the spectacular **Nakalay Beach** and **Kelim Beach** before descending into busy Patong Beach.

After visiting Patong, continue along the new road that cuts through the hills to Karon and then Kata Beach, before climbing steeply through astoundingly beautiful countryside to a viewpoint with awesome views of the bay below.

Afterwards, continue to Nai Harn, home of the Yacht Club and, further around, to **Promthep Cape**, renowned for having some of the finest sunsets on the island.From Promthep, the road leads a further 3 km (2 miles) to Rawai, where you can shop for shells before continuing to Chalong, the yachters pier, signposted to the right at the roundabout.

From Chalong drive the remaining 11 km (7 miles) back to Phuket on Highway 4024, in time for an early evening drink at the top of Khao Rang.

Watersports and Island Tours

Water-skiing, yachting and windsurfing can be found in abundance on almost every beach and especially on Patong. They offer almost every available form of equipment, price range and standard of instruction.

Make sure though, if you haven't tried any particular sport, to check that your instructor has his full licence, because accidents, though few, are not unknown.

For day trips to the offshore islands catch a boat to **Bon Island** and **Coral Island**, both easily reached by long-tail boat rom Rawai Beach or Chalong Beach and offering good snorkelling.

Further south lies **Raja Yai**, with its two sandy bays enclosed by rocky capes, containing a few basic bungalows and a couple of restaurants. Boats can be chartered from Chalong Beach for the two- to three-hour journey or packages arranged through the Phuket Tourist Centre on 125/7 Phang Nga Road, Tel: 211 849.

For those seeking greater luxury, cruises can be arranged aboard old-fashioned schooners or, for the more energetic, on a brand new 52-foot Jeanneau Sun Odyssey, a contender in the King's Cup.

One other island not to miss: **Naga Noi Pearl Farm**, home to the biggest cultivated pearl in the world, weighing a massive 30 g. Tours of the island can be organized by contacting Naga Pearl Tour and Resort, Tel: 213 723. Alternatively just drive to Po Bay, 25 km (15 miles) to the north of town. The island lies a short distance offshore.

For trips to the Surin Islands, Ko Phi Phi and Ko Tarutao contact Songserm, Tel: 214 272 in the Rasda Complex off Rasda Road. They organize scheduled day trips, but only at some times of year, since during the monsoons, the crossing can be dangerous.

After Sundown

From the famous crustacean, the enormous ugly turquoise-mottled Phuket lobster to tiger prawns, garoupa and squid, Phuket offers every kind of delicious seafood and countless places in which to eat it.

In many of the local restaurants, you may also come across Phuket specialities like *ho mok* (curried fish with coconut milk steamed inside a banana leaf cup) or *nam prik kung siap* (a hot fermented shrimp paste with sweet crispy shrimps eaten with fresh and steamed vegetables).

After dinner the main nightlife is situated at Patong and in the numerous beer bars along Beach Road. For crowds and colour and a transvestite floor show, there is Le Crocodile off

Bangla Road, and for a smaller, more typical nightclub, the Banana Disco, on Tawiwong Road, which is part of Patong Beach Hotel. Elsewhere there are discos on all the major beach strips, cinemas in town, videos almost everywhere and, for a quiet drink, the bar on the terrace or the roof at the Boat House Hotel.

Side Trip to Phang Nga

The most popular of all the day trips from Phuket is to Phang Nga, the spectacular limestone-studded bay which achieved fame as the setting for the James Bond film *Man with the Golden Gun*. Almost every travel agent organizes trips to it, boats do it and the place crawls with tourists and with tour organizers taking videos of them.

The only way to escape the crowds is to do the trip yourself, either by public transport or by car or motorbike, and to arrive early or stay overnight in Phang Nga where there's a range of accommodation. The town is situated 90 km (55 miles) to the north-east and can be easily reached by following Highway 403 over the Sarasin Bridge and then taking the right fork, Highway 4, at Khok Kloi junction. From here it's a further 50 km (30 miles) to the turn-off for Tha Dan Pier where you can either arrange boat trips at the Visitors Centre or, alternatively, negotiate directly with the boatmen at the pier.

Most boats will take you down the mangrove swamps of Klong Khao Thalu, past the overhanging cliff formations known as Khao Ma Chu (Small Dog) and to Khao Khian (Cave of Writing). The paintings are said by the Fine Arts Department to be over

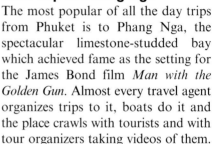

3,000 years old, and the outlines of a dolphin and fish are clearly visible along with some geometric patterns, said to be the work of fishermen sheltering from a storm. Further on, clustered around Ko Pannyi, is a Muslim village on stilts, once a small fishing community, now a thriving commercial centre with markets selling seashells, mangrove woodcarvings and expensive and rather ordinary seafood. Ko Pannyi, surprisingly, does have a life of its own apart from tourist shops and it is worth wandering through the streets of the village to the schoolyard, made of wooden planks above the water, and to the mosque beyond.

But the biggest highlight of the trip is **Ko Phing Kan**, more popularly known as James Bond island. The island—which actually means two islands leaning back to back—was formed thousands of years ago when an earthquake split the island vertically; and, despite large numbers of tourists and hawkers selling Coca Cola and dried squid, it is an impressive sight, with the offshore island of Ko Tapu (Nail Island) rising straight up out of the water to a height of 200 m. From Ko Phing Kan, you return to Tha Dan pier. The round trip takes a couple of hours and will cost around Bt400–500 per boat, but be prepared to bargain hard and make sure that all the major sites are included in the trip.

*I*t took James Bond to propel Phang Nga's mushroom-like rock formations to international fame. Now thousands of tourists arrive by the day to play "007".

For those who prefer to enjoy the surroundings in solitude, a better alternative is to hire boats to the more distant, uninhabited islands, which rise sheer from the water on all sides. Some of the islands have inner lagoons unknown until recently when they were spotted from the air. The trip takes around four to five hours and will cost considerably more than the normal circuit, but you will be rewarded by weird limestone formations and caves where the only sound is from egrets and the lapping waves.

For the adventurous, it is also possible to explore the inner caves and lagoons in inflatable canoes. The trips are organized out of Phuket for anything from a day to a week. Only limited numbers of people are taken and prices are high. Enquire at Phuket Sea Canoe Centre, Tel: 076 214 173 for further details.

Around town there are a number of other small caves and temples, easily visited by *songthaew*. Seven km (4 miles) to the south before you reach the small village of Takua Thung, is a turning-off to the temple of **Wat Suwan Khuha**, filled with Buddha images, *chedis* and *prangs,* whilst near the municipal hall is the **Phung Chang Cave** (Temple Cave in the Elephant's Stomach) and the nearby cave of **Rusi Suwan**, a hermit cave said to have magical powers.

From Phan Nga to Krabi

The journey from Phang Nga to Krabi, is worthy of a side trip in itself. It takes you through gargantuan limestone cliffs and spectacular rock formations curving through magnificent countryside.

Wise people stop off at the beautiful **Than Bokkharani Botanical** gardens near the town of Ao Luk, 50 km (30 miles) from Phang Nga, with its caves and large lotus pool filled with emerald green water.

For those without transport, an alternative means of arrival is by boat from Phuket and Ko Phi Phi. But you would be missing out on one of the highlights of the southern region.

Krabi

This rather ordinary little fishing town lies 95 km (60 miles) south of Phang Nga and is the chief stepping-stone for one of Thailand's most beautiful provinces.

Before heading to the beaches and islands, several sights are worth visiting. Drive north on Highway 4 and just after the 107 km (66 miles) mark turn right to **Wat Tham Sua** or Tiger Cave Monastery, one of South Thailand's most famous forest *wats*. There is a temple, partly recessed into the rock, with several golden Buddha figures and photographs of the abbot, a proponent of a school of Buddhist thought that advocates the contemplation of human internal organs. On display are several rather gory-looking pictures of autopsies, reminders of the temporal nature of mankind. Beyond the temple, a flight of steps leads up and over the rock into a grove of trees enclosed by limestone cliffs and to a huge seated Buddha figure at the foot of the cliff and small huts built into the rockface for meditation.

Continue along the road past the turning to Wat Tham Sua and you will come to a turning for the remote and rarely visited Khao Phanom Bencha National Park. This dirt track is passable by car or motorbike and leads to several waterfalls and caves, though you would be wise to make enquires in town.

One other attraction within the vicinity: the **Shell Cemetery,** which lies 20 km (12 miles) west of town and contains fossilized shells said to be 75 million years old. Not every one impressed though, since they have been compressed into slabs out of all recognition. If you do go, make sure it is at low tide, otherwise the sea almost completely covers the shells.

Ao Nang and Ao Phra Nang

Two beaches lie within easy reach of town. Ao Nang, is the most popular of the two, reached either by boat from Krabi Pier, taking 55 minutes, or by a road that curves through limestone cliffs. It comprises a long stretch of white sand fringed by palm trees and has several places to stay.

Ao Phra Nang is more beautiful, but less accessible. To get there you must catch a boat leaving from Krabi pier or from Ao Nang. The beach is, however, one of the most spectacular in the whole of the region—with white sand stretching between two massive headlands; offshore, a jutting limestone cliff; and behind the beach, a profusion of vegetation.

When you are bored with beaching, explore **Princess Cave**, situated at the southern end. The cave is believed to be the womb of a sea princess, who for many years provided the local inhabitants with food. Today fishermen still leave offerings of small phalluses and flowers, both in gratitude for deeds done and in the hope that they will catch more fish.

After exploring the cave—guides are available with torches—the more adventurous can continue along the nearby wooden walkway, and up an extremely steep rocky path to the right. At the end of a 20-minute climb you will reach a watchpoint with spectacular views of a crescent beach curving around with turquoise seas on either side.

Branching off this path is another steeper path descending to a hidden salt water lagoon called **Sa Phra Nang** (Princess Pool). Ropes are provided for guidance, but good shoes and a certain relish for heights are essential. Check before leaving that the tide is not due to be low since, if it is, when you finally reach the lake there will be no water.

Accommodation is basic, though plentiful. Still at some times of year, it can be very hard finding anywhere. If Ao Phra Nang is full, cross over the headland to Railae East, situated in a bay of mangroves, or to Railae West, near a pretty sandy beach.

Ko Phi Phi

Two hours off shore from Krabi lie two of the great gems of the South.. The legendary islands of Ko Phi Phi nestle amidst turquoise seas, a jumble of jagged limestone outcrops and lofty hills, mirrored underwater by a variety of colourful fish and coral formations.

First port of call for most visitors is **Ton Sai Pier**, the arrival point for Phi Phi Don. From here, paths circle the entire circumference of the island, bordered by hundreds of new bungalows,

evidence of the island's unstoppable popularity.

Finding accommodation is unlikely to be a problem. Lines of touts carry lists of available bungalows and will save you trekking from place to place.

For an awesome view of the island, climb up Sunset Point, signposted towards the south-eastern tip of the island. It's a steep 30-minute walk from Ton Sai up a slope strewn with boulders. But from the top you can stare down on the two bays of Phi Phi Don joined by a narrow strip of land with crescent-shaped stretches of sand on both sides fringed by palm trees.

For snorkelling and diving, try **Tong Sai** or **Cape Laemthong**, 3 km (2 miles) to the east. Finding a boat to take you there is easy. Just wander down to the seafront and almost inevitably there will be someone to arrange a the excursion. Deep-sea fishing trips can also be arranged at any of the travel agencies by the pier. Elsewhere life revolves around swimming, sunbathing and the clusters of bars and restaurants, which stretch out along the bay.

Island Tour

To see some of the most spectacular beaches and limestone cliffs, take one of the day tours of **Phi Phi Don** and twin island **Phi Phi Le**.

First stop is the **Viking Cave** home to prehistoric paintings and to thousands of swallows' nests, used for the precious soup that the Chinese eat around the world.

Such is the value placed on nests that visits to the cave can only be made after the mating season has ended. Flash photography is banned as this might frighten the birds.

*P*icture of paradise. The locals simply call it Phi Phi, one of the most beautiful islands in the world.

Boosting the Libido

Not only is bird's nest soup considered a rare delicacy amongst the Chinese community, but recent scientific tests indicate that certain compounds found in the nests provide a medicinal cure for skin and lung problems, virility and loss of appetite. Hardly surprising, then, that connoisseurs fly halfway around the world to taste it, served up with chicken broth. Some nests can command prices as high as US$1,000 a kilo. Others, where the saliva is less pure and contains feathers, sell for a measly US$20. Still, when it's a matter of libido, that's quite a bargain.

Afterwards the boat will take you to **Shark Point** and to the turquoise waters of beautiful **Maya Bay,** situated on the south-western side of the island. The cost is normally Bt150 and includes a picnic lunch comprising a bottle of water and a plastic box of cold fried rice. Trips can be arranged by any of the local agents and usually leave at 9 a.m. and return at 5 p.m.

Islands dot Thailand's coasts like gems from the sky. Tourists just hire a boat and take their pick of the pile.

Island Hopping

Opportunities for island hopping from Krabi and Ko Phi Phi abound. Indeed for those with the time and the money, it is possible to travel all the way south to the islands of Trang province and beyond to the Ko Tarutao National Park.

Start from Ko Phi Phi and catch one of the regular boats—they only run from October to April—to Ban Sala Din on Ko Lanta Noi. From here cross to **Ko Lanta Yai**, the most popular island, which has stunning white beaches and basic wooden bungalows situated right on the seafront. The biggest concentration of bungalows lies to the north-west, although several other resorts can now be found near the southern tip.

From Ko Lanta, either catch a boat to Bo Muang on the mainland, 70 km

(43 miles) from Trang, or take one of the organized trips to **Ko Hai**, which lies further to the south. The island offers good reefs for snorkelling and has a couple of bungalow resorts. From Ko Hai boats leave irregularly to the islands of Ko Mook with palm-fringed beaches and good coral, and Ko Kradan, a more upmarket resort. To be safe, you should try to arrange bungalows prior to arrival.

An abundance of other small islands lie within the vicinity of Trang and Krabi leading all the way down to Ko Tarutao in Satun Province. But in practice, the only regular boats are mailboats from the mainland to individual islands and the only other option, to charter a boat, can be an expensive alternative.

When the gods made Thailand they sprinkled it with islands, blue seas and glistening white sands. Somehow Maya Bay got more than its fair share.

Ko Tarutao

This vast and, until recently, unknown National Park lies 250 km (150 miles) beyond Krabi near the small town of Pakbara and comprises 51 islands extending as far as the border with Malaysia.

To get there, catch a boat from the pier to **Tarutao Island**, the largest in the group. Boats leave twice daily—last one at 2.30 p.m.; although occasionally, for a price, local fishmermen will take you over at a later hour.

The island is made up largely of ancient Cambrian sandstone and covered in mountains and forest, with waterfalls and caves that once played host to political prisoners. For in 1939, a penal colony was built there. During

Being on a penal colony in Tarutao during World War II can't have been all bad. Indeed so much of a liking did the prisoners take to it that in 1940 they rebelled against the wardens and took over the island.

World War II, however, faced with starvation, prisoners and guards alike rebelled, teaming up to become the most savage pirates in the region. After the war, the British Navy was sent in to deal with them. New settlers arrived, displacing the sea gypsies and pirates, and in 1974, after prolonged struggles, the island was declared Thailand's first marine National Park.

Even today, you won't find many comforts on the island, but you will find swimming and snorkelling and the opportunity for long hikes into the forest. Anyone considering venturing into the inland areas should, however, consult park staff, and women should on no account camp out alone as there have been stories of disappearances.

A pleasant side trip can be made from Ko Tarutao to the more beautiful and less explored islands beyond. Catch a regular boat to bring you to **Ko Lipe** or **Ko Adang**, where accommodation is available. Long-tail boats can also be hired for day snorkelling trips to the nearby islands. **Hin Ngam** (the Beach of Beautiful Stones) is most popular, made up entirely of enchanted black pebbles. **Ko Yang** still has fine coral, although like many of the reefs in the Andaman Sea, it is suffering the effects of dynamiting and increasingly, anchor damage from fishing and tour boats.

Stung with Vitality

Allergic to early mornings? Hungover or jet lagged ? A pint of snakes' blood could be just the thing. This great provider of health and vitality is said not only to make the skin fairer, but according to Chinese doctors, will increase stamina, boost longevity and even improve the eyesight. Choosing the snake is a matter of taste. The poisonous banded krait are cheaper, but have less bite to them. The crème de la crème is the King Cobra. But at Bt600 a kg, it is considered a luxury. To enjoy the liquid reptile at its best, collect the blood from a freshly gutted snake, add a little alcohol or some honey, and drink it down in one. Try it at any of the stalls outside Lumpini Park in Bangkok every morning at 6 a.m., or at Tanon Ngoo (Snake Road) in Hat Yai.

Hat Yai

Nightclubs and massage parlours are the chief attractions of Hat Yai, the principal town in the southern region and one of the fastest growing towns in the country.

Unless you are heading to Malaysia or arriving by train or air, there is little reason to spend much time here, except to watch the Malaysians who come over in droves to do all the things they can't do back home. Still, you can visit the main shopping area off Niphat Uthit 2 & 3 Road with its abundance of cheap electrical goods and the stalls around the Mitra Hotel, home to the popular snake vendors.

Head west of town off Phetkasem Road to find the other local tour de force: the temple of **Wat Hat Yai** containing an enormous reclining Buddha, 35 m long, 15 m high and the third largest in the world. If so inclined, you can even enter its abdomen which is complete with sculptured heart and lungs—the heart is said to contain a relic of the Buddha.

One other speciality is reserved for those in Hat Yai during the first Saturday of the month when the town even holds a bull fight, although not of the Spanish variety. The spectacle is held at the **Klong Wa Stadium** off Rajyindee Road, but you should make enquiries before you leave.

Drop by the Tourist Office at 1/1 Soi 2 Niphat Uthit 3 Rd, Tel: 243 747, for maps and information.

Songkhla

This sleepy town, 25 km (15 miles) from Hat Yai is the very antithesis of its neighbour. Quiet, dignified, charming, it seems like a different world.

Yet Songkhla has a surprisingly colourful history. For centuries it was an important commercial and trading centre and a part of the great Srivijaya kingdom that ruled much of maritime South-east Asia from the 8th to the 13th century.

At one stage in 1654, it even declared itself an independent state from Ayutthaya. But the kingdom's rule was short and, in 1679, King Narai the Great of Ayutthaya attacked the city with cannons, tore down the walls and left the place virtually abandoned.

To see what little remains there are of the old town, head to the Fort on Red Mountain where you can see 18 turrets and the ruins of a Buddhist temple. Afterwards, visit the charming old wooden houses off Nakhon Nai Road, reminders of the early influence of the Chinese and Portuguese.

Songkhla also has a fine **National Museum**, open Wednesday–Sunday 9 a.m.–4 p.m., situated just off Vichianchom Road, in a beautiful old house dating back more than 100 years. It contains collections of old furniture and local archaeological finds, as well as items from the prehistoric site of Ban Chiang.

Two other attractions lie within easy reach. The first is the fishing port on Jana Road to the west of town—best at dawn when piles of fish line the wharf, for this is the busiest fishing port in the South and possibly in Asia. To get to the second, head to Samila

Beach, a grubby but pleasant stretch of sand, which runs for more than 3 km (2 miles) past casuarina trees and the Statue of Mermaid. Continue east along Samila and you will reach the fishing village of **Kao Seng**, famous for its handpainted *kolae* boats used by Muslim fishermen.

Often you can hire boats to the offshore islands. There is little to see on Koh Nu (rat) or Koh Maew (cat), but trips are pleasant and boats can be hired from in front of the Samila Hotel on Ratchadamnoen Road.

In the evening Songkhla is the place to come for fine seafood. Try the Nai Wan Cafe on Samila Beach or the Kok Thaion on Ngan Nam Road, renowned for its 1000-year-old eggs, bird's nest soup and fried frogs.

Side Trip to Khu Khut Bird Park

One of the great bird parks in the Kingdom lies north of Songkhla, on the edge of the lake.

To get to the Khu Khut Bird Park, cross the bridge to the west of town then head north, on Highway 408, along the edge of Songkhla lake and past the ruined Te Noi fort. Shortly before Wat Ja Thing Phra and the ancient town of Sathing Phra, you will see a sign for the Khu Khut Wildfowl Sanctuary, the largest of its kind in Thailand and home to over 100 different species of birds, ducks and kingfishers.

Long-tailed boats carrying up to ten people are available for rent. Bring a camera and a sun hat, and get there early in the morning or late in the afternoon. During the middle of the day you will be roasted.

*K*ing Narai's bloody assault on Songkhla in 1678 did nothing to undermine the prosperity of its seafaring inhabitants. Their successors quickly turned it into one of the busiest fishing ports in the world.

The Far South

Beyond Songkhla and Hat Yai, the isthmus narrows, bordered to the east by the Gulf of Thailand and to the west by Malaysia. Few visitors make it this far. Troubles in the predominantly Muslim region and poor tourist infrastructure—few people speak English—have seen to that.

Still the provinces of Yala, Narathiwat and Pattani do have their attractions in the form of mosques, long empty beaches, tiny farming communities and, for the most part, a friendly people. Before leaving enquire about the conditions and never drive at night.

Khu Khut can be reached by bus from the terminal on Rong Muang Road in the direction of Ranut, and basic accommodation is available near the sanctuary headquarters.

Inhabitants of the deep South may be a Muslim minority, but when it comes to dress they can teach their compatriots a few things about style.

Pattani

Drive south from Hat Yai along Highway 43 and Highway 4086 past the delightful little town of Chana and the first provincial town you will come to is Pattani, situated a few km inland from the Gulf of Thailand

For such a modern looking town, Pattani has a wealth of history. During the early centuries, the town was part of a string of city states which thrived on trade with India and China. At one stage in the early 17th century Pattani even joined forces with a local pirate named Yong Da Na who attacked and razed Songkhla.

Little of that past remains though— and besides a few old wooden houses near the river, there is not a lot to see.

Still, the famous **Mosque on Yarang Road**, is worth a visit. It's a vast green building that was built in the early 1960s and is said to be one of the largest in the kingdom.

Pattani is also the place to indulge in some of the food for which the South is renowned. Try *kaeng lueang* (yellow curry) made with fish, meat and bamboo shoots, cooked in a hot sour sauce or *kaeng tai pla* (fish-kidney curry)

made with fermented fish innards and an assortment of potent spices and vegetables. Both dishes can be bought almost anywhere and have an after-taste like a cannon.

If you are lucky enough to be in the vicinity of Pattani at the end of February, you may well see the famous Lim Ko Nieo Festival, where religious devotees perform ascetic feats such as walking through fire and piercing themselves with metal spikes in order to pay homage to the goddess Chao Mae Lim. At this time of year, it is extremely difficult to get accommodation in Pattani and you may have no option but to stay in nearby towns. At other times, reasonable accommodation can be found.

*B*ird *cooing is more than just a fad in the South. Successful doves sell for up to Bt400,000. No wonder the inhabitants put them in such nice cages.*

Narathiwat

This charming town lies 100 km (60 miles) further to the south of Pattani beyond a string of deserted beaches. Narithiwat has both the lazy air of a French provincial town and some wonderful old wooden houses to recommend it.

At dawn, explore the tiny alleys that lead off Pupaphakdi Road and then head north to the fruit and vegetable

Of Patavi

The inhabitants of Pattani, formerly known as Patavi, were said to be an effeminate and boisterous lot, much given to cohabitation and to wife-swapping. But what impressed early travellers more than anything was their sheer joy of good food and drink. One Thomas Herbert recorded in 1638 "They take great delight in the eating of beetle and opium and love Areck (a strong liquor) exceedingly: they usually eat in plates of gold".

market situated a short distance from the colourful fishing village. For most of the day, it's thronged with women in veils and men in sarongs and headdresses purchasing garlic and spring onions. Nearby stalls sell *musaman* and *kari* and other Islamic foods, although for those still yearning for a European repast, eggs and bacon are served around the corner at the Rex Hotel on Chamroonnara Road.

Continue 2 km (1 mile) to the north of town to **Narathat Beach**, a long peaceful stretch of sand some 4 km (2.5 miles) long, shaded with casuarina pines and dotted with beach stalls selling soft drinks and snacks. It can be easily reached by tricycle, the town's main form of transport.

Narathiwat's other major attraction lies 6 km (4 miles) south-west of town on Highway 42. **Wat Khao Khong** is the largest Buddha image in the south, measuring 15 m (49 ft) from knee to knee, and was nearly blown up in the late 1980s by Muslim separatists. Today it sits on a small hill in the centre of a park staring out peacefully over the surrounding countryside. From Narathiwat, Highway 4084 leads south

for 40 km (25 miles), passing Taksin Ratcha Niet Palace to the border town of Tak Bai. There are a number of beaches stretching as far as the eye can see, but there is little infra-structure or accommodation, and camping is not recommended.

Yala

The third of the major provincial towns in the extreme South and by far the most prosperous is Yala, situated 40 km (25 miles) south of Pattani and reached by Highway 420.

The town lies in the hills set amongst abundant rubber plantations and dominated by a large central mosque, the tallest in Thailand. During the 1970s and 1980s, the province of Yala was home to some of the most serious ethnic troubles, and today there is still a big armed presence in the area. But with its fine parks and sports ground and its wide boulevards the town reflects little of the underlying tensions .

Whilst exploring the town, keep your eyes open for the beautiful bird cages found throughout the region. Every year in March, Yala holds an Asian Dove Festival and dove lovers from all over the Kingdom descend in droves. Doves are believed to bring good luck, and one that wins a string of competitions can be sold for as high a price as Bt400,000. At other times of the year, Yala is also popularly known for its sheep and goat fighting contests.

The Route to Betong

South of Yala, the route, Highway 410, becomes more mountainous, curving spectacularly through limestone cliffs alongside the Bang Lang Dam.

Two National Parks can be easily reached: one, after 60 km (37 miles), at **Thanto** with a fine waterfall of seven levels; the other 10 km (6 miles) beyond **Charoparai** village with hot water springs where eggs can be boiled in seven minutes. These are clearly marked in English and are good places to break the journey.

From here the road leads to the wild frontier town of Betong and over the border to the Malaysian state of Perak. Taxis run from Yala to the Malaysian city of Alor Star via Betong, but only during the day. At night you are strongly advised to stay off the roads, since trouble is not unknown.

Phattalung

The sleepy town of Phattalung has an impressive setting, overshadowed by the two huge limestone mountains known as Khao Ok Thalu (Punctured-Chest Mountain) and Khao Hua Taek (Broken Head Mountain). It is linked to Bangkok and Hat Yai by the main railway line and by Highway 41.

Although best known for its famous *manorha* puppets and shadow plays –which are not much in evidence—the town does have several attractions.

Walk some 2–3 km (1–2 miles) to the north along the railway track and you will reach the pleasant monastery of **Tham Malai**. Tham Malai has three inhabitants—an old monk, a young monk and a white-robed *maichee* or nun.

The monastery is arranged in tiers up the mountainside connected by a path and steps. Halfway up, steps descend into a cave, with stalactites and stalagmites, housing 32 Buddha statues. From the top level there is a stunning view across the plain with its chequerboard of rice terraces stretching towards the western mountain ranges.

Afterwards, if you have the energy, visit **Khuha Savan Cave** on Kuhasawan Road to the west of town, which enshrines several rather ordinary looking Buddha images. Steps lead up inside the cave to another good viewpoint looking westward. There's a couple of other nearby sights including **Saensuk Beach**, 8 km (5 miles) east of town, and **Khao Chaison Hot Water Pond**, 20 km (12 miles) to the south of town; but little to detract from the chief attraction, which lies 30 km (19 miles) to the north-east at the **Thale Noi** (Little Sea) **National Park**.

Side Trip to Thale Noi

To reach the Thale Noi Bird Park, you either take Highway 4048 or catch a bus from the local bus station on Poh Saat Road near the How Hua Hotel.

The Park comprises a freshwater lake covered by *kok* and *krachood* grasses and by lotus flowers, which provide a habitat for more than 150 different species of waterbird and covers 475 sq km (185 sq miles). Some of them migrate to Siberia during the rainy months, but between January and May, when the waters of the lake recede, up to 100,000 birds are estimated to gather within the park precincts to breed.

The best way to see them is to hire one of the boats for an hour or two to take you out into the lake. Early morning and late evening are the recommended times, although if you visit at other times, bring a sun hat.

The most common bird on the lake is the Nok I Kong, which resembles a peahen, but countless other species of waterfowl, ducks and kingfishers can also be spotted bathing amongst the lotus leaves, or flying in swarms overhead.

From the boat, keep an eye out for the local people pushing huge rollers across *krachood* grasses. The grasses have been used for over a hundred years to weave the beautiful mats as well as colourful hats and handbags which are sold at major tourist destinations throughout the Kingdom.

With such magnificent lotus flowers it's easy to attract more than 150 different types of bird.

Side Trip to Nakhon Si Thammarat

Visitors interested in history, should not miss out on the town of Nakhon Si Thammarat (Glorious City of the Dead) situated 100 km (62 miles) to the north-east of Phattalung.

Archaeological finds suggest that 1200 years ago it was part of the powerful Sri Vijaya empire that dominated the Malay Peninsula and much of Java. The town subsequently became an important religious centre, strongly influenced by Ceylon, and with trade links extending to China and Southern India.

In the 18th century, Nakhon Si Thammarat even had its own King. But Phra Palat's reign was brief, lasting for only three years, before it was brought to an end by King Taksin.

For a brief tour of the town start at the southern end of Ratchadamnoen Road at the **National Museum**, open Wednesday–Sunday, 9 a.m.–4 p.m., which houses beautiful southern sculptures, many from the Nakhon Si Thammarat School of Art. These Buddhas, often known as *khanom tom*, are distinguished by their chubby features and rounded faces, and date mainly from the Ayutthaya period. The school of Buddhism in Nakhon Si Thammarat was so strong and attracted so many devotees that for many years neighbouring city states called the area *Muang Phra* (Land of Monks).

The Museum also houses a particularly famous copy of a Vishnu figure with a female attendant—the original is in Phuket's National Museum. In 1966 she had her head cut off and stolen, but it was returned to Thailand by a British antiques dealer in 1973.

Climb up the stairs to see the other local exhibits including traditional shadow puppets, supposed to date from as early as the 9th century, as well as the two-metre high *Nai Yang* puppets used for court performances of the *Ramayana*.

From the Museum, catch a *songthaew* and head north along Ratchadamnoen Road to the 12th-century **Wat Phra Mahathat**, the town's most impressive temple, situated on the left hand side. It is made up of a 78 m high pagoda covered in gold leaf, with a colonnade of seated Buddha figures and numerous *chedi* in Ceylonese style.

Nearby is a small shrine within a government compound to the north, which contains one of the most sacred images in Thailand. **Phra Buddha Singh** is said to have been brought

The hardy members of the town of Nakhon Si Thammarat are known not only for their chubby faced khanom tom *Buddhas, but also for their shadow puppets—beautifully made from dried buffalo hide.*

from Ceylon many centuries ago. But uncertainty surrounds its origins. For there are now three images of Phra Buddha Singh in the kingdom: one in Nakhon Si Thammarat; one in the National Museum in Bangkok; and another in Wat Phra Singh in Chiang Mai. Each one is claimed to be the original.

Nakhon Si Thammarat has two other boasts: puppets and silver jewellery—both can be seen in several shops at the Bazaar on Ratchdamnoen

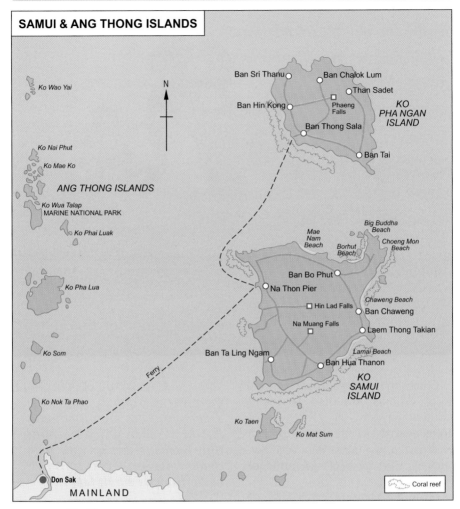

SAMUI & ANG THONG ISLANDS

*M*ap of Samui and
Ang Thong Islands.

Road and along Tha Chang Road. The puppets are especially beautiful, made from dried buffalo hide, softened in water and intricately stencilled, then painted. The best puppets are to be seen at Suchart's in Si Thammasok Road.

The TAT office in the Bazaar off the main road near the Thai Hotel distributes maps and should be able to provide further information on the city and the surrounding area.

Ko Samui

The best-known island in Thailand after Phuket lies 80 km (50 miles) offshore from the mainland town of Surat

Thani. It is surrounded by palm trees and turquoise seas. Centuries ago Ko Samui was inhabited by fishermen who sought refuge from the winds in the protected waters of Bophut bay.

More recently it became a major exporter of coconuts, sending some two million a month to Bangkok, and has the distinction of being probably the only place in the world with a four-headed coconut tree.

In the 1970s Ko Samui made its name as a popular escape for backpackers. But today, with an airport, a handful of international-class hotels, countless bungalows and restaurants, Ko Samui is slowly being groomed as a holiday destination for more up-market tourists. There is little in the way of massive development unlike Phuket though, and for those who want to get away from things, Ko Samui still offers some of the most idyllic surroundings with the option of comforts to go with them.

Orientation

Getting to Ko Samui from Surat Thani is easy. Depending on which ferry you have taken, you will either arrive at the main town of Na Thon or at the car ferry pier further south.

From outside the market at Na Thon, songthaews depart for all the major resorts and beaches, although only before 6 p.m. After that you will have to negotiate your own price for hiring the whole vehicle.

From Na Thon or from any of the main beaches, jeeps and motorbikes can easily be hired by the day or week, but check to see that they are in good condition as in most cases you will be liable for any damage.

Beaches

Ko Samui has beaches for almost the entire length of the island, each with its own attractions. Still you must choose. We list the four main areas.

Chaweng

Of the main beaches, the longest and arguably the most beautiful is Chaweng, a curving stretch of sand that extends more than 6 km (4 miles). To the south at the smaller, quieter Chaweng Noi lies the exclusive Imperial Samui Hotel and in the centre, the biggest concentration of bungalows. At the northern end of the beach you will also find quiet secluded places near Matlong, where the shallow water disappears at low tide leaving a vast expanse of sand.

Lamai

South of Chaweng at Lamai Beach are to be found the cheaper bungalows and a few smaller hotels.

The beach is broken up by strangely-shaped rocks and is backed by a road with beer bars and restaurants and the popular Flamingo disco. People tend to stay on Lamai longer, there is a more laid back feel to the place, and a higher concentration of backpackers.

Bo Phut and Big Buddha Beach

At the northern end of Ko Samui is Bo Phut—quieter, calmer, but a less beautiful beach and less clear water, but particularly good for windsurfing. Continue east from here to Big Buddha Beach, a small bay with a view of two offshore islands and a white sandy beach, suitable for swimming but only at certain times of the year.

Choeng Mon Beach

This beautiful bay lies at the north-eastern tip of the island, and is home to two exclusive hotel developments: the Imperial Tong Sai Bay Hotel and the Boat House Hotel, and to a handful of bungalows. It's a small, peaceful bay, a world away from the bars and discos at Chaweng.

What to Do

Ko Samui may have less to offer than neighbouring Phuket, but there is still an abundance of attractions for those who can tear themselves off the beaches. Watersports are concentrated on Chaweng, and to a lesser extent Lamai, with sailing, fishing and water-skiing amongst the most popular pursuits. Tennis is available at several hotels, but generally for guests only.

At Lamai, beyond the old village, you can get a glimpse of the old days before the tourist boom by visiting an intriguing museum of articles from traditional Thai life.

Walks can also be taken into the hills. One of the best excursions is along a trail which starts in **Mae Nam** climbing through coconut and durian plantations for about two hours to the highest point on the island. The view from the top is exquisite, but bring your own water and lunch, and wear reasonable shoes as snakes abound. After a rest on the top, it is all downhill for a further two hours until you reach Lamai Beach where after a cool beer you can catch a *songthaew* back to your hotel.

Ko Samui even has two waterfalls: the **Hin Lad Waterfall** near Ban Lip Yai, with a pleasant walk up along a forested hillside; and the **Na Muang**

Waterfall near Baan Thurian where there are pools for swimming, and where three former kings have left their initials on the rocks.

In the evening Ko Samui has good restaurants, but the standard of food is not as high as Phuket. Most restaurants are part of bungalow resorts. For discos, try the Green Mango and the Reggae Pub, which are in Chaweng, and the Flamingo and Time Spacedrome in Lamai.

Above all, however, Ko Samui is a place where people come to rest; where walks generally extend no further than from the hut to the beach to the restaurant, and where at sunset the place is lined with people on deckchairs staring dreamily out at the waters of the Gulf of Thailand.

Island Excursions

Islands abound in the surrounding archipelago. Three in particular are worth visiting, with trips organized by countless travel agents, tour groups or simply by catching a regular boat yourself. Closest is **Ko Pha Ngan**, the younger sister, which is less developed

---

Competing on Coconuts

Ko Samui's coconut pickers came a cropper at the hands of an unlikely competitor. The small, brown and hairy local was able to pick up to 1,000 coconuts a day, could climb trees on all fours, and could be coaxed into action by the offer of a banana. The threat—a form of monkey known as the Ling Nang. Word soon got around to other plantations, and the famed monkeys now work the area around, helping to contribute to Ko Samui's record of producing some two million coconuts a month.

Wua Ta Lap (Sleeping Cow Island), where the Park Headquarters is located. Using this as a base, you can explore the other islands such as Ko Mae Ko (Mother Island), Ko Praya (Economical Island), Ko Sam Sao (Tripod Island), Ko Nai Pud (Mr Pud's Island) and Ko Wua Teh (Kicking Cow Island). For details of departures and tours to the islands, enquire at any hotel, bungalow or travel agency on Ko Samui or Surat Thani.

From Surat Thani to Chumphon

Forty km (25 miles) north of Surat Thani lies the old town of **Chaiya**, famous throughout Asia for its salty eggs soaked in brine, and its 100-year-old eggs—which are generally only a few months old. The eggs are duck eggs not chicken eggs, are regarded by the Chinese as aphrodisiacs, and are sold throughout the kingdom.

If you compete with the monkeys to provide more than two million coconuts a month, climbing a tree becomes second nature on Ko Samui.

Chaiya may also have another claim to fame. A group of historians now believe that the town was capital of the great Srivijaya Empire, which from the 8th–13th century ruled a string of principalities in Indonesia, Thailand and Malaysia. Besides **Phra Boromathat**, a revered shrine thought to be more than 1,200 years old, the town, however, bears little sign of any such glory and, with the exception of eggs, there is little to justify spending much time here.

yet equally beautiful, with countless cheap bungalows, white beaches and inland forest. It is reached in an hour by express boat from Na Thon.

A further three hours from Ko Phangan is the island of **Ko Tao**, (Turtle Island) with its picturesque coves and beaches where people often spend weeks in their own little island hideaway, exploring the reefs and wandering along the rocky coastline.

One last major attraction is the **Angthong Marine National Park**, situated 30 km (19 miles) north of Ko Samui—and popularly seen on a one-day trip. The group comprises 40 islands, made up of limestone formations jutting out spectacularly to sea

For those who are taken with it, accommodation can be found on Ko

To get from Chaiya to Chumphon, most people follow Highway 41, a dull concrete road full of trucks. A better alternative is to take Highway 4112, which follows the coast for 70 km (45 miles) past delightful bays and fishing villages before joining the main road to Chumphon and the route back to Bangkok.

Whether You Are Energetic or Easy-going Thailand Offers a Wide Choice of Activity

From shopping to dancing, and from kite flying to boxing, the Thais indulge in every form of joyous activity. To foreigners, it's merely relaxation, to the locals *pai thiau* or pleasure, that insurmountable and most important passion in life. And wherever you go, you will see them at it.

Want to buy an elephant tusk or a lacquered garden pot, or watch a display of Thai boxing? You will always be able to find something to do or see whether you are in Bangkok or in almost any of the main provincial towns. Most major hotels have information counters, which will be able to tell you what leisure activities are available. Many organize tour groups, for example to a boxing match or to dinner at a floating restaurant, and almost all are at reasonable prices.

It is just as easy to put together your own leisure itinerary if you do not want to join an organized group. But before you leave your hotel make sure that you have got any address written in Thai, as well as directions on how to get there.

Below are a few general ideas for various shopping, sporting and cultural activities. For up to date details of addresses, prices and ticket-booking, all of which are constantly changing, your best bet is to contact the local Tourist Authority Office (TAT).

W̶ho needs rain when you can have a colourful umbrella. Chiang Mai's artists not only manage to produce them in abundance, they even export them.

Shopping

Once eclipsed by neighbouring Hong Kong and Singapore, Thailand has recently become one of the best shopping destinations in the region offering some of the widest and cheapest selections of goods.

Indeed besides electrical goods and cameras, which are for the most part expensive and in short supply, Thailand's artisans produce almost every kind of textile, handicraft and jewellery. What's more they even export them and "made in Thailand" items are now sold in some of the most exclusive boutiques in the world.

The key word is selectivity as quality does vary enormously. As a rule, bargain for anything except in shopping centres, department stores or five-star hotels. Sometimes even travel agents have been known to lower the price of an air ticket by a couple of thousand Baht, although this is certainly not a normal practice.

The Art of Bargaining

Want a Gucci ? or a T-shirt ? or even a ride in a tuk tuk ? Then remember to bargain for it. First ask how much the item is. Then name a price considerably lower, and somewhat less than what you want to pay, and eventually agree on a compromise. A few hints to help you along: always check out several stalls to get an idea of the cost; don't get sentimentally attached to blind, or deaf, shopkeepers or smiling ten-year-old children, most of whom are the smartest traders in the game; never admire any object unduly or the price will naturally go up; and finally remember nobody gives anything away for free.

Finally, do not get taken in by the ubiquitous fake. Rolex and Cartier watches, Gucci handbags, and tapes are more often than not imitation, despite assurances from their smiling vendors. They are, however, a speciality of Bangkok and of most major towns, and although not up to the standards of the original, are often of reasonable quality, and can prove handy and remarkably cheap gifts. Many shops have been awarded the official stamp of approval by the judicious TAT. Lists of these shops can be obtained from any of their offices.

Best Buys

Antiques

More tourists probably leave Bangkok clutching mass-produced monstrosities or so-called century old artefacts than even the fake Rolex watches. If you want to be sure that your Chinese porcelain, silver betel nut boxes or old jade are original, stick to a reputable dealer.

The Tourist Authority of Thailand (TAT) provides lists of dealers in its shopping booklet and will also fix you up with the necessary export permits. If you do not have a permit you may find yourself having to convince sceptical customs officials on departure.

Much-prized objects include stone and bronze statues of the Dvaravati period—6th–11th centuries—opium pipes and antique paintings, as well as artefacts smuggled from over the border with Burma. Occasionally you may even be offered a beautiful old Buddha statue, but unless you can be sure that the shop can arrange export papers, you would be unwise to buy it.

Brass, Bronze and Nielloware

Thai artists excel in metalwork. Big brass plates, bronze vases, cutlery and bowls come in numerous shapes and sizes and are specialities in Thailand dating back to the Ayutthaya period. Probably the most exquisite art, however, is that of *nielloware,* which is made of silver or gold engraved with black alloy. *Nielloware* is often used for tea sets, elaborately ornamented cigarette boxes and buttons. The best place to buy these pieces is at Chiang Mai in the North or at Nakhon Si Thammarat in the South, where you can actually see the craftsmen at work.

Celadon *Pottery*

Since the times of King Ramkamhaeng in the 13th century, the distinctive high-fired green *Celadon* pottery has had something of a following in central and northern parts of Thailand. Today, it is available in many forms—lamp bases, vases and bowls—and is made only from earthenware materials with no chemical additives. The main centre of *Celadon* production is Chiang Mai, though beautiful pots are widely sold in many shops in Bangkok and the other major towns.

Clothes

Tailor-made suits, made-to-measure trousers, shirts, skirts, dresses and even boxer shorts are just some of the items available to the selective shopper in just about any cloth, colour or style. Clothes are considerably cheaper in Bangkok than in Singapore or Hong Kong and can often be designed at a day's notice. But beware the quality of the cloth, and if possible try to bring along an article which can be copied.

Gems and Jewellery

Bangkok is often called the coloured stone capital of the world and claims to account for anything up to 70 per cent of the gem cutting trade. It is also renowned for its mastery in imitation. Many tourists find that what was sold to them as a native sapphire or ruby turns out to be no more than an imported piece of glass. To avoid disappointment, go to a TAT approved jeweller or one of the big hotels and ask for a certificate of authentication. Shops opposite the Oriental Hotel in Bangkok and along Silom Road are said to be reputable with gem cutters, goldsmiths and designers making pieces that attract buyers from all over the world.

Lacquerware

Lacquerware is light, widely available and easily transported home. Items are made by covering a thin wooden or bamboo frame shaped in the form of a bowl or vase with a fine coat of black lacquer. After the first coat has dried and been polished, anything up to another 15 coats are added. The objects are then painted and decorated with gold and other colours and sold throughout the country.

Leather Goods

If you want a handbag made from ostrich skin, a belt from snake or a wallet from sting ray, this could be your chance. Thailand has the raw materials and tanneries to cater to every whim and the cheap labour to ensure that leather products are both plentiful and good value. Shoes, bags and jackets can be picked up in many outdoor markets as well as the smarter stores. In some areas, it is even possible to buy leather made from elephant hide, although since this is an endangered species it should be avoided.

Silk

The modern silk industry in Thailand is synonymous with the name of Jim Thompson, an American secret agent who did for silk what Henry Ford did for cars. Largely handwoven, and produced in a sumptuous variety of colours, weights and sizes, silk has justifiably become known as one of Thailand's greatest gifts to the world. Some of the best shops are in Bangkok, although, in practice, silk is to be found almost everywhere, and especially in Chiang Mai or around Nakhon Ratchasima in the North-east. Silk can be purchased either by length or as ready made items of clothing.

Silverware

Silver is generally cheap and of good quality. Often it is melted down from old coins, cooled and chiselled into shape against a wooden mould. The quality of the products is strictly controlled by the government which prescribes that the content of pure silver products must not be less than 92.5 per cent. The three main production centres of silverware in Thailand are Bangkok, Chiang Mai and Nakhon Si Thammarat.

Woodcarving

Woodcarving should in theory be one of the great buys. Until recently, the raw material was in abundant supply. What's more it has a long tradition dating back to the Sukhothai period more than 700 years ago. But whilst

*T*he art of woodcarving handed down from King Ramkamhaeng's times remains one of Thailand's most precious crafts. There's only one problem: a shortage of wood caused by the recent ban on logging.

there are beautiful carvings still to be found, especially in the North around Chiang Mai, there are many relatively poor quality, mass-produced tourist works. If you are looking for an ornate picture frame, a salad bowl or a wall plaque, be prepared to shop around. The best woodcarved products are made of teak. But because of the government imposed logging ban, prices tend to be higher.

Sport

Thais are enthusiastic participants in almost every sport. Most major hotels now have swimming pools, and often tennis courts and a fitness centre. Some even have their own golf range.

In Bangkok, especially, fitness mania has reached fever pitch. At dawn and dusk, Lumpini Park is a mass of heaving human bodies running, walking, shadow boxing or, in a fit of machismo, pulling car tyres along. Further afield, there are pony rides, trekking, sailing and some of the most beautiful coral reefs in the world.

For the best gymnasiums in the capital try the Landmark Hotel, Tel: 254 0404, the Dusit Thani Hotel, Tel: 236 0450, or the Menam, Tel: 289 0352–all of which are open to non-members. The gyms of The Oriental, Tel: 236 0400, Hilton, Tel: 253 0123 and the Siam Inter-Continental, Tel: 253 0355 are usually reserved for hotel guests.

Public tennis courts are at 13/1 Soi Attakarnprasit, Sathorn Road, Tel: 286 7202 and 7 Soi Soonvijai 1, New Phetchburi Road, Tel: 318 1651, as well as at the Ambassador Hotel, Tel: 254 0444, the Shangri-La, Tel: 236 7777 and the Imperial, Tel: 254 0111.

Outside Bangkok, in some of the smaller towns fitness parks have sprung up, with paths for running, and often weight racks and pull-up bars. The relevant TAT offices should be able to provide further details of public sports facilities.

Deep-Sea Fishing

In Thailand, you don't need to be a tycoon to participate in the joys of one of the greatest marine sports. Nor do you need to have had any previous experience. Local operators in Pattaya and Phuket, Krabi, Ko Samui, and even Ranong and Chumphon now offer anything from lightweight hobby-type excursions to serious big game fishing, with catches likely to include barracuda, as well as blue marlin, king marlin, sailfish and *wahoo*.

Trips can be arranged either locally, or through Bang Saray Fishing Lodge in Bangkok, Tel: 233 7719, or Game Fishing Club Pattaya, Tel: (038) 429 645. In Phuket, there are 35 charter boats operating. Philip Watkins is an experienced game fishing consultant at:

Phuket Tourist Centre
125/7 Phang Nga Road
Phuket Town
Tel: (076) 211 849

Prices range from Bt1,500–Bt2,000 a day to join a charter, or from Bt7,000–Bt 15,000 a day for an exclusive charter.

Diving

Along the coasts of Thailand are some of the finest diving spots in the world. Some, like the Similan Islands and Surin Islands, are National Parks with abundant marine life, but only limited accommodation. Others like Phuket and Pattaya, are highly established centres with all the latest types of diving equipment.

Both Phuket and Pattaya can be used as diving locations or as jumping-off points for other destinations. Day or longer trips are easy to arrange and can be booked at almost any travel agency. Some companies offer the option of a combined dive and cruise.

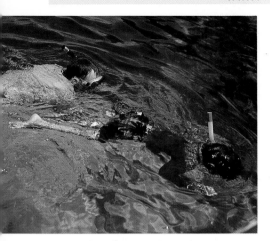

*A*ll you need is a face
mask and snorkel and the
underwater world is your oyster.

There are many diving schools in Phuket and Pattaya whose instructors are qualified members of PADI (Professional Association of Diving Instructors) or NAUI (National Association of Underwater Instructors). Ensure you use a reputable company.

Diving courses can be arranged costing around US$60 for a one-day introductory course, US$340 for a five-day Open Water course, or US$660 for the Divemaster course. A one-day diving trip on the west coast of Phuket costs approximately US$30, while a seven-day diving cruise to the Similan and Surin Islands would be about US$700. The following should all be able to hire out equipment and offer diving instruction.

Fantasea Divers
PO Box 20
Patong Beach
Phuket 83150
Tel: (076) 321 309, 321 020 ext. 8177

Poseidon Memrod Club,
Phuket Island Resort
Tel: (076) 215 950-5

Phuket International Diving Centre
Le Meridien Hotel
Relax Beach
Tel: (076) 321 480-5

Siam Diving Centre
Kata Karon Beach
P.O. Box 244
Phuket 83000
Tel: (076) 212 901/4

Seafari
Royal Garden Resort
Beach Road
Pattaya
Tel: (038) 428 126/7

International Divers Centre
Siam Bayview Hotel
Beach Road
Pattaya
Tel: (038) 423 325/9

Golf

It may not necessarily be a reflection of priorities, but the first thing that almost every visitor will see in Bangkok is not a *wat* or a *tuk tuk*, but a caddy and a golf ball. For in the centre of Bangkok's international airport is the unusual site of an 18-hole course with wide open fairways, greens and an unimpeded view of the plane hangars.

Probably no other sport in Thailand has attracted so much attention in so short a time span as the universally popular game of golf. It's not only that it is cheap and that there are an abundant supply of caddies, but also that the Kingdom boasts some of the most

288

spectacular courses, open all the year round. There are now numerous practice ranges and more than 50 courses throughout the country.

Many of the leading courses such as Navatanee, Tel: 374 6127, Krungthep Kritha, Tel: 374 0491 and Unico, Tel: 377 9038, are situated within Greater Bangkok. Others like the Rose Garden Golf Course, Tel: 253 0295, are within easy reach, whilst away from the capital, 18-hole courses have sprung up in Khao Yai, Chiang Mai, Hua Hin, Phuket and some of the greatest beauty spots in the Kingdom.

There is usually little need to bring your own clubs. Most major courses have full or half sets of clubs for rent, along with shoes, umbrellas and other useful accessories. But remember to book in advance, especially at weekends when almost all the courses are fully booked.

Several Bangkok hotels now have driving ranges and putting greens. The Oriental's Sport Centre on the banks of the Chao Phya River opposite the hotel, has a range and resident pro. The spacious gardens of the Siam Inter-Continental Hotel on Rama I Road include a floodlit 30-m (98.5 ft) driving range and a putting green, complete with sand bunkers.

Lists of golf courses are available from any TAT Office. Alternatively, contact Bogart's International, who specialize in golf vacations and package tours in Thailand at:

Bogart's International
CCT Bldg
109 Surawong Road
Bangkok 10500
Tel: (236) 2910

Kite Flying

Legend has it that during Ayutthayan times, kites were put out into the winds to disturb the clouds and would inevitably lead to rain. Those beliefs largely disappeared with the advent of the weather man. But the Thais' enthusiasm for the things on bits of string did not. Indeed fanatics of one of Thailand's most popular sports still crowd Bangkok's Sanam Luang park on many weekends to participate in one of the Kingdom's oldest and most colourful displays.

Kite fighting contests comprise two kites. The male kite is called *Chula* and is large, cumbersome and nearly two metres long. The female kite is called Pakpao and is smaller, more graceful and agile. During the contest, Chula, tries to catch Pakpao with his hook and bring her to the ground in his territory. Pakpao tries to evade capture and fell her male opponent.

The spectacle is held at Sanam Luang, opposite the Grand Palace on most weekends during the dry season, and especially from February to April. To enjoy it to the full, get there in the early afternoon, bring a picnic and sit back on the grass eating prawns and watching the Thais pursuing one of their favourite sports.

Riding

Equestrian activities have a long tradition going back to the days when the kings would send out their armies on horses and elephants to scare the opposition. Now, increasingly, they are becoming a major tourist attraction, included as part of a number of treks.

One of the best-known horse riding schools caters largely for expatriate children, offers supervised riding or lessons for beginners, intermediate and advanced riders and is at:

River Kwai Family Camp
Box 20
Kanchanaburi
Tel: (034) 512 733

There's also:

Phuket Riding Club
82/2 Patak Road
Tel: (076) 381 667-8

Pattaya's Reo Ranch offers 6 km (3.7 miles) of trail rides on thoroughbreds imported from Australia. For more leisurely rides, there are horses for hire on the beaches of Cha-am and Hua Hin.

If you are keener to watch than to participate, horse racing takes place in the capital on Saturdays and Sundays—except in the rainy season—at:

Royal Bangkok Sports Club
1 Henri Durant Road
Tel: 282 3770

Royal Turf Club
183 Phitsanulok Road
Tel: 282 3770

Tickets should be obtained from their offices in advance.

Sailing

November to April are the best months for sailing around the waters of the Andaman Sea, and Pattaya and Phuket are the best places to organize it. From either of these centres, sailing dinghies, catamarans or windsurfers can be hired out by the hour, and various forms of yacht charter are available ranging from a day to a week or two.

Some yacht charters now offer pampered luxury cruises as well as bareboat charter. And within easy sail of these centres can be found some of the most beautiful tropical paradises, giant limestone rock formations and coral reefs.

Bareboat charter prices range from about US$200 a day for a 32-footer (9.8-m) to about US$1,000 for a 66-footer (20.1 m);a catered cruise on a 17-metre (55.8 ft) schooner costs US$700 a day—for six people.

Below is a list of companies that organize yachting tours.

Asia Voyages
Charn Issara Tower
942 Rama IV Road
Bangkok 10500
Tel: (02) 235 4100-4

Thai Yachting Co, Ltd
Ratchadamri Arcade 7th Floor
Ratchadamri Road
Bangkok 10300
Tel: (02) 253 1733

Star Yachting Co. Ltd
924/126-7 Charn Issara Tower
4th Floor
Rama IV Road
Bangkok 10500
Tel: (02) 233 0232

Alternatively, turn up and organize your own sailing trip through one of the local charter companies, tour operators , dive shops or even individual yachtsmen.

T here is not a lot to worry about when you are breezing along in the Andaman Sea, sails to the wind. These yachters have no time for the intricacies of temples.

Thai Boxing

Muay Thai or Thai-style kick-boxing is the ultimate spectator sport in the Kingdom, and a fine demonstration of speed and agility. Bouts take place in traditional boxing rings and are accompanied by a three-man orchestra beating drums and high-pitched cymbals, and by avid betting amongst the

291

spectators, in first-, second- and third-class seats and stands.

Rules permit lashing kicks to the upper and lower half of the opponent's body as well as punching. Indeed, despite the startlingly frail appearance of the combatants, skilful positioning of elbows, knees and feet makes them formidable opponents. The Thais are not the only ones to practise the sport. Recently Dutch boxers have come to Bangkok and have been building a considerable reputation.

Thai boxing is held in Bangkok at:

Ratchadamnoen Stadium (Mondays, Wednesdays, Thursdays and Sundays)
Ratchadamnoen Nok Avenue
Tel: 281 4205

Lumpini Stadium (Tuesdays, Fridays and Saturdays starting at 6 p.m.)
Rama IV Road
Tel: 251 4303

There are demonstrations in Phuket, Pattaya, Ko Samui and most other major tourist destinations as well.

Bettas Splendens

Outlawed it may be, but fishfighting *(bettas splendens)* continues to draw unprecedented support in Bangkok and outlying rural areas. The main protagonist is a male fish with short sturdy round fins. When placed in a tank with his opposite number, the fish rapidly changes colour from the dullest grey-green to the most brilliant red and blue, and goes on the attack. Observers place bets and cheer. The game is over when one of the fish dies or flees to a corner.

Things of Special Interest to Children

Thai sanuk is not merely reserved for grown-ups, but for anyone who has the good fortune to be spending time in the country. Throughout the Kingdom there are a host of attractions that should appeal to children of any age. What's more the people are extremely child-minded and will constantly pamper them, offering them seats on crowded buses and giving you advice on what to do with them.

If Bangkok is the first stop there are a couple of attractions, which though some distance from the centre, are generally worth the effort, especially if you go on Sundays when traffic is less of a problem. There is a Disney castle with rides, games and cartoon characters at **Magic Land** (*Daen Neramit*), 72 Paholyothin Road, Tel: 513 3126, open daily 10 a.m.–6 p.m.

Bangkok also has a **Planetarium** at 928 Sukhumvit Road, Tel: 392 2598, with two shows in the morning and two in the afternoon.

Further out, on the road to Pattaya there's **Ocean World** at Bangsaen Beach Road, Chonburi, Tel: (038) 377 562, with rides, water-slides and a wave pool.

At the **Rose Garden**, 32 km (19.8 miles) west of Bangkok, Tel: 253 0295, cultural shows are held daily at 3 p.m. with local dances and sports, traditional fights and elephants. There are also numerous zoos, snake farms and crocodile farms (see BANGKOK).

Perhaps the most pleasant morning's outing, and certainly one of the easiest to organize is to hire a speedboat on the Chao Phya River for an hour

or two. This will stop at the Snake Farm and the Royal Barges—as well as provide brief glimpses of temples and of village life. The trip can be organized at almost any hotel or by merely turning up at the jetty near the Grand Palace, Wat Po, the Oriental and a host of other riverside stops.

Outside Bangkok, the biggest attraction is likely to be the beautiful white sandy beaches that are strung along the 2,500 km (1553 miles) of Thailand's southern coasts. Pony rides on beaches, boat trips to the outlying islands or a few hours in a fishing village, are likely to placate even the most demanding child.

*E*ven small *north-eastern villages have a special place in their hearts for the junior members of society.*

Away from the coast, the best inland destinations for children are probably Chiang Mai and the cool mountains of the North, where caves, tribal villages, waterfalls, elephants, butterfly farms and zoos are within easy reach.

If nothing succeeds, there is one simple alternative. Many hotels and associations now offer childcare services so that whilst your little child is being amused, you can peacefully discover the real Thailand.

*M*ore than 1,000 species of flowers and plants dot Thailand's 52 National Parks. No wonder the animals like it.

Wildlife and Nature

Thailand's tropical climate and widely varied terrain have acted as a magnet to a variety of birds and beasts as well

as to plants and trees. Although rapid economic development has taken a heavy toll on the environment, visitors can still enjoy wildlife in its natural habitat as well as beautiful forests, untouched beaches, and sheer limestone crags, almost without parallel.

Within the Kingdom, 52 National Parks have been declared as nature reserves. Within these are to be found the richest examples of flora and fauna that Thailand has to offer.

Some of the Parks like Khao Yai are easily accessible from Bangkok—even as a day trip. They provide basic, but reasonable accommodation and sometimes even meals. Others like Khao Phanom Jura can only be reached by private transport or by trips organized through local travel agents.

As growing numbers of foreign visitors turn their back on the more developed public areas and resorts, the Parks are likely to improve facilities and offer greater numbers of English-speaking guides.

Most Parks charge a small fee to visit. Advance bookings for accommodation are advisable at the more popular parks, especially at holidays and weekends when hordes of locals descend with their guitars and their bottles of Mekong whisky. Most National Park bungalows cost around Bt500–Bt1,000 a night, but will sleep five to ten people. Some Parks, however, offer smaller two-person bungalows for Bt250 or dormitory accommodation, and many provide tents at Bt50–Bt80. Camping in your own tent is allowed in almost all the Parks. In principle, the Parks also provide guides and maps to point out the greatest beauty spots. In practice, you should be prepared to wander off the beaten track with what few signs there are often being in Thai.

Anyone visiting the Parks should make sure that they have a hat—to guard against the sun—and insect repellent, as well as some comfortable walking shoes. If you are staying the night, bring a torch, and, in winter, a sweater or blanket for the cool hours of the morning.

And finally, don't expect too much. Thailand does still have elephants, tapirs and big cats, but they are not always easy to see. The biggest highlight may well turn out to be not the wildlife, but beautiful scenery and a world that is as different from the chaos of Bangkok as it is from the flat rice fields of the Central Plains.

Amongst the most popular Parks are Khao Yai, Ko Samet, Nopparat Thara (Ko Phi Phi), Hat Nai Yang, Phu Kradung and Ko Similan. To get further information on these and other National Parks, ask at:

The National Parks Division of the Forestry Department
Paholyothin Road
Bangkok
Tel: 579 4842 or 579 0529

Birds

Thailand was once a paradise for the ornithologist. These days, birds have in many cases fallen victim to hunters, to deforestation and to the endless forays of smugglers who make their fortune by depriving the Kingdom of one of its most endearing assets.

Colourful birds can, however, still be seen in many National Parks, although

Thale Noi National Bird Park at Phattalung and at the Khu Khut Bird Sanctuary near Songkhla, some 150 different species of waterbird such as the purple heron, egret and purple swamp hen.

Fish

Even the rice fields have fish in Thailand. They are called *pla duk* and they live in the muddy sediment, providing the farmers with an endless source of nutrition. At the other end of the scale is the monster of the Mekong, *pla buk*, which can grow up to three metres long and weigh more than 250 kg.

Some of the fish such as the climbing perch known as *pla maw* and the shooting fish have become worldwide celebrities. The climbing perch can cover considerable distances in mud and on land and has even been known to climb plants.

Also much in demand is the *pla kat*, a tiny fighting fish, which provides the Thais with the sort of excitement reserved by Europeans for a football match.

In the seas, beautifully coloured reef fish abound with angel fish, parrot fish and mantarays all seen in large numbers. Prized gamefish such as barracuda, marlin and wahoo also attract numbers of anglers.

Off the coasts, there are also sharks including hammerhead, tiger, nurse and bull sharks, but they are usually only seen by those who seek them ouy—divers and fishermen—and attacks are almost unheard of.

*B*irds are no longer easy prey even for the most dedicated ornithologist. But in the National Parks, with a bit of stalking, you may still come across the flighty individuals.

you should bring binoculars. Orange-breasted and red-headed trogons, moustached barbets and hornbills can all be found in large numbers at Khao Yai National Park, whilst in Doi Inthanon the rare ashy-throated warbler and yellow-bellied flowerpecker are commonly spotted.

In the South, and especially around Krabi, many species of swallow build their nests in rock crevices and under the crowns of palm trees. One, known as the sea swift, even makes its nest of tiny twigs glued together with saliva. The nests are regarded as a great delicacy and are collected from caves and rockfaces to be served up as soup in Chinese restaurants, where they command high prices.

If you are lucky, you may come across parrots and lorikeets, and in the

Forests

In the beginning, the countryside was an endless carpet of lush and green vegetation, of evergreen forest, red forest and teak forest. Then came the settlers with their slash and burn techniques, the foresters, the illegal loggers and property developers. Today less than 25 per cent of Thailand is forest-covered. Much of this is eucalyptus, a cash crop which grows rapidly, but which drains the soil of valuable nutrients.

There are still, however, forests around Kanchanaburi and Umpang and, in the North, near Mae Hong Son and Mae Sariang. Loei province still has pine, and the teak forest, which once covered the land, can still be seen in the provinces of Nan and Prae. Elsewhere, there's red wood and oak and, along the coast, mangrove—although rapidly being depleted by the development of new sea resorts.

Perhaps the biggest hope for the country's remaining forests lies in a logging ban introduced in 1989 following mud slides and flooding, which left 350 villagers dead. If the Forestry Commission has its way then trees could again cover 40 per cent of the kingdom. For beautiful Thailand, the costs will be severe if it fails.

Insects

Except in tropical America, no region offers such a variety of butterflies as Thailand. There are butterflies from Malaysia, from Borneo and Sumatra, and even from India. The most conspicuous is the *Papilio aeacus*, which on account of its size is known to the Thais as *Phiseua yak* or giant butterfly. Also common is the striking *Kallima inachus*, known as the leaf butterfly. The upperside of the wings is blue-brown in colour and crossed by

---

Of Men and Mosquitoes

Explorers who came to Siam in the early centuries took on not only the elements, the fearsome chillis and the threat of crocodiles, but also, and most punishing of all—mosquitoes. Henri Mouhot, whilst travelling down the Chao Phya River in the 19th century, called them the greatest evil of the lot. "Thousands of these cruel insects suck our blood night and day. I would rather have to deal with the wild beasts of the forest" he wrote. Mouhot's words were to prove truer than he thought. The great man died of a fever said to be malaria. His last words were "Have pity on me, O my God".

---

an orange bar, the underside like a dead leaf. When it alights with wings closed it becomes invisible.

Elsewhere, huge atlas moths with reddish-brown wings, dragonflies, crickets, cockroaches and tortoise beetles are common, as well as rhinoceros beetles, which destroy cocoa-palm, and the ubiquitous mosquitoes, which somehow seem undeterred by even the strongest repellants.

Generally, the only insects you need worry about are of the malaria-carrying kind. Spiders are for the most part harmless, and cockroaches a common but impartial resident in all but the finest hotels.

Mammals

The first animal you are likely to see is a water buffalo, glistening in glutinous mud, wading through rice paddies, with the somnolence of a tourist in a deck chair. But there are a variety of other mammals: monkeys, elephants, bears, wild boar, deer, tapirs and even tigers.

The most legendary is the white elephant, which in fact was never white, but was nonetheless a much-prized beast of the Indian variety, noted for its strength, courage and docility. White elephants were kept at the Royal Palace where they were lavishly waited upon by some of the Kingdom's greatest poets and chefs, and were commonly introduced to visiting dignitaries. Almost a dozen of them are still in residence at the Chitralada Palace in Bangkok.

But in the forests, where a century ago there were more than 20,000, their numbers have rapidly dwindled. Only around 4,000 of them are still to be found, mainly in the North and in the Tenasserim mountains along the border with Burma. A few are still trained to carry wood out of the jungle, a task now fast disappearing, or to pose in the tourist camps which have sprung up in the North and the North-east.

This is becoming a common story amongst Thailand's animal kingdom. Almost 16 species are now listed as endangered, with a further eight close to extinction. But there are still several unusual and commonly seen wild animals, one of the most famous being the tragulus or mouse deer, which is no more than 20 cm tall and is said to be the world's smallest hoofed animal.

In the forests of the North and in the thickly wooded hills around Phetchburi and Kanchanaburi, there are also gibbons and pig-tailed monkeys, as well as weasels, wild pig and flying squirrels. The world's smallest known mammal even comes from Thailand. The bat is known as the khun kitti bat, weighs 2 grams and lives in the Sai Yok National Park.

Reptiles

Snakes live in people's gardens, up their mango trees and measure as long as ten metres. There are thought to be around 100 species, ranging from the python to the krait, cobra and russel viper.

The most dangerous snake is the king cobra, which is occasionally found in dense jungle and measures up to five metres (16.5 ft). So potent is its bite that it has been known to kill an elephant. The longest snake is the reticulated python, which can grow to ten metres and weigh as much as 140 kg (308 lbs).

The snakes have aroused considerable interest amongst zoologists, who occasionally mount expeditions in search of them. Travellers, however, rarely encounter them except when trekking in the northern hills. Even then, there have been few reported cases of fatalities, with the majority of snakes in the country appearing to end up as handbags or cowboy boots.

Along the waterfronts and in the cities, other reptiles are found in abundance—lizards and tortoises, turtles and flying frogs.

The most friendly and beloved are geckos, of which there are some 17 species. They often choose to live in the luxury of people's kitchens, or even in their electric kettles, where they reside perfectly harmlessly, eating insects.

Another popular lizard is the *Liolepis belliana*, a beautifully marked species traditionally found in the provinces. Sadly it is in great demand as food among the country people, who catch the animal in a snare set over the entrance to its burrow, and its numbers are declining fast.

There are also some 47 species of frog, the most notable being the burrowing frog, which is most active during the rainy season, and is occasionally spotted in Bangkok at the time of the monsoons.

Ubiquitous Orchids

Figures vary, but it is estimated that between 500 and 1,000 different types of orchid flourish in Thailand, along with numerous species of bougainvillea and hibiscus.

Orchids were first cultivated in Siam by Prince Tivakornwongpravat more than 100 years ago. These days, Thais have not only become big exporters of the flowers, earning an estimated Bt700 million a year in foreign exchange, but they have also been keen developers of their own hybrids, produced by breeding different species together. One of the most popular is the *Sirikit,* named after Her Majesty the Queen. Other popular species include *Amber Glow, Nellie Morley, Bow Bells, Norman's Bay Emperor* and *Dorset Gold.*

The best time to see the flowers is after the rains have ended and before the heat of summer begins. In February, the area around Chiang Mai is a sea of colours, of purples and pinks, with thousands of rhododendrons and more than 100 types of flowering plants—with hibiscus, bougainvillea, acacia, lotus, frangipani, jacaranda and countless other flowers vying for attention. Even in Bangkok, there are said to be between 500 and 600 species of plants, of which about 73 per cent are truly indigenous, although most of them have a widespread tropical distribution.

Language Guide

Although English is widely used in hotels and shops, you should try to express some simple phrases in Thai.

Below is a basic guide which should at least get you off the ground. As you master some of the most elementary words, you may find that people still find it hard to understand you. This is because Thai has five different tones and one word can often have several meanings depending on which tone is used. Keep on trying though and eventually you will be rewarded.

For those wanting something less rudimentary, try the *Thailand Phrasebook* written by Joe Cummings or *Hugo's Phrasebook* published by Asia Books. Alternatively, there are language courses at the AUA, Tel: 251 1606 and YMCA, Tel: 287 1997, in Bangkok for those contemplating a longer stay.

Pronunciation

Because many Thai vowels do not have English equivalents, the words below have been translated phonetically to the most approximate sound. L and R are interchangeable. Assume *kap* for men or *ka* for women after every statement or question.

Numbers

0	Soon
1	Nung
2	Song
3	Sam
4	See
5	Ha
6	Hok

7	Jet
8	Baet
9	Gao
10	Sip
11	Sip-e
12	Sip-song
13	Sip-sam
14	Sip-see
15	Sip-ha
16	Sip-hok
17	Sip-jet
18	Sip-baet
19	Sip-gao
20	Yee-si
21	Yee-sip-et
22	Yee-sip-song
23	Yee-sip-sam...
30	Sam-sip
40	See-sip
50	Ha-sip
100	(Nung) Ro
200	Song roi
300	Sam roi...
1,000	(Nung) Pan
10,000	(Nung) Meun

Time

When?	Meu arai
Today	Wan nee
Tomorrow	Proong nee
Yesterday	Meua wan nee
Now	Diao nee
Later	Tee lang
Minute	Na tee

Hour	Chua mong
How many hours?	Kee chua mong?
Day	Wan
Week	Athit
Month	Deuan
Year	Pee

Persons

I	Pom (men) Chan (women)
You	Khun
He/she/they/him/her/ them	Khao
Respectful you/he/she	Thun

Shopping

Do you have?	Mee...mai, ...mee mai?
Yes	Mee
I don't have	Mai mee
I want	Ao
I don't want	Mai ao
How much (is this)?	(Nee) tao rai?
How many Baht?	Kee Baht?
Expensive	Paeng
Too expensive	Paeng pai
Too small	Lek pai
Big	Yai
Bigger	Yai kwaa
Cheap	Mai paeng or tuuk
Cheaper	Tuuk kwaa
Do you have something bigger?	Mee yai kwaa nee mai?

Food

Deep-fried chicken in pandanus leaf	Gai haw bai toey
Fried fish cakes	Tot man pla
Fried shrimp cakes	Tot man kung
Fried spring rolls	Po pia tot
Spring rolls, not fried	Po pia sot
Spicy soup with chilli and lemongrass	Tom Yam
Spicy shrimp soup	Tom Yam Kung
Chicken in coconut milk soup	Tom Ka Gai
Thai vegetable soup	Kaeng Liang
Noodle soup	Kuai tiao nam
White (rice) noodles	Kuai tiao
Yellow (egg) noodles	Ba mee
Fried thin white noodles with egg, vegetables, meat and peanuts	Pat Thai
Wide white noodles with meat and vegetables	Kuai Tiao rat na
Fried yellow noodles with pork	Ba mii na muu
with chicken	Ba mii na kai
with crab	Ba mii na pu
with shrimp	Ba mii na kung
Crispy fried yellow noodles	(Ba) mee grob (rat na
with pork	mu
with chicken	kai
with shrimp	kung
Rice	Khao
Fried rice	Khao pat
Sticky rice	Khao niao
Roast duck with rice	Khao na pet
Chicken sauce on rice	Khao na gai
Purple sticky rice with coconut milk in bamboo	Khao lam
Curry	Kaeng

Hot Thai curry	Kaeng pet Thai
Sweet green curry with fish chicken or beef	Kaeng khiaw wan
Rich beef curry	Kaeng mat sa man
Fish and vegetable curry	Kaeng som
(Hot) chicken curry	Kaeng phet gai
Beef curry	Kaeng neua
Catfish curry	Kaeng pla duk
Duck curry	Kaeng pet phet
Mild Indian curry with chicken	Kaeng kari kai
Seafood	Aahaan thaleh
Fried fish	Pla tot
Crispy fried prawns	Kung tot krop
Fried garoupa with sweet and sour sauce	Pla tot sam roi
Sweet and sour fish	Pla priaw wan
Steamed fish	Pla neung
Steamed crab (claws)	(Kam) pu nung
Stuffed crab	Pu jaa
Stir-fried mixed vegetables	Pat pak
Fried Thai vegetable (morning glory)	Pat bung pak bung
Thai spicy salad with chilli and mint	Yam
with squid	Yam pla meuk
Bean-thread noodle	Yam wun sen
with beef	Yam nua
with deep-fried catfish	Yam pla duk foo
Lobster	Gung yai
Eggs	Khai
Plain omelette	Khai jiao
Omelette stuffed with vegetables and pork	Khai yat sai
Chilli	Prik
Black pepper	Prik thai
Salt	Kleua

Fish sauce (with chilli)	**Nam pla (prik)**
Vinegar (with chilli)	**Nam som (prik dong)**
Soy sauce	**Sii yu**
Sticky rice in coconut milk with mango	**Khao niao ma muang**
Coconut ice cream	**Ai-sa-krim kathi**
Custard	**Sang kha ya**
Coconut custard	**Ma phrao sang kaya**
Banana in sweet coconut cream	**Kluai buat chi**

Fruit

Banana	**Kluai**
Young coconut	**Maphrao-on**
Custard apple	**Noi na**
Durian	**Thurian**
Guava	**Farang**
Jackfruit	**Khanun**
Lime	**Manao**
Longan	**Lamyai**
Lychee	**Linchi**
Mango	**Ma muang**
Mangosteen	**Mangkut**
Orange	**Som**
Papaya	**Malako**
Pineapple	**Sapparot**
Pomelo	**Som oh**
Watermelon	**Taeng moh**

Drink

Water	**Nam**
Cold water	**Nam yen**
Tea	**Chaa**
Coffee	**Cafee**

No sugar	**Mai sai nam-taan**
Hot (spicy)	**Pet**
Not hot	**Mai pet**
Medium hot	**Pet noi**

Food-related Comments

Delicious	**Aroy**
I can't eat	**Pom/ chan kin…. mai dai**
I'm vegetarian	**Pom/ chan kin jeh**
What is this?	**Nee arai?**

Health

(I'm) ill	**(Pom/chan) Mai sabai**
(Where's the) hospital?	**Rong payabaan (yoo tee nai)**
Ambulance	**Rot payabaan**
Doctor	**Maw**
Pharmacy	**Raan khai yaa**
Diarrhoea	**Tong ruang**
Dysentery	**Rohk bit**
Headache	**Puat sii-sa**
Flu	**Khai wat yai**
Venereal disease	**Kaama rohk**
Painkiller	**Yaa kae puat**
Allergic	**Phae**

Accommodation

Hotel	**Rongraem**
Do you have a (double) room?	**Mee hong (kuu) mai?**
Where is the bathroom?	**Hong nam yoo tee nai?**

I want an air-conditioned room	Ao hong air (ae)
Fan	Pat lom

Be careful	Tong rawang
It doesn't work	Mai tit
Garage	Rong rot
Help	Chuay pom/diichan

Getting Around

Where are you going?	Pai nai?
I'm going to	Pom/diichan ja pai
Where is the?	Yu tii nai
Bank	Tanakaan
Beach	Hat
Market	Talaht
Street	Thanon
Side street	Soi
Restaurant	Raan ahaan
Bus	Rot meh
Bus station	Sa-tanee rot meh
Train	Rot fai
Railway station	Sa-tanee rot fai
Airport	Sanam bin
Police station	Sa tanee tamruat
Police	Tamruat
Post office	Prai-sanee
Boat	Reuah
Car	Rot Keng
Motorbike	Rot Motorcye
Please drive slowly	Prot put cha cha
Stop	Yut
Turn right	Lieo Khwa
Turn left	Lieo sai
Drive straight on	Khap trong pai
Petrol	Naman
Diesel	Benzene/ Solar
I have run out of petrol	Naman mot leo

Conversation

Thank you (men)	Kop khun kap
Thank you (women	Kop khun ka
Hello/goodbye (polite)	Sawatdee Sawatdee kap/ka
Good luck/goodbye	Chok dee (kap/ka)
Yes	Chai or Kap/ka
No	Mai
Please	Karuna or prot
How are you?	(Khun) sabai dee ru?
I'm fine (thanks)	Sabai dee (kop khun)kap/ka
I'm not feeling well	Mai sabai (kap/ka)
Never mind	Mai pen rai
Do you understand?	Kao chai mai
I don't understand	(Chan) mai kao chai
Do you speak English?	Puut Angrit dai mai?
I cannot speak	Thai Puut Thai mai dai
I speak Thai a little	Puut Thai nit noi
Please speak slowly	Prot puut cha-cha
What is this in English?	Thai riak wa arai?
I'm sorry	Chan Sia chai
Excuse me	Kor thot
Very good	Dee mak
No good	Mai dee
Better	Dee kwa
What is this?	Ni Arai
Hot	Rawn
Cold	Yen

303

Information to Help You Have a Good Trip

Emergency Services

Ambulance
Tel: 252 2171/5

Fire
Tel: 199

Police
Tel: 191

Tourist Police Centre
Tel: 225 7758

Tourist Assistance Centre
Tel: 281 5051 or 282 8129

Embassies

Australian
37 Sathorn Road
Tel: 287 2680

Canadian
11 & 12/F Boonmitr Bldg
131 Silom Road
Tel: 234 1561-8

Irish
United Flour Mills Building
11th floor
205 Rajawongse Road
Tel: 223 0876

New Zealand
93 Wireless Road
Tel: 251 8165

British
1031 Wireless (Withayu) Road
Tel: 253 0191-9

American
95 Wireless (Withayu) Road
Tel: 252 5040-9

Ayutthaya

Ayutthaya is 80 km (50 miles) north of Bangkok and can be reached by train, bus or boat.

Trains leave Hualamphong Railway Station some 20 times daily. Regular buses leave the Northern Bus Terminal on Paholyothin Road. There are also numerous tours organized by hotels and travel agents. The most pleasant way of getting to Ayutthaya is by river. The Oriental Hotel, Tel: 236 0400, organizes daily tours leaving the hotel at 8 a.m. and arriving at Ayutthaya around 11.30 a.m. A buffet lunch is served on board and is followed by a coach tour of the major temples, and a visit to Bang Pa-In. The Ayuthaya Princess, Tel. 255 9200, does a similar trip. Both return to Bangkok in the early evening.

Bangkok

The ubiquitous guesthouses of Khao-san Road deserve a mention as proof of what money can buy. Prices go as low as Bt50 for dormitory-style rooms. Standards vary enormously with new guesthouses regularly springing up and old ones disappearing. The only way to check them out is to go in person.

Useful Telephone Numbers
Medical Emergency
Tel: 252 2171

Directory of Assistance
Tel: 13

Tourism Authority of Thailand (TAT)
Tel: 282 1143

Tourist Police
Tel: 195

Immigration Office
Tel: 286 4231

Airport
Tel: 535 1253

Railway
Tel: 223 7010

Bus Station:
Northern Terminal   Tel: 279 4484/7
Eastern Terminal   Tel: 392 9227
Southern Terminal   Tel: 411 4978

Chiang Mai

Chiang Mai is 691 km (428 miles) north of Bangkok and can be reached by train, bus, aeroplane and road.

Trains from Hualamphong Railway Station take 12 hours and leave five times daily.

Sleepers are recommended on night trains, but you should book them in advance.

Both air-conditioned and non-air-conditioned buses leave regularly from the Northern Bus Terminal on Paholyothin Road, taking around ten hours.

Thai Airways operates five scheduled flights a day from Don Muang Airport, taking one and a half hours.

Car Rental
Avis
14/14 Huay Kaew Road
Tel: 221 316

Hertz
12/3 Loi Khlao Road
Tel: 235 925

Useful Telehone Numbers
Tourist Police
105/1 Chiang Mai-Lamphun Rd
Tel: 222 977
Emergency Tel: 195

Lanna Hospital
Superhighway
Tel: 211 037

Tourism Authority of Thailand (TAT)
105/1 Chiang Mai-Lamphun Road
Tel: 248 604

Thai Airways
240 Phrapoklao Road
Tel: 211 044-7

Chiang Rai

Chiang Rai is 882 km (547 miles) from
Bangkok and can be reached directly
by bus and air.

Planes leave Don Muang Airport
daily, taking about one and a half
hours. Buses leave Bangkok's Northern Bus Terminal on Paholyothin
Road, taking about 11 hours.

From Chiang Mai, Thai Airways
has three flights, taking 50 minutes, every day.

Alternatively, buses leave from the
Arcade Bus Station in Chiang Mai,
taking about four hours. There are
also connecting buses with Mae Sai,
Chiang Saen and all the other major
northern destinations.

Cafes and Bars

Try Dusit Island Cafe at 1129 Kraisorasit next to the river, Tel: 715 777,
which offers northern specialities such
as *sai asa* (pork with chilli) and *kaeng
hung le* (pork curry with ginger).

The popular Golden Triangle Cafe,
Tel: 711 339, is at 190 Paholyothin
Road.

Around the clock tower on Punyo-
dana Road, the liveliest strip that Chiang Rai has to offer, you can eat
steaks at the Cat House Grill, Italian
food at the Cantina and barbecues at
the simpler Eugene's Place.

Afterwards, there is a host of small
bars and pubs with live bands—and
even a topless "go-go" bar.

Car Rental

Yiamsawat
opposite Wangcome Hotel
Tel: 713 946

P.D Tour & Car Rental Services
834/6 Paholyothin Road
Tel 711 164

Useful Telephone Numbers

Thai Airways
Tel.: 711 464

Kohn Song Bus Station
Tel: 711 369

Tourist Information Centre
Tel: 713 009

Chiang Rai Hospital
Tel: 711 300

Police
Tel: 711 444

Chantaburi

Chantaburi is 245 km (152 miles) from
Bangkok on Highway 3 and can be
reached by bus from the Eastern Bus
Terminal on Sukhumvit Road opposite
Soi 42, as well as from Pattaya, Trat,
and Chonburi.

Several tour agencies in Pattaya also
organize day trips to the mines and af-
terwards to the surrounding waterfalls.
For details contact:
Malibu Travel Co
Tel: 038 426 229

Doi Inthanon

Accommodation is available adjacent to the Hmong village of Ban Khun Klang behind Park Headquarters and advance reservations should be made through the National Parks Division, Tel: Bangkok 579 4842.

Far South

Pattani, Yala and Narathiwat can all be reached by bus from Bangkok or Hat Yai. Yala is also on the main train line to Hat Yai and Bangkok with three trains daily from Hualamphong Railway Station, taking 18 or 19 hours.

For further information about the Far South, contact the Tourist office in Hat Yai, Tel: (074) 243 747, or any other of the TAT offices.

Hua Hin

Hua Hin is 220 km (136 miles) south of Bangkok and can be reached by train bus, plane or hydrofoil.

Trains leave Bangkok's Hualamphong Railway Station nine times daily for the four-hour journey.

Both air-conditioned and non-air-conditioned buses leave Bangkok's Southern Bus Terminals on Charoen Sanitwong Road in Thonburi every hour, taking four hours.

From Hua Hin, minibuses to local destinations leave from opposite the market on Sra Song Road.

Bangkok Airways also flies to Hua Hin on Fridays and Sundays with a flight time of 25 minutes.

Hydrofoils run from the Thai Intertransport Building near the Menam Hotel in Bangkok, Tel: 291 9613.

Cheap places to stay near the beach, can be found along Naretdamri Rd, where there many guesthouses.

Kaeng Krachan National Park

Accommodation in dormitories and bungalows is available at the Visitors Centre. Bungalows should be reserved in advance through the National Parks Division in Bangkok, Tel: 579 4842. There is a restaurant open at weekends or when there is sufficient demand.

Kanchanaburi

Kanchanaburi is 129 km (80 miles) west of Bangkok and can be reached by train, bus and road.

One train daily leaves Thonburi Railway Station, rather than Hualamphong, at 8 a.m., arriving at Kanchanaburi two and a half hours later, and continuing to Nam Tok station, the end of the line. At weekends, a special return trip is organized by the State Railways with stops to allow time for sightseeing

Regular buses leave Bangkok's Southern Bus Terminal, Tel: 435 1199, to Kanchanaburi town, taking two hours.

Buses for Sai Yok and Erawan National Parks also leave from Kanchanaburi Bus Station off Saengchuto Road.

A wide range of accommodation is available from hotels and luxurious raft houses to guesthouses and simple bungalows. Several more upmarket resorts lie outside of town. Reservations should be made well in advance at their Bangkok offices. Often the hotels will arrange for transfer from Kanchanaburi or even from Bangkok.

In town there are several places to rent jeeps and motorbikes. Most of them organize trips into the surrounding region. Enquire at the Tourist Authority (TAT) which has an office on Saeng Chuto Rd, Tel: 511 200.

Khao Sam Roi Yot

Accommodation is available at the Park Headquarters, but you need to make a reservation in advance at the National Parks Division in Bangkok, Tel: 579 4842.

Khao Yai

Khao Yai National Park is 170 km (105 miles) north-east of Bangkok off Highway 2 and Highway 2090, and can be reached by bus and train via Pak Chong.

At weekends a special daily return package is offered by the State Railway with trains leaving at 6.00 a.m. and returning in the early evening.

Until recently, accommodation was available in the National Park. Since a ban on overnight stays was introduced in 1991, visitors must now arrange accommodation outside on the road to Pak Chong. For further information contact the National Parks Division in Bangkok, Tel: 579 4842, or the TAT, Tel: 282 1143.

Ko Chang

Laem Ngop, the departure point for Ko Chang and the surrounding islands is situated around 330 km (205 miles) from Bangkok and can be reached by *songthaew* from Trat.

Regular buses leave Bangkok's Eastern Terminal opposite Sukhumvit Soi 42, taking around five or six hours. Buses also operate between Chantaburi and Trat.

Boats theoretically leave the pier at Laem Ngop twice a day at 8 a.m. and 3 p.m. for the two-hour trip to White Sands Beach on Ko Chang before continuing on to the other beaches.

For Ko Maak a daily boat leaves at 3.30 p.m. taking three hours.

If you miss a boat, there are several places to stay at Laem Ngop including the Paradise Hotel and a number of cheap, but pleasant guesthouses.

For up to date information on accommodation on the islands, enquire on arrival at the small travel agent on the pier.

Kong Chiam

Accommodation is available in the Park, but should be booked in advance through the National Parks Division, Tel: 579 4842.

Ko Hai

Bungalows can be arranged prior to arrival—contact Ko Hai Villa,Tel: Bangkok 318 3107, Ko Mook Resort, Tel: (075) 219 49, or Kradan Island Resort, Tel: (075) 211 391.

Khon Kaen

Khon Kaen is 449 km (278 miles) from Bangkok and can be reached by train and bus.

Trains leave Bangkok's Hualamphong Station three times a day, taking eight hours.

Regular buses leave from the Northern Bus Terminal on Paholyothin Rd, taking seven hours.

Useful Telephone Numbers
Police Station
Klang Muang Rd
Tel: 211 162

Provincial Hospital
Si Chan Rd
Tel: 236 005

Ko Phi Phi

Most of the accommodation at Ko Phi Phi is aimed at backpackers, with bungalows arranged after arrival.

Korat

Korat is 259 km (161 miles) northeast of Bangkok and can be reached by plane, train and bus.

Planes leave daily from Don Muang Airport, taking 40 minutes.

Regular trains leave from Hualamphong Railway Station, taking five hours.

Buses leave the Northern Bus Terminal on Paholyothin Rd, taking approximately four hours.

Useful Telephone Numbers
Police Station
Sapphasit Rd
Tel: 242 010

Provincial Hospital
Tel: 241 117

Thai International
14 Manas Rd
Tel: 257 211

Ko Samet

Ban Phe is situated 220 km (136 miles) from Bangkok and can be reached by buses leaving approximately every hour from the Eastern Bus Terminal off Sukhumvit Soi 42.

From the pier at Ban Phe, boats generally depart for Ko Samet every 20 minutes, taking 40 minutes for the 6 km crossing, although during weekdays in the low season, it may be only a couple of times a day. If you miss the last boat, generally around 6 p.m., there's accommodation in Ban Phe.

Cheaper and more basic bungalow accommodation is found all the way around the island and especially at Hat Sai Kaew, but this can only be arranged on arrival.

Ko Samui

Ko Samui is situated 80 km (50 miles) from Surat Thani, which is the nearest provincial town on the mainland, and can be reached directly by air or by boat, or via Surat Thani by bus or train and boat. Bangkok Airways flies seven times daily to Ko Samui airport, in the north-east of the island. Boats from Surat Thani to Ko Samui depart from three different piers. The car ferry leaves from Don Sak, about three-quarters of an hour on a bus to the south.

Samui Tours in Talat Mai Rd, Tel: 272 452, runs a connecting bus from the town to the ferry. The whole trip takes two and a half hours.

Songserm, Tel: 272 928, operates the Express Boat, and a connecting bus for the half-hour journey to Tha Thong Pier, taking three hours altogether.

There is also a two-storey sleeping boat, which leaves Ban Don Pier at around midnight taking around four hours, but conditions are cramped with only dormitory-style mattresses lined on the floor.

Trains from Bangkok to Surat Thani arrive four times a day. From the railway station, a bus service brings you to the Ban Don Pier from where express boats leave for Ko Samui twice a day at 10 a.m. and 2 p.m. for the one and a half-hour crossing.

There are five air-conditioned buses leaving Bangkok's Southern Bus Terminal on Charoen Sanitwong Rd in Thonburi daily, as well as two non-air-conditioned buses.

A number of private bus companies organize daily coach trips from Bangkok to Surat Thani, and vice versa, including Krung Siam, Tel: Bangkok 282 0261, and Muang Tai, Tel: Bangkok 412 0697.

Many companies in Na Thon and along the road at Chawengalso rent out jeeps and motorbikes.

Useful Telephone Numbers

Airport
Tel: 077 311 233

Tourist Police
Tel: 077 421 245

TAT office
Talat Mai Rd
Surat Thani
Tel: 077 282 828)

Car and Jeep Hire

Avis
Imperial Samui Hotel
Tel: 421 390-4

Tongsai Bay
Tel: 421451-6

Ko Tarutao

Pakbara, the departure point for the Tarutao Islands National Park, can be reached by *songthaew* from the town of La Ngu, which is in turn connected to Trang by bus.

Boats leave for Tarutao twice daily at 10.30 a.m. and 2.30 p.m. after which time you may have to spend the night in Pakbara, where there is basic accommodation.

Beware though. Ferry services to the park run only from November to May.

Accommodation on Ko Tarutao should be booked in advance through the National Park Division in Bangkok, Tel: (02) 579 0529, or Tarutao National Park branch office in Pakbara, Tel: (074) 711 383.

Loei

Loei town is 520 km (322 miles) from Bangkok and can be reached by buses leaving the Northern Bus Terminal on Paholyothin Rd, which take around ten hours.

An alternative is to take the train to either Nong Khai or Udon Thani, from where regular buses leave to Loei.

Buses from Loei to Phu Kradung leave from the main bus station on Ruamjai Rd and take around one hour. From the bus stop it's a short *songthaew* ride to the park.

From Loei it is possible to continue down to Phitsanulok and then up to the North on Highway 203 and Highway 12, via the beautiful Nam Nao National Park. Buses do the journey, but you have to change in Phitsanulok.

Be warned! The park is closed during the rainy season from July to mid-October.

Lopburi

Lopburi is 153 km (99 miles) from Bangkok on Highway 1, and can be reached by train or bus.

Trains leave Hualamphong Railway Station regularly between 6.40 a.m. and 10 p.m. Buses leave from the Northern Bus Terminal on Paholyothin Rd every hour.

Mae Hong Son

Mae Hong Son is 270 km (167 miles) north-west of Chiang Mai and can be reached by bus, road or air.

Thai Airways operate scheduled flights twice daily from Chiang Mai to Mae Hong Son taking half an hour.

Buses leave from Pratu Chiang Mai (Chiang Mai Gate), five times daily via Mae Sariang District, taking about eight hours.

There are also direct air-conditioned and non-air-conditioned buses from the same bus station, as well as buses running via Pai.

Tours can be arranged by almost any agency and motorbikes and jeeps rented from shops along the main road.

Mae Sai

Mae Sai is 68 km (42 miles) north of Chiang Rai and can be reached by regular buses taking one and a half hours.

There are also buses from Chiang Mai, Chiang Rai and Chiang Saen. Sethee Tour and Siam First Tour, both located on Paholyothin Road operate VIP buses to and from Bangkok taking around 13 hours.

Accommodation in Mae Sai is mainly in the form of guesthouses frequented by backpackers and budget travellers. Most of them are to be found along the river and include the idyllically situated Mae Sai Guest House with a small restaurant and hot showers and the Mae Sae Plaza built into the side of the hill with fine views and more upmarket rooms.

Almost all guesthouses now rent out motorcycles.

Mae Salong

Mae Salong is 67 km (41 miles) from Chiang Rai and can be reached by taking a bus from Chiang Rai or Mai Sai and alighting at Ban Basang. From Ban Basang, there are regular *songthaews* up the mountain.

Mae Sot

Mae Sot is 500 km (310 miles) north-west of Bangkok and can be reached by regular buses from Tak or by a bus leaving once a day from the Northern Bus Terminal in Bangkok.

Thai Airways also flies between Phitsanulok and Mae Sot via Tak four times a week.

From Mae Sot there is now a highway leading along the Burmese border all the way to Mae Sariang, some 200 km (120 miles) to the north. The road was built by the army and is paved for all but the last 20 km (12 miles). *Songthaews* ply the route, but you should enquire about local conditions before leaving.

Mukdahan

Accommodation in town can be found at the Mukdahan Hotel, 8/8 Samut Sakdarak Road, Tel: 611 619, and at the cheaper Banthorm Kasem at 4/1 Samut Sakdarak Road, Tel: 611 235.

Nan

Nan is 668 km (414 miles) from Bangkok and can be reached by bus from the Northern Bus Terminal on Paholyothin Road.

Regular buses also run from Chiang Mai, Chiang Rai and Phrae.

Nan has an airport with direct flights to and from Phitsanulok and Phrae.

Tours and trekking are organized by Fhu Travel at 314 Sumondeavarag Rd and Kiwi Guest House, Tel: 054 710 636.

Nong Khai

Nong Khai is 615 km (381 miles) from Bangkok and can be reached by train or bus. Trains leave Hualamphong Railway Station three times a day for the 12-hour journey.

Buses leave the Northern Bus Terminal on Paholyothin Rd, taking ten hours. There are also bus connections with Khon Kaen, Udon Thani, Chiang Khan and Korat.

Along the main road, you can rent cars, motorbikes and bicycles.

Visas for Laos can currently be arranged at travel agents near the ferry terminal in Nong Khai. They cost around Bt 3,000 for a 15-day visa, and take two to three days to be processed. The situation can, however, change at very short notice. Often it is better to get a visa through the Laotian embassy, which is in Bangkok at 193 Sathorn Rd, Tel: 286 0010, where it is not only official, but is also considerably cheaper.

Useful telephone numbers
Police Station
Michai Rd
Tel. 411 020

Provincial Hospital
Michai Rd
Tel. 411 504

Pattaya International Hospital
Soi 4, Beach Road
Tel: 428 374/5

Nong Nooch

There is accommodation available in bungalows, and these need to be booked in advance at the Pattaya office, Tel: 429 321.

Pattaya

Pattaya is 147 km (91 miles) south-east of Bangkok.

Both regular air-conditioned and non-air-conditioned buses leave Ekamai Eastern Bus Terminal next to Sukhumvit Soi 42 in Bangkok, and take about three hours to reach Pattaya Bus Station, situated on North Pattaya Road.

Travel within the resort is generally by minibuses which continually ply Beach Road and Pattaya 2 Road in anticlockwise circuits.

Motorcycles, jeeps and cars can also be hired by the day or by the week.

Car rental
Avis Rent-A-Car
Dusit Resort
Tel: 429 901/902/903

Useful Telephone Numbers
Tourist Office (TAT)
382/1 Beach Road
Tel: 429 113

Tourist Police
382/1 Beach Road
Tel: 429 371

Phu Kradung

Accommodation is available in bungalows and tents at the top of the mountain near the Information Centre. Tents can be arranged on arrival, but for bungalows you should book in advance at the National Parks Division in Bangkok, Tel: 579 0529

Around the Park—and especially around the camping ground—there are stores selling local snacks, fried rice, noodles and ominous quantities of whisky.

Be warned though: the Park is closed between the months of July to October because of the monsoons.

Phitsanulok

Phitsanulok is 377 km (209 miles) from Bangkok and can be reached by train, plane and bus.

Trains leave Hualamphong Railway Station seven times a day, taking six and a half hours.

Regular buses leave the Northern Bus Terminal on Paholyothin Rd eleven times a day.

Flights leave Bangkok's Don Muang Airport daily for Phitsanulok.

Car Rental
Golden House Tour
55/37 Sithamtraipikok Rd
Tel: 259 973
Phitsanulok Tour Center
Tel: 242 206.

Phuket

Phuket lies 890 km (552 miles) from Bangkok and can be reached by plane, bus or car.

Thai Airways operates eight flights a day from Bangkok, as well as international connections with Penang, Kuala Lumpur, Singapore and Hong Kong. Bangkok Airways operates daily flights between Ko Samui and Phuket

Both air-conditioned and non-air-conditioned buses leave from Bangkok's Southern Bus Terminal on Charoen Sanitwong Rd in Thonburi, taking about 15 hours.

There is no rail service to Phuket. The nearest railway stations are at Surat Thani, 6 hours north-east by road, 25 minutes by air, and Hat Yai, 8 hours south-east by road, 20 minutes by air.

Local buses *(songthaews)* to all the beaches leave at frequent intervals from the market on Ranong Road, but make their last return trips in the mid- to late afternoon.

Tuk tuks will take you anywhere on the island.

Car Rental
Avis
Airport
Tel: 311 358
Le Meridien Hotel, Karon
Tel: 321 480-5
Holiday Inn, Patong
Tel: 321 020-1

Hertz
Airport
Tel: 311 162
Patong Merlin
Tel: 321 070-4
Pearl Village, Nai Yang
Tel: 311 376-83

Pure Car Rent, Rasda Rd
Tel: 211 002

Useful Telephone Numbers
24-Hour Emergency Ambulance
Tel: 212 297

Local Police
Tel: 212 115/046

Emergency Police
Tel: 161

Tourist Police
73/75 Phuket Rd
Tel: 212 213, 211 036 (day)
     212 486 (night)

Tourist Office
73/75 Phuket Rd
Tel: 212 213

Immigration Office
Tel: 212 108

Phuket Airport
Tel: 311 205

Ranong

Ranong is 568 km (352 miles) south of Bangkok and can be reached by bus from the Southern Bus Terminal on Charoen Sanitwong Rd in Thonburi or alternatively from Phuket or

Chumphon. The Jansom Thara runs an air-conditioned minibus service to and from Phuket and will also arrange transfers from Bangkok and Surat Thani.

Getting around Ranong can be done by *songthaews,* which leave regularly for Hot Springs and Hat Charndamri.

Sangkhlaburi

Sangkhlaburi is 340 km (211 miles) from Bangkok and can be reached by bus or by organized tours from Kanchanaburi.

Buses leave Kanchanaburi Bus Terminal every half hour for Tong Pha Phum and every couple of hours for Sangkhlaburi.

Songthaews from Tong Pha Phum occasionally leave for Pilok, but there is no fixed departure time.

There are also irregular *songthaews* which leave from Sangkhlaburi to the Three Pagodas Pass. Before leaving, it is imperative to check on local conditions with the authorities, or to ask at your hotel.

Sangkhom

Perhaps the most idyllic place to stay in the area is Grandpa's River Retreat; it is situated on the river Som Sowan, 14 km (9 miles) east of Sangkhom, next to a wooden bridge, in some of the most unspoilt countryside in the region. Currently there are just three cottages, but the owner has plans to build a further three. There's no other guesthouse for miles and it is the perfect place to rest for a couple of days and

to explore the surroundings from a simple, but comfortable base.

Songkhla

Songkhla is 950 km (590 miles) south of Bangkok and can be reached via Hat Yai, the major transportation hub of the province.

Hat Yai has regular trains, buses and air connections with Bangkok, Phuket and Malaysia.

Bus number 1871 leaves the stand in front of the Hat Yai Plaza Theatre on Phetkasem road for Songkhla every 30 minutes until 7.30 p.m.

Numerous air-conditioned minibuses leave as soon as they fill up from near the TAT office.

From Bangkok there is also a passenger ferry, which leaves for Songkhla once a week. For further information, contact the Tourist Office (TAT) in Hat Yai at 1/1 Soi 2, Niphat Uthit 3 Rd, Tel: 074 243747, which also provides information on all the Southern Region.

Sukhothai

Sukhothai is 427 km (265 miles) north of Bangkok and can be reached by bus as well as by organized tour.

Buses leave the Northern Bus Terminal on Paholyothin Rd some ten times a day. Sukhothai can also be reached by regular bus from Phitsanulok, which is served by train and by direct flights from Bangkok.

From the intersection across from the Sukhothai Hotel on Singhawat Rd, buses leave approximately every hour

315

for Si Satchanalai and every one and a half hours for Kamphaeng Phet.

Surin

Surin is 457 km (283 miles) north-east of Bangkok and can be reached by train and bus.

Trains leave Hualamphong Railway Station seven times a day and there is a sleeper at 9 p.m. which arrives in Surin at 4.20 am.

Surin can also be reached by buses which leave the Northern Bus Terminal on Paholyothin Rd, taking six hours. The town has a couple of very modern, but slightly characterless luxury hotels.

Useful Telephone Numbers
Police Station
Lak Muang Rd
Tel: 511 007

Provincial Hospital
Tambon Nai Muang
Tel: 511 757

Provincial Governor
Lak Muang Rd
Tel: 512 039

Surin Islands

Accommodation is available in Park bungalows at Ao Mae Yai. For further details, enquire at the Provincial Governor's office, Tel: (076) 411 140.

Thale Noi

National Park accommodation is available on the lake. Contact the National Parks Division, Tel 579 4842, for reservations.

That Phanom

Simple accommodation is available at the Saeng Thong Hotel on 34 Mu 1, Phanom-Phanarak Road.

Ubon Ratchathani

Ubon Ratchathani is located 629 km (390 miles) from Bangkok and can be reached by train, bus and air.

Trains leave Hualamphong Station seven times a day, taking ten hours.

Buses leave from the Northern Bus Terminal on Paholyothin Rd for the eight-hour journey.

There are also flights on Thai Airways.TAT Office, Tel: 377 008, at 264/1 Khuan Thani Road

The best place to hire chauffeur-driven cars is from CH Wattana, Tel: 242 202. For other rentals enquire at the TAT.

Useful Telephone Numbers
Police
Sapphasit Road
Tel: 254 216

Hospital
Sapphasit Road
Tel: 254 906

The Right Place at the Right Price

Hotels

Thailand's hotels have an unrivalled reputation for excellence and for *nam chai* —an irrepressible desire to please. At least five are listed amongst the world's top 100 hotels and many others are vying for secondary honours.

Bangkok, Pattaya, Chiang Mai, Phuket and Ko Samui brim over with luxury establishments; even off the main tourist track top-class hotels are mushrooming. Further down the scale there is no shortage of budget hotels, often with swimming pools and gardens, almost always clean and friendly. And at the bottom of the scale, there is a range of cheap guesthouses and hostels with spartan rooms and dormitories and cockroaches, to boot.

Prices vary as much as standards. In Bangkok, a deluxe suite at the Oriental will cost as much Bt15,000 and a standard room Bt5,000, whilst on Khaosan Road, you may be able to pick up a bed for as little as Bt60. As a general rule, clean rooms are plentiful and extremely good value. Only in the really far-flung provinces is choice limited, with the smaller, cheaper hotels tending to double as brothels.

The prices of hotels are:
▯ less than Bt500;
▯▯ Bt500–Bt1,500;
▯▯▯ over Bt1,500.

These ranges should be viewed only as rough guides, as hotels may have some rooms in the price band above or below the one in which they have been placed, and prices vary from season to season.

Ao Nang (Krabi)

Krabi Resort ▯▯
Mu 2 Tambon Ao Nang
Tel: 612 160
40 rooms and 46 bungalows.Luxurious bungalows and a swimming pool

Phra Nang Inn ▯
Tel: 612 173
60 rooms.

Ayutthaya

Holiday Inn ▯▯▯
Soi 80
131 Lardtrow
Bangkapi
Tel: 254 2709
200 rooms. Luxury amenities including swimming pool, gardens and river view.

Si Samai ▯
12 Talad Chao Phrom
Tel: 251 228
58 rooms.

U-Thong Inn ▯▯
210 Mu 5
Rotchana Road
Tel: 242 618
100 rooms.

U-Thong Hotel ▯
86 U-Thong Road
Tel: 251 136
65 rooms. Swimming pool and coffee shop.

Bangkok

Atlanta Hotel ▯
78 Soi 2
Sukhumvit Road
Tel: 252 1650
Lackadaisical air of dilapidated grandeur. Swimming pool but no room service.

Comfort Inn ▯▯
Soi 11
Sukhumvit Road
Tel: 251 9250
Spotless but fairly small rooms and a quiet but central location.

Dusit Thani ▯▯▯
946 Rama IV Road
Tel: 236 0450
Recently refurbished to the highest international standards and situated over the road from Lumpini Park.

Federal Hotel ▯▯
27 Soi 11
Sukhumvit Road
Tel: 253 0175/6
80 rooms. Popular, modern establishment with a good swimming pool and patio.

Hilton International ▯▯▯
2 Wireless Road
Tel: 253 0123
525 rooms. Set in lush tropical gardens with central location and light, open rooms.

Impala Hotel
9 Soi 24
Sukhumvit Road
Tel: 2590053
200 Rooms. Located in the Sukhumvit area with swimming pool, sauna and health club.

Malaysia Hotel
54 Soi Ngam Dupli
Rama IV Road
Tel: 286 3582
120 rooms. Budget backpacker's paradise with adjacent swimming pool and notorious 24-hour coffee shop.

Manohra Hotel
412 Surawong Road
Tel: 234 5070
250 rooms. Within walking distance of the Chao Phya River. Sports a cocktail lounge, roof garden and an indoor swimming pool.

Menam Hotel
2074 Charoen Krung Road
Yannawa
Tel: 289 1148/9
727 rooms. The cheapest of the big river hotels with swimming pool, health club and terraces.

Opera Hotel
16 Soi 11
Phetchburi Road
Tel: 252 4031/2
One of the best-value and most popular hotels in the lower price range.

Oriental Hotel
48 Oriental Avenue
Charoen Krung Road
Tel: 236 0400/39
394 rooms. Nominated one of the world's best hotels and boasting fine views of the river.

Park Hotel
6 Soi 7
Sukhumvit Road
Tel: 255 4300
139 rooms. Newly refurbished with swimming pool, fitness centre, sauna and jacuzzi.

Regent Hotel
155 Ratchadamri Road
Tel: 251 6127
400 rooms. Popular businessman's hotel with swimming pool, business centre and famous Spice Market Restaurant.

Royal Hotel
2 Ratchadamnoen Klang Road
Tel: 222 9111/26
300 rooms. One of Bangkok's venerable old institutions, situated near the Grand Palace.

Shangri-La Hotel
89 Soi Wat Suan Plu
Charoen Krung Road
Tel: 236 7777
694 rooms. Offers superb river fronted rooms, swimming pool and top class service.

Swan Hotel
Soi 36
31 Charoen Krung Road
Tel: 234 8594
64 rooms. Quiet situation with swimming pool and smallish rooms.

YMCA Collins International House
27 Sathorn Road
Tel: 287 1900
50 rooms. High standard accommodation with restaurant and adjacent swimming pool.

Bang Saen

Bang Saen Beach Resort
55–150 Bang saen Beach Road
Tel: 376 675
29 rooms and 102 bungalows.

Bang Saen Villa
190 Mu 13
Bang saen Beach Road
Tel: 377 088
70 rooms.

Buriram

Krung Rome
78/2 Niward Road
Tel: 611 740
81 rooms.

Thai Hotel
38/1 Romburi Road
Tel: 611 112
90 rooms.

Chanthaburi

Chanta Nimit
116–118 Rimnam Road
Tel: 312 388
57 rooms.

Chanthaburi Hotel
42/6 Tha-Chalab Road
Tel: 311 300
70 rooms.

Eastern Hotel
899 Tha-Chalab Road
Tel: 312 218
142 rooms.

Chiang Khan

Amnat Siri
282 Chai Kong Road
15 rooms.

Suk Sombun
243/3 Chai Kong Road
Tel: 821 064
17 rooms.

Chiang Mai

Chiang Mai Plaza
92 Sri Donchai Road
Tel: 270 050
450 rooms. Popular business man's hotel with large swimming pool and disco.

Chiang Mai Orchid
100 Huey Kaew Road
Tel: 222 099
450 rooms. Class establishment with swimming pool, fitness centre and nightclub.

Dusit Inn
112 Changklan Road
Tel: 251 033
200 rooms. Bright elegant hotel in central location.

Diamond Hotel
33/10 Charoen Prathet Road
Tel: 234 153
145 rooms. Popular family hotel

Galore Guest House
91 Charoen Prathet Road
Tel: 273 885
30 rooms. Upmarket guesthouse on the river.

Holiday Garden Hotel
16/16 Huey Kaew Road
Tel: 210 901
Quiet family hotel set around courtyard with swimming pool.

Hotel Top North Centre
41 Moonmuang Road
Tel: 213 309
Situated in a quiet cul de sac off Tapei Gate.

Lai Thai Guest House
111/4–5 Kotchasarn Road
Tel: 271 725
90 rooms. Modern chalet-style hotel, clean friendly and built around courtyard.

318

Lek Guest House
22 Chaiyapoom Road
*14 rooms. Backpacker's paradise
with garden and restaurant.*

North Star Guest House
Moon Muang 2 Road
*Good, popular and relatively
cheap.*

Once Upon a Time
385/2 Charoen Prathet Road
Tel: 274 932
*Eccentric wooden buildings in
exotic beautiful gardens.*

Prince Hotel
3 Taiwan Road
Tel: 236 396
*121 rooms. Centrally located with
swimming pool.*

Rim Ping Garden
411 Charoen Prathet Road
Tel: 281 080
*20 rooms. Idyllic location on river
with swimming pool, fine
restaurant and charming rooms
with balconies.*

Riverview Lodge
25 soi 2
Charoen Prathet Road
Tel: 251 110
*36 rooms. Riverbank setting with
big garden and fine views.*

Top North Guest House
Soi 2
15 Moonmuang Road
Tel: 213 900
*Pleasantly situated with swimming
pool.*

Chiang Rai
Boonbundan Guest House
105/13 Jetyod Road
Tel: 712 914
*Friendly guesthouse in the centre
of town.*

Dusit Thani Island Resort
1129 Kraisorasit Road
Tel: 715 777
*International facilities and fine
river views.*

Golden Triangle Inn
590 Paholyothin Road
Tel: 711 339
*Quietly situated in the heart of
town. Charming staff and an
excellent cafe.*

Gratom Rim Kok
339/1 Soi Homnuan
Paholyothin Road
Tel: 716 370
*Set on the river with small rooms
or smarter log cabins.*

Maekok Villa
445 Singhakai Road
Tel: 311 786
*44 rooms. Charming bungalow
style rooms with bath and hot
water.*

Rama Hotel
34/1 Trairat Road
Tel: 311 344
*43 rooms. Central location with
coffee shop and a pub called
'Cheers'.*

Rimkok Resort
6 Mu 4
Tha Thon Road
Tel: 716 445
*248 rooms. Set on the banks of
the river some five km (3 miles)
from town with swimming pool,
jogging facilities.*

Wang Din Place
34/1 Kwae Wai Road
Tel: 713 363
*12 huts. Comfortable, wooden huts
on the river, but a good two km
(1 mile) from the centre of town.*

Wiang Inn
893 Paholyothin Road
Tel: 711 533
*260 rooms. Central location,
swimming pool and disco.*

Chiang Saen
Baan Boran Resort
Tel 716 678
*International resort overlooking
the Mekong.*

Chiang Saen Guest House
45 Mekong Riverside
10 rooms.

Golden Triangle Resort
222 Golden Triangle
Tel: 714 801
*Exclusive resort on the banks of
the Mekong.*

Lanna Guest House
39 Rhim Khong Road

Hat Yai
JB Hotel
99 Juti Anusorn Road
Tel: 234 300
212 rooms.

King's Hotel
126–8 Niphat Uthit 1 Road
Tel: 243 966
88 rooms.

Laem Thong Hotel
44 Thamnoonvithi Road
Tel: 244 433
133 rooms.

Regency Hotel
23 Prachathipat Road
Tel: 234 400
169 rooms.

Hua Hin
Chan-Chai Bungalow
117/1–18 Phetkasem Road
Tel: 511 461
18 rooms.

Hua Hin Highland Resort
Phetkasem Road
Tel: 211 2579
*13 rooms. Situated to the north of
town, near the golf course.*

Royal Garden Resort
107/1 Phetkasem Road
Tel: 511 881/4
*217 rooms. Swimming pool, roof
terrace, tennis courts and a view
of the sea from every room.*

Sailom
29 Phetkasem Road
Tel: 511 890/1
*60 rooms. Swimming pool and
tennis courts.*

Sofitel Central
1 Damnoen Kasem Road
Tel: (032) 512 021/30
*218 rooms. Colonial-style hotel,
recently renovated and set in
beautiful grounds.*

Kamphaeng Phet
Chakangrao Hotel
123/1 Thesa Road
Tel: 711 315
120 rooms.

Phet Hotel
99 Wichit Road
Tel: 712 810
234 rooms.

Thepnakorn Hotel
Soi 10
12 Ratchadamnoen Road
Tel: 711 091
25 rooms.

Kanchanaburi
Home Phu Toey
Tel: Bangkok 280 3488
Chalet-style accommodation and swimming pool overlooking the river.

Jungle Rafts
Tel: Bangkok 246 5679
Away from it all. Simple bamboo rafts moored to the river bank and with no electricity.

Kasem Island Resort
27 Chaichumphon Road
Tel: 511 603
12 rooms. On an island in the Mae Klong River.

Pung Waan Resort
Tel: Bangkok 281 3221
Floating houses or brick huts in extensive landscaped gardens with swimming pool

River Kwai Hotel
284/3–16 Saeng Chuto Road
Tel: 511 565
127 rooms. Swimming pool and disco.

River Kwai Village
Tel: Bangkok 251 7552
Swimming pool, mini-zoo and hoards of package tours.

Sam's Place
Song Kwai Road
Simple, but charming, river bungalows.

Khao Yai
Juldis Khao Yai Resort
54 Mu 4
Thanarat Road
Tel 235 2414
Top of the range, with swimming pool, a golf practice course and tennis courts.

Pak Chong Guest House
Soi 3
752/11 Kongvaksin Road
Pak Chong
Friendly guesthouse situated 40km (25 miles) from Khao Yai in Pak Chong. Organizes daily tours.

Wan-Ree Resort
Thanarat Road
Tel: 399 4271
Simple huts with communal balcony.

Khon Kaen
Kaen Inn
56 Klang Muang Road
Tel: 237 744
162 rooms.

Khon Kaen Hotel
43/2 Phimphasut Road
Tel: 237 711
140 rooms.

Kosa Hotel
250–252 Si Chan Road
Tel: 225 0148
123 rooms.

Roma
50/2 Klang Muang Road
Tel: 236 276
142 rooms.

Sawaddi Hotel
177/9 Na-Muang Road
Tel: 221 600
146 rooms.

Suksawad
2/2 Klang Muang Road
33 rooms.

Ko Phi Phi
Phi Phi International Resort
Tel 214 297

Phi Phi Island Cabana
Tel: 611 496
112 rooms.

Phi Phi Island Village
Tel: 215 014

Ko Samet
Malibou Garden Resort
Tel: 321 0345
16 rooms

Wong Duan Resort
Tel: 250 0423
12 bungalows.

Wong Duan Villa
Tel: 321 0789
15 rooms.

Ko Samui
Boat House Hotel
Tel: 421 460
Old teak klong barges from Bangkok converted into luxury land-based suites.

Chaweng Garden
Tel: 421 403
Pretty wooden bungalows in a leafy setting near the middle of the beach.

Coral Bay Resort
Bo Phut Beach
Tel: 286 902
Large thatched bungalows with spacious balconies, a swimming pool and terrace.

Imperial Ko Samui
Chaweng Beach
Tel: 421 390–7
One of the island's finest hotels with beautiful gardens, two swimming pools and fine views.

Imperial's Tong Sai Bay Hotel
Choeng Mong Beach
Tel: 421 451/60
Mediterranean-style hotel with swimming pool and spectacular views.

The Island
Chaweng Beach
Tel: 421 026
A wide range of bungalows, good restaurant and a popular bar.

Matlang Resort
Chaweng
Tel: 272 222
At the quiet northern end of the beach in a pretty garden.

Marina Villa
Lamai Beach
Tel: 421 426
One of Lamai's more upmarket bungalows with simple but pleasant accommodation.

PS Villa
Choeng Mong
Tel: 286 956
Situated on a quiet beach offering fine views.

Sandy Resort
Bo Phut Beach
Tel: 421 353
Inland bungalows with charming wooden terrace for sundowners.

Korat
(Nakhon Ratchasima)

Chomsurang Hotel
2701/2 Mahatthai Road
Tel: 257 088
*Swimming pool and pleasant
garden.*

Kings Hotel
85 Mittraphap Road
Tel: 253 3360
62 rooms.

Sripattana Hotel
346 Suranaree Road
Tel: 242 883
*183 rooms. Swimming pool, coffee
shop and banquet facilities.*

Thai Hotel
640 Mitrapharp Road
Tel: 241 613
110 rooms.

Krabi Town

Thai Hotel
7 Issara Road
Tel: 611 122
108 rooms.

Wiang Thong
155/7 Uttarakit Road
Tel: 611 288
154 rooms.

Lampang

Asia Lampang Hotel
229 Bunyawat Road
Tel: 217 844
72 rooms.

Lampang Hotel
696 Suan Dok Road
Tel: 217 311
50 rooms.

Siam Hotel
260/9 Chat Chai Road.
Tel. 217 472
84 rooms.

Thip Chang Hotel
54/22 Tha Krao Noi Road
Tel: 218 078
*125 rooms. Two restaurants, live
bands and swimming pool.*

Loie

King Hotel
11/9–12 Chumsai Road
Tel: 811 701
48 rooms.

Phu Luang Hotel
55 Charoen Rat Road
Tel: 811 532
86 rooms.

Thai Udom Hotel
122 Charoen Rat Road
Tel: 811 763
56 rooms.

Lopburi

Asia Hotel
1/7 Surasak Road
Tel: 411 892
111 rooms.

Holiday Hotel
3 Soi Suriyothai 2
Narai Maharat Road
Tel 411 343
99 rooms.

Thai Pe Hotel
24/6–7 Surasongkhram Road
Tel: 411 524
104 rooms.

Mae Hong Son

Baiyoke Chalet
90 Khunlumprapas Road
Tel: 611 486
*Upmarket Swiss-style chalet with
cosy rooms, restaurant and central
location.*

Holiday Inn
114/5–7 Khunlumprapas Road
Tel: 611 231
*114 rooms. International-class
hotel with swimming pool, disco
and convention facilities.*

Mae Hong Son Guest House
Soi 2
18 Khunlumpraphas Road
*Comfortable wooden house built
on stilts.*

Mae Hong Son Resort
24 Ban Huey Dua
Tel: 611 504
*40 bungalows. Five km (3 miles)
outside town with river-style
bungalows.*

Mae Tee Hotel
55 Khunlum Phra Athit Road
Tel: 611 150
38 rooms.

Rim Nam Klang Doi Resort
Ban Huay Dua
Tel: 611 086
*Five km (3 miles) from town,
with pleasant huts on the river
bank.*

Sangthom Huts
off Khunlumpraphas Road
*Beautifully positioned, intimate
and run by a charming couple.*

Tara Mae Hong Son
149 Mu 8
Tambon Pang Mu
Tel: 611 473
*Luxury development set in
extensive landscaped gardens with
swimming pool and charming
views.*

Mae Sai

Sin Wattana Hotel
Paholyothin Road
Tel: 731 950
*Deluxe 8-storey hotel due to be
completed by the end of 1992 with
swimming pool and health club.*

Tai Tong Hotel
Paholyothin Road
Tel: 731 975
*Clean, recently renovated with
adequate sized rooms.*

Mae Salong

Khumnaiphol Resort
Tel: 712 485
*The newest development with
comfortable modern bungalows set
on the hillside.*

Mae Salong Resort
Tel: 714 047
*Comfortable bungalows with fine
views of neighbouring Burma.*

Mae Salong Villa
Tel: 713 444
*44 rooms. Situated shortly before
you reach town with sun terrace
and pleasant views.*

Mae Sot

First Hotel
444 Inthakhiri Road
Tel: 351 233
38 rooms.

Mae Sot Hill Hotel
100 Asia Road
Tel: Bangkok 532 600
*120 rooms. Swimming pool, tennis
courts and a disco.*

Siam Hotel
185 Prasat Withi Road
Tel: 531 376
70 rooms.

Mukdahan
Banthorm Kasem
4/1 Samut Sakdarak Road
Tel: 611 235
11 rooms.

Mukdahan Hotel
8/8 Samut Sakdarak Road
Tel: 611 619
55 rooms.

Nakhon Phanom
River Inn Hotel
137 Sunthon Wichit Road
Tel: 511 305
16 rooms.

Windsor Hotel
692/19 Bamrungmuang Road
Tel: 511 573
60 rooms.

Nakhon Phathom
Mitraworn Hotel
305/1–3 Rot Fai Road
Tel 243 115
70 rooms.

Nakhon Inn
55 Ratwiti Road
Tel: 251 152
70 rooms.

Whale Hotel
151/79 Ratwiti Road
Tel: 251 020
136 rooms.

Nakhon Si Thammarat
Nakhon Garden Hotel
Pak Nakhon Road
Tel 344 831/5

Thaksin
Si Prat Road
Tel: 356 788
155 rooms.

Udon Hotel
1461/8–9 Yommarat Road
Tel: 356 310
53 rooms.

Nan
Dheverag Hotel
466 Sumonthewarat Road
Tel: 710 094
154 rooms. Modern air-conditioned rooms and coffee shop, with Thai and European cuisine.

Nan Fah
438–440 Sumonthewarat Road
Tel: 710 284
24 rooms.

Sukkasem
29/31 Ananworritdet Road
Tel: 710 141
40 rooms.

Naratiwat
Rex
6/1–3 Chamrun-Nara Road
Tel: 511 134
39 rooms.

Tanyong Hotel
16/1 Sopa Pisai Road
Tel: 511 477
83 rooms.

Nong Khai
Phantawee Hotel
1241 Hai Sok Road
Tel: 411 568
67 rooms.

Pongwichit
1244/1–2Banthoengchit Road
Tel: 411 583
39 rooms.

Prajak Bungalows
1178 Prajak Road
Tel: 411 116
28 rooms.

Pattani
My Garden Hotel
Charuenpradit Road
Tel: 348 655
130 rooms.

Palace Hotel
3840 Soi Prida
Tel: 349 171
42 rooms.

Pattaya
Diana Inn
216/6–7 Mu 10
Pattaya 2 Road
Tel: 421 622
59 rooms. Air-conditioned rooms and swimming pool.

Dusit Resort
240/2 Beach Road
Tel: 425 611
500 rooms. Swimming pool, tennis courts, fitness centre and sauna.

Garden Lodge
Mu 5
Naklua Road
Tel: 429 109
58 rooms. Swimming pool and breakfast buffet.

Ocean View Hotel
10 Beach Road
Tel: 428 084
112 rooms. Fronting the beach road with swimming pool and terrace.

Pattaya II
216 Pattaya Beach Road
Tel: 429 239
79 rooms. Swimming pool and coffee shop.

PK Villa
Beach Road
Tel: 418 462
120 rooms. Set in a villa with lovingly cared- for gardens and swimming pool.

Royal Cliff
Cliff Road
South Pattaya
Tel: 428 511/3
700 rooms. The finest hotel in town, with its own private beach and several swimming pools.

Seaview Resort
Naklua Soi 20
Tel: 429 317
80 cottages. Away from the crowds beyond north Pattaya with private beach and bungalows.

Siam Bayshore
Beach Road
Tel: 428 678
265 rooms. Located at the southern tip of Pattaya and set in eight hectares (20 acres) of woods and tropical gardens.

Phang Nga
Lak Muang
1/2 Phetkasem Road
Tel: 411 218
23 rooms.

Phang Nga Valley Resort
Phetkasem Road
Tel: 411 201
15 rooms.

Phang Nga Bay Resort
20 Tha Dan Road
Tel: 411 067–70
90 rooms.

Phayao

Bua Resort
Two km (1 mile) along road to
Chiang Rai
Tel 481 596
26 brick cottages.

Tharn Thong
55–57 Donsanam Road
Tel: 431 772
96 rooms.

Watthana
69 Donsanam Road
Tel 431 086
32 rooms.

Phetchburi

Chom Klao Hotel
1–3 Phongsuriya Road
Tel: 425 398
36 rooms.

Khao Wang Hotel
174/1–3 Ratwiti
Tel: (032) 425 167
50 rooms.

Phetkasem Hotel
86/1 Phetkasem Road
Tel: 425 581
50 rooms.

Phimai

Phimai Guest House
Mu 1 Chomsudasadet Road
*Friendly guesthouse with simple
rooms.*

Phimai Hotel
305/1–2 Haruthairom Road
Tel: 471 689
50 rooms.

Phitsanulok

Amarintr Nakorn Hotel
3/1 Chao Phra Road
Tel: 258 588
134 rooms.

Indra Hotel
103 Sithamtraipidok Road
Tel: 259 188
47 rooms.

Pailyn Hotel
38 Boromtrailoknart Road
Tel: 252 411
200 rooms.

Rajapruk Hotel
89/9 Phra Ong Dam Road
Tel: 258 788
100 rooms.

Phuket

Amanpuri
118 Srisoonthorn Road
Pansea Beach
Tel: (076) 311 394–9
*40 rooms. Phuket's finest hotel
with exclusive bungalows
overlooking a secluded bay.*

Boathouse Inn
Kata Beach
Tel: 381 557–60
*Charming hotel modelled on
traditional Thai boat houses with
swimming pool.*

Casuarina Bungalows
Patong Beach
Tel: 321 123
*10 rooms. Conveniently located
bungalows in a pretty garden.*

Club Andaman
77/1 Patong Beach
Tel: 321526
*Thai-style thatched bungalow,
swimming pool and extensive
landscaped gardens.*

Jungle Beach Resort
11/3 Vised Road
Nai Harn
*38 rooms. Set in its own small
rocky bay,with swimming pool and
a wooden terrace.*

Le Meridien
8/5 Karon Beach
Tel: 321 480–5
*470 rooms. Big international hotel
with swimming pool, balconied
rooms and a vast wooded area
with tennis courts.*

Pansea Phuket Bay
Pansea Beach
Tel: 311 249
*100 rooms. Luxurious designer
thatched bungalows on stilts, a
swimming pool and variety of
watersports.*

Patong Beach Bungalow
96/1 Patong Beach
Tel: 321 117
*34 rooms. Small swimming pool
and beach-front terrace.*

Pop Cottage
2/12 Moo 2 Patak Road
Tel: 381 794
*Tiny bungalows on the hillside
with fine views and a swimming
pool.*

Sunset Bungalows
Nai Harn Beach
*Old-style beach bungalows ranged
up the hillside.*

Prachuap Khiri Khan

Thesaban Bungalow
Su-Suk Road
Ao Prachuap
Tel: 611 150
26 rooms.

**Provincial Administration
Bungalows**
Su-Suk Road, Ao Prachuap
Tel: 601 014
9 rooms.

Suk San Hotel
131 Su-Suk Road
Tel 611 019
60 rooms.

Ranong

Asia Hotel
39/9 Ruangrat Road
Tel: 811 113
90 rooms.

**Jansom Thara Beach
Resort**
Hat Chamdamri
Tel: 811 511
*Spacious bungalows. Swimming
pool.*

**Jansom Thara Hot Springs
Resort**
2/10 Phetkasem Road
Tel: 811 511
*230 rooms. Backed by lush
mountain scenery with jacuzzi,
fitness centre and swimming pool.*

Sin Ranong Hotel
28/23 Ruangrat Road
Tel: 811 454
120 rooms.

Sangkhlaburi

P Guest House
Signposted from the centre of
town
*Charming bungalows overlooking
the reservoir.*

Runtee Palace
Tel: Bangkok 314 2656
*18 raft houses. Fifteen minutes by
boat from Tha Saphan Runtee.*

Si Deng Hotel
Tel: 595 039
Located opposite the bus station.

Songkhla

Lake Inn Hotel
301–303 Nakhonnok Road
Tel: 314 240

Narai Hotel   ▯
12/2Chaikhao Road
Tel: 311 078
12 rooms.

Pavilion Hotel   ▯▯
17 Pra Tha Road
Tel: 311 355

Samila Hotel   ▯▯
1/11 Ratchadamnoen Road
Tel: 313 505
70 rooms.

Sukhothai

Pailyn Sukhothai   ▯▯
Jarodvithithong Road
Tel: 613 310
*120 rooms Four km (2.5 miles)
from the historic town with fine
views and swimming pool.*

Rajthannee   ▯▯
229 Chodwithithong Road
Tel: 611 031
*81 rooms. In the new town with
two restaurants and rooms with
balcony.*

Sawaddiphong Hotel   ▯
56/2–5 Singhawat Road
Tel: 611 567
51 rooms.

Somprasong Guest House   ▯
off Jarodvithithong Road
New Sukhothai
*Charming. friendly and extremely
good value. Situated to left of
bridge on the west bank.*

Surin

Memorial Hotel   ▯
186 Lak Muang Road
Tel: 511 288
56 rooms.

Petchkasem Hotel   ▯▯
104 Chit Bamrung Road
Tel: 511 274
162 rooms.

Pirom Guest House   ▯
242 Krungsrinai Road
*Extremely cheap and friendly.
Run by one of the most
knowledgeable people in the area.*

Tarin Hotel   ▯▯
Sirawat Road
Tel: 514 281
Swimming pool and disco.

Tak

Tak Hotel   ▯
18/11 Mahadthai Bamrung Road
Tel 511 234
29 rooms.

Viang Tak Hotel   ▯▯
25/3 Mahadthai Bamrung Road
Tel: 511 095
100 rooms.

That Phanom

Saeng Thong Hotel   ▯
34 Mu 1
Phanom-Phanarak Road
17 rooms.

Tong Pa Phum

Boonyong Bungalows   ▯
61 Mu 1
Tambon Tha Khanun
Tel: 599 049
15 bungalows.

Tong Pha Phum Bungalows   ▯
28/1 Mu 1, Tambon Tha Khanun
28 rooms.

Ubon Ratchathani

Patumrat Hotel   ▯▯
173 Chayangkun Road
Tel: 241 501
137 rooms.

Ratchathani Hotel   ▯▯
229 Khuan-Thani Road
Tel: 254 599
100 rooms.

Ubon Hotel   ▯
333 Khuan Thani Road
Tel: 254 952
120 rooms.

Udon Thani

Charoen   ▯▯
549 Pho Si Road
Tel: 221 331
120 rooms.

Charoensi Palace   ▯▯
60 Pho Si Road
Tel: 222 601
110 rooms.

Paradise Hotel   ▯
44/29 Phosi Road
Tel: 221 956
90 rooms.

Udon Thani   ▯
81–89 Mak-Khang Road
Tel: 222 166
90 rooms.

Yala

Si Yala   ▯
16–22 Chaicharati Road
Tel: 212 299
93 rooms.

Thep Wiman   ▯
31–7 Si Bamrung Road
Tel: 212 400
82 rooms.

Restaurants

Thai cuisine brings together some of the finest culinary traditions of India, China, Malaysia, and even Portugal. It has the spiciness of hot chillis and the sweetness of coconut milk, the pungency of fresh herbs and the saltiness of fermented fish. More than anything it has the inspiration and beautiful presentation which are inextricably Thai.

If you are a newcomer to Thai food, start off with something mild (*mai phet*) and work up towards the heights of chillied serpent's heads or pigs' intestine soup. Curries (*kaeng pet*) particularly those with a coconut cream base are often less piquant than in Europe or India. Steamed sweet and sour fish with ginger and garlic (*pla priawan*) is another exquisite dish and is often served with pineapple and green peppers.

Each region has specialities. The North-east includes large numbers of Laotians and is famed for its sticky or glutinous rice (*khao nia*), normally served alongside barbecued meat (generally buffalo); and *som tam*, a hot salad that combines shredded green papaya, dried shrimps or curried crab claws, lemon juice, fish sauce, garlic and chillis. In the North, a local sausage called *naem* is popular. The South has many dishes influenced by the Muslim-style cooking of Malays; and, of course, all kinds of seafood.

There are a variety of sweet desserts. Many are based on rice flour, coconut milk, palm sugar and sticky rice. Others are soaked in jasmine and aromatic flowers in water.

Bangkok

Akbar
Soi 3
Sukhumvit Road
Tel: 253 3479
Good Indian curry, vegetarian and non-vegetarian tandoori and Halal food in a bright and tastefully decorated dining room.
Indian. Medium price.

Angus Steak House
9/4–5 Thaniya Road
Tel: 234 3590
Specialities include all forms of steaks and grilled dishes.
European. Medium price.

Ban Chiang
14 Soi Srivieng
Pramuan Road
Silom
Tel: 236 7045
Turn of the century residence with mainstream/regional Thai cuisine.
Medium price.

Ban Khrua
29/1 Soi Saladaeng 1
Silom Road
Tel: 233 6912
Comfortable, simply decorated but with delicious local specialities to recommend it.
Medium price.

Bussaracum
35 Soi 2 Piphat
Convent Road
Tel: 235 5160
Authentic Thai cuisine featuring sakunna chom suan (shrimp birds with taro) and kao tang na tang (crispy rice chips with minced pork and mint dip).
Expensive.

Cabbages and Condoms
Soi 12
10 Sukhumvit Road
Tel: 252 7349
Supports the Family Planning Association. Don't miss the mah haw (minced pork, prawns, nuts and onions).
Medium price.

China House
Oriental Hotel
48 Oriental Avenue
Tel: 236 0400
Fine Cantonese cuisine served in elegant wooden house. Especially recommended—superior shark's fin soup and roast pigeon stuffed with herb.
Cantonese. Expensive.

China Restaurant
231/3 Soi Sarasin
Tel: 251 0737/8
Cantonese, Shanghai, Mandarin, Szechuan and other Chinese regional dishes.
Chinese. Medium price.

D'Jit Pochana
62 Soi 20
Sukhumvit
Tel: 258 1597
Favourite Thai dishes on an English menu in pleasant atmosphere. Popular with long-term residents.
Medium price.

El Gordo's Cantina
Soi 8
130/8 Silom
(opposite Bangkok Bank)
Tel: 234 5470
Known as the best Mexican restaurant in town with home-made tortillas, enchilladas and cornchip and avocado dip.
Mexican. Medium price.

Harlequin
118 North Sathorn Road
Tel: 234 3259
Bangkok's new jet set restaurant and wine bar. Good selection of good European and American cuisine and excellent wine cellar.
European and American. Medium price.

Jade Garden
Montien Hotel
54 Surawong Road
Tel: 233 7060
Popular dim-sum as well as delicious noodles, Peking duck and steamed dumplings.
Chinese. Medium price.

La Grenouille
Soi 1
220/4 Sukhumvit
Tel: 252 0311
Cosy atmosphere and good French food. Favoured dishes include champignons fricasse, sea bass and coq au vin along with daily plat du maison.
French. Medium price.

La Tache
Shangri-La Hotel
89 Soi Wat Suan Plu
Charoen Krung Road
Tel: 236 7777
Grand-style dining with a lavish menu featuring oysters, paté de fois gras, caviar and Chateabriand.
European. Expensive.

Laicram
11/1 Soi 49
Sukhumvit Road
Tel: 392 5864
Popular and long-established with wide selection of Thai dishes.
Medium price.

Lemon Grass
Soi 24
5/1 Sukhumvit Road
Tel: 258 8637
Set in a delightful old house with a charming terrace. The food is excellent, but order lots as the portions are small.
Medium price.

L'Hexagone
4 Soi Thonglor
25 Sukhumvit Road 55
Tel: 381 2187
Newly opened and tastefully decorated with some of the best French food in town.
Medium price.

L'Opera
55 Soi 39
Sukhumvit Road
Tel: 258 5605
Italian cuisine served in a charming house with glass conservatory.
Italian. Medium price.

Maharaj
Situated upriver from the Grand Palace. Get there at sundown and feast on a good curry and spicy Tom Yam Kung (prawn soup).
Low Price.

Moghul Room
Soi 16
1/16 Sukhumvit Road
Tel: 221 6989
Offers a lavish choice of dishes from the North and the South Indian. Medium price.

Neil's Tavern
58/4 Soi Ruam Rudee
Tel: 251 5644
Extremely popular with meat eating foreigners. Good steaks and seafood in lively atmosphere.
European. Medium price.

Normandie
Oriental Hotel
48 Oriental Avenue
Tel: 236 0400
*The most exclusive French
restaurant in town with exquisite
food and a wine list to match.
French. Expensive.*

Ristorante Sorrento
66 North Sathorn Road
Tel: 234 9841
*Set in an old Neapolitan style villa
on busy Sathorn Road.
Specialities include baked scallops,
oyster soup, and Phuket lobster
thermidor.
European. Medium price.*

Royal India Restaurant
392/1 Chakraphet Road
Tel: 221 6565
*Small and extremely popular with
fine tandooris, Madras curries and
Indian sweets.
Indian. Medium price.*

Sala Rim Naam
Oriental Hotel
48 Oriental Avenue
Charoen Krung Road
Tel: 437 9417
*Charming situation on the banks
of the Chao Phya River. Classical
dancing every night at 8.30 p.m.
Expensive.*

Seafood Market
388 Sukhumvit Road
Tel: 258 0218
*Choose your own seafood in a
shopping trolley, select how you
want it cooked then sit outside and
feast on some of the best fish in
Bangkok.
Medium price.*

Silom Village
286 Silom Road
Tel: 235 8760
*Open air and indoor restaurants
serving fresh fish, Chinese and
Thai specialities. Accompanied by
Thai classical music.*

Spice Market
The Regent Hotel
155 Ratchadamri Road
Tel: 251 6127
*Captures the feel of old Siam fine
seafoods, green curries and spicy
Tom Yam. Expensive.*

Tam Nak Thai
131 Rachadapisek Road
Tel: 277 8833
*The largest restaurant in the
world, seating up to 3,000 diners,
attended by 120 chefs and 400
waiters on roller skates.*

Thanying Restaurant
10 Pramuan Street
Off Silom Road
Tel: 236 4361
*Beautifully presented Thai food.
Try the wild pork stir-fried with
lesser galangal and basil and the
duck curry.
Medium price.*

Trattoria Da Roberto
Plaza Arcade
Patpong 2 Road
Tel: 234 5987
*Situated in Bangkok's infamous
gogo heartland. Good Italian food
and selection of wines.
Italian. Medium price.*

Whole Earth
93/3 Soi Lang Suan
Ploenchit Road.
Tel: 252 5574
*One of Bangkok's only vegetarian
restaurants but also serves a wide
selection of non-vegetarian and
Thai dishes. Classical guitar
between 8 p.m.–11 p.m.
Vegetarian. Medium price.*

Chiang Mai
Ban Suan
51/3 Sankamhaeng Road
Tel: 242 116
*Situated in several teakwood barns
on the outskirts of town, but worth
going out of the way for.
Medium price.*

Butcher's Shop
193/15 Sri Donchai Road
Tel: 272 493
*Cafe-style dining with delicious
French food.
European. Medium price.*

Cafe de Paris
14/16 Kotchasarn Road
Tel: 234 804
*Fine French fare with lively cafe
atmosphere and good wine menu.
French. Medium price.*

Chiang Mai Culture Centre
185/3 Wualai Road
Tel: 275 097
*Set khantoke dinner including
gaeng hang le (pork curry) and
namprik ong (minced pork
cooked with tomatoes and chillis).
Expensive.*

Daret Restaurant
Chaiyapoom Road
(near Tapae Gate)
*Budget backpacker's paradise with
good Thai and European food.
Cheap to medium price.*

Diamond Hotel
33/10 Charoenprathet Road
Tel: 234 155
Khantoke *dinner in beautiful old
teak house Reserve in advance.
Expensive.*

Gallery
5–29 Charoenrat Road
Tel: 248 601
*Set in a delightful 100-year-old
teak house. Delicacies include
spicy curry and banana flower
salad.
Medium price.*

Kai Tong Restaurant
67 Kotchasarn Road
Tel: 276 584
*Delicious fried frog, tortoise and
monitor lizards. Claims to be the
only restaurant in the world with
python steak on the menu.
Medium price.*

Kaiwan Restaurant
181 Nimanhemin Road
Tel: 222 147
*Set in peaceful veranda.
Specialities include the* kratong-
tong, *a pancake filled with
chicken in a white sauce and peas.
Medium price.*

La Villa Pizzeria
145 Ratchadamnoen Road
Tel: 215 403
*Famed for the best seafood pizza
in town.
European. Medium price.*

Nang Nual
27/2–5 Koa Klang Road
Nong Hoy
Tel: 241 771
*Grand ornate with probably the
best seafood on town.
Expensive.*

The Pub
88 Huay Kaew Road
Tel: 211 559
Heralded by Newsweek *as one of
the world's best bars.
Medium price.*

Rajawadee Restaurant
411 Charoenprathet Road
Tel: 281 060
*Riverside hotel restaurant
specializing in Thai and Chinese
dishes.
Medium price.*

Riverside
9/11 Charoenrat Road
Tel: 243 239
*Thai and European cuisine with
bands and a beautiful river setting.
Medium price.*

Whole Earth Restaurant
88 Sridonchai Road
Tel: 282 463
Northern-style house serving
vegetarian and non-vegetarian
Indian and Thai dishes
Medium price.

Pattaya

Dolf Ricks
Sri Nakorn Centre
North Pattaya
Tel: 418 269
Good Indonesian and European
food including the house speciality
of rijstafel, *a combination of 18*
different dishes.

El Toro Steakhouse
215–31 Pattaya 2 Road
Tel: 426 238
Serves the most popular steak in
town to capacity crowds.

Hafen Suble
Nipa Lodge
Central Pattaya Road
Tel: 428 195
Much in demand for its
Oktoberfest Brathendl, grilled
chicken in Octoberfest style, and
its pickled pork knuckle with
sauerkraut.

La Gritta
Beach Road
Tel: 428 161
Good authentic Italian food.
specialities include La Gritta pasta
with clams, herbs and white wine.

Noble House
310 Mu 10
Beach Road
Tel: 423 639
Popular for its marinated spare-
ribs, fillet steaks and baked
lasagna served on a ground floor
terrace.

Pattaya Seafood Palace
Mu 10
Tel: 427 396
Good lobster, mussels and freshly
caught fish in ideal setting.

PIC Kitchen
Soi 5
off Beach Road
Tel: 428 374
Some of the most authentic Thai
cuisine served in traditional Thai
architecture.

Ruen Thai Restaurant
Pattaya 2 Road
South Pattaya
Tel: 425 911
Set in beautiful gardens with fine
Thai cuisine and classical dancing.

Tam Nak Nam
252 Central Road
Tel: 429 059
Chinese-style seafood restaurant
raised on concrete pillars over a
pond.

Thang Long
Soi 3
201 Pattaya
Tel: 425 487
Classical Vietnamese food served
by waitresses in traditional
Vietnamese costume.

Villa Seafood Restaurant
Soi 7
Pattaya Beach Road
Tel: 422 523
Original Chinese recipes used to
prepare Peking Duck, stir-fried
black pepper crabs and five-
flavoured broiled king lobster.

Phuket

Ban Rim Pa
100/7 Kalim Beach Road
Tel: 723 0386
Pucket's finest restaurant set in an
open teak house at the north end
of Patong Beach. Specialities
include duck curry, tom yam *and*
salad of exotic fruits.

Buffalo Steak House
95/24–26 Soi Patong Resort
Renowned for its steak, its
Scandinavian specialities and
occasionally even elephant's ear.

Fishermen's Tavern
Kamala Beach Estate
Tel: 723 0379
Renowned for exquisite French
cuisine under the hand of well
known chef Christopher Moulard.

Kan Bang
9/3 Chaofa Road
Chalong Bay
Tel: 381 323
Delicious seafood and stunning
views. Specialities include steamed
lobster in fresh milk.

Malee Seafood
Thawiwong Road
Tel: 321 205
An abundance of seafood and
steaks served from inside a
beautiful indoor garden.

Patong Seafood
Thawiwong Road
Patpong
Tel: 321 247
Popular fresh seafood,
conveniently located near the
centre of night life.

Phuket View Restaurant
Khao Rang Hill
(Phuket Hill)
Tel: 216 865
Good seafood. Fine views.

Pizzeria Napoli
Soi Post Office
Patong Beach
Pizzas galore with bottles of wine
and the odd Italian waiter.

Ruam Thep Inn
Karon Beach
One of the first seafood
restaurants in Karon and still one
of the most popular, with a vast
menu of Thai, Chinese and
Western dishes.

Terrace Restaurant
Amanpuri Hotel
118 Srisoonthorn Road
Pansea Beach
Tel: 311 394–9
One of the most expensive, but
exquisite spots on the whole
island. Serving Thai cuisine.

Thai Gourmet
Thavorn Palm Beach Hotel
Karon Beach
Upmarket Thai seafood with
waitresses dressed in traditional
costumes.

Tung Ka Cafe
Khao Rang Hill
(Phuket Hill)
Tel: 211 500
Set in beautiful leafy surroundings
with fine views of the island. Try
the excellent seafood curry served
in a coconut or the glass noodles
with crab.

Vecchia Venezia
82/16 U Thit Road
Patong
Good Italian food. Especially
recommended: cockles and mussels
paesana, *homemade pasta or one*
of 25 pizzas.

Index

Page references in **bold** refer to main entries; those in *italic* refer to illustrations.